Should the FDA Reject *Itself*?

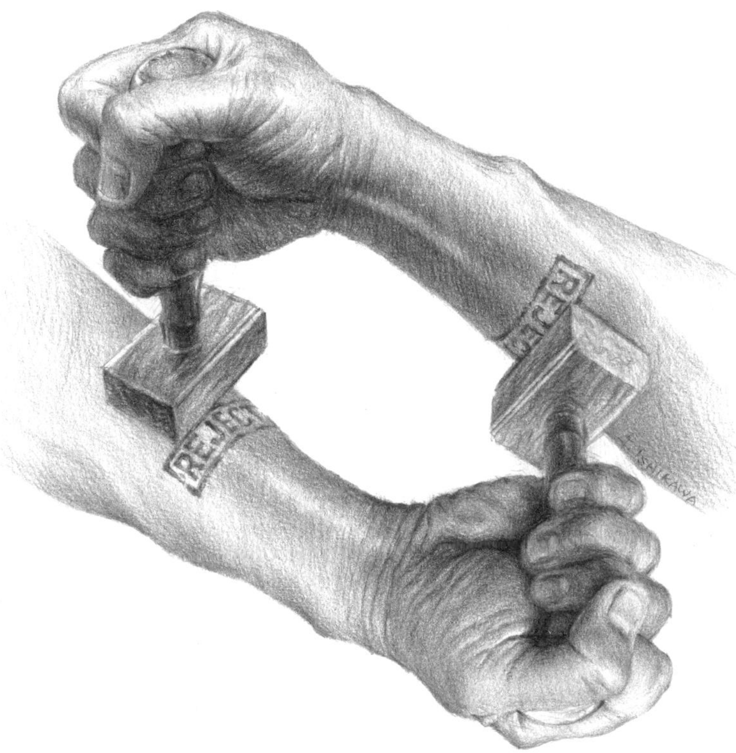

Should the FDA Reject *Itself*?

Charles L. Hooper

Chicago Park Press

Should the FDA Reject *Itself*?
RejectFDA.com

First edition.

CharlesLHooper.com
Hooper@ObjectiveInsights.com

Published by Chicago Park Press
P.O. Box 542, Chicago Park, CA 95712
ChicagoParkPress.com

Cover design by Russell T. Hooper
• RussellHooper.com

Cover illustration by Jeff Ishikawa
• JeffIshikawa.com/paintings/
• JeffIshikawa@hotmail.com

Illustrations within book by Mark Lawler
• ILoveTheUSA@live.com
• MarkLawler777@outlook.com

Library of Congress Control Number: 2021951283
ISBN-13: 978-0-9768541-3-5

CHAPTER 5: THE PERILS OF HUMAN TESTING 119

CHAPTER 6: THE REAL COST OF THE FDA 159

CHAPTER 7: IT'S NOT EASY BEING THE FDA205

Introduction

There are some remedies worse than the disease.
Publilius Syrus, 85-43 B.C.

This book explores the pharmaceutical industry, the U.S. Food and Drug Administration (FDA), and the practice of medicine, with an eye toward questioning the assumptions that many people hold.

Like many readers, I grew up believing that government agencies protect us in the same ways that our parents protected us when we were young; they understand the world well, know us well, and put our interests before their own. But later, I began to question that view: why would a huge government agency manned by people who are complete strangers to me care so much about my well-being? Even if those people do care, do they have the right information to make good decisions about my health and welfare? Do they know anything about me? What if my childhood assumptions were wrong? (To know more about me, please see About the Author at the end.)

Let's start by considering four people and their stories; then I'll explain what this book is about.

Maurice Hilleman's Vaccines

Maurice Hilleman, an employee of Merck & Co., might have saved more lives than almost any other person in history. According to one count, he saved 129 million lives.[1]

What did Hilleman do? He almost singlehandedly developed 40 vaccines over his 60-year career at Merck. Of the fourteen vaccines routinely recommended in current vaccine schedules, he developed eight. What's more, his vaccines save primarily children—otherwise healthy people with long lives still in front of them.

His ingenuity, persistence, and diligence are legendary. In 1963, when Hilleman's oldest daughter developed a fever and swollen glands that were symptoms indicative of mumps, he made a late-night trip to his laboratory to retrieve some equipment to culture her virus. Using the isolate from his daughter, Hilleman carefully reduced the virulence of the virus and shepherded the new vaccine through testing and production in his typical focused fashion. His younger daughter was a subject in early clinical trials. Happily, both daughters survived, and Hilleman's ubiquitous mumps vaccine has since brought a classic childhood disease to the verge of extinction.

The editors of *The Atlantic* listed the vaccines that Hilleman and others developed as number eight on its list of the "50 greatest breakthroughs" over the last 6,000 years. (Penicillin, incidentally, was number three).[2]

In addition to their life-saving value, vaccines are a fantastic economic value. Of the total value of vaccines, a mere two percent accrues to the companies that develop and manufacture them, while 98 percent is enjoyed by those patients who are vaccinated and by society overall.[3]

What was life like before vaccines? One couple that I read about had six children who all died, one after another, from typical childhood diseases. The father was so heartbroken that he slept at the cemetery.

Magic Johnson's HIV

On November 7, 1991, basketball great Magic Johnson shocked the sports world by announcing, at the peak of his career, that he had tested positive for HIV and would retire immediately. In 2004, ESPN ranked this announcement as the seventh most memorable sports moment of the previous 25 years.

HIV was seen as a death sentence during that era. People in San Francisco and other big cities were seen venturing out into public with visible opportunistic infections, as they inevitably wasted away from AIDS. Clouds of pessimism and fear hung in the air like the ubiquitous San Francisco fog, motivating Oprah Winfrey to report in 1987: "Research studies now project that one in five—listen to me, hard to believe—one in five heterosexuals could be dead from AIDS at the end of the next three years. That's by 1990. One in five. It is no longer just a gay disease. Believe me."[4]

We should all be thankful that Oprah's prediction went so horribly askew. That happened for two reasons. First, she had a profound misunderstanding of the actual situation. Second, the pharmaceutical industry worked hard to prove her wrong.

HIV, while a killer in 1991, is now treated like many other chronic conditions. What changed? At first, with a paroxysm of public outcry, AIDS activists convinced the FDA to be more lenient and expeditious, and the agency approved Burroughs Wellcome's AZT[5] in the astounding time of 107 days. Most FDA reviews at that time took a couple of *years*. Since then, we've had Abbott, Agouron, Boehringer Ingelheim, Bristol-Myers Squibb, Gilead Sciences, GlaxoSmithKline, Johnson & Johnson, Merck,

Pfizer, Roche, and ViiV to thank for their alphabet soup of single-agent and combination products to treat HIV. Physicians now have nucleotide/ nucleoside reverse transcriptase inhibitors, non-nucleoside reverse transcriptase inhibitors, protease inhibitors, integrase inhibitors, and entry inhibitors to choose from—and HIV patients benefit daily. Even patients' daily mound of pills has been squeezed into easy-to-take single-tablet regimens. All said, the pharmaceutical industry has reduced the mortality rate of HIV/AIDS by 92.5 percent.[6]

Magic Johnson is as alive today as he was 30 years ago, thanks to AIDS activists, pharmaceutical companies, and an FDA that saw the light.

Allen Tower: Hero, Criminal

Allen Tower is a hero to doctors and the parents of small children with heart defects. To the FDA, he's a criminal.

Doctors treating dying babies with congenital heart defects rely on Tower to make and quickly deliver customized cardiological devices, often within hours. Without these devices used to widen the aortas or open the valves in their hearts, afflicted babies would die. Not surprisingly, time is critical. The government hasn't questioned the safety and efficacy of Tower's devices, but it is making it more difficult for him to provide them, requiring Tower to file documents with the agency for specific approval *each time* he sells a "custom device." Of course, each device is custom—that's the whole point. Why should he be required to submit paperwork each time?

Worse, federal prosecutors have charged Tower with a crime, claiming that he marketed "unapproved" stents for use in children. Tower could even be charged with a felony.

In response to these threats from the FDA, 650 cardiologists and parents have signed a petition stating that the actions against Tower could cause "a devastating loss to patients . . . should Mr. Tower be relieved of his freedom or ability to continue his work." Larry Latson, director of the congenital cardiac catheterization lab at the Cleveland Clinic, calls the FDA rules "terrible," and he lists specific instances of children who, as a result of the FDA's scrutiny, died because they couldn't get Tower's devices. "The FDA wants more data, yet there are few patients to acquire the data," Latson said. "The FDA's system does not work well for fields like ours, where there are small numbers of widely varying patients."[7]

Tower pleaded guilty to selling medical devices without FDA approval and paid a $2.3 million fine. Nine years later his company, NuMed, did receive FDA approval to sell the devices.

Howard Root's Cardiac Arrest

Howard Root was CEO of Vascular Solutions when he faced his "cardiac arrest" moment. Root was arrested and charged with a felony, for which he faced prison time and expulsion from the medical profession. What had he done wrong? It turns out—nothing.

A disgruntled Vascular Solutions sales representative reported the company to federal prosecutors for allegedly selling unapproved medical devices. The product in question was of a slightly different length than an approved cardiac catheter and accounted for less than one percent of the company's sales. This product was almost identical to other, already approved medical devices, and not a single patient had ever claimed to be hurt by it. Facing a resolute Root who defended his case and didn't knuckle under, federal prosecutors resorted to "threatening witnesses, misleading grand juries, and strategically leaking secret documents. Whatever it took to pressure a headline-grabbing settlement."[8] Their dirty tactics didn't work.

Root's marathon case lasted five years, took 121 attorneys, cost $25 million in legal fees, and even launched a Congressional investigation, but he was eventually acquitted.

One juror, shortly after the trial, confided to Root: "What the federal government did to you . . . is nothing short of criminal."

What, exactly, is this book about?

The pharmaceutical, biotechnology, vitamin, supplement, diagnostic, vaccine, and medical device industries are comprised of real people, people like Hilleman, Tower, and Root, who are helping real people like Magic Johnson. Unless you follow the news very closely, you might miss their stories and you might miss any discussion of how the FDA affects the people who struggle to bring us the next big medical advances.

Pro-FDA Thesis

The FDA's powers are predicated on six straightforward concepts:

One, that some drugs are so dangerous that they shouldn't be used. Dangerous drugs harm patients in three ways: the drugs cost money, they are used in place of other drugs that might help, and they directly harm patients.

Two, that ineffective drugs can be recognized and should be prohibited. Ineffective drugs harm patients in two ways: the drugs cost money and they are used in place of other drugs that might help.

Three, that someone can clearly judge drugs based on points one and two and, further, that that "someone" is a federal government agency. Most of us haven't been trained as medical professionals and we are unable to assess the relevant scientific information. Other experts in the field, such as doctors and drug companies, may have perverse incentives to sell us useless or harmful medicines. It helps to have an objective third party—the FDA—pore over the data and decide what's right.

Four, that the FDA must have enforcement powers to ensure that companies abide by the best research, manufacturing, and marketing practices. We need to trust that the medicines we purchase are honestly and accurately labeled and promoted.

Five, that the FDA can and should tell us which drugs work for which diseases and inform us of optimal dosing schedules. This government agency should also warn us of possible side effects and drug-drug interactions. If safety issues do arise with marketed drugs, the FDA should alert manufacturers, pharmacists, doctors, and the media. If marketed drugs are deemed unsafe, they should be pulled from the market.

Six, that by testing new drugs before they are put into widespread use we will know what to expect when and if we ever require one. With the FDA on our side we face fewer health risks and are healthier overall.

If you believe that these six concepts justify a regulatory agency such as the FDA, congratulations, you're in the majority. You can take comfort in knowing that most reasonable people agree with you.

What the FDA Does

The FDA assesses new drugs to make sure they are safe and effective. To better understand the FDA and how it works, we will first explore safety through the lens of dangerous drugs and then explore efficacy through the lens of ineffective drugs.

This exploration will start to chip away at the six ideas comprising the pro-FDA thesis and we'll see how quickly they crumble. What follows are some aspects that are little discussed in the pharmaceutical industry, yet they should be.

Dangerous Drugs

Consider some specific examples of dangerous drugs: first, the infamous thalidomide.

In a tragedy in the early 1960s, more than 10,000 babies, mainly in Europe and Australia, were born deformed after their pregnant mothers took a sedative called thalidomide. Women took it as a sleeping pill and for morning sickness.

While many people think that thalidomide was an awful drug that has been forever banished from the market, they would be wrong. Even the dictionary gets it wrong. The WordBook dictionary on my smartphone says: "…withdrawn from sale after discovered to cause severe birth defects." While it was withdrawn from sale in those places where it had been used—not in the U.S.—thalidomide and some close variants are available and are widely used today. You may be surprised to learn that years after the birth defect tragedy, thalidomide was found to be effective in adults for a number of serious diseases, including some skin conditions arising from leprosy and certain cancers, such as multiple myeloma.

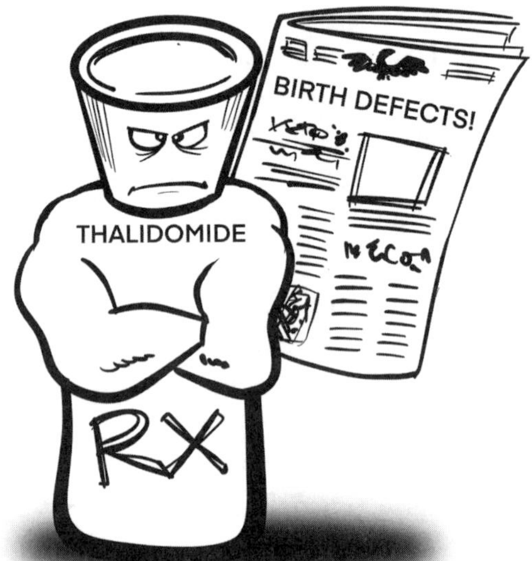

Celgene's Revlimid (lenalidomide), a slightly tweaked version of thalidomide, is the second largest selling drug in the United States—with U.S. revenues of about $10 billion in 2019—and it is helping thousands of people, including a friend of mine who suffers from multiple myeloma.

Is thalidomide dangerous? Yes. Thalidomide is exceptionally dangerous. Is thalidomide safe enough to treat people with multiple myeloma? Yes. It's both.

Consider something even more dangerous than thalidomide: rat poison. Imagine the hypothetical, but extreme, case where a drug company asks the FDA to approve rat poison as a medicine for human consumption.

What should the FDA do? This situation actually happened and the FDA, you may be surprised to learn, approved rat poison as a safe human medicine. And the FDA was right to do so!

I have a friend who successfully takes rat poison to prevent blood clots from moving into his heart and his brain. What he takes isn't actually called rat poison; the brand name is Coumadin and the generic name is warfarin, but it is nothing more than rat poison. Former secretary of state Hillary Clinton also takes Coumadin for the same condition.

Historical evidence suggests that warfarin was used to murder Soviet strongman Joseph Stalin: "...he may have been poisoned with warfarin, a tasteless and colorless blood thinner also used as a rat killer, during a final dinner with four members of his Politburo."[9] One of the dinner guests, Lavrenti P. Beria, later bragged about killing Stalin, saying, "I did him in! I saved all of you."

Here's a drug that is a known rodent and human killer and yet my friend and Clinton are using it to stay alive.

Is warfarin dangerous? Yes. Is warfarin safe enough for my friend to use? Yes. It's both.

For something even worse than rat poison, consider a substance that was *banned* as a *weapon* by the Geneva Protocol of 1925. It's something so ghastly that you can't use it even when you're trying to dispel invading enemy troops: mustard gas.

> In July 1917, troops based in Ypres, Belgium, reported a shimmering cloud around their feet and a strange peppery smell in the air. Within 24 hours they started to itch uncontrollably and developed horrific blisters and sores. Some started coughing up blood.
>
> They'd been poisoned by mustard gas—one of the most deadly chemical weapons deployed in battle.
>
> And because mustard gas can be absorbed through the skin, gas masks were useless. Even fully clothed soldiers weren't fully protected. It could take up to six weeks to die from mustard gas, and it was a terrible way to die.[10]

Mustard gas is actually not a gas—it's a yellowish-brown liquid that evaporates readily. It has been used to kill approximately 100,000 soldiers in battle.

A slightly modified form of mustard gas later became a treatment for cancer and is now commonly referred to as chemotherapy. You undoubtably know a number of people who have been successfully treated with chemotherapy. There are now various types of chemotherapy, but a handful of them are still derivatives of mustard gas. One, cisplatin, is largely responsible for the fact that 96 percent of men with testicular cancer now survive the disease long term.[11] It didn't use to be that way.

Are mustard gas and chemotherapy dangerous? Yes. Are they safe enough for treating cancer patients? Yes.

Can we take this too far? If some poisons have health benefits, should the FDA boldly advocate, say, venomous snake bite treatments? Of course not. But there are beneficial components found even in snake venom. Millions of people rely on snake venom to keep their blood pressure in check. Popular ACE inhibitor drugs were isolated from Brazilian pit vipers, which employ a key molecule to make their prey pass out from low blood pressure.[12] Another drug derived from snake venom is the anticoagulant, aka blood thinner, Aggrastat (tirofiban).

Can venomous snake bites kill people? Yes. Is snake venom safe enough for patients with certain cardiovascular diseases? Yes.

Is there nothing so dangerous that it would fail the FDA's tests? The most dangerous toxin known to mankind is the neurotoxin produced by the bacterium *Clostridium botulinum*—the completely natural cause of botulism.

Surely if anything will fail the FDA's testing process it will be the most toxic substance known. As you may have guessed, botulinum toxin has been approved as a "safe drug" and is available and on the market today as Allergan's Botox (onabotulinumtoxinA), used for removing facial lines and preventing migraines. Botox's U.S. revenues were about $3.6 billion in 2019.

If the most dangerous toxin known can pass the FDA's tests as a safe drug, then really, anything can pass.

On the other end of the spectrum, it seems as if nothing is safer than water. Of course, one can drown in water, but can water hurt us otherwise? Yes, it can.

In 2009, Sacramento radio station KDND held a contest to see how much water contestants could drink in the studio. It was jokingly called "Hold Your Wee for a Wii," referring to the popular Nintendo Wii gaming system. Eighteen people entered, including a 28-year-old mother of three, Jennifer Strange. Strange drank nearly two gallons of water on the show, joked about the size and shape of her belly, won second place, and then died just hours later in her bathroom. She died from hyponatremia—she drank too much water while not getting enough electrolytes.

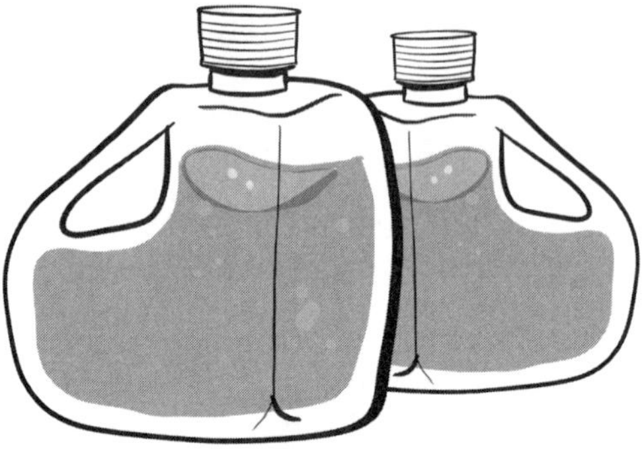

Marathon runners occasionally succumb to the same condition if they drink too much during their long runs.

Is water necessary for life? Yes. Can water kill? Yes.

Even the most dangerous toxin—botulinum toxin—can serve as a safe drug under the right conditions and the safest substance—water—can kill under the right circumstances.

What conclusion can we draw?

As wise people have known for centuries, the dose makes the poison. A substance can be benign or harmful, depending on your situation and your exposure.

> *All things are poison and nothing is without poison; only the dose makes a thing not a poison.*
> **Paracelsus**, the founder of toxicology (1493-1541)

Too much water killed Jennifer Strange. Most of us drink water safely every day. Too much warfarin may have killed Stalin; the right amount of warfarin keeps my friend alive. Thalidomide can harm fetuses; thalidomide treats multiple myeloma patients. There is no such thing as a completely "dangerous" or "safe" substance, an insight that makes the FDA's job difficult if not impossible.

Ineffective Drugs

Now consider efficacy, whether drugs offer a therapeutic benefit or not.

David Kessler, who served as FDA commissioner under both Presidents George H.W. Bush and Bill Clinton, confidently stated, "When the industry sells a drug, the drug works, and it does what it says on the label. Take that away and we go back to snake oil."[13]

Consider Genentech's Herceptin (trastuzumab), which many consider a "miracle drug." Herceptin is among the better drugs in oncology and in 2019 it was the 6th biggest selling drug in the U.S., with sales of approximately $3 billion.

Before Herceptin, chemotherapy was the standard of care for breast cancer. For doctors to give Herceptin to patients in conjunction with chemotherapy, it must offer an incremental advantage over chemotherapy alone. What is the incremental advantage of Herceptin? It turns out that 23 percent of patients benefit.[14] That's less than a quarter of patients.

Merck's Keytruda (pembrolizumab) has recently become one of the hottest drugs on the market. Keytruda received some favorable press after former President Jimmy Carter reported that he was "cancer free" after therapy with Keytruda. Keytruda, too, is given in conjunction with chemotherapy to help patients with melanoma. What incremental advantage does Keytruda offer over chemotherapy alone? It helps 36 percent of cancer patients to live longer.[15] Keytruda—which was the second biggest-selling drug globally in 2020 and brought in worldwide revenues of $14.4 billion —is far from a sure thing.

Kessler's "When the industry sells a drug, the drug works…" makes it sound as if FDA approval confers an ironclad guarantee. It doesn't.

We haven't yet touched on the worst aspect. The FDA can't tell *which* patients will benefit. Can the FDA tell if you will benefit from Herceptin? No. Can the FDA tell if you will benefit from Keytruda? No.

After the FDA approves a medicine as safe and efficacious, what happens next? Patients, advised by their doctors, must actually try a medicine to see if it works for them. It's called **trial and error** and *it was the foundation of medicine in the past and it still is today*.

What is described on the drug's label is what happened to strangers in another time and place. You want to know if a drug will help *you* today.

An FDA approval for efficacy is largely duplicative because you'll still need to decide if the medicine is right *for you* and then test it yourself to see if it works *for you*, which is exactly what people did before the FDA existed.

Is the FDA Helping?

Maybe the FDA's job isn't so simple and obvious. Dangerous things can still help people. Safe things can still hurt people. A drug that works for one person doesn't work for another. One patient suffers an adverse event and the next patient doesn't.

Are there downsides to the FDA trying to protect us from unsafe foods and unsafe and ineffective drugs?

The real cost of the FDA stems from the expenses, delays, and hassles of getting new medicines approved. With higher costs and lower probabilities of success, fewer companies—especially smaller ones—will be in business; fewer drugs will be discovered, developed, and marketed for the patients who need them; and, with the reduced competition, drug prices will generally be higher. Plus, even successful drugs will be delayed by many years, precluding their use by patients during the time they are being reviewed.

The cost to discover and develop one new drug is now a shocking $3.2 billion.[16] This price tag has been increasing at 7.5 percent annually for decades. If this growth rate persists, costs will more than double every ten years and, in a decade, that new drug will likely cost $6.4 billion.

If costs are so high, have fewer drugs actually been developed? That's a hypothesis that has already been tested. But before we address it, here's some useful background information.

Around 1960, Senator Estes Kefauver of Tennessee held hearings and wrote bills that were, essentially, anti-big business. One industry that caught his attention due to its high profits was the pharmaceutical industry. To solve some perceived problems, Kefauver wanted to dramatically shorten patent lives, curtail marketing practices, substantially reduce drug prices, and require drug companies to prove that drugs were both safe and efficacious before they were marketed. At that time, drug companies needed only to prove safety.

He wasn't getting much traction.

And then, the thalidomide disaster hit. The issue might have blown over except that Kefauver persuaded the press to focus on it and, subsequently, instead of blowing over, the issue blew up. With the press and public focused on this tragedy, something had to be done. And it was. In just a few weeks, president John F. Kennedy went from opposing Kefauver's bill to saying it was too weak.

The FDA's rules were altered with the Kefauver-Harris Amendments of 1962, that required drug companies to prove both safety and efficacy before a new drug could be marketed.

Let's review some facts about the thalidomide tragedy because they are central to the discussion.

The FDA never approved thalidomide. Nor did it reject it. Thalidomide was in the middle of the FDA's review process. And yet there's no reason to think that, given the FDA's approach and the technology of the time, the FDA wouldn't have eventually approved thalidomide.

The FDA never uncovered thalidomide's dark secret about birth defects. In fact, it was only after the tragedy was exposed in Germany and Australia that the FDA became aware of the issue.

If you were a drug regulator, what lesson might you have learned from this tragedy? Delay, delay, delay, and hope that some other people in some other country act as your guinea pigs and Sherlock Holmes.

But the most interesting and important aspect of the tragedy is that drug companies are now required to prove both safety and efficacy before a new drug can be marketed. What kind of problem did thalidomide have? Did thalidomide have an efficacy problem? No. Did it have a safety problem? Yes. *The FDA already had rules in place to prevent unsafe drugs.* The FDA could have rejected thalidomide based on rules that had been on the books since 1938.

"You never want a serious crisis to go to waste," said President Obama's chief of staff, Rahm Emanuel. Congress and President Kennedy didn't waste this one.

Kefauver got his bill because of the thalidomide tragedy even though his bill had almost nothing to do with the thalidomide tragedy.

Have fewer drugs been developed since the FDA's rules were changed? This question has already been asked and answered.

Sam Peltzman

In 1973, economist Sam Peltzman of UCLA analyzed the effect of the 1962 rules by comparing the number of new chemical entities approved by the FDA before and after the law was changed.[17] He found that the actual number post-1962 was a shocking 61 percent below his projections.

Was it just the bad drugs that were weeded out? No. Multiple researchers have come to the conclusion that it wasn't just the bad drugs. Peltzman, himself, came to this same conclusion, seeing the culling as if "an arbitrary marketing quota...had been placed on new drugs after 1962." Peltzman's findings are worth exploring in more detail, something we'll do in Chapter 6.

Frank Lichtenberg

Columbia University's Frank Lichtenberg has studied the effects of pharmaceutical innovation.[18] His analysis suggests that three quarters of the increase in life expectancy we've enjoyed in recent decades is due solely to our adoption of modern drugs. New pharmaceuticals are more friends than foes; they are more lifesavers than killers.

And with the FDA, evidently, we have 61 percent fewer lifesavers. *That's* the real cost of the FDA.

Already, the six concepts justifying the FDA are starting to look shaky. What are the arguments of those on the other side of the issue?

Anti-FDA Thesis

The counterpoint to the pro-FDA thesis is based on thirteen straightforward concepts:

One: substances themselves aren't dangerous or safe. The safety of a substance depends on the situation and the exposure of the individual.

Two: efficacy can't be determined without decentralized trial and error by doctors and patients. The FDA's assessments of efficacy are duplicative.

Three: drugs work for some but not others. The FDA often can't tell which patients will benefit.

Four: animal studies and human clinical trials often can't tell us which drugs work and which don't. When they do give a clear answer, that answer is often wrong.

Five: with the FDA's rules, new drugs are presumed guilty until proven innocent. The FDA reduces our therapeutic choices by making it difficult for companies to develop new medicines.

Six: pharmaceuticals are more beneficial than they are detrimental; they should be presumed innocent until proven guilty.

Seven: the FDA slows new drug development and availability.

Eight: the FDA doesn't bring any unique skills to the table. There are other organizations that can and do evaluate drugs.

Nine: doctors and researchers, when given the freedom to do so, find the best uses for each new drug, accentuating the positive aspects and reducing the negative.

Ten: both you and your doctors seek drugs that work and have manageable side effects and reject drugs that don't work or have bad side effects.

Eleven: you are a unique individual and you will sometimes make different choices than others who appear to be similar. The FDA has little or no idea who you are and what you want.

Twelve: the FDA has a fundamentally different perspective from you and your doctor, and that perspective has some serious shortcomings.

Thirteen: politicians and government employees are no less attached to their jobs and the prospect of potential gain than the rest of us. Sometimes that leads them to act in ways which directly or indirectly harm us.

This book will explore these ideas and other important aspects of drug development and regulation. Toward the end of this book, I present possible solutions—often multiple ones for each issue—with the objective of fostering and furthering a debate on a topic that affects all of us directly and personally. You can agree or disagree with these solutions, but my goal is to contribute to a consequential conversation, something I hope you will join.

---

[1] Steven Pinker, *Enlightenment Now, The Case for Reason, Science, Humanism, and Progress*, Viking, 2018, p. 64. Hilleman's employment at Merck & Co. overlapped my own, but I never met him. My good friend, Tim Wissman, however, worked closely with Hilleman.

[2] "The 50 Greatest Breakthroughs Since the Wheel," *The Atlantic*, November 2013, https://www.theatlantic.com/magazine/archive/2013/11/innovations-list/309536/#list

[3] Tomas Phillipson, Julia Snider, et al, "The Social Value of Childhood Vaccination in the United States," *American Journal of Managed Care*, 5 December 2016, 2017;23(1):41-47.

[4] Michael Fumento, http://fumento.com/aids/pish.html

[5] Note that Duke University and the National Cancer Institute helped with the development of AZT.

[6] Zohar Mor et al, "Causes of death and mortality trends of all individuals reported with HIV/AIDS in Israel, 1985–2010," *Journal of Public Health*, 17 June 2017.

[7] Thomas Burton and Shelly Banjo, "How Maker of Stents for Kids Ran Afoul of FDA," *The Wall Street Journal,* 5 July 2007.

[8] Howard Root, Stephen Saltarelli, "*Cardiac Arrest*," BookBaby, 2017.

[9] Michael Wines, "New Study Supports Idea Stalin Was Poisoned," *The New York Times*, 5 March 2003.

[10] "Mustard gas – from the Great War to frontline chemotherapy," Cancer Research UK, http://scienceblog.cancerresearchuk.org/2014/08/27/mustard-gas-from-the-great-war-to-frontline-chemotherapy/

[11] "Mustard gas – from the Great War to frontline chemotherapy," Cancer Research UK, http://scienceblog.cancerresearchuk.org/2014/08/27/mustard-gas-from-the-great-war-to-frontline-chemotherapy/

[12] Carl Zimmer, "How a pit viper saved millions of lives: Snakes as drug factories," *Discover*, 11 March 2011.

[13] "Donald Trump Looking Beyond Traditional Medical Experts for FDA Commissioner," *Wall Street Journal*, 13 January 2017.

[14] See Chapter 3.

[15] See Chapter 3.

[16] See Chapter 6.

[17] See Chapter 6.

[18] See Chapters 9 and 10.

Chapter 1: History

The U.S. Food and Drug Administration (FDA) is a federal government agency that is, in its own words, responsible for:

- protecting the public health by assuring the safety, effectiveness, quality, and security of human and veterinary drugs, vaccines and other biological products, and medical devices
- the safety and security of most of our nation's food supply, all cosmetics, dietary supplements and products that give off radiation

It is surprising to us today, but before the FDA existed, people could legally buy any medication that existed. For example, any buyer could acquire morphine, which Merck began selling commercially in 1827, from any willing pharmacist.

Medicine was much simpler back then.

> *You could count the basic medicines on the fingers of your two hands. Morphine, quinine, digitalis, insulin, codeine, aspirin, arsenicals, nitroglycerine, mercurials, and a few biologicals.*
> **Former Merck & Co. president discussing products sold in the 1930s**

The history of the FDA can be traced from a single chemist in the U.S. Department of Agriculture in 1862 to a powerful agency with a staff of over 17,000 employees today. Here's how the industry publication *BioCentury* introduced its "Inside FDA's Archives" broadcast:

> Americans take it for granted that government ensures foods are safe, and medical products are safe and effective. But that wasn't always the case.
>
> FDA started out during the Civil War as a single chemist with little authority, and the following decades have seen a consistent pattern

> of opposition to the agency's oversight, followed by a tragedy or scandal that leads to expansion of FDA's mission and power.[1]

Note the implicit assumptions: drugs weren't safe before, but now they are; drugs weren't effective before, but now they are. After certain scandals and tragedies, the FDA's powers increased, meaning that, previously, the fledgling FDA could not ensure the safety of medical products and foods in America, but now, as a regulatory powerhouse, it can. It stands to reason, given this view, that the problems experienced in this country were far worse before the FDA acquired these powers. What types of problems?

Tragedies

Here's what I wrote in "Pharmaceuticals: Economics and Regulation" for *The Concise Encyclopedia of Economics* (free on the web[2]):

> In 1937, to make a palatable liquid version of its new antibiotic drug sulfanilamide, the Massengill Company carelessly used the solvent diethylene glycol, which we now recognize as antifreeze. Elixir Sulfanilamide killed 107 people, mostly children, before it was quickly recalled; Massengill was successfully sued and the chemist responsible committed suicide. This tragedy led to the Food, Drug, and Cosmetic Act of 1938, which required that drugs be proven safe prior to marketing. In the next infamous tragedy, more than 10,000 European babies were born deformed after their mothers took thalidomide as a tranquilizer to alleviate morning sickness. This led to the Kefauver-Harris Amendments of 1962, which required that efficacy be proven prior to marketing.[3]

Elixir Sulfanilamide

With Elixir Sulfanilamide, sulfanilamide—which had just seven years earlier saved President Franklin Roosevelt's 22-year-old son from a grave illness—wasn't the problem; its diethylene glycol base was. One physician wrote the following about his personal involvement in the Elixir Sulfanilamide debacle:

> But to realize that six human beings, all of them my patients, one of them my best friend, are dead because they took medicine that I prescribed for them innocently, and to realize that that medicine which I had used for years in such cases suddenly had become a deadly poison in its newest and most modern form, as recommended by a great and reputable pharmaceutical firm in Tennessee: well, that realization has given me such days and nights of mental and spiritual agony as I did not believe a human being could undergo and survive. I have known hours when death for me would be a welcome relief from this agony.[4]

According to the late legal scholar David F. Cavers, the momentous Food, Drug, and Cosmetic Act of 1938—designed to address the Elixir Sulfanilamide problem—ended up affecting every American and numerous large industries, however it "...never became the object of widespread public attention, much less of informed public interest. I suspect that today [shortly after the law was passed] only a small fraction of the public knows that a new law has been enacted."[5]

Thalidomide

The FDA had not approved thalidomide—not because it had specifically rejected the drug, but because the drug's application sat on the desk of FDA reviewer Frances Kelsey, mainly due to delays in answering some remaining questions. Kelsey and the two other reviewers had no reason to suspect the now infamous birth defects until the problem became apparent in Germany and Australia. The linkage between thalidomide and birth defects was first made public by Australian doctor William McBride in December 1961 and this bombshell heralded the beginning of the end for thalidomide. The history of thalidomide is especially important given its sizable influence on regulatory policy.

Some think blocking thalidomide was the FDA's greatest achievement. Can you find evidence of FDA heroism in the following abbreviated timeline for thalidomide?[6] [7]

- October 1957: Grünenthal launches thalidomide for over-the-counter sales in West Germany
- April 1958: Distillers Co. Ltd. launches thalidomide for sale in the United Kingdom
- October 1959: Grünenthal receives reports of nerve damage in patients taking thalidomide (note: this issue was not related to fetal birth defects)
- February 1960: Scottish doctor Leslie Florence contacts Distillers about nerve damage in patients taking thalidomide
- August 1960: Distillers launches thalidomide in Australia and New Zealand
- September 1960: William S. Merrell Co. submits new drug application to the FDA
- October 1960: Merrell distributes thalidomide tablets to 1,231 U.S. doctors as part of a "clinical trial"
- November 1960: FDA reviewer Kelsey, noting that the submitted clinical studies were incomplete, requests that Merrell conduct further studies of thalidomide
- December 1960: *The British Medical Journal* publishes a letter by Florence about nerve damage in patients taking thalidomide
- Early 1961: Kelsey reads Florence letter in *BMJ*
- May 1961: Grünenthal moves thalidomide to prescription-only status in West Germany
- May and August 1961: Distillers and Grünenthal put warning labels on thalidomide, warning of nerve damage in patients taking thalidomide
- June 1961: Australian obstetrician William McBride phoned Distillers to request that sales be suspended
- Mid-November 1961: German pediatrician Widukind Lenz phoned Grünenthal to warn that birth defects might be caused by thalidomide
- Mid-November 1961: Physicians Wilhelm Kosenow and Rudolf Pfeiffer present findings of limb deformities at a scientific meeting in West Germany
- Mid-November 1961: Lenz states publicly that the limb deformities reported by Kosenow and Pfeiffer were due to a specific, unnamed drug
- Late-November 1961: German newsmagazine *Welt am Sonntag* calls for the withdrawal of the still-unnamed drug
- Late-November 1961: thalidomide is pulled from market in West Germany, Britain, and Australia
- December 1961: *The Lancet* publishes a letter from McBride linking congenital abnormalities to thalidomide

- March 1962: Merrell voluntarily withdraws U.S. new drug application for thalidomide and calls back all unused tablets from U.S. doctors
- 1962: sales stop in Belgium, Brazil, Canada, Italy, and Japan
- July 1962: *The Washington Post* publishes an article about Kelsey and thalidomide
- August 1962: Kelsey receives award from President Kennedy
- October 1962: Kefauver-Harris Drug Amendments bill signed into law

Kelsey was hailed as a heroine and received the President's Award for Distinguished Federal Civilian Service from John F. Kennedy, and yet she never suspected or discovered thalidomide's dark secret, nor did she directly reject William S. Merrell Co.'s new drug application. The link between thalidomide and birth defects was uncovered in Germany and Australia and then events overtook and obviated an FDA review.[8] The sponsoring company, Merrell, voluntarily withdrew the new drug application when the risks of thalidomide became apparent to everyone involved. This belies a supposed benefit of the FDA: isn't the FDA expected to uncover problems *before* they become obvious? While we are fortunate to have avoided this teratogenic compound's widespread use in America, what many see as the FDA's greatest achievement—stopping thalidomide—was ultimately the result of red tape and dumb luck.

Interestingly, the Kefauver-Harris Amendments, had they been in place at the time, probably would not have prevented FDA approval of thalidomide due to the FDA's methodology and the low level of medical sophistication at the time.

> Amazingly enough, the 1962 amendments would still not have kept thalidomide off the market in the United States. The precise strain of rodent that would have been required to identify the lesion was not in common use, and the adverse event frequency in neonates [newborn babies], in the average-sized NDA [new drug application] of the day, might not detect adverse events of such low frequency.[9]

The thalidomide episode demonstrates that if the only objective is to prevent the marketing of dangerous drugs, a failsafe strategy is delay, delay, and delay. Act like a bureaucrat and make sure that every box is checked; take as much time as possible, allowing other people to function as our coal mine canaries. Clearly, that's not what the typical person wants because new drugs, in addition to potential health risks, also have potential health *benefits*, and delaying those benefits harms people.

Note that even though thalidomide's problem was clearly one of *safety*, an issue for which the FDA already had regulations, the laws were changed to add proof of *efficacy*. This is the non sequitur we presently deal with: because one drug had a safety problem and was withdrawn by its manufacturer, a government agency now must determine that all future drugs provide useful clinical benefits before a single dose is sold.

Certainly, others were hurt by ineffective or unsafe drugs outside of the Elixir Sulfanilamide and thalidomide sagas, but if we limit this to Americans, the combined number of those involved in such prominent tragedies is, perhaps, in the thousands (there were 17 thalidomide babies in the U.S.). If we expand the scope to include Europeans, Canadians, New Zealanders, and Australians, the numbers are, perhaps, in the tens of thousands.

These were certainly tragedies, and even one death is one too many. But in the grand scheme, these thousands of American deaths pale in comparison to estimates that 100,000 Americans die *each year* from FDA-approved drugs—drugs that are supposedly safe—and to the *millions* who die because they lack adequate medicines. Thankfully, these relatively small tragedies were contained, in the sense that people learned what had gone wrong and presumably worked hard to avoid making the same mistake later.

> *Life is a perpetual instruction in cause and effect.*
> **Ralph Waldo Emerson**

The role of the countless tragic mistakes made throughout history is widely recognized as an impetus for learning and preventing subsequent mistakes. Consider the Donner Party, which suffered through the snowy winter of 1846-47 on its journey west to California. Only 45 of the original 89 survived, and they did so, in part, by eating the bodies of those who had perished. This was a tragedy by any definition, but people learned

from it—presumably not to cross a mountain pass in the winter or, at least, to be better prepared to do so.

What if the official response to the Donner Party incident had been to prohibit all further migrations westward? Or consider an official response —not unlike FDA regulations—requiring all future wagon trains, before embarking, to prove to a government agency that they could safely and successfully travel to California. Both solutions seem overbearing, expensive, and unnecessary, given that people could, and did, learn from and avoid the Donner Party's mistakes. How do we learn and improve? By trying things, sometimes succeeding, sometimes failing, and by watching others do the same. The goal of all parties traveling west was to get there safely, easily, and quickly, meaning that immigrant parties were already motivated to plan and act properly; these immigrants didn't need a government official to tell them what they already knew. Warning people of risks and reminding them to avoid bad outcomes might have some benefit, but prohibiting them from getting into situations that might lead to bad outcomes is entirely different.

Those who were put directly at risk from traveling long distances by wagon train were the wagon train parties themselves. Thus, the outcomes of the wagon trains' treks, whether good or bad, were internalized, so to speak—and did not put others outside the expeditionary parties at direct risk, an aspect of public health that needs to be considered when discussing regulatory policies.

Today, we are protected by the FDA. But consider for a moment that a doctor who is determined to give a pregnant patient thalidomide theoretically could do so. If this is true, then why don't we have "thalidomide babies" today? The answer is straightforward: the medical establishment—doctors, nurses, scientists, guideline committees, watchdogs, the press, third-party payers, hospitals, pharmacists, and patients—learned long ago that thalidomide shouldn't be given to pregnant women (it is teratogenic—able to disturb the development of the fetus). This is a good thing. This is learning.

The primary difference between our attitude toward thalidomide now and pre-1962 doesn't necessarily have to do with the FDA. Rather, it's what we have learned through experiences that have been deposited, just like sedimentary layers, throughout our society. Give thalidomide to a pregnant woman? No way!

Pre-FDA

Before the FDA existed, drugs were "tested" by patients and their doctors through regular clinical, medical practice. Of course, there were home remedies and quack treatments, and people made mistakes. However, patients had a strong incentive to take only medicines that would help them, and physicians—some of the most intelligent and highly educated members of society—had a strong incentive to help their patients become well. As illustrated above by the disconsolate physician's tale in the Elixir Sulfanilamide tragedy, it has always been a poor business practice to kill your customers.

It is easy to look back at the pre-FDA period in medicine and believe that, if the FDA had existed, people wouldn't have been exposed to so much quackery and so many dubious drugs. If we compare today's medical world—with its anesthesia, antibiotics, immune-oncology drugs, and gene therapy—with the world of the 18th century—with its treatments based on camel's urine, cigarettes laced with mercury, and being wrapped in the bowels of a freshly slaughtered sheep—it might be easy to conclude, "Aha!, the FDA must be the driver of our vaunted medical improvements." We need to stop and remind ourselves that that period in history wasn't just the pre-regulation period but was also the pre-scientific, pre-technology, pre-medical knowledge, and pre-wealth period. There wasn't enough scientific knowledge, scientific infrastructure, medical experience, medical infrastructure, technology, wealth and, for that matter, electricity, refrigeration, and decent transportation to support the types of medical care that the FDA requires and we expect nowadays.

Let's face it—an absence of government regulations was not the reason cavemen lacked smoke detectors and Roman chariots traveled sans air bags.

It is startling to realize that George Washington, who was treated with mercury pills and bleeding by his doctors,[10] had largely the same medical care available to him as did Julius Caesar. Even barely 70 years ago, there were no effective treatments for most medical conditions. Gradually, we entered a period with a few treatments, and the current era continues to see more treatments available for many conditions. In previous periods, patients chose whether or not to take the one available drug. The current environment often allows us the choice among multiple drugs, but also the burden of figuring out which is best. Yet we should be very clear that this is still the dark age of medicine: good diagnostics are the exception, not the rule; most medicines are severely deficient; and there are numerous serious conditions without a single good treatment. As this was being written in early 2020, there were no effective therapies and vaccines for SARS-CoV-2, the virus that causes COVID-19. We need better technology and better medicines, and we need them now, not 50 or 100 years from

now. This lack of good medicines and good medical care is killing your friends, family, and neighbors at an alarming rate.

In America alone, 2.4 million people die each year from disease, degradation, and old age. Many of us take these afflictions and their death toll for granted, with a shrug of the shoulders, but we shouldn't. Imagine that there were a cell of terrorists lurking in this country killing 2.4 million people per year, or 6,500 per day, for the equivalent of two 9/11 terrorist attacks *per day*. How many people would blithely accept this murderous band? I wouldn't. You wouldn't and shouldn't. Doctors, nurses, hospitals, and the pharmaceutical industry don't accept the death toll from "natural causes" because they see that many, many deaths and disabilities can be prevented, ameliorated, or delayed. Here, and in many other situations, "natural" does not equal "good."

FDA Powers

Food, Drug, and Cosmetic Act of 1938

With the passage of the Food, Drug, and Cosmetic Act of 1938, pharmaceutical companies were required to test their drugs for safety. As has been known for centuries, and is evident upon examination, the dose makes the poison. For instance, virtually all of us have minute concentrations of mercury in our blood—with no adverse effects—but only a few of us have mercury concentrations high enough to cause concern. However, there is no reason to imitate George Washington and swallow mercury pills, purposely raising our blood levels of mercury to dangerous levels.

As discussed in the Introduction, a large dose of warfarin may have killed Joseph Stalin and a smaller dose is successfully used by my friend to manage his blood clots.

When new drugs are tested for safety, the dosage must be considered. A low dose of warfarin provides no danger, but also no benefit. A high dose is effectively a poison. The middle dose balances efficacy and safety, but reasonable people can question what "safety" means and where best to balance safety and efficacy—is it necessarily in the "middle"? Plus, as with disease, safety announces itself door-to-door: you might have an adverse reaction to a widely-prescribed drug, while I might not.

Kefauver-Harris Amendments of 1962

After the Kefauver-Harris Amendments of 1962, pharmaceutical companies were required to test their drugs for both safety and efficacy. Testing for efficacy introduced a new wrinkle: efficacy for what? Testing for efficacy requires the sponsoring drug company to clearly state *exactly* which condition the drug is supposed to treat. Is it for headaches or migraines? If it is for migraines, is it for chronic or episodic migraines? Is it for the treatment of migraines or the prevention of migraines? Is it for people with chronic migraines resistant to other treatments or just the run-of-the-mill kind? Pre-migraine aura or not? Known migraine triggers or not? Et cetera.

Breast cancer is even more bifurcated. What does the new drug treat: Monotherapy or combo? Hormone receptor-positive? Human epidermal growth factor receptor 2-negative? Triple-negative? BRCA-mutated? Advanced? Postmenopausal patients? Patients who have received endocrine therapy? First-line therapy? Second-line therapy? And on and on.

Further, because even efficacious drugs don't benefit all patients—a normal range is 20 to 70 percent of patients— each individual patient, under the care of a doctor, must experiment to see if the new drug successfully treats that particular person at that particular time. Even after the FDA determines that the drug is sufficiently efficacious, each patient must still run his or her own experiment. This duplicative process is necessary because each patient is unique and the FDA can't tell, beforehand, which patients will benefit.

Safe, Efficacious . . . and Better?

These days, the FDA is empowered to judge whether a drug is safe and efficacious, and that's all. In its literature, the FDA confirms this role, saying: "Once a new drug application is filed, an FDA review team—medical doctors, chemists, statisticians, microbiologists, pharmacologists, and other experts—evaluates whether the studies the sponsor submitted show that the drug is safe and effective for its proposed use."[11] But in many cases, the FDA slyly adds a third requirement: Is the new drug better than what is currently on the market? Is there a need for it?

Robert Myer, director of the FDA's Office of Drug Evaluation II, told reporters that, "simply having another drug on the market wasn't sufficient reason to approve the product [a new drug being evaluated] unless there was a unique role defined." Under the law, that was outside the FDA's mandate[12] and, using a more familiar product to illustrate, consider how difficult and expensive it would be to show that Ford trucks are safe, useful, *and* better than Chevy and Dodge trucks before even selling a single Ford truck. What would the FDA do in this truck example? If Chevy and Dodge were on the market first, the FDA might reject outright Ford's application to sell trucks. "Why do we need Ford when we've already got Chevy and Dodge?"

Me-Too Drugs

Some critics disdainfully refer to drugs that are similar to, and not materially better than, existing drugs as "me-too drugs." The implication is that once we have one drug with a certain mechanism of action, that's all we need, and somehow biopharma companies are cheating us or are wasting everyone's time by developing me-too drugs. Note that they are agreeing with the FDA that "simply having another drug" isn't sufficient.

Think, again, about automobiles: Ford is a me-too Chevrolet and the Accord is a me-too Camry. And yet some people prefer Ford to Chevy and Accords to Camrys, choosing the one that best suits their needs. And, just as important, competition from Ford keeps Chevrolet on its toes and helps keep prices lower.

There are good reasons for having another drug (or truck) on the market. Take pretty much any medicine and ask around. You'll find that each product has its adherents and its critics. Isn't it possible that at least some segments of the population would find that a new safe and effective drug addresses their needs? Even if the clinical results of a new drug look identical to those of the existing one, we can't tell, based on most clinical trials, whether the two drugs will help the same patients. What if Drug A helps 50 percent patients and Drug B helps the *other* 50 percent?

The final reason that drug companies shouldn't have to prove that their drug is better than existing drugs is summed up in one word: competition. Take the worst case and assume that a new drug is no better for anyone than any existing drug but is equally good for some patients. In that "worst case," the new drug would compete with existing drugs. Two centuries of economic theory and evidence show that competition is good. A new drug that competes with existing drugs is likely to keep those competitors on their toes and put downward pressure on their prices.

This issue is not theoretical.

Non-Inferiority Tests

When the FDA wants a company to measure how a new drug compares to an existing drug, it requires the drug company to run a non-inferiority trial, to prove, at a minimum, that the new drug is no worse than the existing drug. In such a trial, that company gives some patients the established drug and other patients the new drug.

In 2017, small California-based Versartis was left reeling after a Phase 3 trial of its lead product failed to show non-inferiority to an existing product. The results were close, with Versartis' growth hormone drug somavaratan producing 9.44 cm of "height velocity" among prepubescent children, while the existing product, Genotropin, produced 10.70 cm.[13] Versartis lost 80 percent of its value in one day as the prospects of approval plummeted.[14] But why? If Versartis demonstrates that somavaratan is safe and effective, the FDA is legally obligated to approve it. Is the FDA saying that Americans and their doctors are so inept that they can't properly choose and use a drug that has been proven to be both safe and effective? If so, we need it to publicly state that. Isn't it possible that some patients will find somavaratan superior to Genotropin? And if they don't, sales of somavaratan will be zero. The market will have solved the problem.

Currently, with growth hormone products, patients—actually the parents of the patients—and their doctors decide between two alternatives: daily doses of short-acting Genotropin with a resulting 10.70 cm boost or no injections and zero boost. Isn't it possible that some parents would choose the more convenient twice-monthly injections of somavaratan with a boost of 9.44 cm? The FDA is implying that height gain is the only thing that matters, and yet many people strongly prefer two injections per month to thirty. Do you really want a government agency making these tradeoffs for you and your children and taking away your choice?

Further, clinical trials artificially force patients to take their medicines punctually, whereas most patients outside of clinical trials are less fastidious.[15] In a squeaky clean, rigidly controlled clinical trial, Genotropin was better than somavaratan, based solely on height gain. But in the real world, where patients regularly miss doses due to poor compliance, even missing as little as 10 percent of doses would likely make the two drugs equivalent in terms of efficacy. If 20 percent of doses were missed, somavaratan could very likely come out the winner.

The FDA doesn't seem to care about this insight.

Another problem with non-inferiority trials is that they compare apples and oranges. While the new product might not give stellar results for the average patient, it might be far better for a subset of patients. For instance, Genotropin might be better for 70 percent of patients, while the Versartis growth hormone formulation might be better for the rest. Now, because the product has been shelved, we'll never get to find out.

There's no clear line above which drugs are safe and below which others are unsafe. How much safety and efficacy are enough? Well, it depends on what else is currently available. How virulent is the disease? What are the alternatives? If all cancer treatments cause patients to lose all their hair (alopecia), a new treatment that causes only half the patients to lose their hair is better. If no cancer treatments cause alopecia, a new treatment that caused hair loss might be unacceptable. In the world of medicine, there is room for both absolute and relative evaluations. And because health care professions and their patients compare the attributes of products, the FDA doesn't need to, and any attempt to do so shows how far the FDA has strayed from its original mission. Moving the FDA from *approving* safe and efficacious drugs to *choosing* them is no small transgression.

Absinthe

We can't conclude any review of government regulation without discussing misfires: foods and drugs that have been incorrectly vilified at one time but later absolved. Absinthe is a perfect example.

Green, licorice-tasting absinthe was one of the most popular liquors during the 19th century. But, because it was later found to be toxic and psychedelic due to one of its components, thujone, the U.S. government banned absinthe in 1912. Absinthe supposedly once caused Oscar Wilde to witness flowers springing up around him at a café. It was also rumored to have influenced Vincent van Gogh's decision to slice off his ear and was implicated in a particularly grisly murder in Switzerland. The ban on absinthe was rescinded in 2007, but only after some dedicated citizens convinced the government that absinthe contains only trace amounts of thujone, a compound also found in other herbs. "The sage in your Thanksgiving stuffing will give you more thujone than any normal absinthe," said Brian Robinson of the Wormwood Society, a nonprofit dedicated to dispelling myths about the spirit.[16]

We can happily drink our absinthe again and take comfort in the knowledge that this simple mistake was rectified in less than a century!

Grape Nuts

If we hopped into a time machine and went back to the "good old days," we would see one of my favorite breakfast foods, Grape Nuts, being advertised as a cure for tuberculosis and appendicitis, along with some early 20th century advertisements for Bayer's aspirin claiming it "does not affect the heart."

Yikes.

Grape Nuts didn't cure my appendicitis, but I have yet to test it with TB. Many people, myself included, take aspirin because it *does* affect the heart, or at least the blood within the heart. Maybe the good old days weren't all that good.

They weren't. But they were getting better, partly from the efforts of people like Arthur J. Cramp, who, through his work with the American Medical Association, personally assumed the task of identifying and exposing quackery.[17] In one humorous example, in 1910 he took on A.W. Van Bysterveld, from Grand Rapids, Michigan, who claimed to be an

"Expert Inspector of Urine." Van Bysterveld declared that he had a secret process of analyzing urine that had been handed down generation after generation and was "most carefully guarded by the old families of Europe." So Cramp created fake urine with tap water, pepsin, aniline dye, and ammonia and mailed it to Van Bysterveld for analysis. Cramp enlisted the help of others in different locations to send in the same fake urine mixture. As you might imagine, the huckster Van Bysterveld provided each of the customers in this sting operation with a different diagnosis, such as "too much acid in the blood," "the back is weak," "malfunctioning liver," "heart problems," "gas," and a "tired, nervous feeling most of the time." Van Bysterveld had simply fabricated these diagnoses as there were no patients and no real urine. Cramp wrote a weekly column in *JAMA* exposing deceptive and outright fraudulent medical products and practices, helping to professionalize American medicine.

What does this story show? There were and are people willing to promote fraudulent products for a quick buck. However, even without government regulation and oversight, there were and are private forces aligned to challenge and attack these medical quacks.

It was in this world of Cramp, Grape Nuts, absinthe, and a supposed urine expert that the FDA was given massive regulatory power to keep dangerous and ineffective drugs off the market. The theory was straightforward: unsafe drugs can harm people directly, and inefficacious drugs give people false hopes, waste their money, and occupy their time and attention when better therapies might be available. In short, keeping dangerous and ineffective drugs off the market helps Americans.

Yet problems persist today. There are still unacceptable drug interactions, adverse events, and drugs that were later pulled from market (see Chapter 2). Even with these problems, many drugs don't work that well. Either they don't help many patients or they don't help them much (see Chapter 3). The cost of drug research and development has grown at 2.3 times the rate of inflation (see Chapter 6), and the FDA, flexing its muscles, has gone so far as to criminally convict a pharmaceutical executive and utterly destroy his career for a press release that even the government admits was factually correct (see Chapter 8). Worse, our medicine cabinets are far sparser than they should be, reducing our ability to keep our loved ones safe and healthy (see Chapter 6). Are there better approaches? Has the FDA succeeded in its mission? Let's take this explication one step at a time. Next, we'll consider safety.

---

[1] BioCentury TV email 25 August 2014.

[2] http://www.econlib.org/library/CEE.html

[3] http://www.econlib.org/library/Enc/PharmaceuticalsEconomicsandRegulation.html

[4] Letter by Dr. A.S. Calhoun, October 22, 1937, from FDA website: http://www.fda.gov/aboutfda/whatwedo/history/productregulation/sulfanilamidedisaster/default.htm

[5] David F. Cavers, "The Food, Drug, and Cosmetic Act of 1938: Its Legislative History and its Substantive Provisions," Duke Law, 1939, http://scholarship.law.duke.edu/cgi/viewcontent.cgi?article=1937&context=lcp

[6] The Conversation, "Timeline: key events in the history of thalidomide," 6 December 2015.

[7] "Thalidomide—Detailed History and Timeline," RMS Consultancy.

[8] Nancy Kriplen, "The Heroine of the FDA," *Discover Magazine*, March 2017.

[9] *Principles and Practices of Pharmaceutical Medicine*, edited by Lionel Edwards, Andrew Fletcher, Anthony Fox, and Peter Stonier, John Wiley & Sons, 2007.

[10] The theory was to debilitate the body to the point where the disease had nothing left to work with!

[11] FDA website, http://www.fda.gov/Drugs/ResourcesForYou/Consumers/ucm289601.htm

[12] David R. Henderson & Charles L. Hooper, "Our Lawless FDA," *The Wall Street Journal,* 17 May 2007.

[13] "Versartis Announces Phase 3 VELOCITY Trial of Somavaratan in Pediatric Growth Hormone Deficiency Did Not Meet Primary Endpoint," Versartis press release, 21 September 2017.

[14] Nick Paul Taylor, "Phase 3 flop puts Versartis on life support," *FierceBiotech*, 22 September 2017.

[15] "Versartis Announces Phase 3 VELOCITY Trial of Somavaratan in Pediatric Growth Hormone Deficiency Did Not Meet Primary Endpoint," Versartis press release, 21 September 2017.

[16] David Marcelis, "Absinthe Was Once Banned for Being Evil—Now It's Just Meh, " *The Wall Street Journal,* 23 November 2017.

[17] Robert Blaskiewicz and Mike Jarsulic, "Arthur J. Cramp: The Quackbuster Who Professionalized American Medicine," *Skeptical Inquirer*, Nov./Dec. 2018.

Chapter 2: Drugs are Still Unsafe

According to *BioCentury*, "Americans take it for granted that government ensures foods are safe, and medical products are safe and effective. But that wasn't always the case." The FDA is charged with ensuring that all medicines we Americans consume are safe, a role that many support. Has it succeeded?

If you, like most people, support the FDA's safety policing, you are probably assuming that it is obvious which drugs are safe and which ones aren't, and that safety is a clear concept with clear measurements, providing unambiguous signals. Further, you are probably assuming that the FDA is doing the job you would do if you had the training and were put in that position—that if you pored over the data, both you and the FDA would come to similar conclusions. But what if safety isn't that black or white? What if the FDA has biases and is employing judgments and values that don't coincide with yours? What if the FDA is using flawed techniques? What if the FDA is just guessing?

What if there are "safe" drugs that are really unsafe and "unsafe" drugs that are really safe?

What Does Safety Mean?

Consider the definition of safety. Safe is defined as not likely to cause or lead to harm or injury; not involving danger or risk. Safety is defined as the condition of being protected from or unlikely to cause danger, risk, or injury.

Does drug "safety" mean that no one will ever be hurt by a medicine? Or is there a threshold of harm below which a drug is considered safe? If so, is that threshold one percent of patients? Five percent? Ten percent? How badly do they need to be hurt? Do they need to die, or would a headache count? How about a swollen purple tongue?

A microwave oven is considered safe if it doesn't short circuit and burn down your house while you are at work, render your leftover Thai food toxic, or shower you with harmful electromagnetic waves. Even a product considered safe can be dangerous if used improperly, either inadvertently ("Wow! Look at the cool colors the aluminum foil on my soup bowl gives off in the microwave!") or purposefully, if, for example, you override the safety features.

The FDA works hard to ensure that the foods and medicines that we Americans consume are safe. But what does safe mean in the context of medicine? Many would assume that it means—as with the microwave oven—that if not abused or used in crazy ways, the foods and medicines approved by the FDA will not directly hurt us. Anyone holding this belief will be disappointed.

Are FDA-Approved Drugs Safe?

Since the passage of the Food, Drug, and Cosmetic Act in 1938, all pharmaceutical companies have been required to test their drugs for safety, and safety is the most important product attribute the FDA considers before approving new drugs—more important than efficacy, tolerability, and dosing. Every new drug marketed during the last eight decades has been certified "safe" by the FDA.

Would it surprise you to learn that some patients who have taken FDA-approved drugs for osteoporosis have had the unfortunate aftereffect of a rotting jawbone? It's called Dead Jaw Syndrome and it has happened, albeit rarely, when the jawbones of patients on osteoporosis drugs have failed to heal after a minor injury, such as getting a tooth pulled. Patients can end up with a rotted, soft jawbone, unable to speak clearly or even eat solid foods. Can we consider these drugs, which otherwise help millions by slowing the deterioration of their bones, "safe"?

Cyanide is one of the metabolites of Nitropress (nitroprusside sodium)—used to treat conditions such as congestive heart failure—creating the risk of cyanide poisoning with longer-term use, particularly in patients with liver dysfunction. You might be interested in the symptoms: an almond odor to the breath, acidosis, tachycardia, mental status changes, and the ultimate of all adverse events, death. Is Nitropress safe?

Sometimes safety warnings can be unexpected and startling. The FDA reported that "Viberzi (eluxadoline), a medicine used to treat irritable bowel syndrome with diarrhea (IBS-D), should not be used in patients who do not have a gallbladder. An FDA review found these patients have an increased risk of developing serious pancreatitis that could result in hospitalization or death."[1] This strange result was discovered *after* the FDA approved Viberzi based on clinical trials involving nearly three thousand patients.

Consider Adriamycin (doxorubicin), a chemotherapeutic agent green-lighted by the FDA in 1991. Approximately 11 percent of patients taking Adriamycin develop acute cardiotoxicity and 1.7 percent develop chronic cardiotoxicity.[2] Cardiotoxicity can lead to cardiomyopathy, for which there is no treatment and carries a 50-percent mortality rate. Should we consider Adriamycin "safe"?

Shine a light on Pfizer's Norcuron (vercuronium bromide), a muscle relaxant that the FDA has approved as "safe and effective." Norcuron is used, against Pfizer's wishes, to carry out lethal injections for executions of condemned prisoners. With convoluted logic suitable for Alice in Wonderland, lawyers for inmates on death row sometimes question whether the drugs to be used in executions are safe and effective.[3] If you are going to kill someone, you should make sure the drug you use is safe! Can we judge Norcuron safe if it is proficient at killing people?

Consider another drug, Reglan (metoclopramide)—used to treat such issues as nausea, vomiting, and heartburn—approved by the FDA in December 1980 and saddled with a "black box warning" on its label in 2009. Is metoclopramide safe? The FDA-approved label for metoclopramide tells us in bold lettering: "**Treatment with metoclopramide can cause tardive dyskinesia, a serious movement disorder that is often irreversible. The risk of developing tardive dyskinesia increases with duration of treatment and total cumulative dose.**"

The side effects of metoclopramide include repetitive, involuntary muscle movements, such as lip-smacking, lip puckering, pursing of the lips, excessive eye blinking, grimacing, tongue movements, and an urge to be constantly moving (extra-pyramidal effects). In a more extreme form, the side effects are termed tardive dyskinesia and include irreversible, uncontrollable body or facial movements. But that's not all. Here is a list of metoclopramide's adverse reactions—reactions that can occur, even if rarely—according to the FDA-approved label, in the order presented:

- Restlessness
- Drowsiness
- Fatigue
- Lassitude
- Insomnia
- Headache
- Confusion
- Dizziness
- Mental depression with suicidal ideation
- Acute dystonic reactions
- Parkinsonian-like symptoms
- Tardive dyskinesia
- Neuroleptic malignant syndrome
- Galactorrhea

- Amenorrhea
- Gynecomastia
- Impotence
- Hypotension
- Hypertension
- Supraventricular tachycardia
- Bradycardia
- Fluid retention
- Acute congestive heart failure
- Nausea
- Bowel disturbances
- Hepatotoxicity
- Urinary frequency and incontinence
- Neutropenia
- Leukopenia
- Sulfhemoglobinemia
- Rash
- Uticaria
- Angioneurotic edema
- Visual disturbances
- Porphyria

I'm not sure that I even want to know what some of those adverse reactions, such as sulfhemoglobinemia, are. Is metoclopramide "safe"? To truly make an informed choice, we would need to know the rates for each of these adverse events. But, on the surface, metoclopramide appears to be anything but safe. Imagine if your microwave oven had such a long list of possible problems, including:

- Explosions
- Fires
- Broken glass
- Electrocution
- Molten metal
- Pealing lead paint
- Chipping plastic
- Effluvium

- Ear-piercing noises
- Mushroom clouds
- Conflagration
- Tumult
- Hazardous flashes of light
- Toxic fumes
- Skin discoloration
- Pandemonium
- Lawlessness
- Shrapnel
- Etc.

Would you consider such an oven safe? Few would. Has the FDA succeeded in ensuring that all drugs are safe? Clearly not. According to Glaxo's former chairman and chief executive officer, J.P. Garnier, "The notion that drugs are perfectly safe 'is Wonderland.'"[4] And metoclopramide is still on the market today, categorized as "safe and effective" by the FDA.

Consider epilepsy. A close relative of mine suffers from epilepsy, and his family can attest to the fact that it is a life-stealing disease, party from the seizures and partly from the nasty treatments. Drugs used to treat or control seizures are responsible for the following side effects:

- Difficulty thinking clearly (66 percent of patients)
- Drowsiness (67 percent)
- Lethargy (66 percent)
- Clumsiness (61 percent)
- Depression (57 percent)
- Weight gain (42 percent)

And the sad list goes on and on. Fifty-three percent of epilepsy patients found their medication side effects to be "extremely frustrating," while 36 percent found them to be "debilitating."[5] Identify people with a bad disease and then hobble them with bad treatments. It's barbaric, really.

Are epilepsy treatments "safe"? No. Are the treatments literally killing people? Scientists aren't sure. But they do know that epileptics suffer from an increased incidence of sudden and unexplained death, perhaps due to the treatments or to the disease itself.

There are two broad actions that the FDA takes regarding drugs that have safety issues. The first consists of drugs that have such imposing problems that they are pulled from the market. The diabetes drug Rezulin (troglitazone) was pulled from the market in 2000 after it was linked to dozens of cases of fatal liver damage. Propulsid (cisapride), a heartburn drug, was pulled from the market in March 2000 after 80 users died. Baycol (cerivastatin), Seldane (terfenadine), Vioxx (rofecoxib), and "Fen Phen" (fenfluramine and phentermine) are well-known examples of FDA-approved drugs that their manufacturers voluntarily withdrew after they were found to be dangerous to some patients. In the case of Vioxx, a non-steroidal anti-inflammatory drug (NSAID), Merck discovered that patients on therapy for 18 months or more faced a doubled risk of heart attack and stroke and promptly pulled its blockbuster product from the market.

The second action regards drugs that have some problems, but whose benefits still outweigh their risks, so they remain available. Xalatan (latanoprost) for glaucoma has caused ten to 20 percent of people's blue and green eyes to permanently turn brown. This amazing side effect was uncovered only after the drug was green-lighted by the FDA.

Just watch any television ad for any drug and you'll hear a long list of potential side effects, some worse than others. For instance, due to repeated advertisements, we have learned that if you take Viagra (sildenafil) for erectile dysfunction, you could develop sudden vision or hearing loss or an erection that won't go away. The more common—but still not very common—side effects of Viagra include headache, flushing, upset stomach, abnormal vision, changes in color vision, blurred vision, stuffy or runny nose, back pain, muscle pain, nausea, dizziness, and rash. "I don't know, honey, I took my Viagra, but I'm just not in the mood tonight. It must have something to do with this headache, upset stomach, blurred vision, and rash."

Taking too much of the popular drug Tylenol (acetaminophen) can poison your liver. Serious liver damage is rare, but of the 100 million people a year who take acetaminophen, 56,000 end up in emergency rooms due to acetaminophen overdoses, and about 100 people die after unintentionally taking too much. Liver toxicity from acetaminophen poisoning is by far the most common cause of acute liver failure in the U.S.

Years ago, I talked to a family friend who nearly died from bleeding due to the analgesic Naprosyn (naproxen). This was especially upsetting to me because at the time I worked for the company, Syntex, that invented and made Naprosyn. Even with her close call and, perhaps, many others that we don't know about, naproxen is still available and widely used today, frequently as Bayer's over-the counter (OTC) drug Aleve.

Vioxx and all the COX-2 inhibitor drugs, such as Celebrex (celecoxib), were specifically designed to be safer than drugs such as aspirin, ibuprofen, and naproxen, all of which are non-steroidal anti-inflammatory drugs that can cause gastrointestinal bleeding. Experts have estimated that in the United States, NSAID-induced gastrointestinal complications result in more than 100,000 hospitalizations and 16,500 deaths per year. This is what happened to the aforementioned family friend who took naproxen and ended up in the hospital.

Safety is an important issue; however, it is vital to realize that safety fears can be overblown. For instance, in clinical trials, children on antidepressants were 1.8 times as likely to have so-called suicidal tendencies as equally depressed children taking placebos. That sounds bad. Is it? Not really. An analysis of 27 studies of young people being treated with antidepressants showed that only 0.7 percent of patients had increased suicidal thoughts—so, that 0.7 percent is 1.8 times an even smaller number (0.4 percent).[6]

How many of the 4,000 children on eight different antidepressants actually committed suicide in these studies? None.[7] Not a single one. While there were no completed suicides in *any* of the studies, there *was* a measured increase in the rate of teen suicides after the FDA, in response to these studies, required pharma companies to put "black box" warnings on all antidepressants' labels, scaring patients and reducing SSRI usage.[8] Moreover, a separate study among teenagers suggests that, as we would expect, antidepressant usage *reduced* suicides.[9] "Many experts credit a rise in use of Paxil, Prozac and other antidepressants known as SSRIs for a 25% reduction in teenage suicides in the past 10 years—to about eight per

100,000 teenagers per year."[10] This makes sense because if you are no longer depressed, you are less likely to take your life.

Many of us, when we hear a statement such as "antidepressants cause suicidal tendencies," imagine that all patients experience these thoughts, which is far from the truth. Also, the relationship identified is correlational —that is, no cause and effect has been established. Information can be scary. Pharmaceutical companies generally provide far more information for their products than do other companies, and some of that information is, frankly, frightening.

Despite all the frightening information, we need to retain perspective and learn what this information really means; people can worry too much about the side effects of drugs. While there has been much press about the muscle pain and weakness problem resulting from statins such as Crestor (rosuvastatin), Lipitor (atorvastatin), Mevacor (lovastatin), and Zocor (simvastatin), we should temper those worries with the startling results from a paper published in the *New England Journal of Medicine.* This paper, published in 2016, examined the results of 12,705 people from 21 countries with "intermediate risk" for cardiovascular disease. After 5.5 years, the statins in the study reduced the risk of heart attack and stroke by a whopping 24 percent, and, surprisingly, more patients on placebos discontinued therapy due to adverse events than did the patients on statins.[11] If more patients on placebos complained of adverse events than did those on the actual drugs, and the statins were so beneficial, how can that not be a ringing endorsement for statins?

Safety is Ambiguous

It's not just the drugs themselves that can be dangerous. Too large a dose, taken either inadvertently or on purpose, can be dangerous. That individual sleeping pill might be safe, but the whole bottle certainly isn't. There isn't much the FDA can do to prevent this danger.

The Dose Makes the Poison

Making the FDA's job that much harder, and complicating the discussion of the FDA's proper powers, is the fact that, as wise people have known for centuries, the dose makes the poison. "All things are poison and nothing is without poison; only the dose makes a thing not a poison," said Paracelsus. A substance can be benign or harmful, depending on your exposure.

For detrimental agents, low doses generally produce no adverse effects, but at a higher dose, the negative effects can be seen. For beneficial agents, the benefit rises as the dose rises and then, at some point, the relationship reverses, and even the beneficial agent can cause serious adverse reactions. Alcohol is one example of such a beneficial agent. Based on a 1995 study of 85,000 women, having one drink every three to four days led to a 17-percent reduction in the death rate. One drink each day led to an 11-percent reduction in the death rate; thus, in that study, alcohol's benefits were already in decline at the higher dose. With *more* than one drink per day, the death rate was higher than with abstinence from alcohol, moving alcohol from the beneficial into the detrimental category at a higher dose.

Is drinking alcohol beneficial? Is it deleterious? Repeat after Paracelsus: it depends on the dose. The dose makes the poison.

> *Even nectar is poison if taken in excess.*
> **Hindu proverb**

Consider something as ubiquitous and essential as water.

Without water, we die relatively quickly. But water can also kill people. We can drown, of course, but there are other risks. In 2002, a runner collapsed and died at the Boston Marathon. Medics later determined that she suffered from hyponatremia, or water intoxication. In common terms, she drank too much water while not getting enough electrolytes during the endurance event. "You can get too much of a good thing," said Arthur Siegel, of McLean Hospital. "With prolonged, strenuous exercise, the combination of too much water plus the muscle injury that shuts down the ability of the kidney to excrete the water produces this dangerous, life-threatening problem."[12]

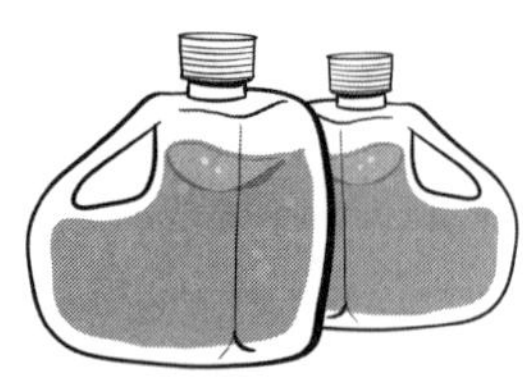

As noted in the Introduction, Jennifer Strange died just hours after drinking water for a radio station contest.[13] She, too, suffered from hyponatremia.

Should water be outlawed or restricted by the FDA? What would the rules be and what would that accomplish? Is water "safe"? Is it "unsafe"? It is both.

As was covered in the Introduction, a large dose of warfarin may have killed Joseph Stalin and yet a smaller dose successfully manages my friend's blood clots. Thalidomide is dangerous for fetuses but safe enough to treat people with multiple myeloma. Mustard gas is very dangerous, but mustard-gas-derived chemotherapy is safe enough to treat cancer patients.

Repeat after Paracelsus: safety depends on the dose.

Finally, if the most dangerous toxin known to humans—the neurotoxin produced by the bacterium *Clostridium botulinum*—can pass the FDA's tests as a safe drug (see Allergan's Botox), then really, anything can pass. We could, somewhat facetiously, simplify the FDA's safety tests to this:

- Rule 1: if it's not more toxic than botulinum toxin, then it can be used safely
- Rule 2: nothing is more toxic than botulinum toxin

Risk Everywhere

The discussion of water highlights the problem with blanket statements about water being safe and thalidomide being unsafe. When people choose treatments for conditions, they try to choose the best treatments within the context of their situations. Blanket statements about thalidomide being unsafe don't help. Instead, the question should be: given what we know, is thalidomide the best therapy or not? At what dose? What is the risk?

We incur a risk whenever we consume a pharmaceutical. But there's also the risk we incur by *not* taking beneficial medicines. Members of Debby Demaree's family in Bethesda, MD were, for years, taking drugs that were generally considered to be somewhat dangerous. What drugs were they taking? Three of her children were taking Adderall, an amphetamine, for attention-deficit disorder; her son took Accutane (isotretinoin) for acne; her daughter took the antidepressant Prozac (fluoxetine); and her husband was taking Vioxx. All of these drugs have had safety concerns. Her perspective: "the side effects of not having those drugs are much more serious than the risks of taking the medications."[14]

Magnitude of Safety Problem

Drug safety is not a small problem. The U.S. government estimates that such staples as cough and cold medicines send 7,000 children to emergency rooms each year.[15] The FDA received 179,855 reports of serious, disabling, and fatal adverse drug events in 2011 but believes that there was significant undercounting.[16] Drugs were mentioned in some 44,000 litigations in 2011.[17] Some researchers have estimated that 128,000 Americans die each year due to adverse events resulting from the use of "safe" FDA-approved drugs.[18] [19] Let's assume a round number of 100,000 deaths each year. As a comparison, during the 20-year period of 1995 through 2014, there were a total of 3,264 fatalities due to terrorism in the United States. That means that, with the 100,000 estimate, FDA-approved "safe" drugs kill 613 times as many people per year as do terrorists. Even compared to gun homicide, FDA-approved drugs kill nine times as often.

Can we consider the drugs that the FDA has approved safe, even when used at recommended doses? Unless you consider sudden vision loss, a rotting jawbone, extreme blood loss, or actual death "safe," the answer is no. It is apparent that the FDA uses a different definition of safe than do you and I.

Should the FDA Require More Testing?

Drugs aren't used in a vacuum, because many people are taking more than one, and doctors have known for a long time that drugs can interact. To understand drug safety, we need to study each drug in isolation and also consider the interactions between multiple drugs.

I have in front of me a *Physician's Desk Reference Companion Guide* from 1999, which, among other things, lists known interactions between drugs. Even way back in the 20th century, this subject took 1,241 pages to detail, highlighting the frequency and significance of drug interactions. For instance, tests show that over-the-counter pain relievers cause depressed patients taking SSRI antidepressants to be 25-percent less likely to have their symptoms relieved.[20]

A clinical trial of two standard drugs for breast cancer—Taxotere (docetaxel) and Adriamycin—was cut short when two patients died and an alarming number of patients developed life-threatening complications. It turns out that Adriamycin doesn't play well with other drugs. There are 492 drugs that are *known* to interact with Adriamycin, and with 83 of those drugs, the interactions are "major."

In another example, aspirin can reduce the effectiveness of the antidepressant drug Celexa (citalopram) by between 45 to 55 percent.[21] You may wonder why we didn't know about that sooner. The answer is simple: The FDA never required the two companies to test the two drugs together. But why didn't it? Should it have? And what *if* it had?

Let's consider our stalwart and ever-mysterious aspirin in the context of drug-drug interactions.

> *We haven't figured out all the complex effects that aspirin has on body chemistry, however, and it continues to make headlines.*
> **Berkeley Wellness Letter**

Aspirin has been on the market since 1899, and we still don't know everything about its complex effect on body chemistry. Celexa has been available only relatively recently, since 1998, so it, too, is not fully understood. So, since we don't fully understand each component, it should be no surprise that we don't fully understand how the two interact.

Let's explore what would be involved in addressing this problem scientifically with rigorous empirical data.

Aspirin would need to be tested more than it has been in its 122-year history. Aspirin has uses or potential uses for headache, inflammation, and the prevention of a first heart attack (myocardial infarction), recurrent heart attack, stroke, and several cancer types (lung, prostate, and colon). We would need to check different doses and make sure that we have captured a representative sample of patients by age, gender, weight, racial origin, health status, and pre-existing conditions. Some reasonable numbers will demonstrate the scope of the problem:

- Aspirin doses: 5
- Age groups: 10
- Gender groups: 2
- Weight groups: 5
- Racial origin groups: 10
- Health status groups: 5
- Pre-existing conditions: 20
- Conditions to treat: 10

We would need to test all possible combinations, which works out to five million potential groups of patients (5 x 10 x 2 x 5 x 10 x 5 x 20 x 10 = 5,000,000). If we assume that we need 10,000 patients in each group to look for rare reactions, then we need 50 billion patients, which is seven

times the world's population. If we sign up one new patient every second, we will need 1,585 years to enroll this clinical trial. And that's just for *one drug*—aspirin.

Aspirin is one of the many drugs available to patients. There are more than 6,700 drugs on the market, but let's use a low estimate and look at just the top 1,000 significant medicines. Doing the type of testing described above for every drug requires 50 trillion patients (50 billion x 1,000). But, of course, we haven't addressed the interaction of two or more drugs, which is what started this whole discussion.

How Many Test Subjects?

Assume that the maximum number of drugs that any one patient takes is five, which is a low estimate because 67 percent of older patients take five or more prescription and OTC medications.[22] If we look at all combinations of drugs, up to a total of five drugs per patient, our 1,000 top drugs balloon into 8.25 trillion combinations. In total, with 1,000 drugs, and the combinations thereof, we would need 4.13×10^{26} patients (that's 413 septillion, or a four followed by 26 zeros) for this clinical trial. Even if we sign up one new patient every second, we will still need *13 million trillion* years to enroll the patients in such a clinical trial. If we wanted to run the trial sooner, we would run out of people on Earth. So, we would need to enlist the help of the "people" on 5.57×10^{16} different worlds just like Earth—assuming they are just like us—and far more money and effort than any of us can possibly imagine. That number of Earth-like planets is, by the way, 100,000 times the number of stars in the

Milky Way. Given that we know of exactly zero other planets with life, the prospects don't look good.

Even if we dramatically scale back the scope of the problem (three doses, four age groups, two genders, and one for everything else; just 3,000 patients per trial), we would still need 40 billion times as many people as currently call Earth home.

There it is. We asked a serious question and ended up with—I think you'll have to admit—a pretty humorous answer. There's no way to test all drugs and all reasonable combinations of drugs in a rigorous, scientific manner, given the constraints on the number of patients, time, and money. Scientists typically discover the information about the interactions between drugs in that huge medical experiment known as "real life" or in smaller clinical trials. This leaves us open to reading in the newspaper, as we do from time to time, that two drugs (or supplements or food: peppermint oil and grapefruit can interact with statins; tea can decrease iron absorption; and vitamin C can increase iron absorption) might interact, either positively or negatively. We might not know beforehand that aspirin and Celexa will interact, but we find out after they have been on the market for some period. While it would be nice to know the answer a priori, that solution just isn't feasible. The solution that is feasible is the one that uses the amazing combination of trained physicians, motivated patients, wary insurance companies, perceptive and persistent scientists, and a lot of experimentation. Is it perfect? No. It is far from perfect; but, alas, perfection is impossible, and this approach is, at least, feasible. Perfection shouldn't be the gauge.

We are all guinea pigs in a giant unguided experiment.
Berkeley Wellness Letter

The usage of real-world, clinical data, while not perfect, does have advantages over the data gleaned from squeaky-clean controlled clinical trials. Former FDA Commissioner Scott Gottlieb, in his advocacy of the use of real-world data for evaluating drugs, argued, "Should a product be marketed based on a data set that speaks to a limited and rigidly constructed circumstance, when the clinical use, and in turn the evidence we might have to evaluate the product, could have been far richer, far more diverse, and more informative?"[23]

Would you prefer sterile, stilted data, or richer, more diverse data? How much richer is real-world, decentralized data? It is many orders of magnitude richer than centralized clinical trial data because it effectively gets more shots on goal.

And note that even if the trials were feasible and the number of patients required was an earthly number, the drugs must be put into *homo sapiens* regardless. In the one approach—the centralized approach—the drugs are put into humans in clinical trials. In the other approach—the decentralized approach—the drugs are put into humans through the normal day-to-day practice of medicine by clinicians. Either way, to learn what will happen, we still need to put actual drugs into flesh and blood people. There is no guaranteed safe way to do this. Someone must be a guinea pig, using unproven and potentially dangerous drugs. It should come as no surprise that problems can arise.

Russian Roulette

Admirably, the FDA is attempting to understand drugs before they are unleashed on the American populace. According to W. Donald Gray, a Senior Investigator with the House Intergovernmental Relations Subcommittee, "we must make certain all existing scientific knowledge and capabilities are employed to determine, insofar as possible, just how dangerous and how useful a given drug may be, *before* subjecting large numbers of people to its effects."[24]

However, even with the FDA's conservatism and attempts to be scientific, critics complain, correctly, that some of the medicines that the FDA approves later reveal problems.

One in five new drugs has serious side effects that do not show up until well after the medicine has received approval, according to a study that exposes what one researcher calls an alarming game of medical Russian roulette.[25]

Based on what we've learned so far, this should be expected. Some side effects are discovered only after a drug has been approved and marketed. In one extreme case, the steroidal hormone DES was given to pregnant women until it was linked to vaginal cancer in the women's female offspring, a full 15 to 20 years after initial exposure in their mothers. This example, with the problem showing up in the adult children of the original patients, is even worse than the problem with thalidomide, which showed up in the newborn children of the patients. Who knows if something you are taking today will negatively or positively affect your offspring when they reach adulthood? I don't. You don't. And, most important in this context, the FDA doesn't.

The unstated implication in the Russian roulette quote above is that the FDA could and should approve only safe drugs. And how are drugs deemed safe? Well, by long-term usage by many thousands of patients. But giving a large number of patients drugs for long-term use before they are proven safe is, to use the critics' words, "Russian roulette." Here we have a Catch-22, an infeasible alternative. The only feasible alternatives are never to use any new drug or to use new drugs that may have problems that will show up later. Which is better: the possibility of finding medicines that will improve our health or the guarantee of illness? If we prevent the risk associated with medicines, then we prevent the possible benefit, too.

Food Safety

Most foods need no FDA approval for placement on your grocer's shelves, but foods have benefits and risks, just as medicines do, and the U.S. Food and Drug Administration is responsible for food, too, as its name clearly states. If a prescription medicine caused life-threatening allergic reactions (anaphylaxis), the odds are high that it would be pulled off the market. But many foods cause the same problem. Some people have adverse reactions to nuts, shellfish, eggs, wheat, soy, legumes, seeds, and dairy products. Approximately 30,000 people visit an emergency room and 125 people die each year in the United States from food-induced anaphylactic reactions. And yet these foods are still available for purchase.

There are, of course, the famously dangerous foods, including pufferfish (a mere milligram of its toxin will kill), some wild mushrooms, and a bird, the Hooded Pitohui, so loaded with the same neurotoxin employed by poison dart frogs that eating part of it would prove fatal and merely licking one feather would make you ill. There are also commonplace fruits, vegetables, and raw sprouts that sicken 80 million Americans a year and kill approximately 5,000.

Consider the story of a 22-year-old man, Bruce, from Minneapolis, who was visiting his father. When he arrived at his father's house, he vomited and asked his brother for an inhaler because he was having trouble breathing. Within two minutes, the brother yelled to his father for help.

They called 911. “In those moments, it was just panic. Pure panic,” Bruce’s dad later recounted. Bruce lay unconscious on the floor, his neck swollen, his lips purple, his face blue. When emergency crews arrived, the family was told, “There's nothing more we can do." Bruce was already dead.

The story of Bruce is a painful reminder of the danger of food, as he suffered an anaphylactic reaction and died, not from peanuts per se, but from a chocolate bar that had been “made in a facility that also processes peanuts.” A chocolate bar, no less, that he had eaten partially, without any untoward effects, the day before.

Varying in severity, peanut allergies affect approximately 1.5 million Americans. Are peanuts “safe”? To 329 million Americans, yes, but to 1.5 million of their friends, family, coworkers, and neighbors, absolutely not. The simple fact is that safe things don’t kill you.

The FDA treats peanuts very differently than it does drugs such as Propulsid or Vioxx, even though all three have benefits but pose serious risks to some segments of the population. If peanuts were subjected to FDA approval, the FDA would discover what we already know—namely, that peanuts are nutritious for 99.5 percent of Americans and markedly dangerous for 0.5 percent. In a hypothetical clinical trial with four thousand people given peanuts, 20 might have an allergic reaction and some of them might even die. Given this, it is unlikely that the FDA would ever approve peanuts. If peanuts were treated like drugs such as Propulsid or Vioxx, they would be kept off the market forever, and the official story would be that they are too dangerous and that Americans are better off without them. Sorry, lovers of peanut butter and jelly sandwiches.

Fortunately, peanut allergies can be ameliorated. One company, Aimmune, has successfully used an oral biologic drug to desensitize 90 percent of test subjects to the offending protein in peanuts. The FDA approved Aimmune’s drug in early 2020. It is possible that, someday, even people such as Bruce may find peanuts safe and nutritious. If peanuts had been banned by the FDA, Aimmune would never have invested the resources necessary to make this discovery.

Society's attitude toward foods such as peanuts is to accept their existence and to learn to avoid them if necessary. Foods aren't bad or good, but sometimes particular people have a bad reaction to certain ones. This is completely different than the attitude expressed by the media, government, and public toward prescription drugs such as Merck's Vioxx and Janssen's Propulsid.

The press painted Vioxx as a bad drug because of the increased heart attack risk. Period. End of story. But some patients and doctors, even after they understood the risks, concluded that the benefits of Vioxx clearly outweighed the risks. One such person was Kathleen Slocum, who said that her life without Vioxx or other drugs like it was "misery." She also pointed out that while OTC analgesics worked well for pain relief, they did nothing for her severe joint swelling and stiffness.[26] Another person was Dave Ellis, a 66-year-old retired pharmacist from Edmond, Oklahoma. For 30 years, he had had degenerative arthritis in his spine. When Vioxx was withdrawn, he stated that he "dreads" the day that he runs out of his supply of Vioxx.[27] Hayes Wilson, a rheumatologist in Atlanta, put it this way: "If you live with intractable pain every day of your life, would you take a chance that you would have a heart attack? A lot of my patients would."

Propulsid is now considered a very dangerous drug and was pulled from the market in 2000. It also happens to be a miracle treatment for patients with cerebral palsy because it allows them to digest food without extreme pain. Propulsid has been used to treat gastric reflux, gastroparesis (in which the stomach cannot empty itself of food properly), ileus (a painful lack of movement in the intestines), and constipation. Propulsid is off limits to people but is still being made by compounding pharmacies for sale to veterinarians for use in cats and dogs.

Peanuts aren't beneficial for all and Vioxx and Propulsid aren't detrimental to all. A reasonable person would conclude that Bruce should have avoided all contact with peanuts—at least until he was desensitized; Slocum should have continued on her Vioxx; and some patients suffering from cerebral palsy should have continued on Propulsid.

Even that menacing malefactor, thalidomide, along with some of its cousins, has a friendly side. It is back on the market for a variety of conditions and is successfully treating patients daily, proving that efforts to paint drugs as black or white are bound to fail.

Have All Foods and Drugs Been Tested for Safety?

Regarding safety, many would assume that the FDA has tested—or, more correctly, required manufacturers to test—all foods and medicines. Not quite.

Consider herbal and natural medicines. Almost none of these products has been evaluated and approved by the FDA. Why? The FDA categorizes these products as "dietary supplements," and their manufacturers don't make specific health claims. A specific health claim would be "lowers blood pressure," whereas a non-specific health claim would be "benefits cardiovascular health." The first statement can be measured and, therefore, proven or disproven. The second statement is too vague to measure and, thus, prove or disprove. The FDA allows these non-specific claims, which are usually followed by the disclaimer, "These statements have not been evaluated by the Food and Drug Administration. This product is not intended to diagnose, treat, cure or prevent any disease."

Homeopathic Drugs

Homeopathic drugs were specifically exempted from the FDA's "safe and effective" requirements, along with the accompanying mandate that ingredients be listed. This allows homeopathic products—perhaps the least effective therapeutics on the market—to legally make explicit claims about treating diseases, while dietary supplements and herbal and natural medicines, which might have some clinical benefit, are forbidden to do so unless they've navigated the FDA's expensive and lengthy process. Homeopathic medicines, inhabiting the fringe of the pharmaceutical industry, may be useless for treating diseases, but can still have distinct safety problems: In 2016, homeopathic teething tablets with elevated belladonna—i.e., nightshade—levels killed ten children and hurt 400 others.[28] Some homeopathic products contain strychnine. Zicam, a homeopathic cold remedy,[29] and other products containing zinc, have caused over 100 people to lose their sense of smell. "People may be putting their trust and money in therapies that bring little or no benefit in combating their ailments, or worse—in products that may cause serious and even irreparable harm," reports former FDA Commissioner Scott Gottlieb.[30]

While natural medicines can cause side effects just as prescription drugs can, consumers are free to use them while real-world experience and scientific evidence is gathered. To remove a natural medicine from the market, the FDA must prove that it is unsafe. We can, however, predict with near certainty that natural medicines would disappear from the market if proof of safety and efficacy were required *prior* to marketing, as they are with prescription drugs. Why? Who would pay the hundreds of millions of dollars to garner approval for a product without any patent protection? No one.

Natural and Deadly

In a print advertisement for an herbal supplement designed for bladder control, a woman is quoted as saying, "And because it's all natural, I can enjoy the results without the worry of dangerous side effects." Yeah, right.

Notwithstanding the current popularity of "natural" foods and "natural" medicines, we should be clear that natural does *not* mean safe and better; natural things can kill you. Nature is often dangerous.

The nasty stuff produced by the bacterium *Clostridium botulinum*—the completely natural cause of botulism—is the most dangerous toxin known to man. Breathe in just 0.00015 milligrams and you'll die. A small jar of this odorless, colorless, tasteless liquid, if somehow put into the water supply, would kill everyone in a large city, perhaps up to 30 million people.[31]

Interestingly, Allergan's Botox is vacuum-dried purified botulinum toxin type A and has been approved by the FDA as safe and effective to treat certain muscular conditions, cosmetically remove wrinkles, and prevent migraines. It does this by temporarily paralyzing muscles. In a low dose, you get a smooth face. With a higher dose, you're dead.

Other bacteria can cause problems. Globally, 1.4 million deaths each year are caused by *Mycobacterium tuberculosis* infections. At least 40,000 people in the U.S. get sick and around 400 die each year from ingesting *Salmonella* bacteria.

What about ricin? It's the highly toxic protein obtained from the pressed seeds of the castor-oil plant. Or mercury? Or radiation? Or arsenic? They are all natural, too. Four of the five most toxic substances are natural.[32] The top synthetic one, VX nerve agent, used to kill North Korean Kim Jong-nam in 2017, doesn't crack the top three.

What many have suspected was verified by Bruce Ames, professor of Biochemistry and Molecular Biology Emeritus at U.C. Berkeley: about half of all manmade chemicals are mutagenic, potentially capable of causing cancer at a high enough dose. That doesn't seem surprising, especially given the image presented by those promoting and advocating natural foods and medicines—that synthetic chemicals can be dangerous. But what proportion of natural chemicals—such as those found in the aforementioned natural foods and medicines—are mutagenic? Take an honest guess. Zero? One percent? Ten percent? Wrong. Again, about half.

> *Half of all chemicals (natural or synthetic) cause cancer if given in high doses.*
> **Bruce Ames**, U.C. Berkeley

Despite advertisements to the contrary, natural does not mean safe and better. Most diseases, after all, are natural, and most of what the medical profession does is to address natural afflictions. If natural things were always good for us, the medical industry could close its doors.

Drugs That Predate the FDA Were Never Evaluated by the FDA

> *Doctors are men who prescribe medicines of which they know little, to cure diseases of which they know less, in human beings of whom they know nothing.*
> **Voltaire** (1694–1778)

The promise of our current pharmaceutical regulatory setup is that if we understand the characteristics of a new drug before it is marketed, we won't be surprised after it is marketed.

Let's apply this logic to the granddaddy of all drugs: aspirin (acetylsalicylic acid).

Aspirin has been available since 1899 and has been used well over a trillion times, with 60 billion tablets consumed worldwide each year. If we are going to know about anything, it will be aspirin. Yet it is humbling to realize how little scientists know about aspirin. One news report announced that seniors who take aspirin daily are twice as likely as non-users to have late-stage macular degeneration, an age-related loss of vision. Was this known in 1899 or even 1999? No.

The FDA usually makes its assessments after a new medicine has been tested for about a decade and in thousands of patients (any given patient will be on an experimental drug for perhaps just a few days and at most a few years). Even if the FDA were to wait until 120-odd years and a trillion doses had elapsed to approve any new drug, we'd still have surprises. If aspirin still surprises us, we can be surprised by *any* drug.

Aspirin—the one-cent miracle drug—was never tested and approved by the FDA since it didn't exist in 1899, when aspirin was first marketed. Moreover, the FDA didn't get the power to prevent untested drugs from entering the market for another 39 years (the FDA required proof of safety in 1938 and proof of efficacy *and* safety starting in 1962, and drugs marketed before 1938 were grandfathered). So, if you have ever taken aspirin for a headache—and who of us hasn't—you have ingested a drug that was never formally evaluated and approved by the FDA. And if aspirin worked for you, then you have proof that you can be successfully treated by a drug that was developed by a for-profit company that skirted the FDA's approval process.

Aspirin was finally approved in 1980, more than eight decades later, for the limited indication of secondary prevention of stroke and acute cardiac events. Aspirin has since received other indications.

Markets Can Improve Drug Safety

We look to the FDA for drug safety. We should also look to markets.

Chemotherapy is still one of the primary weapons used to attack cancerous cells in patients. Unfortunately, chemotherapy can be brutal on patients because it attacks not only cancerous cells but other cells in the blood, gut, brain, and scalp.

Patients getting chemotherapy for colorectal cancer often get a concoction of drugs that includes one called 5-FU (fluorouracil). These 5-FU regimens frequently cause severe diarrhea that must be treated in a hospital. For some patients, the diarrhea is fatal. In 2003, 5-FU regimens caused severe diarrhea in 17 percent of patients, while in 2016, the number had dropped to 11 percent.[33] Can the FDA take credit for fewer people ending up in hospitals? No. Oncologists around the world tried various tweaks to 5-FU chemotherapeutic regimens and found ones that worked better. Plus, they discovered how to provide better supportive care. The international market for colorectal cancer improved the safety of the drug regimens and saved many patients a trip to the hospital. For some, their very lives were saved. No drug regulators needed.

Wrap-up

When we consider foods, natural and herbal medicines, grandfathered drugs, OTC drugs, and prescription drugs that are used for conditions other than what they were officially approved for, we see that the U.S. Food and Drug Administration, for its good intentions, legal power, and name, has evaluated only a portion of the foods and drugs we ingest. And those that it has assessed and approved as "safe" still cause enormous problems.

To fully test drugs in all reasonable segments of patients and for possible interactions, we would need to employ 4.13×10^{26} patients. That's a really, really big number. Even if we signed up one new patient every second, it would still take over 13 million trillion years to enroll such a clinical trial.

Does everything the FDA touches invoke heaven on Earth? No. Is everything not touched by the FDA reminiscent of hell? No. Both are a mixed bag of good and bad. Does the FDA have an impenetrable wall with some foods and drugs on the "good" side, with everything else on the "bad" side? No. If the FDA's regulatory powers are so essential to public health, then how can we explain the huge gaps in the FDA's supposedly protective wall and the presence of dangerous products on both sides of that figurative wall? Maybe those regulatory powers weren't so imperative. When studying this situation, it becomes less and less clear what effect the FDA has had and on what.

We can summarize thus: an FDA certification of "safety" doesn't mean much, and the FDA, which has been given awesome regulatory powers, a huge budget, big buildings, and an army of employees, has still failed in its mission to ensure the safety of our foods and medicines.

If things are going well, FDA defenders say, or at least imply, that it's all due to the FDA. "You'd all be stricken with rodent feces-infested quack medicines if the FDA weren't here." If things aren't going so well, FDA defenders say that the agency needs more money and power: a lot more money and a lot more power.[34] And yet we can see that many products are never assessed for safety by the FDA, such as natural and herbal medicines and foods, and those that are assessed for safety are still killing 100,000 Americans each year due to adverse reactions. If this is success, what would failure look like?

FDA proponents might reply that all drugs have some risk of side effects and adverse reactions. That's true. But then how can the FDA say with a straight face that it "is responsible for protecting the public health by assuring the safety, efficacy, and security of human and veterinary drugs, biological products, medical devices, our nation's food supply, cosmetics, and products that emit radiation"?[35] The usage of the word "assuring," by the way, may be a Freudian slip (*assuring* is something you do to someone to remove doubt or anxiety), but the FDA certainly has not *assured* the people that drugs, such as metoclopramide, are safe.

FDA proponents might counter that, while drugs aren't completely safe today, they are *safer* than before the FDA got its powers. They might tell us to think on the margin. To this, we can ask, "Where is the proof?" And, if things are better, would they have gotten better anyway? Are improvements a result of increased knowledge, such as knowing that thalidomide shouldn't be given to pregnant women, along with increased wealth and technology? In addition, even if drugs are safer with the FDA hovering and doing its appointed tasks, is the increment in safety worth the additional cost? When calculating the cost per quality-adjusted life year[36] saved by the FDA, we know that the numerator—cost—is large and the denominator—lives saved—may be large, small, or even negative. We aren't even sure of the sign of the denominator.

For instance, if each year, the FDA cost $10 billion and helped add 500,000 quality-adjusted life years, the cost per year added would be $20,000— a good deal. If the FDA cost the same amount but helped add only 5,000 quality-adjusted life years, the cost per year would be $2 million—a worse deal. If the FDA *reduced* quality-adjusted life years (see Chapter 10), we could save money and live longer by abolishing the agency. It would be nice to have a full cost/benefit analysis, as we will discuss later. Unfortunately, little research has been done in this area.

> *Relatively little explicit research has been done by economists on the efficiency trade-offs involved in the policies of the Food and Drug Administration.*
> **Economists Tomas J. Philipson and Eric Sun**[37]

While the drugs that the FDA regulates are highly scrutinized and are often criticized for the marketing messages used to promote them, the FDA itself is not immune to false advertising. If the FDA is truly helping make medicines safer, truth in advertising would dictate that the FDA scale back some of its hyperbole: "safer" is not the same thing as "safe."

If a drug manufacturer were using contaminated equipment that caused some fraction of patients to get ill, the following day's headlines would be abundant and accusatory. If a drug manufacturer makes an FDA-approved medicine properly, but some fraction of patients fall ill due to a side effect, there's a collective shoulder shrug. But medical problems are medical problems, regardless of the cause. The shrug is more a sign of our sense of exhausted solutions, that we've done everything we can.

If all the safety problems we have cataloged happened within the context of a self-regulated free market, people would argue that the system wasn't working and that more government regulation was necessary. Such a conclusion would seem self-evident. Because these problems occur within a system already heavily encumbered by government regulations, people are either resigned to accepting them or they are calling for more regulations. Both reactions assume that muscular government regulation is the pinnacle of possibility. If we are already regulating fully, they reason, what else can we do? If we aren't regulating fully, well, then we should. Such assumptions show a lack of vigor and creativity. In the rest of this book, we will challenge those and other hypotheses and assumptions.

[1] www.FDA.org, 16 March 2017.

[2] "Doxorubicin Cardiomyopathy," National Institutes of Health, https://www.ncbi.nlm.nih.gov/pmc/articles/PMC2848530/

[3] Eric Palmer, "Pfizer, McKesson try to stop Arkansas executions, say state lied to get drugs," *FiercePharma*, 17-Apr-17.

[4] Ron Winslow, "What Makes a Drug Too Risky? There's No Easy Answer." *The Wall Street Journal*, 16 February 2005.

[5] James W. Wheless, "Intractable epilepsy: A survey of patients and caregivers," *Epilepsy & Behavior*, 8 (2006) 756-764.

[6] Elizabeth Bernstein and Jennifer Corbett Dooren, "Antidepressants Get a Boost For Use in Teens," *The Wall Street Journal*, 18 April 2007.

[7] Amanda Gardner, "Caution Urged on Antideppresants and Children," *Healthfinder News*, 23 August 2004.

[8] Sarah Rubenstein, "Elevated Rate Of Teen Suicide Stirs Concern," *The Wall Street Journal*, 3 September 2008.

[9] "Antidepressants Seem to Have Reduced Teen Suicides," *Archives of Internal Medicine*, 20 October, 2003.

[10] Ron Winslow, "What Makes a Drug Too Risky? There's No Easy Answer." *The Wall Street Journal*, 16 February 2005.

[11] "Cholesterol-lowering statin drugs help prevent heart attacks and stroke," *University of California, Berkeley Wellness Letter*, vol 33, issue 1, October 2016.

[12] "Doctors: Marathoner Died From Too Much Water," WCVB, http://www.wcvb.com/Doctors-Marathoner-Died-From-Too-Much-Water/11334548.

[13] Suzan Clarke and Rich McHugh, "Jury Rules Against Radio Station After Water-Drinking Contest Kills Calif. Mom," ABC News, http://abcnews.go.com/GMA/jury-rules-radio-station-jennifer-strange-water-drinking/story?id=8970712.

[14] Ron Winslow, "What Makes a Drug Too Risky? There's No Easy Answer," *The Wall Street Journal*, 16 February 2005.

[15] Mike Stobbe, "Cold Meds Send 7,000 Kids to Hospitals," Associated Press, 29 January 2008.

[16] QuarterWatch, Monitoring FDA MedWatch Reports, 31 May 2012.

[17] QuarterWatch, Monitoring FDA MedWatch Reports, 31 May 2012.

[18] This assumes 40 million annual admissions to U.S. acute care hospitals with 0.32 percent of these patients dying due to adverse reactions to drugs. Donald W. Light, Joel Lexchin, and Jonathan J. Darrow, "Institutional Corruption of Pharmaceuticals and the Myth of Safe and Effective Drugs," *Journal of Law, Medicine and Ethics*, 2013, Vol. 14, No. 3: 590-610.

[19] QuarterWatch, Monitoring FDA MedWatch Reports, 31 May 2012.

[20] *Berkeley Wellness Letter*, August 2011

[21] Aspirin and Prozac Can Mix Badly, Study Say, *The Wall Street Journal*, 26 April 2011, pg D1

[22] Laura Landro, "Medication Overload," *The Wall Street Journal*, 11 October 2016.

[23] "Gottlieb gets real," *BioCentury Extra*, 19 September 2017.

[24] Arthur Daemmrich, "Invisible Monuments and the Costs of Pharmaceutical Regulation: Twenty-Five Years of Drug Lag Debate," *Pharmacy in History*, Vol. 45 (2003) No. 1

[25] The Associated Press, *The Union*, 1 May 2002, "Questions raised on medication's safety," page A1.

[26] "The Truth About Vioxx? Ask an Arthritis Sufferer," *The Wall Street Journal*, November 22, 2004; Page A15.

[27] Heather Won Teroriero, "Patients Weigh Pain vs. Risk," *The Wall Street Journal*, December 21, 2004.

[28] Matthew Perrone, "FDA to Target High-Risk Homeopathic Medicines," Associated Press/*Time Health*, 18 December 2017.

[29] There is dispute whether Zicam is actually a homeopathic medicine. Steven Coward, ND and Kristina Lewis, ND report that Zicam is not homeopathy on naturopathic.org.

[30] Matthew Perrone, "FDA to Target High-Risk Homeopathic Medicines," Associated Press/*Time Health*, 18 December 2017.

[31] By the Numbers: Bacteria, *Science Illustrated*, September/October 2010, pg 74-75.

[32] Simon Cotton, "Handle with care—the world's five deadliest poisons," *The Conversation*, 12 April 2016.

[33] Internal analysis conducted by Objective Insights, Inc.

[34] FDA Commissioner Scott Gottlieb argued that the FDA needed a 13 percent boost in its budget for 2019 on 18 April 2018.

[35] FDA website, viewed 27 November 2017.

[36] Quality-adjusted life year (QALY) is a measure of the state of health of a person in which the benefits, in terms of length of life, are adjusted to reflect the quality of life. One QALY is equal to one year of life in perfect health. An additional QALY is a benefit and frequently the ratio of cost per QALY is considered.

[37] Tomas J. Philipson and Eric Sun, "Is the Food and Drug Administration Safe and Effective?," *Journal of Economic Perspectives*, Volume 22, Number 1, Winter 2008, p. 85–102

Chapter 3: Drugs are Still Ineffective

Let's again consider the *BioCentury* statement that opened Chapter 2: "Americans take it for granted that government ensures foods are safe, and medical products are safe and effective. But that wasn't always the case." We've considered safety. Now let's ponder efficacy.

Efficacy is Ambiguous

David A. Kessler, who served as FDA commissioner under both Presidents George H.W. Bush and Bill Clinton, confidently stated, "When the industry sells a drug, the drug works, and it does what it says on the label. Take that away and we go back to snake oil."[1]

Let's scrutinize Kessler's statement vis-à-vis the current state of the pharmaceutical industry.

First, we need to ask what counts as efficacious ("the drug works"). Obviously, if 100 percent of patients were forever cured, that would count by anyone's definition. But what if only 30 percent of patients show a slight improvement? Would that count? If a drug helps only one person, and only moderately, can we say that the drug is efficacious? It is somewhat efficacious for that one person, certainly, but it is efficacious in general? If that one individual used that drug and everyone else ignored it, the overall health of society would increase because everyone minus one would be unaffected, while one would improve. Can a drug be universally "efficacious" or "inefficacious"? It's not clear how to think about efficacy from a global perspective.

We can ask, however, whether drugs on the market are universally efficacious, now that the FDA mandates it.

Consider Genentech's Herceptin (trastuzumab), which many touted as a "miracle drug." Before Herceptin, chemotherapy was the standard of care for breast cancer. For doctors to give Herceptin to patients, it must offer an incremental advantage over chemotherapy alone. What is the incremental advantage of Herceptin? In a clinical trial of Herceptin as a first-line treatment for metastatic breast cancer, the overall response rate among the patients who got Herceptin plus chemotherapy was 45 percent, while it was only 29 percent among the patients who received chemotherapy alone.[2] Herceptin certainly helped some patients, but not all patients. Looking at the increment due to Herceptin, or the patients who weren't helped by chemotherapy but did benefit from Herceptin—assuming the two groups were otherwise identical—we calculate 23 percent.[3] Herceptin benefited fewer than one-quarter of the patients who were not helped by chemo. And Herceptin, a leading light, was the sixth biggest selling drug in the U.S. in 2019, with sales of approximately $3 billion.

Merck & Co.'s Keytruda (pembrolizumab) had become one of the hottest drugs on the market. Keytruda received some favorable press after former President Jimmy Carter reported that he was "cancer free" after therapy with Keytruda. Carter was lucky. In one clinical trial for melanoma, Keytruda destroyed or reduced the tumors in only 34 percent of patients.

In one study for lung cancer, Keytruda plus chemotherapy helped 48 percent of patients, while chemotherapy alone helped only 19 percent, and the test subjects on Keytruda lived over three months longer.[4] While Keytruda helped 36 percent of the patients,[5] and living longer is wonderful, the great majority of those who benefited had what is called a "partial response." Keytruda—which was the second biggest-selling drug globally in 2020 and brought in worldwide revenues of $14.4 billion—is far from a sure thing.

During the 2017/2018 influenza season, the CDC estimated that the flu vaccine was just 34-percent effective against influenza A viruses and 56 percent against B viruses.[6] This means that up to two thirds of those who rolled up their sleeves were just wasting their time.

AstraZeneca's Iressa (gefitinib) was approved by the FDA even though in one key clinical trial (IDEAL-2) only ten percent of patients enjoyed a clinical benefit, a so-called "objective response."

Triptans (serotonin-receptor agonists), those gold-standard drugs used to treat migraines, demonstrate that drugs can achieve stellar reputations while being effective in approximately only 70 percent of sufferers. Roughly a third of patients see no benefit.

There are, no doubt, the occasional stars in the efficacy arena. Gilead Sciences tested a triple-combination therapy for hepatitis C infections in the POLARIS-1 clinical trial. Vosevi (sofosbuvir, velpatasvir, and voxilaprevir) produced a "sustained virologic response"— the hepatitis C virus was undetectable for 12 consecutive weeks—in 96 percent of patients, while the placebo helped exactly zero patients.[7] Now that's impressive, especially given the rough state of many of the patients infected with hepatitis C.

Are the drugs that the FDA has approved universally efficacious? Well, just study the results of clinical trials and you'll typically see that 20 or 50 or 70 percent of patients benefit. Completely efficacious drugs would benefit all patients. Not all drugs are as good as Gilead's Vosevi, and, unless you consider a drug that helps only ten percent of patients "efficacious," the answer to the question is no.

Efficacy can also be evaluated on how strongly a drug works—does a drug eliminate a risk or remove all symptoms? In 2018, Novartis was studying a new drug, canakinumab, which was shown in a trial of 10,000 patients to reduce the risk of cardiovascular events by 18 percent and ten percent, respectively, in patients with chronic kidney disease and diabetes.[8] That's substantial. But it is still a far cry from reducing the risk by 100 percent, which is the ideal. Canakinumab, like most drugs, is not perfect.

Kessler's "When the industry sells a drug, the drug works…" makes it sound as if FDA approval confers an ironclad guarantee. Not quite. Have we gone back to the era of snake oil? Using Kessler's definition, it sounds as if we have. Or maybe we never left.

At Least Drugs Are Tested Nowadays, Right?

You might have been led to believe that prior to the FDA's broad powers, the pharmaceutical market was devoid of science and evidence. But thanks to the FDA's tireless efforts, the drug industry has been forced into the modern world. If you believe that, then you probably believe that all drugs are thoroughly tested and certified as safe and effective. Let's consider that assumption.

Who Are You?

A *Wall Street Journal* article told the story of eight-year-old Gage Martindale, who had been taking Merck & Co.'s once-a-day Vasotec (enalapril) for his blood pressure since he was a toddler and underwent surgery to fix a heart defect.[9] Most "adult" medicines haven't been tested in children, especially those who have survived heart surgery. Such clinical trials would be difficult to recruit—imagine how hard it would be to find enough kids like Martindale who have rare conditions and whose parents would consent to have them treated like guinea pigs. Even if enough subjects could be found for such a trial, it could dramatically increase the cost and time to develop a new drug and would open up the pharmaceutical company to a round of lawsuits if things didn't go well. In addition to eight-year-old heart surgery survivors, how many other patient segments would Merck & Co. be required to run clinical trials on? Dozens? Hundreds?

Here was an eight-year-old with prior heart surgery who was on a drug that hadn't been proven safe and effective in eight-year-olds with prior heart surgery. And it is possible that Martindale would be on Vasotec for 80 or more years. Vasotec, which was launched just 16 years before Martindale was born, had not been used by *any* patients for 80 years, for obvious mathematical reasons.

If you think Martindale's case is unusual, consider Taylor Muhl, who is even more peculiar. She is her own twin, with a distinct line down the middle of her torso, one side with lighter pigmentation and the other with darker. Doctors report that she was a fraternal twin who fused together with her sibling in the womb and now carries that twin's DNA within her own body, manifesting in two different immune systems and two different bloodstreams, causing some expectedly unusual problems.[10] How many people could we find for a clinical trial who, like Muhl, are chimeric?

Upon further reflection, there really is no clear distinction between the pre- and post-FDA worlds. In both worlds, countless people take pills that were never tested and certified for patients *in their situation*.

> *It is well to remember that the entire population of the universe, with one trifling exception, is composed of others.*
> **Andrew J. Holmes**

If all the clinical trials for a particular drug were conducted in men—the early studies that found that a daily dose of aspirin prevented heart attacks were done on middle-aged white men—then we have a legitimate question about the efficacy and safety in women.[11] If the men in the trial were aged 30 to 50, then we can reasonably ask about elderly men or younger boys like Martindale. If all the men in the trial were overweight, then what about the subsets of normal-weight or even underweight men?

If all the men in the trial ate typical American diets, what would happen to vegetarians, vegans, or paleos? Were the men in the trial all Caucasians? Then what about African Americans, Hispanics, Pacific Islanders, Asians, Inuits, and Native Americans? In one study, scientists found that black men had higher dihydrotestosterone levels and higher dihydrotestosterone-to-testosterone ratios than white and Hispanic men.[12] Does this matter? Perhaps. Perhaps not. It may matter in some areas and not in others. We simply don't know.

One company, NitroMed, tilted the odds in its favor by launching a drug, BiDil, in 2005 for one racial group: African Americans, a group in which it reduced the deaths due to heart failure by half. Due to disappointing sales, however, the product was pulled in 2008, and 80 percent of NitroMed's workforce was laid off. The idea behind BiDil is still solid: scientists have shown that a person's genetics determine how well they'll respond to hypertension medicines.[13]

Russ Altman, professor of bioengineering at Stanford University, observed that, "[g]enetic variation can have profound effects on your clinical response to medications."[14] Altman has been collecting his findings and has built a pharmacogenomics database that cross-references 708 drugs, 151 metabolic pathways, 165 dosing guidelines, and 780 drug labels (see pharmgkb.org).[15] He gives the example of gene CYP2C19, which if tweaked, "...for hundreds of drugs, the average dose is the wrong dose for you." In another example, children with acute lymphoblastic leukemia (ALL) may have a severe reaction to the drug Purixan (mercaptopurine) if they have the TPMP gene. Luckily, doctors can test for TPMP and then give lower doses or use a different drug.

We are all incredibly complex and even our blood types matter. Blood type O is associated with lower rates of cardiovascular disease, cancer, diabetes, cognitive impairment, and malaria. Scientists have found that the malaria parasite secretes a protein that binds more tightly to type A than to type O red blood cells, causing the cells to clump in capillaries and result in tissue damage.[16]

Scientists have discovered that not all of us taste food the same and have categorized people into “non-tasters,” “average tasters,” and “super-tasters.”[17] There’s even a straightforward way to tell the difference using strips of paper soaked in chemicals that people perceive either has a bad taste, a plain paper taste, or a “glittery” taste. One quarter of Americans are non-tasters; one quarter are super-tasters—with a heightened sensitivity to bitterness, sweetness, and fat; and the rest of us are average. Could this affect our health? Perhaps.

According to one study of 1,935 people, just three percent of super-tasters came down with COVID-19 and their symptoms lasted five days. Among non-tasters, 29 percent became infected and their symptoms lasted 24 days.[18] Average tasters were in the middle. Can this be true? There’s some logic to this result while, on the other hand, this could be a statistical artifact. As scientists everywhere say, more research is needed.

Clinical Trials

In the male-only clinical trial example above, is anyone going to tell us with a straight face that because a drug benefited 60 percent of 50-year-old overweight European-American males with typical American diets, we know what the effect will be on a certain skinny, 11-year-old, prepubescent Chinese vegetarian girl? We can’t even predict the outcome in any *particular* white, 50-year-old, overweight, American male who shares the outward traits of the patients in the trial.

Imagine that you’re a 50-year-old male in good shape, with a normal weight with decent blood pressure, but with a family history of cardiovascular disease. You are considering taking cardiovascular Drug X. You look at the clinical trial results and find that 50 percent of patients taking Drug X improved, while only 20 percent improved with a placebo. You look at the patient segmentation (results broken down by patients’ characteristics) to see what someone with your characteristics can expect. Unfortunately, the patient segmentation isn’t perfect, but you believe that

55 percent of patients who are like you improved. However, you remember that you take an aspirin a day, exercise vigorously, are Hispanic, and eat a fatty diet. The results don't cover these finer breakdowns.

One solution would be to increase the number of patients in each clinical trial by a factor of 10 or 100 or 1,000 and clearly specify every attribute of every patient. At some point, perhaps, there would be enough segmentation so that you could view the results for someone just like yourself. But the costs of the clinical trials would increase dramatically, and, with such high costs, fewer new drugs would be developed. Plus, there might not be enough qualified patients willing to enroll in such large clinical trials, which is a difficult problem that drug companies face today, even with smaller trials.

Still, two huge problems would remain:

(1) Those clinical trial results apply to you (Hispanic, male, 50-years-old, exercise, daily aspirin, etc.) only if you are similar to those tested. And yet you may never know if some hidden but key attribute is different, such as blood type, triglyceride levels, creatinine levels, genetics, diet, exercise levels, attitude, family structure, wealth, hormonal levels, sleep patterns, stress levels, hydration levels, sunshine exposure, alcohol consumption, fat consumption, fiber consumption, smoking, kidney health, liver health, mitochondrial health, vitamin supplementation, environmental pollution, enzymes present, or gut bacteria.

(2) Even with such a fine level of segmentation, perhaps only 60 percent of the patients in your group improved. You still don't know whether Drug X will help you or not. You could get lucky and end up in the 60-percent group or be unlucky and end up in the 40-percent group.

We can't tell if a drug will work in terms of safety, efficacy, and tolerability in a certain person without putting that drug in that person. This fact is due to the overwhelming complexity of the biology of our bodies, combined with unpredictable interactions between endogenous and exogenous chemicals and other stimuli. Scientists understand that with complex systems, such as the human body, slightly different initial conditions, such as genetics, diet, and health status, can lead to wildly different results. In the medical field, we witness that up close, day after day.

At their core, clinical trial results are like weather forecasts—"there's a 60 percent chance of rain"—while trying a drug yourself is like walking outside into the weather; once outside, you *know* whether or not it's raining.

Off-Label Uses

Even drugs that have successfully navigated the FDA's rigorous procedures may not have been fully tested for the particular condition your doctor wants to treat. Why? Because once they are marketed, drugs can be used in ways not specifically approved by the FDA. Such usage is called off-label.

While off-label usage may initially sound bad, conjuring up the image of a sleazy company trying to make an extra buck by misleading doctors and hurting patients, if you are like me, when you learn what's really going on, you'll be flabbergasted.

Off-label usage helps American patients because they get what their doctors believe are the best available drugs for their conditions. The fact is that off-label uses of drugs save lives. Consider Genentech's Rituxan (rituximab), which the FDA approved in 1997 for relapsed or refractory CD20-positive B-cell low-grade non-Hodgkin's lymphoma (NHL). In a matter of years, sales surpassed what would have been expected even if all the Americans with this type of NHL took Rituxan. What happened? Oncologists reasoned that a drug that worked for relapsed and refractory patients might also work for previously untreated patients or even for other cancers. Since cancer is often a deadly disease, it's better to try something that might work rather than trying nothing at all. In many cases, Rituxan *did* work. According to *Oncology Business Review*, "Rituxan has not only changed the natural history of NHL, it has significantly changed the way cancer is treated and how cancer research is approached...."

Rituxan has since received FDA approval for a number of indications (different diseases or patient types), some of which, such as rheumatoid arthritis, are even outside the cancer arena. Physicians' off-label usage of Rituxan, far from being inappropriate or rogue, reflected the best medical thinking at the time and was ultimately vindicated by the FDA itself. Off-label usage naturally precedes formal FDA approval because off-label usage comes from the latest research, while the slow, official FDA approval process is initiated only after the research is released. The FDA is typically one of the *last* organizations to acknowledge that a drug works for other diseases.

Off-label usage is often just a small step away from on-label. A 2017 *New England Journal of Medicine* editorial discussed off-label usage for Imfinzi (durvalumab).[19] Instead of using the drug only for patients with brain metastases whose tumors *couldn't* be surgically excised (on-label), the author discussed its use in patients with brain metastases whose tumors *could* be surgically excised (off-label). You'll be forgiven if that difference —couldn't and could be surgically removed—doesn't seem considerable. To the FDA, it's a huge difference, effectively night and day. To the FDA, those are very different groups of patients.

It frequently doesn't make economic sense for a drug company to put the time and money into getting another approved use, especially if the new disease afflicts only a few patients, if the patients are already being treated anyway, and/or if the drug's patent is running out. Despite the evidence that off-label uses tend to help rather than hurt patients, the FDA merely tolerates off-label usage. Is it possible that the FDA sees off-label prescribing as a threat to its powers? After all, if you can sell a drug for a usage that the FDA hasn't formally approved, why endure the expensive and lengthy FDA approval process?

The U.S. government itself, through the Medicare program, for example, regularly pays for drugs prescribed off-label, and Congress has pushed to expand Medicare to reimburse all drugs prescribed off-label.

In addition to reimbursing for off-label prescriptions, the government sometimes funds studies to explore off-label uses. The National Institutes of Health's National Eye Institute, for example, funded a clinical trial of Genentech's Avastin (bevacizumab), already approved for cancer, for use on wet age-related macular degeneration (AMD). Genentech had not designed Avastin for use in patients' eyes, and so it had never funded a head-to-head trial to compare the cheaper Avastin to the more expensive Lucentis (ranibizumab), which *was* designed for eyes. That's why the government stepped in, hoping to save money on AMD treatments. If off-label usage threatens public health, then Congress, the National Institutes for Health, Medicare, the Veterans Administration, and the National Cancer Institute never got the memo.

Consider this related question: Who would want to take a drug that has not been shown, to the FDA's satisfaction, to be effective? The answer: almost everyone. According to WebMD, "More than one in five outpatient prescriptions written in the U.S. are for off-label uses."[20] Alex Tabarrok[21] has cited studies showing that 80 to 90 percent of pediatric patients are prescribed drugs for off-label uses. The National Cancer Institute stated, "Frequently the standard of care for a particular type or stage of cancer involves the off-label use of one or more drugs." For some medicines, 90 percent of the usage is off-label, and off-label uses account for up to 56 percent of drug usage in oncology and 81 percent in AIDS.

Consider gastroparesis, a poorly understood upper gastrointestinal disorder in which the contents of the stomach do not move efficiently into the small intestine. Diabetics are particularly susceptible to this condition. The FDA has approved only one drug to treat it: the previously discussed Reglan (metoclopramide). But doctors have found that, for some patients, an antibiotic called erythromycin reduces nausea, vomiting, and abdominal pain. Erythromycin is not FDA-approved to treat gastroparesis.

But it works. For some diseases, like AL amyloidosis, there are no approved medicines.[22] Not a single one. What do doctors do? They use medicines such as Velcade (bortezomib), developed to treat related diseases such as multiple myeloma, even though they and their patients would prefer medicines that treat AL amyloidosis directly.[23]

As this was written, 160 million Americans have had at least one dose of a vaccine to prevent an infection of SARS-CoV-2, the virus that causes COVID-19. How many of these folks knew that the vaccine they were accepting was not FDA approved? The three current vaccines have Emergency Use Authorizations (EUA), but the FDA is clear that an EUA is not a regular approval as EUA's apply to "unapproved medical products, or unapproved uses of approved medical products."[24] None of these vaccines are approved for other indications, so they fall into the first category: unapproved medical products. Whether the 160 million recipients knew it or not, they were rolling up their sleeves for a medical product that had not been approved by the FDA.

The argument against off-label prescribing is that it amounts to an uncontrolled experiment. Some patients get better and others don't, and some have unexpected adverse events. Yet this same complaint could be levied against *on-label* prescribing.

Examples of Off-Label Uses

There are many, many examples of FDA approved drugs being used off-label.

Soon after Merck launched Proscar (finasteride) to treat enlarged prostate glands, physicians started sharing stories of men reporting new hair growth. "One of the doctors said that was impossible," recalled Merck spokeswoman Janet Skidmore. It wasn't impossible. Proscar lowers levels of the hormone dihydrotestosterone, making it effective for both shrinking prostate glands and growing hair. Merck turned this off-label usage into a

second product, specifically designed for hair growth: Propecia (finasteride).

Eli Lilly's Prozac (fluoxetine) was originally approved to help people deal with depression. But doctors found that it often helped women with premenstrual syndrome, and they started prescribing it for that. Prozac was later approved by the FDA for a severe form of PMS. In this case, the drug came first, the usage came second, the definition of the condition came third, and the FDA approval was dead last.

Symmetrel (amantadine) was originally developed to treat influenza. Some Parkinson's patients taking amantadine for the flu serendipitously noticed symptomatic relief of their Parkinson's disease, which scientists later discovered came about because amantadine increases dopamine release and inhibits dopamine reuptake; dopamine reduces the symptoms of Parkinson's disease.

Doctors at the University of Utah found that anti-clotting drugs used to treat cardiovascular conditions could restore blood flow to frostbitten fingers and limbs, greatly reducing the need for amputation. Will the companies that make these drugs run full clinical trials and seek FDA approval for such a rare condition? It's unlikely; the cost-to-benefit ratio of testing probably won't be appealing, meaning that all future uses of anti-clotting drugs for frostbite will likely be off-label.

Researchers noticed that patients with tuberculosis had lower rates of cancer. This led some urologists to treat cases of bladder cancer by filling patients' bladder with a mixture containing BCG, a live, but weakened, tuberculosis-causing bacteria. As incredible as it seems, BCG, previously used as a vaccine to prevent tuberculosis, is now the standard of care to treat some types of bladder cancer, and has received FDA approval for that indication.

Roche's Accutane (isotretinoin) is indicated for severe acne, specifically "severe recalcitrant nodular acne," but the FDA once estimated that 90 percent of the prescriptions for Accutane were for off-label mild to moderate acne.

Hundreds of thousands of prescriptions have been written off-label for antibiotics used to treat stomach ulcers caused by the bacteria *Heliobacter pylori*, which is a known cause of ulcers.

Some off-label uses spontaneously suggest themselves when they show up as side effects of FDA-approved drugs. We discussed hair growth with Proscar. When Oleptro (trazodone) was prescribed for depression, drowsiness was a common side effect. People can be perceptive, and they turned that relationship around: people *wanting* drowsiness started taking Oleptro.

As mentioned above, off-label usage is widespread. Below is a list of some drugs used both on- and off-label, and what they are used for.

Table 1: Off-Label Uses

Medicine	Approved Indication	Off-Label Usage
Abilify (aripiprazole)	Bipolar disorder, schizophrenia	Alzheimer's disease, dementia
Actemra (tocilizumab)	Rheumatoid arthritis	COVID-19
Accutane (isotretinoin)	Severe acne	Mild and moderate acne
Anti-clotting drugs	Cardiovascular conditions	Frostbite
Avastin (bevacizumab)	Cancer	Macular degeneration
Botox (botulinum toxin A)	Facial frown lines, certain muscle disorders, preventing migraines	Back pain, stroke recovery
Catapres (clonidine)	High blood pressure	Hot flashes
Cialis (tadalafil)	Erectile dysfunction	Enlarged prostate (BPH)
Corgard (nadolol)	Angina, high blood pressure	Migraines
Coumadin (warfarin)	Atrial fibrillation	Hypertensive heart disease
Dolobid (diflunisal)	Pain, osteoarthritis, rheumatoid arthritis	ATTR amyloidosis
Elavil (amitriptyline)	Depression	Prevention of migraines
Gabitril (tiagabine)	Seizures	Depression
Inderal (propranolol)	High blood pressure, heart disease, migraines	Anxiety

Medicine	Approved Indication	Off-Label Usage
Lamictal (lamotripgine)	Bipolar disorder, epilepsy	Depression
Neurontin (gabapentin)	Nerve pain from herpes zoster (shingles)	Nerve damage from diabetes and fibromyalgia
Oleptro (trazodone)	Depression	Insomnia
Paxil (paroxetine)	Depression in adults	Depression in teenagers and children
Prozac (fluoxetine)	Depression	Pre-menstrual syndrome
Proventil (albuterol)	Asthma	Bad coughs
Provigil (modafinil)	Excessive sleepiness from narcolepsy	Enhanced wakefulness and alertness
Pulmicort (budesonide)	Asthma	COVID-19
Risperdal (risperidone)	Bipolar disorder, schizophrenia	Alzheimer's disease, dementia, eating disorders
Stromectol (ivermectin)	Anti-parasitic	COVID-19
Symmetrel (amantadine)	Influenza	Parkinson's disease
Topamax (topiramate)	Seizures, migraines	Bipolar disorder, depression, nerve pain
Velcade (bortezomib)	Multiple myeloma and mantle cell lymphoma	AL amyloidosis
Viagra (sildenafil)	Erectile dysfunction in men	Sexual problems in women, obtaining stem cells for bone marrow transplants

Medicine	Approved Indication	Off-Label Usage
Wellbutrin (bupropion)	Depression	Weight loss, sexual dysfunction, substance addiction, and ADHD
Zonegran (zonisamide)	Epilepsy	Mania, bipolar disorder, migraine, chronic headaches, and eating disorders

Many approved drugs are used for off-label purposes

Actually, the concept behind off-label usage long predates the FDA and drug regulation. Captain Cook gave his crew limes for scurvy long before anyone knew what vitamin C was. People had no idea why it worked, but Cook's limes prevented scurvy. That's similar to off-label usage today. If it works, why not use it?

Off-label usage does not mean that physicians are making a mistake or are being duped. Physicians have eyes, ears, and brains and can see whether a medicine works based on published studies, talking to their colleagues, and their own experience. It's a case where the medical community thinks the drug works, but the FDA hasn't agreed for one of several reasons: because the FDA sees things differently; the sponsor hasn't yet borne the cost of presenting that medicine to the FDA for that specific indication; or the sponsor has done all the work, but the FDA is still working through the details.

For my company, Objective Insights, I regularly talk to physicians to assess their likely use of new medicines. When asked about possible off-label usage, the physicians usually report that they don't care what the FDA says; they will use it if it works and won't if it doesn't. Here's what one infectious disease specialist said about off-label usage: "I would put an FDA indication at the bottom of the [priority] list, not at the top. We used propranolol for migraine for ten years before the FDA approved it. As long as there is literature to support a use, we can use anything we want." Two other physicians concurred: "FDA indications are semi-irrelevant"; "ID's [infectious disease specialists] move fast. We don't have time to wait for FDA indications."

In a survey, doctors correctly identified only half the time whether the FDA had approved a particular indication for a given drug.[25] Of course, this does not mean that all off-label usage is always appropriate or safe. Off-label usage, like on-label usage, can be good or bad—it depends on the situation.

Markets Can Rapidly Incorporate New Information

How well do markets work, absent government regulation? If we wanted to assess the market for non-FDA-approved medicines, we would face a formidable problem: the market for non-approved drugs is nonexistent because the FDA requires that all drugs be approved before they can be sold. You can't study something that doesn't exist. But we can still get important information about how markets work in other situations. Consider the following.

In 2007, the *New England Journal of Medicine* published a study that stated that patients on the diabetes drug Avandia (rosiglitazone) faced a higher risk of heart attacks. This was important new information for diabetics. What happened next? If, indeed, markets don't work, we might expect sales of Avandia to have remained about constant because people wouldn't have received the message or, due to lack of medical sophistication, might have been incapable of properly processing the message. Or the company's marketing messages would have overwhelmed the conclusions from this one study. That's not what happened; Avandia's sales were hit almost immediately. Avandia's share of all newly prescribed oral anti-diabetic drugs fell from around ten percent to almost zero just two days after the article was published. This caused Avandia's annual revenues to drop from $3 billion before the controversy to $183 million in 2011.

Did the market overreact? It appears likely. Glaxo, the manufacturer of Avandia, insisted that the scientific evidence supported its use. Glaxo asked the FDA to take a closer look at the data, and, after eight long years, the FDA finally cleared Avandia of these charges; the agency determined that the data did not show an increased risk of heart disease.

This example shows that markets work, whether the signals they obey are real or exaggerated. There was no government action to hamper the usage of Avandia; rather, the impetus came from doctors, payers, patients, and their families. Within a market of countless dispersed individuals, all acting in their self-interest, the new information about Avandia was quickly processed and acted upon. I have no doubt that if patients on thalidomide had heard reports of its teratogenic behavior in 1960, sales of thalidomide would have dropped to zero, based on the same behavior we saw with Avandia.

Off-label prescribing relies on decentralized clinicians deciding what to prescribe. Another name for decentralized clinicians: a market. We can describe what off-label prescribing is and how it works, but we should expand our analysis to markets in general. What information do we have that suggests that markets work?

Markets Can Determine Drug Efficacy

Markets Can Pick the Best Drug

There's a very serious medical condition called status epilepticus. It's defined as an epileptic seizure lasting longer than five minutes and it includes situations where seizures occur so frequently that the patient doesn't have time to recover between them.

There are currently three predominant drugs used to treat this dangerous condition. Two have an FDA-approved indication while the third is used off-label.[26] Curiously, the third product is used about twice as often as the other two.

What insights can we learn from this market?

Does the FDA always pick the best products for approval? No. The third drug, the one that doesn't have an approval for status epilepticus, is considered the best product. Doctors give it high ratings for efficacy, safety, tolerability, and ease of use. Success came from the bottom up, not the top down.

Did the most widely used product—Keppra (levetiracetam)—find its success because of aggressive marketing? Were doctors duped into using it? No. The company that makes the third drug is forbidden from advertising it in even the slightest manner due to laws prohibiting off-label promotion. Use of the drug grew organically through information passed from person to person.

The success of the off-label product is an example of scientists, doctors, pharmacists, and hospitals—with no help, and even some amount of hinderance, from the FDA—discovering which product offers the best treatment and adopting that product. The success of the winning product came from customers looking for and finding the best drug. Sound familiar? That is how markets work.

Ignoring Efficacy to Speed Access

Pay attention and the world is full of insights, sometimes from unexpected sources.

When Representative Henry Waxman (D-Calif.) wanted to get new drugs into the hands of patients quickly and cheaply, he knew just what to do—waive some or all of the FDA's clinical trial requirements.[27] In 1984, Waxman championed legislation that waived the requirement that all small-molecule, or "regular," generic drugs had to be clinically tested for safety and efficacy. With the new rules, generic drug manufacturers simply needed to show that their generic drugs were, as far as could be determined, equivalent to the original drugs. In 2009, Waxman tried to do the same thing with a bill that extended those standards to another category of generic drugs that wasn't included in the original Hatch-Waxman law: biosimilar drugs.

To help consumers save money, Waxman was willing to allow certain drugs, called biosimilar drugs—biologic knockoffs—to enter the market without clinical testing proving their efficacy. He realized that requiring clinical testing for efficacy would slow down development and needlessly keep important drugs out of the hands of suffering patients.

Here was someone who supported the FDA's regular process for vetting normal drugs, but when he could help bring knockoffs to the market to save customers a few bucks, he was all too happy to jettison those rules. A more consistent solution would be repealing the requirement for *all* new drugs.

How much harm is there in giving the FDA the power to exclude new drugs until they have proven effective? Plenty. Approximately 35 percent of drug development costs are for safety testing, while 65 percent are for efficacy testing.[28] Because of this, good drugs are being delayed or not developed at all due to the added expense of efficacy testing. I have personally helped kill drugs for brain cancer, ovarian cancer, melanoma, hemophilia and other important conditions—not because they weren't good drugs, but because the projected development costs were greater than the anticipated probability-adjusted financial returns.

Just as Waxman's proposal would get drugs into patients' hands more quickly and create more competition, so too would a wholesale repeal of the efficacy requirement. The case for repealing the efficacy requirement for all new drugs, moreover, is just as strong as the case for repealing such requirements for small-molecule and biologic knockoffs.

Traditional drugs are small molecules made through chemical reactions; a chemist can attest, for example, that the 21 atoms of Bayer's and Teva's aspirins are equivalent. Biologics are large molecules, often with tens of thousands of atoms. Biologic drugs are protein-based and derived from living matter or manufactured in living cells using recombinant DNA biotechnologies. Even small changes in the manufacturing process can result in variances in a biologic drug's structure and efficacy, and there can be variation between batches of the same drug produced at the same facility. According to the FDA, the technology for a company to create an exact replica of a biologic drug does not exist. Therefore, as the name implies, all new generic "biosimilars" or "follow-on biologics," are similar—but not identical—to the original drugs.

Waxman's H.R. 1427 bill, introduced in the House of Representatives on March 11, 2009, recognized that the drugs would be different, and the Federal Trade Commission agreed in its June 2009 report, *Emerging Health Care Issues: Follow-on Biologic Drug Competition*, which said: "Unlike small-molecule generic drugs, FOB [follow-on biologics] products will not be designated as 'therapeutically equivalent' with the pioneer biologic drug product. The lack of therapeutic equivalence means that, like pioneer manufacturers, FOB manufacturers will have to market their products and negotiate individual contracts with purchasers."

Waxman hadn't forgotten safety for biosimilars. H.R. 1427 mandated safety testing, requiring "(i) information derived from chemical, physical, and biological assays, and other non-clinical laboratory studies; and (ii) information from any necessary clinical study or studies sufficient to confirm safety, purity and potency." But H.R. 1427 did not require clinical testing to prove efficacy and, in fact, stated, "Any studies under clause (ii) shall be designed to avoid duplicative and unethical clinical testing." It is generally considered unethical to shunt patients into clinical trials, where they might receive a placebo, if the active drug has already been proven to work. Those patients on the placebo would, therefore, be denied a good therapy. That's what Waxman was trying to avoid.

In a break with the 1962 drug law, H.R. 1427—which was never enacted—would have allowed the FDA to approve new, unique drugs *without any proof of efficacy*. Waxman said that it is okay for the market to ascertain efficacy—and it's easy to agree with him. If it's reasonable to jettison efficacy requirements for biologic knockoffs, then it's not much of a stretch to eliminate them for all new medicines.

As a postscript, these biosimilar drugs—which now have a formal regulatory pathway and some successful FDA approvals—appear to be very close to their branded cousins in terms of safety and efficacy. Many pioneer biologic drugs are receiving substantial competition from biosimilars.

Disease Drift

Here's another problem with determining efficacy: disease drift.

A measurement of efficacy might be misleading because the disease in question might have changed. The first two vaccines for COVID-19 boasted efficacy rates of around 95 percent. Two months later, the Johnson & Johnson vaccine displayed efficacy in the 70 percent range. Did this mean that the J&J vaccine was that much less efficacious than its peers? Not necessarily. The pandemic had progressed during those months and the J&J vaccine was tested in places where there were multiple strains of the SARS-CoV-2 virus, potentially muffling its efficacy. The coronavirus had quietly become harder to conquer. J&J faced a steeper hill to climb.

Wrap-up

> *If it's not approved and no one has tested it, we can't be sure that it's safe and effective.*
>
> **Harry M. Lever**, Cleveland Clinic cardiologist[29]

Dr. Lever's quote is true, but it tells only half the story. We can't be sure that *any* drug, approved or unapproved, is safe and effective, as we see that many drugs approved by the FDA demonstrate dubious safety and efficacy.

There is no clear distinction between the pre- and post-FDA worlds, at least in one regard, because in both, countless people take pills that were never tested and certified for patients *in their situation*.

As explained in Chapter 2, to fully test each drug in all reasonable segments of patients, we would need 50 billion patients. If we signed up one new patient every second, we would need 1,585 years to enroll the clinical trial. And that's just for *one drug*.

The current call for diversity in clinical trials seems to address this issue but it really doesn't because the problem is extrapolating clinical results for a population—be the population white males or Pacific Islanders or a broad mix of people—to one individual. We don't have enough test subjects or enough time to conduct the required trials. And if the test subjects experience a range of results, we don't know which result our particular individual will experience.

When a new drug appears, we know little about it. If we want to learn about such medicines, we must accept our role as guinea pigs, whether that happens in a centralized, rigid clinical trial or in real world, decentralized medical practice. At the present time, we can't tell if a drug will work in terms of safety, efficacy, and tolerability in a certain person at any specific time without putting that drug in that person at that time. Until our scientific understanding improves, and improves a lot, we are consigned to the role of guinea pigs and lab rats for the foreseeable future.

Markets function better than most people understand and are especially good at determining whether or not individual products work. Read an issue of *Consumer Reports*. Read product reviews on retail Internet sites, such as Amazon, Tire Rack, and Crutchfield. Do we need the government to tell us which televisions and toaster ovens work? When we already have better information than the government can provide, the answer is no.

The widespread application of off-label prescribing shows that markets function properly and can be used to determine efficacy, outside of official government agency proclamations.

The benefits of removing the FDA's efficacy requirements are arguably far greater than the costs. Of all the actions that policy makers could take to improve the practice of medicine with regards to pharmaceuticals, this is the one to focus on.

Clinical trials in humans are still a messy and problematic business. What can we do? We could test drugs in animals, as is commonly done, saving people from the exposure to potentially dangerous or ineffective drugs. Animal testing has some interesting challenges, as will be explored in the next chapter.

---

[1] "Donald Trump Looking Beyond Traditional Medical Experts for FDA Commissioner," *Wall Street Journal*, 13 January 2017.

[2] Table 11, Study 5, Overall Response Rate, Herceptin label, http://www.gene.com/download/pdf/herceptin_prescribing.pdf

[3] Herceptin plus chemotherapy helped 45 percent of patients. Chemotherapy alone helped 29 percent. Subtracting the two numbers gives 16 percent. Next, we need to calculate the percentage of patients not helped by chemotherapy: 100 percent minus 29 percent is 71 percent. Next, we divide the 16 percent by 71 percent and get 23 percent. Herceptin helped 23 percent of the patients not helped by chemotherapy.

[4] Keytruda package insert (aka label, prescribing information), study KEYNOTE-189, Merck & Co., https://www.keytruda.com/non-small-cell-lung-cancer/combination-therapy-clinical-trial-results/

[5] Keytruda plus chemotherapy helped 48 percent of patients. Chemotherapy alone helped 19 percent. Subtracting the two numbers gives 29 percent. Next, we need to calculate the percentage of patients not helped by chemotherapy: 100 percent minus 19 percent is 81 percent. Next, we divide the 29 percent by 81 percent and get 36 percent. Keytruda helped 36 percent of the patients not helped by chemotherapy.

[6] Doug Campos-Outcalt, "Latest recommendations for the 2017-2018 flu season," *Journal of Family Practice*, 2017 September; 66(9); 570-572

[7] "Gilead reports data for latest HCV combo," *BioCentury Extra*, 10 October 2016.

[8] Eric Sagonowsky, "ACC: Novartis' canakinumab cuts CV risks in patients with kidney disease, diabetes by up to 18%," *FiercePharma*, 13 March 2018.

[9] Anne Wilde Mathews, "So Young and So Many Pills," *The Wall Street Journal*, 28 December 2010.

[10] Cindy Arboleda, "'I am my own twin': Woman's rare genetic condition," *Yahoo Lifestyle*, 19 December 2017.

[11] One major study found that aspirin helps women avoid strokes but does not reduce their risk of heart attacks, unless they're 65 or older—effectively the opposite of how it affects men.

[12] Heather Litman, et al, "Serum Androgen Levels in Black, Hispanic, and White Men," *The Journal of Clinical Endocrinology & Metabolism*, 91(11):4326–4334, 2006.

[13] Amanda Gardner, "Genetics Influence Blood Pressure Medications," *The Washington Post*, 22 January 2008.

[14] Hanae Armitage, "A new tool helps tailor prescriptions to complement a patient's genome," *Stanford Engineering*, 22 February 2018.

[15] As of May 2018.

[16] "What's your type?," *Berkeley Wellness Letter*, October 2017.

[17] Sophia Hollander, "Let Your Genes Do the Ordering," The Future of Everything, *The Wall Street Journal,* November/December 2017.

[18] F. Perry Wilson, "Can Bitter Taste Perception Predict COVID Outcomes?" *Medscape*, 26 May 2021.

[19] Naiyer Rizvi, "Immunotherapy for Unresectable Stage III Non-Small-Cell Lung Cancer." *New England Journal of Medicine*, November 2017.

[20] Kelli Miller, "Off-Label Drug Use: What You Need to Know," WebMD, 2009 at: http://www.webmd.com/a-to-z-guides/features/off-label-drug-use-what-you-need-to-know#1

[21] Alexander T. Tabarrok, "Assessing the FDA via the Anomaly of Off-Label Drug Prescribing," *Independent Review*, Vol. V, No. 1, Summer 2000: 25-53. At: http://www.independent.org/publications/tir/article.asp?articleID=240&issueID=21

[22] The case when this was written in 2020.

[23] This paragraph covers some of the same ground that we covered in David R. Henderson and Charles L. Hooper, "To Increase Innovation and Make Drugs More Affordable, Deregulate," *Journal of Clinical Pathways*, September/October 2015. At: http://www.journalofclinicalpathways.com/increase-innovation-and-make-drugs-more-affordable-deregulate

[24] "Emergency Use Authorization for Vaccines Explained," FDA website, "content current as of 11/20/2020.

[25] "When doctors prescribe 'off-label'," *Consumer Reports on Health*, December 2009.

[26] Phenytoin and fosphenytoin are FDA-approved for status epilepticus while levetiracetam is not.

[27] From an article by David R. Henderson and Charles L. Hooper: "Markets Can Determine Drug Efficacy," *Forbes*, 7 August 2009.

[28] Joseph A. DiMasi, Henry G. Grabowski, and Ronald W. Hansen, " The price of innovation: new estimates of drug development costs," *Journal of Health Economics*, Journal of Health Economics 22 (2003) 151–185, Table 5.

[29] Natasha Singer, "F.D.A. Says Millions Got Unapproved Heart Pills," *The New York Times*, 26 March 2010.

Chapter 4: The Perils of Animal Testing

> *Cancer has been cured a thousand times.*
> **Christopher Austin**, National Center for Advancing Translational Sciences

Hurray! Cancer has been cured a thousand times...*in mice*. You and I will need to wait our turn.

Two decades ago a class of cancer-fighting drugs called MMP inhibitors showed great promise in mouse versions of metastatic cancer. The catch? They failed miserably in human clinical trials.[1]

It is commonly accepted that new drugs should be tested in the laboratory first, on cell cultures and such, and then, before they are tested on humans, tested on animals. The two implicit assumptions, which are somewhat contradictory, are that humans are different—and more valuable—than animals, and yet animals are good proxies ("models") for humans. Using logic from George Orwell's *Animal Farm*, we're equal, but so much more than equal.

Scientists believe that mice and humans descended from a common ancestor about the size of a small rat and, while each possesses about 30,000 genes, only a limited number of genes are unique to either organism. If we shared 100 percent of our DNA with mice, then mice biology would be a flawless "model" for our own, but we could no longer argue that humans are different and more valuable. So, for animals to work as a model for human physiology, they must be close enough but not too close. Sharing 97.5 percent of our genes seems to fit the bill and, from an ethical standpoint, it helps that mice don't look like us and can't tell us their feelings.[2] When was the last time you saw mice stage a protest rally?

In addition to mice, studies use rats, rabbits, guinea pigs, hamsters, gerbils, cats, dogs, and non-human primates. Ugh. My dislike for animal testing has remained constant throughout my three decades in the industry.

Does Safety in Animals Equate to Safety in Humans?

Animal testing got a big boost in 1921, when a pancreatic extract was successfully tested in diabetic dogs, helping to elucidate how insulin would help humans with the same disease.

Assume for a moment that animal testing of new drugs is a good idea and that dogs are appropriate test subjects. Given this, and buoyed by the success of the pancreatic extract, imagine that scientists start testing new compounds on man's best friend. They find that the first new compound that they put into dogs causes kidney failure, which, understandably, slams the brakes on all further development. Is this a triumph for science and drug safety? No. We later discover that this new "drug" contained some amount of plain old raisins and currants, innocuous to people but harmful to dogs.

The purpose of animal testing is to find drugs that are safe for humans, but it is burdened by two types of errors: dangerous drugs could incorrectly pass animal testing and end up in humans; and safe drugs could incorrectly fail during the animal testing phase, with humans missing out on beneficial therapies. Here are more examples of the latter type based on our hypothetical testing in dogs:[3]

- Dark chocolate? Safe in humans but toxic to the hearts and nervous systems of dogs.
- Anemia from blood cell damage results from the third compound. Later, we find that it is derived from onions and garlic.

- An experimental compound causes kidney failure in dogs. What is it? Something toxic to humans? Nope. Just grapes.
- Alcohol? It can cause coma and death in dogs.
- Avocados? Vomiting and diarrhea in dogs.
- Many varieties of mushrooms? Shock death in dogs.
- Caffeine? Vomiting and diarrhea in dogs.
- Xylitol, which is an ingredient in some gums and candies, produces yummy goodies for humans but liver failure, hypoglycemia, and death for dogs.

Based on this "logical" process for testing new drugs in dogs and the "scientific" evidence that comes from it, the FDA could have potentially prevented us from consuming raisins, currants, grapes, onions, garlic, chocolate, alcohol, coffee, tea, avocados, nuts, mushrooms, caffeine, milk, cheese, chives, yeast dough, and xylitol, had researchers tested these compounds in dogs before humans had ever had the chance to consume them. While the foods listed above can cause adverse reactions in dogs, other foods (bleu cheese, carbonated drinks, dried corn, green bananas, licorice, mango, orange juice, poppy seeds, rhubarb, and spinach) can harm mice, rats, guinea pigs, monkeys, or rabbits. And the list of foods that would be eliminated from our diets due to this "scientific approach"—foods that are nutritious and delicious and enjoyed by billions of humans daily—grows. I, for one, am drinking a delicious glass of iced tea as I write this, appreciating the fact that tea was well established as safe before the FDA was formed.

Maybe this scientific approach isn't so scientific, and maybe animals aren't perfect substitutes for us.

While researching this topic, I came across a website that listed "people foods" that can be harmful to pets. One category was medicine, and it called out acetaminophen and ibuprofen, saying that they are extremely toxic to dogs and cats. This is sadly ironic. The FDA's thinking is that medicines should be tested in animals to see if they are safe for us. Yet that implies that medicines that are fine for us are also fine for animals. But if some of the most widely used medicines can't be given to animals, lest they lead to gastric ulcers, liver damage, and kidney failure, then we can be certain that the process of testing drugs in animals as a precondition for testing them in humans is logically flawed. This can go forwards and backwards. If drugs are supposed to work in animals first and humans second, then logically, we should be able to take drugs that have been approved by the FDA for human consumption and give them to animals. We should, but we can't. The FDA's approach is seriously flawed.

To recap, there are two types of problems with animal testing: first, drugs that would be beneficial in humans are rejected due to adverse results in animals; second, drugs that pass animal testing are later found to be dangerous or useless in humans. The first mistake potentially reduces the number of new drugs that are available to humans. Not only does the second mistake waste time and money, it raises false hopes in humans and exposes countless animals to needless suffering. Is this a serious problem? Yes, it is. *Ninety percent of drugs that pass animal testing subsequently fail when tested in humans.*[4] While many of these failures aren't for reasons of safety, success in animal studies clearly does not translate into success in human studies. The numbers are so extreme that we can fundamentally question the value of animal testing.

A comparison that's more relevant is the probability that a drug that passed safety tests in animals then passed safety tests in humans. That number is more like 75 percent, with three drugs passing for each drug that falls short.

Animals are clearly hurt. Are there real examples of people being hurt by this "test in animals first" approach? Yes.

In 2006, six men in the U.K. were made seriously ill by the use of an experimental drug in a clinical trial. Observers were alarmed at the violent reaction, called a "cytokine storm" and involving multi-organ failure, caused by the drug, TGN1412, which is a CD28 superagonist antibody.[5] [6] What is noteworthy about TGN1412 is that it stimulates a protein found *only in humans*. What use is animal testing if the animals lack the required hardware? The scientists admitted that the animal testing might have caused "falsely reassuring results."

You might think that the discussion above is hyperbole and that, in real life, the FDA would never disallow something like tea or chocolate just because of animal testing. The truth is even worse than that. There have been examples of drugs that have been successfully marketed—meaning that they have worked in humans for decades with good safety and efficacy. And then, based on subsequent animal testing results, these drugs were almost recalled for problems that showed up only in test animals but not in humans. We'll explore some real examples.

Which Species Does the FDA Care About?

One can reasonably ask: which species does the FDA care about more, humans or rats? This is a serious question that deserves a serious answer.

Rats

In 2010, the FDA rejected XenoPort's new drug, Horizant (gabapentin enacarbil), a next-generation version of gabapentin.[7] It was just like the original gabapentin except that it was more easily transported through the intestinal wall. That is the crucial fact to know to understand how strange and destructive was the FDA's rejection of Horizant.

In 1993, Pfizer had launched Neurontin (gabapentin) for treating seizures, postherpetic neuralgia, neuropathy, and other nerve pain. The FDA approved Neurontin, even though, in animal testing, some male rats given ten times the highest human dose got a certain type of pancreatic cancer. Yet the rats still did fine. The tumors did not metastasize, were not locally invasive, and did not affect the rats' survival. Interestingly, neither mice nor female rats given gabapentin developed the tumors. And, most important, neither did humans. In 2010, after 17 years of experience with Neurontin, no increase was seen in pancreatic cancer among humans. The FDA even acknowledged this fact.

So, when Horizant came along, the Neurontin results should have been enough to assuage any alarm if Horizant showed the same tumors in some male rats, right?

Not for the FDA.

As could be expected, Horizant showed the same tumors in male rats given up to twenty-five times the highest human dose. Because of this, the FDA put the brakes on Horizant. Said the FDA: "[P]reclinical finding of pancreatic acinar cell tumors in rats was of sufficient concern to preclude approval of Horizant for RLS [restless legs syndrome] at this time."

It gets worse. The FDA had already determined that Horizant was effective and associated with no clinical (human) safety problems. Ronald Barrett, XenoPort's CEO at the time, said, "This one came out of left field."[8] Indeed,

XenoPort's stock dropped a whopping 66 percent the next day. The FDA

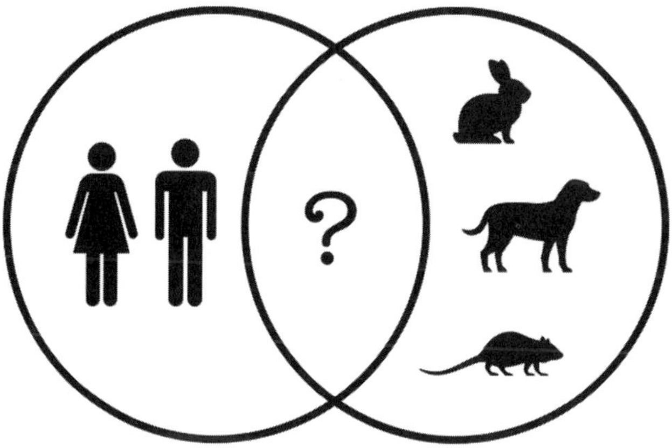

Figure 1: A Venn diagram of the overlap between the "hardware" for humans and animals. The problem is we don't know how much overlap there is.

acknowledged that this safety "signal" occurred only in rats, not humans Researchers had previously shown that the pancreatic exocrine tumors induced by gabapentin in rats do not correspond to human tumors. These are tumors that humans typically aren't susceptible to; acinar cell carcinoma was very uncommon in humans before Neurontin launched, and it was still uncommon 17 years later. Again, our hardware is different from rats'.

Now, you might say that with Neurontin already on the market, rejecting Horizant was no big deal. But it *was* a big deal. Horizant is more convenient and effective because it can be dosed twice a day with fewer milligrams than Neurontin's three-times-per-day regimen and still provide more stable levels in the blood. Ask most doctors what their biggest frustration is with patients and their medicines, and they will likely tell you that it's hard to get patients to keep taking their pills. Easier dosing causes patients to better adhere to their therapy.

Prior to Horizant, there were only two approved medications for restless legs syndrome. Unfortunately, they were associated with significant side effects and could cause the symptoms of RLS to *worsen*. According to the National Institute of Neurological Disorders and Stroke, RLS is a neurological disorder characterized by unpleasant sensations in the legs and an uncontrollable urge to move them for relief. People with RLS report feelings of burning, creeping, or tugging, and they sometimes feel as if they have insects crawling inside their legs. The sensations range in severity from uncomfortable to painful. RLS is generally a life-long condition for which there is no cure. Should these sufferers thank the FDA for trying to make them suffer for a lifetime?

Beyond the damage inflicted on people with RLS is the damage inflicted on drug companies. Yes, drug companies. Biopharmaceutical companies are in business to make money by curing or ameliorating disease. When the FDA gives them the green light to go beyond animal studies and do the more-expensive studies on humans, drug companies believe that they have some assurance that if the drug works on humans without untoward side effects, the FDA will approve the drug. But now the FDA has established a bad precedent. It can say, in effect, "We know we approved this next phase of testing, but we've changed our minds. We're worried about the effect on male rats that we ignored earlier." This creates enormous uncertainty for drug companies. If they see this decision on Horizant as a precedent, they will be less likely to invest in new medicines. And that will hurt all of us.

Remember that one of the primary purposes of testing new drugs in clinical trials of humans is to look for possible dangers to humans. That is exactly why Horizant was tested in clinical trials, where it passed. Is the FDA going to admit that human clinical trials aren't that useful? And if they aren't useful, why does it persist in requiring them?

Seventeen years of human data from millions of patients showing that gabapentin doesn't cause pancreatic cancer in humans were trumped by a two-year study in 200 rats given extremely high doses. The FDA needs to be reminded that it should be reviewing drugs for humans, not for rats.

As explained above, the FDA did reject Horizant in 2010. Thankfully, a little more than one year later, the FDA finally saw the light and approved Horizant, which is still on the market today.

Mice

In a similar story, the popular sleep drug Lunesta (eszopiclone) was almost derailed by the FDA because of tumors that developed in rat and mice test subjects. As with Horizant, scientists later determined that the incidence of cancer in rodents didn't apply to humans.[9]

Monkeys

Diabetes drug Galvus (vildagliptin) was delayed at the FDA because some monkeys who had been given high doses developed skin lesions. The agency took this action even though this problem hadn't arisen in the 5,500 patients exposed to Galvus in (human) clinical trials.[10] While caution is often warranted with such safety signals, we are left to wonder what would have happened to Galvus if the monkeys had developed these problems *before* the new drug ever had a chance to be tested on thousands of humans. It, too, might have ended up in the scrapheap of failed drugs.

Horses

In 2011, after Peyton Manning, the star quarterback for the Indianapolis Colts, had his third neck surgery in 19 months, he was still not healthy enough to play professional football. Willing to try something else and frustrated that nothing had worked, he agreed to try stem cell therapy to further his recovery. Unfortunately, this procedure came with a mandatory trip to Europe. Why? Because the FDA had not reviewed and therefore not approved such a treatment for humans, Manning couldn't stay in

Indianapolis or a nearby city, close to his family and friends; he had to go overseas.

The FDA doesn't regulate therapies for animals, and so racehorses, which are valuable and prone to injuries, have been the lucky recipients of stem cell therapies for years. "Orthopedically, the horse is a disaster waiting to happen," says veterinarian Bob Harman. "They're so big—a 1,000-pound animal on little toothpick legs—and they're working at high capacity." Harman has more than a passing interest in racehorses—he is the CEO of Vet-Stem, a California company that treats racehorses with stem cell therapy. As of 2011, Vet-Stem had treated 4,141 horses for soft-tissue injuries such as tendinitis and muscle contusions. He claimed that 70 to 80 percent had healed completely.

The clinical benefits of stem cell therapy in horses are impressive. In a study of 170 horses, researchers found that nearly 80 percent of them could return to racing, compared with previously published data showing a 30-percent success rate for horses given traditional therapies. After three years, the re-injury rate was 23 percent versus 56 percent.

Stem cell therapy has produced some exciting results in humans, too. A trial conducted at Stanford University and the University of Pittsburgh

Medical Center injected modified human stem cells—derived from the bone marrow of adult donors—into the brains of stroke victims. Many of these patients benefited so profoundly that they earned the nickname "miracle patients." If you or I ever contract a deleterious medical condition, we should be so lucky to earn the moniker of miracle patient. A larger study is planned.

Some colts are just luckier than others. If Manning had been a horse instead of a Colt, he could have gotten the cutting-edge therapy here in this country. Unfortunately, he was a human, so it was off-limits to him. To recap: The FDA "cares" too much about Peyton Manning to let him have this new therapy. It doesn't "care" as much about racehorses, so they get the green light. Make sense?

Manning played four more seasons, was named league MVP, and won a Super Bowl in his final year. While we can't say with confidence that his stem cell therapy helped him, the timing of his comeback after the therapy suggests that it did.

The case studies of Horizant, Galvus, and Lunesta demonstrate how animal testing results should *not* be used. How is animal testing supposed to work? Let's consider a few—admittedly extreme—hypothetical examples and follow their logic, assessing how well they address certain problems.

The Dangers of Dihydrogen Monoxide

In the first example that we'll consider, scientists want to study the safety of dihydrogen monoxide, a substance commonly consumed by humans. To do this, they follow standard procedures and give small doses to humans and exceptionally large doses to laboratory mice and rats. The usual tactic is to increase the human dose, such as one milligram per kilogram, by a factor of 100 to 10,000, to get a clear reading in a short amount of time. One three-month study was run in dogs at 300 times the human dose. In another study, a marketed drug was given to rabbits at 32,000 times the maximum human dose. So, for instance, if you took two tablets per day of this medicine, the dose given the rabbits would be equivalent to 64,000 tablets per day, or 1,067 bottles of 60 pills. That's a lot, to say the least.

The result of our hypothetical dihydrogen monoxide testing? Scientists showed that high doses of it caused asphyxiation in mice and rats, a result that was later reproduced by other researchers and led to a general warning against continued dihydrogen monoxide consumption by humans.

Should you be worried? No. This is a farce. Dihydrogen monoxide is a fancy name for water, which we all drink every day. Why did the rats and mice die in the study? Those poor rodents were given the human equivalent of thousands of glasses a day. The "dose" given to the rats and mice was enough to drown them, hence the cause of death—asphyxiation. If asphyxiation didn't doom the rodents, hyponatremia, or water intoxication, probably would have. While this example was made up to demonstrate a point, this is the standard approach to determine whether substances are toxic to animals in high doses and, therefore, potentially toxic to humans at regular doses. In such extreme examples, we can see the weaknesses of this approach.

If the dose makes the poison, perhaps any problems observed, such as tumors in male rats given gabapentin or drowning due to water, are due to the high dose instead of the compound itself. The FDA doesn't seem interested in this insight.

Rat Poison

In the second example—a worst-case scenario—an unethical pharma company decided to greedily push rat poison as a new medicine on unsuspecting human victims. Because of established FDA rules, before the company could make any money hurting customers, it needed to conduct animal testing on several types of animals, including rats and mice. The results showed that this new "drug" killed rodents with certainty; it was rat poison, after all. The FDA, seeing these results, resolutely prohibited this drug from entering human clinical testing, potentially saving countless people from the ill effects of ingesting a rodenticide pushed by an unethical company.

Success! We can see the FDA's processes working as designed.

Not so fast. Is this really what success looks like? If so, then "success" would include seeing my friend, the father of two wonderful daughters and the CFO of a public company, dying in the prime of his life. You see, this man suffers from blood clots in his lungs and has been hospitalized repeatedly. You, too, undoubtedly know several people who would have died had they not had access to oral anticoagulants, as their untreated blood clots gradually moved into their hearts, lungs, and brains.

Luckily, my friend is still alive—because of this very same rat poison.

Warfarin was introduced in 1948 as a potent rodenticide for use against rats and mice. Later, it was developed for humans as Coumadin (warfarin), an anticoagulant to prevent the formation and migration of blood clots in blood vessels. Americans have successfully used Coumadin since its approval by the FDA in 1954 as "safe and effective," and it is still a widely prescribed oral anticoagulant.

Coumadin has its challenges, as the wrong dose can kill humans as easily as it does rodents. As discussed in the Introduction, evidence suggests that warfarin was used to kill Soviet strongman Joseph Stalin.

Coumadin is a good example of the rule that the dose makes the poison and the concomitant insight that human utility can derive from a drug that produces harmful effects in animals. Think about it. If a drug that was *designed* to be highly dangerous to animals has utility for humans, why should any drug that *incidentally* appears to have issues with animals not be considered for human use? Indeed, this insight can cast doubt on the value of animal testing in general: many drugs have failed animal testing but are still useful to humans, and many drugs have passed animal testing but aren't useful for humans. With such a poor correlation and resulting uncertainty, why espouse the requirement of animal testing as a hurdle for drug development?

Mustard Gas

Coumadin was originally developed to kill rodents but has found use in humans. Could there be drugs that were originally developed to harm or even kill *humans* that exhibit some clinical value? Yes. As discussed in the Introduction, mustard gas is so ghastly that it was banned by the Geneva Protocol of 1925 as a weapon during wartime. It's been *banned* internationally as a *wartime weapon*. Nonetheless, a slightly modified form of mustard gas later became a treatment for cancer and is now commonly known as chemotherapy.

How could something that destructive have any medical value?

In 1942, two doctors at Yale University, Louis Goodman and Alfred Gilman, were examining the medical records of World War I soldiers who

had been exposed to mustard gas, when they noticed that many of the victims had a low number of the type of immune cells in their blood that, if mutated, can develop into leukemia and lymphoma. They hypothesized that if mustard gas could destroy normal white blood cells, it would also destroy the cancerous ones responsible for leukemia and lymphoma. Could mustard gas be a treatment for cancer, they wondered? Their discovery led to the first chemotherapeutic agent.

The first patient treated by such a chemotherapeutic agent was in pitiful shape. He had tried everything, and his outlook was considered hopeless. With a massive tumor on his jaw, he couldn't swallow or sleep or even fold his arms across his chest because the tumors in the lymph nodes in his armpits were too big. Acting as a human guinea pig, this patient received many treatments with mustard gas and with each one he became a little better. He could sleep, swallow, and eventually eat. Even his pain receded. From a shimmering cloud of death on the battlefield to a hopeful medical treatment in the hospital, the shining age of chemotherapy was born through odd and unexpected circumstances.

Here we have a "drug" that was *designed* to *kill* humans. Can anything that was designed to kill people be considered safe for people to consume? In a manner, yes. Chemotherapeutics have been used for decades to help cancer patients. Further, there are other examples of such poisons. Botox's botulinum toxin type A works by paralyzing muscles. Take too high a dose and you'll die. Norcuron is used, off-label, to kill inmates on death row. Is it safe? Safe things don't kill you. From these examples, we can see that even drugs that were originally intended to kill humans or rodents—or incidentally kill humans or rodents—can have therapeutic benefit.

The problems with animal testing don't end there; they just keep piling up. Consider the following startling realization that arose relatively recently, in 2016.

Painful Problems with Animal Studies

Scientists who studied pain with an animal model typically used male mice, under the assumption that both males and females would respond similarly, and that by using males only, one potentially confounding variable—sex, and the hormones and offspring that go with it—could be counteracted. What was known was that in male mice, immune system cells called microglia processed pain signals through the spinal cord and onto their final destination in the brain. Scientists assumed that this process held in all mice and, therefore, in humans. “These are perfectly reasonable assumptions. It just turns out that the assumptions are wrong,” says Jeffrey Mogil of McGill University in Montreal.

Not just wrong, but fundamentally wrong. Scientists discovered that pain signals in female mice are transmitted by an entirely different immune system pathway. Who knew? And why did mice evolve this way? It’s a mystery.

This new finding has demanded a fundamental reassessment of pain management.[11] If male and female mice use a different pathway to transmit pain signals, it holds that they might benefit differentially from pain medications. It’s not as if we didn’t have any warning: it has been well known that in humans, males and females demonstrate different sensitivities to pain. Even the color of someone’s hair has been shown to affect pain sensitivity.

Scientists have found that women with red hair need extra anesthesia during surgery. This finding is supported both by anecdotal evidence from anesthesiologists and by a test conducted at the University of Louisville. Researchers there administered electric shocks to women who were totally unconscious from anesthesia. (I hope the women volunteered for this!) It turns out that the ten natural redheads needed more anesthesia to keep their bodies from jerking or twitching from the shocks than did the ten dark-haired women.[12]

Half of what you will learn in medical school is wrong. We just don't know which half.
Statement from first day in medical schools

Although I am loathe to admit it, even with the above discussion of animal testing, such "pre-clinical" studies do often provide important findings. What needs to change is the FDA's animal testing requirements. Animal studies should be ancillary, not central, to the drug development process.

Wrap-up

The gold standard of animal testing, it turns out, isn't a gold standard after all; it's more like an aluminum foil standard.

We know that animal testing has some fundamental flaws, making the FDA's reliance on animal safety data problematic. For instance, approximately 25 percent of drugs that pass animal safety trials fail human safety trials, and a full 90 percent of drugs that pass animal safety tests still fail human safety or efficacy clinical trials.

This is not to say that human and animal testing is useless but, rather, that all test results need to be considered critically and skeptically, and their weaknesses must be known and understood. However, it does call into question the FDA and its rigid regulations.

The very approach that the FDA uses to "prove" that some drugs are safe or unsafe for human consumption is fatally flawed, and we see proof of this in the fact that some compounds known to *kill* animals and humans have found valuable uses in treating human diseases. If compounds known to kill animals can be valuable therapeutics, then the FDA should no longer halt the testing of new drugs in humans based on poor results in animals. If compounds known to kill humans can be valuable therapeutics, then the FDA should cease its pointless segregation of drugs into "safe" and "unsafe" categories. Any drug can be unsafe if used in the wrong dose in the wrong person, while any drug can be safe if used in the right dose in the right person at the right time.

The FDA's rigid rules don't work in real life.

---

[1] Arlene Weintraub, "A two-fisted punch against cancer metastasis," *FierceBiotech*, 25 January 2019.

[2] Any Coghlan, "Just 2.5% of DNA turns mice into men," *New Scientist*, 30 May 2002.

[3] Based on a poster in a veterinarian's office.

[4] Erin Biba, "From Chimp to Chip," *Popular Science*, December 2013.

[5] Anna Wilde Mathews, "Recent Cases Point To the Limitations Of Animal Drug Tests," *The Wall Street Journal*, 30 March 2007.

[6] Henry Miller, "Drug Testing, Drug Hazards," *TCSDaily*, 15 September 2006.

[7] First published as: "We Smell a Rat," Charles L. Hooper & David R. Henderson, *Medical Progress Today*, 8 March 2010.

[8] Donna Young, "XenoPort Shares Collapse After FDA Rejects RLS Compound," *BioWorld*, 6 March 2010.

[9] Anna Wilde Mathews, "Recent Cases Point To the Limitations Of Animal Drug Tests," *The Wall Street Journal*, 30 March 2007.

[10] Anna Wilde Mathews, "Recent Cases Point To the Limitations Of Animal Drug Tests," *The Wall Street Journal*, 30 March 2007.

[11] Christian Millman, "Of Mice and Pain," *Discover Magazine*, May 2016.

[12] "Anesthesia and hair color." *Consumer Reports on Health*, Vol. 15, No. 11, November 2003, p 10.

Chapter 5: The Perils of Human Testing

Alas, we can't just gaze at the chemical structure of a new medicine and appreciate which patients will benefit, what the proper dose should be, and which side effects may crop up.

To understand how drugs work in human bodies we need to actually put those drugs into human bodies. We do this through personal experimentation and, when we strive to be more scientific, organized clinical trials.

The use of clinical trials to determine the safety and effectiveness of pharmaceuticals nominally relies on the assumption that one human is a good proxy, or "model," for another. If a drug works in Arnold, it will work in Aimee. If it doesn't work in Arnold, it won't work in Aimee. As soon as we state this assumption, we realize its weaknesses. Men and women have key differences, for sure. Older patients are different than younger ones. The really sick differ from the merely sick. Diabetics face unique problems and pregnant women are not like average people. Diets, genetics, ancestral makeup, and a hundred other factors might swing the results one way or another. This is why clinical trials test drugs in thousands of subjects—because one person *is not* a good proxy for another. What if the situation were even more precarious? In this chapter, we'll explore the perils of human drug testing and the statistical conclusions that such testing yields.

Patients are Not Fungible

Fungible goods are interchangeable. If I take your dollar bill and give you a different one back, you shouldn't care; a dollar is a dollar is a dollar.

Mice aren't fungible, as we have seen. People, too, are not fungible.

Roughly 40 percent of people of East Asian descent have variations in their genes that convert alcohol into the chemical acetaldehyde, resulting in nausea, increased heart rate, and a severe flush.[1] No laboratory tests are needed, as the outcome—turning red at a dinner party due to "Asian flush" — is obvious, especially to the person consuming the alcohol.

Those of East Asian descent are clearly not fungible.

It's not just alcohol. For one of my brothers, treatment with the pain medication Vicodin (hydrocodone and acetaminophen) results in a paroxysm of vomiting. It doesn't have that effect on me, but it does give me brutal constipation. Why the difference? My brother and I are not fungible. Let's consider how and why we humans aren't fungible.

Who You Are Determines What You Should Take

If We Are the Same, I'm a Monkey's Uncle

Our differences aren't all in our minds. That is, our differences *are* in our minds, but the physiologies of our bodies are also maddeningly unique. Erbitux (cetuximab) is a successful drug that treats many types of cancer. There's one potential problem with Erbitux that didn't show up in Europe, New York, or even Boston. But the people in North Carolina now know that they must be alert to it. It turns out that some people, after being bitten by certain ticks found in North Carolina, react to a sugar in Erbitux, effectively making them allergic to the treatment.[2] Who knew?

The health effects of rubella, or German measles, depend on the person infected. In most patients, rubella leads to a trivial illness with a mild fever and rash. But in pregnant women, rubella causes miscarriages or babies born with blindness, deafness, microcephaly, and heart malformations. After a rubella epidemic in the U.S. in 1964-65, 20,000 children were born with birth defects.[3] When the FDA approves a vaccine or treatment for rubella, which type of patient—man, woman of childbearing age, or other type of woman—does it have in mind? One type? More than one? A blended average of all patient types?

Nicole, a communications executive in Brooklyn, is different from most of us. She reported that, "Instead of putting me to sleep, drugs such as NyQuil and Tylenol PM would make me hyper." She eventually learned that she had a sensitivity to two decongestants: diphenhydramine and pseudoephedrine. After she switched to Claritin, which contains neither of these, the problems went away.

Merck's finasteride, which is used by men to shrink enlarged prostate glands and to prevent baldness is so dangerous to pregnant woman that women are forbidden to even work in the factory that produces the drug.

Steven Pete and Pam Costa live 100 miles apart in Washington state. In terms of pain, they are worlds apart. Costa has "man on fire" syndrome, where even normal fabrics feel like a blowtorch on her skin, while Pete has a condition called congenital insensitivity to pain, which has a particularly awful downside: those who can't feel pain get hurt a lot, and Pete estimates that he has broken 70 to 80 bones in his 37 years.[4]

Lance Armstrong

Unique people benefit from tailored treatments.

Let's get this out of the way: Bike racer Lance Armstrong lied to almost everyone about his doping and made a general mess of his life and the sport of professional bicycle racing. The sport is still recovering from Armstrong's doping scandal.

If you can ignore this enormous black mark, this doping pariah's comeback story is still one of the greatest in sports history. On his deathbed with advanced testicular cancer—admittedly among the worst his doctors had

ever seen—Armstrong managed not only to survive, but to become the only seven-time consecutive winner of the Tour de France, one of the most physically and mentally grueling and highly-contested sporting events in the world. After his extensive doping was uncovered, of course, his seven Tour de France victories were nullified.[5]

You may hate him for what he did, but his story is still amazing from both physical and perseverance standpoints, and it was enabled by his physicians who understood his particular situation and needs. His first set of oncologists had wanted to give him the standard combination of drugs for testicular cancer: bleomycin, etoposide, and cisplatin. Armstrong got a second opinion from another oncologist who pointed out that while bleomycin was the right choice for many patients, it was extremely toxic to the lungs and liver. If Armstrong had any hope of returning to the competitive athletic world, bleomycin was a horrible choice. Armstrong's eventual oncologist, Craig Nichols, prescribed, instead, a regimen of vinblastine, etoposide, ifosamide, and cisplatin, allowing Armstrong to preserve his lung capacity and have a chance at returning to competition.[6]

Armstrong's doctors were alert enough to see that this unique patient needed a uniquely tailored treatment.

We are unique. Even pariahs.

Problems with Human Studies

A number of problems with clinical trials in humans become apparent once you think about them.

If patients have access to a medicine, they will be less willing to participate in clinical trails in which not all participants are dosed with that medicine. Hence scientists must somehow restrict the access to the medicine being tested until the research has been completed. The perfect vehicle for this: the FDA.

Second, in some rare diseases, it would be impossible to show a statistical survival advantage for a new drug because of the small number of patients available. Third, some conditions manifest so slowly that clinical trials would take decades or longer to show a benefit. Fourth—something that annoys drug companies and the FDA alike—placebos often work. Fifth, if patients can assess how they feel and, in fact, the very response being measured is how they feel, then patients are not "blinded."

These are not small problems.

Unexpected Placebo Responses

Many a clinical trial has been blindsided by the unexpected success of the placebo control arm. Medical experience may tell us that perhaps ten percent of patients with a certain condition will get better even with no treatment. When a drug company sets up a clinical trial to test a new medicine, it may rely on this ten-percent value to determine how many subjects to enroll in the trial. If the goal is to show that the new drug is better than nothing—a placebo—but some people will get better anyway, then more subjects will be needed in the trial to show statistically significant results. This ten-percent value, the level of statistical significance desired, along with an estimate of the effect from the new drug, are used to "power the trial," or to determine how many test subjects are needed to show a clear difference between the active and control arms.

After running the trial and analyzing the results, the drug company is gratified to see that 40 percent of patients got better on the new medicine but is astonished to realize that a whopping 30 percent got better with the placebo. This 30-percent "baseline" number makes it hard to show that the 40-percent value was truly better, especially if the trial was powered based on the ten-percent placebo estimate. Even higher placebo responses are possible: two trials that I'm aware of showed rates of 54.6 percent and 60 percent.

Why would, say, 30 percent of the patients get better on a placebo? There are three main reasons. First, sick people get better all the time. If you were a subject in a clinical trial to treat head colds and were assigned to the placebo arm of the trial, you would feel better after a week or so anyway. Second, the patients in clinical trials are treated like royalty, and even those who get placebos enjoy otherwise excellent care, including numerous doctor visits, individualized attention, etc. That original ten-percent base level might have included many in the community who don't typically get good care. Think of a poorly served group of patients, such as residents of ghettos with diabetes, who, in their normal circumstances, are likely to get substandard care for their diabetes. The "standard of care" that the patients in the trial receive will be far better than these patients' normal level of care, or, even the community's average level of care. The FDA does not seem to care about this insight and requires all patients to get "standard of care" therapy, even if it is far above the norm.

This one fact has prevented the development of many drugs. If Drug X plus an average level of care leads to clinical success, but a placebo plus standard of care therapy does too, the FDA will never approve Drug X because it won't be able to show a benefit over the placebo. But in the real world, patients would certainly benefit from Drug X because they *won't* be receiving such good baseline therapy. The placebo pill's good baseline therapy is pure fantasy.

Once again, the FDA doesn't seem to care.

Third, sometimes placebos work. And they work for two very different reasons: they cause people to believe that they *should* get better, and that belief leads, through mechanisms that aren't fully understood, at least by me, to real improvements; and they sometimes cause the body's own internal medicine cabinet to deliver real medicine to the patient.

Regarding the first—the psychological aspect—how you think about a disease affects how the disease affects you. As a case in point: after patients in one study were taught to "re-evaluate" their pain emotionally, they perceived less pain. "There is a growing recognition that drugs are only part of the solution and that people who live with chronic pain have to develop a strategy that calls upon some inner resources," said Josephine Briggs, director of the National Center for Complementary and Alternative Medicine. Research into the placebo effect has shown that anticipating relief seems to make it happen.

> Already, neuroscientists know that how people perceive pain is highly individual, involving heredity, stress, anxiety, fear, depression, previous experience and general health. Motivation also plays a huge role—and helps explain why a gravely wounded soldier can ignore his own pain to save his buddies while someone who is depressed may feel incapacitated by a minor sprain.[7]

Mind over matter; point of view over pain.[8]

Regarding the second aspect of the placebo effect—the physiological aspect—placebos can cause the brain to release beneficial chemicals. When runners get their "runner's high," that's from the body's own endorphins (the name endorphin was derived from "endogenous morphine," or endo-orphine), and placebos can do something similar, releasing actual chemicals to reduce pain.

A friend of one of my brothers used to attend Grateful Dead concerts while high on marijuana. Years later, he gave up smoking pot but still reported feeling high when listening to music of that famous band. Was his mind just reliving the "good old days" and making him feel nostalgic? When marijuana is consumed, it affects our bodies via cannabinoids, such as THC. The cannabinoids that we get from the cannabis plant are called phytocannabinoids. But there's another type, called endocannibinoids, which our *own bodies* produce on demand, and they activate the same cannabinoid receptors.[9] This means that our own bodies can produce some of the very chemicals that we get by smoking pot. So, years after he gave up smoking marijuana, my brother's friend might really have gotten "high" just by listening to the Dead's music.

We are familiar with actual drugs being ingested and releasing active ingredients into a patient's body. With a placebo, the patient is convinced that she[10] will receive a benefit, and that belief causes her brain to release real drugs that produce real benefits. It's not the placebo, per se, that's releasing the drugs—the brain does that part—but the placebo gets the whole thing rolling, so it deserves a good chunk of the credit. It's like a runner's high without the running: the running activates physiological changes that cause the brain to release endorphins; the placebo, similarly, activates psychological and physiological changes that cause the brain to release certain chemicals. In essence, the process of taking the placebo "convinces" the brain to release the beneficial chemicals.

In a controlled study, the brains of men who were told that they had received a genuine analgesic, but had actually received a placebo, released natural painkilling endorphins. "This deals another serious blow to the idea that the placebo effect is a purely psychological, with no physical basis," said Jon-Kar Zubieta, associate professor of psychiatry and radiology at the Michigan Medical School. "The mind-body connection is quite clear."[11]

In studies of subjects with fMRI (functional MRI) scanning machines, Kathryn Hall, a molecular biologist, reports that: "Now through imaging you can literally see the brain lighting up when you give someone a sugar pill."[12]

Nonetheless, even though it's real, the placebo effect has been the bane of researchers everywhere.

Imagine that you are a researcher and you believe that salt-water injections will reduce the number of migraine attacks experienced by chronic sufferers. You run a clinical trial and, sure enough, the patients who received the salt-water injections saw a reduction from 20 to 13 headache days a month. That's a huge difference. Do you celebrate? No. On the contrary, you didn't *want* the salt water to work; you wanted botulinum toxin, the drug you were actually testing, to work. You believed that botulinum toxin, not salt water, would reduce the number of headache days a month, but you included the salt-water injections as a sham procedure for a placebo control. Your hypothesis was that the botulinum toxin would help the patients while the salt water would not. Based on the trial, the patients who got salt water saw their headache days drop from 20 to 13, while the botulinum toxin recipients saw their headache days drop from 20 to 11. While 11 is better than 13, you were hoping to compare 11 to 20 to show a bigger benefit and, perhaps, a statistically significant difference between the two therapies. Your study might not have been powered to show a statistical difference between 11 and 13.

Maddening Placebos

Thinking about placebos can be mind-bending, which is one reason that they aren't fully understood. As discussed earlier, a paper published in the *New England Journal of Medicine* in 2016 examined the medical records of 12,705 people from 21 countries with "intermediate risk" for cardiovascular disease. Those who follow news on statins were surprised when the study showed that more patients in the placebo arm than in the statin arm discontinued therapy due to adverse events.[13]

Ponder that. Some of these people were given placebos, or inactive pills. At some point in their "therapy," these patients noticed negative side effects from the placebos, significant enough to stop "therapy." Perhaps one person had headaches he blamed on the placebo, while another was tired and listless. Later, after they stopped therapy, we can assume that these adverse events stopped. And this from an *inactive* pill. We humans are amazing creatures.

In many clinical trials, placebos produce half of the reported side effects of real drugs. What would happen if a patient "overdosed" on placebos? While bizarre to consider, it has happened. In 2006, a patient in a trial of antidepressants tried to overdose on his pills. After taking 29 pills, he started to feel faint, his blood pressure plummeted, and physicians had to administer intravenous fluids to stabilize him. It turns out he was in the placebo arm of the trial, and, when he realized the embarrassing truth, his symptoms quickly disappeared.[14]

A writer for the *Wall Street Journal* swears that a combination of Coke, Snickers, and ibuprofen successfully treats his migraines. Unless we think he's mistaken or lying, it's either a real treatment that works for him or it's a placebo that works for him. Either way, it works for him. How does it work? He replied, "My best theory is that the combination of the caffeine in the Coke with the salt, sugar and calories in the candy bar fixes some chemical imbalance in the body."[15] Would the FDA ever approve this triplet of common products for the treatment of migraines? It's doubtful. Also, who would ever invest the millions of dollars required to run the trials? Plus, what if this therapy benefits only a few patients, such as this WSJ writer?

Given that placebos can produce results, why not let people use them? If you think like a scientist, you'll probably shudder at this and say no. If you want good medical outcomes and don't need the scientific proof, you may say yes. What's to lose? We "know" that placebos are safe. American doctors clandestinely agree with this logic and about half of them admit to regularly giving patients placebo treatments—drugs or vitamins that shouldn't really help.[16]

The twin of the placebo response—a patient gets better without taking a "real" drug—is the nocebo response, where patients suffer side effects because they *expect to*. We've already discussed the adverse events seen by those on placebos in the statin trial.

In February 2018, Donald Trump Jr.'s wife, Vanessa, opened an envelope addressed to her husband that contained a mysterious white powder.[17] She called 911 and reported that she was coughing and nauseous. Was she okay? Yes. While she did go to the hospital, the powder ended up being harmless, meaning that her symptoms were manufactured in her mind. She thought she was being poisoned, and her body reacted appropriately by manufacturing a nocebo response.

Television and print ads for drugs include long lists of potential side effects, and sometimes those lists of pitfalls sound as if they have much larger probabilities than they really do. While maybe only five percent on a certain drug reported a headache and, perhaps, three percent taking placebos also reported a headache, the ads list "headache" as if virtually *everyone* who takes the drug will experience one. How many people have had one of those side effects precisely because they were influenced by the lists in the ads?

Studies have looked at the nocebo effect. In one study of approximately 20,000 people that included both blinded (patients didn't know what they were on) and non-blinded periods (patients knew what they were on), patients reported higher rates of adverse events during the non-blinded period, when they knew they were on a statin. During the non-blinded phase, these patients on statins reported muscle-related problems 41 percent more frequently than those not on statins. However, during the blinded phase, the rates of reported muscle-related problems were the same between the placebo and statin groups. That sounds suspicious.

> These analyses illustrate the so-called nocebo effect, with an excess rate of muscle-related AE [adverse event] reports only when patients and their doctors were aware that statin therapy was being used and not when its use was blinded. These results will help assure both physicians and patients that most AEs associated with statins are not causally related to use of the drug and should help counter the adverse effect on public health of exaggerated claims about statin-related side-effects.[18]

Other studies have corroborated this. In one study of patients who had previously complained of muscle aches while on statins, 26.5 percent of them still had "statin muscle aches" even after they had been unwittingly switched to a placebo.[19]

Some people are convinced that statins are the culprit—the evidence be damned—illustrating the power of nocebos.

For clinical trials, we have generally assumed that the "real" result of an active drug is the result that the active drug gets minus the result the placebo gets. If the active drug's results are better than those of the placebo, the active drug is "doing something." But that's an assumption. Perhaps a better way to think of it, instead of Real Drug versus Placebo, is Therapy That Includes Real Drug versus Therapy That Includes Placebo. The "therapy" part (the clean medical office, educated people in white coats who seem to care, getting to talk about bothersome ailments, having tests and scans run, being administered a promising "drug," observing the awesomeness of modern scientific medicine, etc.) might be the biggest contributor.

Placebo-controlled clinical trials—jokingly called trick or treatment—have another tendency that inflates the measured value of placebos and reduces the measured value of active drugs. Consider a clinical trial where half the patients are on the active drug and half are on a placebo, but they don't know which. Assume that the active drug will help patients increase their health by 100 points, whereas a placebo will offer zero benefit. Further, assume that the patients in the trial understand and *believe* these benefits of 100 and 0. Now, the half of the patients on the active drug will expect to improve 50 points (100 times a probability of 0.5—a coin toss—plus 0 times 0.5 equals 50). Their expected benefit will be 50 points lower than their "actual" benefit, and, given that beliefs do matter, this will tend to reduce the measured value of the active drug. The half of the patients on placebo will also expect to improve their health by 50 points (the equation is the same as the one above), which means that their expected benefit will be 50 points higher than their "actual" benefits. As the mirror image of the patients on the active drug, the placebo patients' inflated expectations of the placebo will tend to increase the measured value of the placebo response.[20] The net result will reduce the difference between the clinical results for the active drug and the placebo. Instead of 100 versus 0 points of health benefit, we might see 70 versus 30.

The downside of these two effects, to the extent they are present: a lot of good drugs have been tossed into the scrap heap because they didn't absolutely crush the placebo-controlled arm in clinical trials. Crush the placebo or go home, in a stadium where the placebo has home-field advantage.

Unblinded Subjective Clinical Responses

Clinical trials are designed to measure the objective differences between groups that have been given different treatments. Blood pressure is one such objective measurement. Blood pressure is also generally asymptomatic, meaning that patients don't feel better or worse while on their hypertension drug, which is why one of my family members once said, "I feel fine. Why do I need to be on this blood pressure drug?" But what happens when the quantity being evaluated and measured isn't objective, but is subjective and observable only by the patient?

A woman once told me that after she stopped drinking soft drinks, all the pain in her joints, especially her hands and knees, disappeared. I believed her, but should I have? She's not a doctor, so how can she diagnose diseases? She also didn't have any empirical proof that her pain went away. How would she convince a third party that her pain had ceased? Perhaps she had misled herself or, perhaps, she was simply lying. Or, most likely, she knows her body better than anyone else does, and she really did notice a cessation of pain when she stopped drinking sodas.

How would I "scientifically" assess and prove or disprove her subjective claims?

> *Not everything that can be counted counts, and not everything that counts can be counted.*
> **William Bruce Cameron**[21]

Many patient experiences are subjective, with pain, libido, dry eyes, fatigue, depression, eye discomfort, brain fog, muscle aches, itching, sleepiness, alertness, vitality, and well-being providing some examples. What's a scientist to do? A zero-through-ten pain scale can be used to measure pain, for example, but it must be the patient who makes the critical observation. I, as an outsider, might be able to tell that someone I know well, such as my son, is in pain, but only he can say how much pain he is experiencing.

Some diseases are maddeningly resistant to outside observations and measurable scales. Consider premature ejaculation. How many "patients" would be willing to hold a stopwatch while engaged in sexual intercourse? With emotions and physical sensations running rampant and ego tied to sexual prowess, would we get accurate measurements? Even with such difficulties, premature ejaculation could theoretically be measured in units of time from the start of sexual intercourse. What about libido? No outside observer can measure it, and even the person himself or herself may have a hard time putting numbers to it, partly because it is so amorphous, partly because it depends on other physical and emotional states, partly because an individual patient can't know how he or she compares to others, and partly because it changes over time.

For diseases that concomitantly lower libido, for instance, a patient's physician may prescribe a drug to improve libido and then say, "Tell me if you feel better over the next few months." That's all the physician can do. Perhaps the patient has symptomatic androgen deficiency (low testosterone levels) and his doctor prescribes intramuscular injections of testosterone. The doctor can measure the man's blood levels of testosterone, but only the patient can say whether or not the injections have ameliorated the libido-related symptoms.

Imagine that no FDA-like regulatory agency judged which drugs were efficacious and, consequently, which drugs could be marketed. (Assume for a moment that safety was still regulated.) Pharmaceutical companies would develop and manufacturer medicines and sell them to patients. If the patient felt better or got better, or if the prescribing physician recommended continuing that therapy, the patient would likely keep taking that medicine. If the patient didn't get better, had a tolerability issue, or didn't see the economic value, the patient would likely stop taking the medicine.

The problem with this, as we all know, is the placebo and nocebo effects. The patient's perceived net benefit is equal to the "real" benefit plus the placebo and nocebo effects, or the net objective plus the net subjective effects. There could be a real effect, such as reduced blood pressure or increased CD4 cell counts—or there could be none at all. The placebo effect could convince the patient that there's a real benefit even when there is none. Placebos and nocebos work both ways, "giving" therapeutic benefits and "causing" side effects.

The FDA's approach to getting around this problem is to separate the real effect from the placebo/nocebo effect via clinical trials with large numbers of patients to determine whether or not the medicine in question is working.

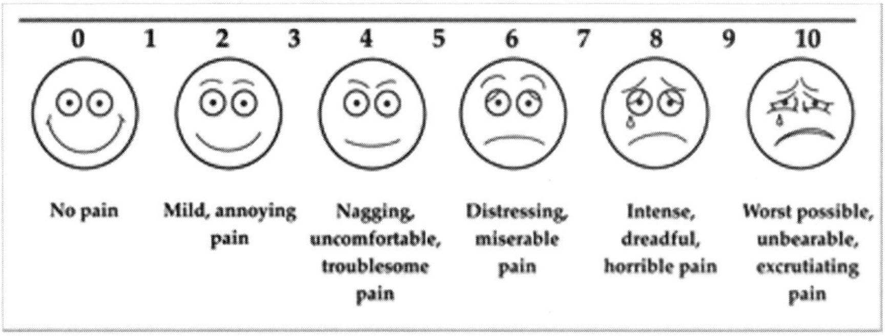

Visual Analog Pain Scale

Consider pain. In clinical trials, the visual analog scale, shown nearby, is used frequently to assess a patient's perceived pain level on a scale from no pain to excruciating pain. This is merely an objective measurement of nothing other than a subjective assessment. What the FDA ends up doing is looking at large collections of these subjective responses to try to infer an objective response.

The FDA's approach is as follows: (1) See if a drug is "really" efficacious. (2) If so, approve it. (3) Once approved, let patients and doctors experiment with the new medicine to see if it works for them. We could just as easily skip steps 1 and 2 and go right to 3. We could let patients and doctors experiment to find what works for them. Because medicines don't work for every patient and the FDA doesn't know how each individual patient will respond beforehand, patients, and the doctors that treat them, are *already* required to discover who responds through such trial and error. Patients need to personally test every drug prescribed by their physician to ensure that it is safe and effective *for them*. Skipping steps 1 and 2 and going right to 3 would be easier, cheaper, faster, and intellectually honest.

After all, if patients can be entrusted with the responsibility of assessing their subjective responses in clinical trials, why can't they be trusted with that same responsibility outside of clinical trials?

Humans are not fungible, and even *groups* of humans are not fungible, making clinical trials challenging. To ponder an even bigger question: Are you even "human"?

Microbiome and You

Do you think you're a bona fide human, deserving of the *homo sapiens* moniker? Think again. Nine out of ten cells in your body are non-human. There are 70 trillion bacteria that reside in and on your body. Six hundred species of bacteria live in your mouth alone, while 400 to 600 species of bacteria inhabit your intestines. You are more of a wild and unexplored ecosystem—think Amazon River basin—than just a plain old human.[22] Your microbiological passengers and partners live amazing and specialized lives: there are 2,368 species of identified bacteria that dwell in the human navel, 19 species that live in the fold behind our ears, and 44 species residing on our forearms. In total, the human microbiome is estimated to include 10,000 microbial species.[23]

A study of the microbiome residing in the mouths of dolphins revealed many types of bacteria unknown to science, and even new phyla—major branches on the tree of life—currently unknown to science.[24] It's not just dolphins. In human mouths, scientists have found that every tooth has a different population of bacteria![25] According to researchers at Stanford University, more than 99 percent of the microbes (e.g., bacteria, viruses, fungi) inside us are currently *unknown to science*. The team studied

the bits and pieces of DNA circulating freely in blood plasma and found that 99 percent of the genetic code failed to match any known patterns in existing genetic databases.[26] Moreover, scientists have estimated that 81 percent of all microbial cells have never been successfully grown in a lab culture, due either to a lack of knowledge or to the inability to create the right conditions.[27] This is a problem because to understand microbes, you need to culture them and study them in the laboratory.

These microbes aren't just hanging out enjoying the commute to and from work each day. They affect you in many ways, such as by helping digest food and regulating bodily functions. They also have a role in diseases. There are an estimated 30 million microbial species, but only 70 are known to directly cause disease. However, research has shown a link between the microbiome— specifically the presence and absence of certain bacteria—and diabetes, allergies, asthma, inflammatory bowel diseases, autoimmune diseases, autism, graft-versus-host disease, obesity, and certain types of cancer. Researchers have discovered that if the beneficial microbes naturally inhabiting an infant‘s gut are disrupted during the first weeks of life, that newborn faces a threefold risk of childhood allergies and asthma.

> *These microbes really have their little fingers on the knobs of all of our biological dials—they're tuning our immune system, they're tuning our metabolism, they can influence our central nervous system.*
> **Justin Sonnenburg**, Stanford University microbiologist[28]

In 2017, PD-1 inhibitors were some of the hottest new drugs and included Keytruda (pembrolizumab) and Opdivo (nivolumab). (Keytruda was the drug that helped Jimmy Carter with his melanoma.) These drugs are among the class of monoclonal antibodies that target either PD-1 or PD-L1, essentially "off switches" that prevent T cells from attacking other cells in the body, sometimes, unfortunately, even cancer cells that *should* be assaulted. The trick performed by PD-1 inhibitors is to flag cancerous cells as "foreign" so the body's natural immune system will attack them.

Understandably, by enlisting the body's immune system to recognize and attack cancer cells, these drugs have achieved fantastic results in treating certain cancers.

The problem with PD-1 inhibitors, as with most drugs, is that some patients respond to them and others don't. An article in *Science* shed some light on this issue, reporting that scientists found significant differences in the diversity and composition of the gut microbiome in melanoma patients who responded to PD-1 inhibitors, compared to those who did not.[29]

The microbiome turns out to be so important that scientists are studying fecal transplants to restore healthy gut bacteria in deficient people. One motivation for this is to fight the bacteria *Clostridium difficile* that has been linked to 14,000 deaths per year in the U.S. from diarrhea. In these transplantation procedures, doctors take fecal matter from healthy donors, dilute it, and use a nasal tube or a colonoscope to deliver it into the recipient's small intestine. While it sounds disgusting, researchers have demonstrated effectiveness in clinical trials.[30] Dutch and Finnish researchers found in a randomized, controlled trial in 2013 that more than 90 percent of the test subjects were cured.[31]

> *Our microbes are a part of human physiology...as much a part...as our liver, or our kidneys, or our heart.*
> **Martin Blaser**, Chair of the Department of Medicine at New York University

When it comes to the microbiome, researchers are looking at a mind-boggling smorgasbord of possible therapeutic approaches: bugs as drugs, removing bugs as drugs, feeding bugs as drugs, drugs for your bugs, drugs from bugs, bugs to fight bugs, bugs to help bugs, keeping bugs in the right place, bugs to activate cells, bugs to deactivate cells, etc. The possibilities are dizzying. But wait, there's more. The species of bacteria and viruses in your body may provide early diagnosis of disease. A little-studied family of viruses—picobirnaviruses—can be detected *before* patients develop graft versus host disease (GvHD), in which immune cells in grafted tissues attack the patient.[32] "To our knowledge, this is the only potential marker that we and others have been able to find that may be actually predictive of whether or not a patient will go on to develop GvHD," reported Charles Chiu, a researcher at UC San Francisco.

Viral strains that predict Type I diabetes have been found in infants and toddlers, long before antibodies become measurable in blood serum.[33] Think of the benefit of diagnosing important diseases years earlier than is possible now. "It is early days in terms of understanding this new biology. As more and more data are available the challenge is how to decide where to place the bets that will result in successful therapies 10 years from now," said Gareth Hicks, VP, Takeda Pharmaceutical Co. Ltd.

Curious about the composition of your microbiome? Those who are motivated can participate in the crowdfunded study, American Gut, which is a growing global database of individual microbiome data (see americangut.org).

Do you think scientists will understand the microbiome soon? I wouldn't bet on it. While our bodies are mind-bogglingly complex, even something seemingly far simpler, such as a drop of seawater, is still beyond our comprehension.

> *Every drop in the ocean has tens of thousands of microbes that are changing the chemistry around them. They are everywhere, and we know almost nothing about them.*
> **James Bellingham**, Monterey Bay Aquarium[34]

Imagine what it must have been like to develop drugs in the 19th century, before scientists even grasped the germ theory of disease. Developing and approving new drugs today without really understanding the microbiome is not all that different.

Antibiotics and Hormones

Did you know that many farm animals have been given large doses of antibiotics? Do you know why? You might guess it was to prevent or cure illnesses, especially considering the close quarters that livestock inhabit. That answer is only partly right. Surprisingly, livestock given antibiotics grow heavier faster. Livestock managers discovered years ago that by killing internal bacteria and altering the microbiome, they caused their livestock to grow fatter. Consider your waistline and the health of your microbiome the next time you doctor hands you a prescription for a course of antibiotics.

Enzymes and You

Billions of adults around the world are unable to digest milk because they no longer produce lactase, the enzyme that takes apart lactose, the key sugar in milk. But even among those of us who are lucky enough to produce lactase, our bodies produce it only when needed, meaning that after our dairy meal is finished and the lactose is digested, our bodies shut down the production of lactase. Your body is far from static.

> *We are all biochemists. Every moment, our bodies perform gazillions of chemical reactions, putting molecules together, taking them apart. While a chemist in the lab uses test tubes and beakers, our bodies use enzymes—tiny machines that can grasp atoms and molecules.*
> **Alan Stahler**, science writer[35]

What if the body's lactase levels determine how a drug is metabolized (broken down and used)? If so, then two people will metabolize a drug differently, and even an individual's ability to metabolize that drug will vary throughout the day. In 1997, the FDA approved Plavix (clopidogrel), a drug to prevent heart attacks. Thirteen years later, it was discovered that Plavix is less effective in a third of patients because of variances in their metabolisms.[36]

How quickly people metabolize caffeine determines their heart attack risk from coffee. "Among slow-metabolizers, those who drank two or more cups of coffee daily were at least 36 percent more likely to have a nonfatal heart attack than those who drank little or no coffee. Even higher risks were found for slow metabolizers under 50. They were up to four times more likely to have a heart attack than slow metabolizers in their age group who drank little or no coffee."[37] This is not to say that coffee is unambiguously dangerous; coffee has been shown to lower the risk of heart disease, type 2 diabetes, liver diseases, and Alzheimer's disease, among other things. Drinking coffee helps protect against Parkinson's disease and decreases the risk of suicide. Coffee is still the world's most popular source of dietary antioxidants. Nevertheless, coffee does have some downsides.

Given all this complexity, can we trust the ostensibly scientific studies that the pharmaceutical industry and the FDA have used to develop and approve drugs? Maybe not. The shocking conclusion is that some large percentage of these studies may not be reproducible for elemental reasons, calling into question the reliability of their conclusions and exposing what might be a very expensive medical castle built on shifting sand.

We can do more than wave our hands and pose hypotheticals; we can concretely quantify the magnitude of the problem using statistics.

Discrimination and Statistical Fractals

Take a moment and leave the world of pharmaceuticals and drug regulatory agencies, and look at something that most of us have experience with: education. Suppose that you suspect some gender discrimination against women in admissions at your university, and so you do some research on admission rates and find the following:

Table 1: College Admissions

Gender	Admission Rate
Men	**66%**
Women	43%

What Percentage of Students are Admitted?

This table appears to be a smoking gun showing discrimination against women because an admission rate of 66 percent for men is much higher than the 43 percent rate for women. Before reporting this to the university president, however, you look deeper, realizing that the results might be different at the department level. You're right. This particular school has only two departments, engineering and art, wherein you find the following results:

Table 2: College Admissions

Department	Men Admitted	Women Admitted
Engineering	70%	**80%**
Art	30%	**40%**

What Percentage of Students are Admitted?

This table appears to contradict Table 1 and show discrimination against *men*. How can you reconcile the two set of results? Upon further thinking, you realize that more women apply to the art department, where the admission rates are lower; at the same time, more men apply to the engineering department, where admission rates are higher. Women have higher admission rates than men in both departments, but they overwhelmingly choose the more selective department, producing lower overall admission rates. Unsettled by these findings, and before reporting this to the university president, you look still deeper, at the sub-department level, of which there are two per department. You find the following:

Table 3: College Admissions

Sub-Department	Men Admitted	Women Admitted
Mechanical Engineering	**95%**	85%
Biomedical Engineering	**60%**	50%
Graphic Arts	**60%**	50%
Watercolor Arts	**20%**	10%

What Percentage of Students are Admitted?

You are unsettled by results that, again, appear to show discrimination against *women*! How can this be? What is the truth in this matter? Do men have higher admission rates or do women? In this case, we can use statistics to show conflicting results. Ultimately, the answer depends on the numbers of men and women applying to each department. (It also depends on the quality of the applicants, but we'll ignore that here.) In this fictitious example, women apply disproportionately more frequently to art—specifically graphic arts—while men apply disproportionately more frequently to engineering—specifically biomedical engineering. The complete numbers in this fictitious but mathematically correct example are shown in the footnote.[38] Disturbingly, all *three* of the conclusions are true, with the caveat that, as always, these results show associations and correlations, not cause and effect. There's no proof of disreputable behavior here. Depending on how deeply you dig, you could report that women were discriminated against or that men were discriminated against. Neither conclusion may be right. We don't have enough information.

The example above was fabricated to illustrate the point. Could this ever happen at a real university? Yes. Below are real data reflecting graduate school admissions to the University of California, Berkeley in 1973. At first glance, it looks as if there's gender discrimination against women, but is there?

Table 4: College Admissions, U.C. Berkeley

Gender	Admitted
Men	**44%**
Women	35%

What Percentage of Students are Admitted?

Just as in the fabricated example, discrimination against women seems clear. But, once again, look at the departmental-level data.

Table 5: College Admissions, U.C. Berkeley

Department	Men Admitted	Women Admitted
A	62%	**82%**
B	63%	**68%**
C	**37%**	34%
D	33%	**35%**
E	**28%**	24%
F	6%	**7%**

What Percentage of Students are Admitted?

Table 5 appears to show discrimination against men because women generally had higher admission rates at the department level.

In Table 4, it looks as if women were admitted at a lower rate, but Table 5 shows that their admission rates were higher in four out of the six departments surveyed. What gives? What was really going on here? The answer is that more men applied to departments A and B, with higher overall admission rates, while more women applied to departments C, D, E, and F, with lower overall admission rates. Men had a higher admission rate at the school level even though women generally had higher admission rates in each department. The women were applying for admission into the more selective departments, which made their overall rates of admission look lower than those of men.

What if we didn't or, worse, couldn't break out these admission rates by department? We might draw the wrong conclusion and perhaps incorrectly report a scandal. But it's worse than that because any wrong conclusion we draw will have the air of statistical rigor. What's even worse, if we further divided the applicants by sub-departments, as we did in the fabricated example above, it is possible that, once again, we would see *lower* admission rates for women. Do you see the problem? Where do we stop? It's like a fractal that goes on forever, repeating its patterns in smaller and smaller scale. When can we say that women appear to have been discriminated against? When can we say that the men were discriminated against? This fractal never reaches a conclusion.

While issues of discrimination are interesting, could the same concept be happening in the hard science of drug testing and clinical trials? In fact, it is. The principle is the same. At a high level, Drug X might appear to help more patients than Drug Y. One level below that, it might be Drug Y that appears to help more patients than Drug X. At the next level below that, the conclusion might be reversed again. And so on and so on. This insight even has a name: Simpson's Paradox.

Simpson's Paradox

Ponder this disturbing fact: clinical trial results can show results that are the *reverse* of reality.

A straightforward example will help.

Consider two groups of men: younger men and their older compatriots. We conduct a survey to ascertain the effect of dieting on body mass to help determine whether dieting helps men lose weight. Once we do that, we come to an unexpected, yet statistically proven, conclusion: those men who diet are 30 pounds heavier than those who don't. Can this be right? Can dieting make you *heavier*, and, if so, why would anyone want to diet? Of course, this is a correlation, not proof of causation, but the statistics clearly display this associative relationship. In actuality, this conclusion is diametrically opposed to the real truth. Here's the complete story.

- Young men who diet all weigh 150 pounds, while those who don't diet weigh 160.
- Older men who diet all weigh 190 pounds, while those who don't diet weigh 200.
- None of the younger men are currently dieting, while all of the older men are.

When we survey and group the men into "dieting" or "not dieting" cohorts, we end up inadvertently segregating them by age (dieting = older, not dieting = younger), hence the conclusion that men who diet are 30 pounds *heavier* than men who don't. When we look at them by age group, we come to the opposite conclusion, which is that men who diet are ten pounds *lighter*.

Table 6: Dieting

Men (weight)	Dieting	Not Dieting	Difference
All Ages	190	160	+30 pounds

Men's Weights, By Diet

Table 7: Dieting, by Age

Men (weight)	Dieting	Not Dieting	Difference
Younger	150	160	-10 pounds
Older	190	200	-10 pounds

Men's Weights, By Diet and Age

Table 6 shows the incorrect conclusion. Table 7 shows the correct conclusion.

We can avoid this trap by knowing that age is a crucial variable and that men need to be segregated by age because weight is a function of age. But what if age were hidden, or "lurking"? What if we didn't suspect its importance or, for some reason, we couldn't or chose not to measure it? We wouldn't be able to separate men into age groups and we would come to the conclusion that men who diet are, indeed, heavier.

We've already discussed how any individual can't know ahead of time if a given medicine will work, or how well it will work, until the person in question actually ingests or injects that medicine. This is due to the amazing complexity of human biology and the unknown effects of any number of factors. Due to the fact that we can't predict that someone with certain characteristics will have a particular result, we are left lumping a number of heterogeneous people into cohorts, putting a new drug into those cohorts and measuring how well the cohorts did. Whenever we do this—and we do it all the time—we potentially run into something known as **Simpson's Paradox**, which is a phenomenon in which a clinical trend appears across groups but disappears or reverses when these groups are combined. The results point one way but then flip and point the other way. The essential insight is that Simpson's Paradox can be in effect when there are "lurking" or confounding variables that either aren't understood or, if they are understood, aren't properly considered in the analysis.

In the fictional example above of men dieting, age was the lurking variable that gave us the incorrect conclusion. When we considered age, the results flipped from "men who diet are heavier" to "men who diet are lighter." In the college admission example, departments and sub-departments were the lurking variables that gave us incorrect conclusions.

> *Nature is full of infinite causes.*
> **Leonardo da Vinci**

When scientists don't understand what causes one person to respond to a drug while another doesn't—in other words, in almost every situation—we are in danger of coming to the wrong conclusion based on the trickery of Simpson's Paradox. There's something driving the results, but it is hidden from us. If we want to quantify our ignorance, however, there's an analytical technique that can help us understand how much we know and how much we don't know. **Multiple linear regression modeling**—a standard analytical tool for teasing out the relationships inherent in such problems—shows two important outputs: how much the individual variables are driving the final answer; and how much of the final answer is explained by the variables present in the model.[39]

To help explain, here are four possible scenarios for a clinical trial along with what multiple linear regression modeling tells us about each:

- **Spectacular drug:** In a clinical trial, 100 subjects take Drug X and another 100 get a placebo. All patients on X improve, while none on the placebo improve. With these stellar results, we can say with certainty that

Drug X helped the patients—the results are not due to chance—and a linear regression model would show that we explained 100 percent of the variance—100 percent of the results. This makes sense. But the example is abnormal; generally, not everyone on a drug gets better, and some on the placebo improve. Life is normally more complicated.

- **Useless drug:** In another clinical trial, 100 subjects take Drug X and 100 get a placebo. Fifty patients on X improve and fifty on placebo improve. A linear regression model of these clinical results shows that X did not help these patients and that we have explained 0 percent of the variance —0 percent of the results. We have no idea why 50 patients on Drug X got better and 50 didn't or why 50 patients on placebo got better. All we know is that Drug X doesn't help patients.

- **Great drug:** In another clinical trial, 100 subjects take Drug X and 100 get a placebo. Ninety patients on X improve, while ten on the placebo improve. We can say with virtual certainty that Drug X helped those patients or, in other words, the results aren't due to chance. And yet a linear regression model of these clinical results shows that we have explained only 64 percent of the variance—64 percent of the results. A full 36 percent of the results are due to...we don't know—something other than just the ingestion of Drug X or the placebo.

- **Average Drug:** In our final example, 100 subjects take Drug X and 100 get a placebo. Forty patients on X improve, while twenty on the placebo improve. This is a realistic example and, while the linear regression model tells us that we can be 99.8 percent certain that X helped those patients who got it, this linear regression model explains only 4.8 percent of the overall results. Why didn't everyone on X get better? We don't know. Why did some on the placebo get better? We don't know. This model explains only 4.8 percent of the variability, and a full 95.2 percent of the results were driven by *something else* that wasn't included in our model. That's huge. There's so much we don't know—something else must be at work, lurking behind the scenes. We may have no idea what it is.

This "lurking variable" issue has far-reaching ramifications for FDA drug approvals.

Here is an illustrative example, comparing drugs X and Y, followed by some conclusions:

- Among all patients, Drug Y worked better than Drug X. With these results, perhaps the agency will approve Y but not X.
- Among healthier patients, X worked better than Y, while among sicker patients, Y worked better than X. What will the FDA do? Approve one drug? Approve both?
- Among women, X worked better than Y, while among men, Y worked better than X. What will the FDA do?

If the companies developing these two drugs picked the "wrong" patient populations to study them in, their drugs may never be approved and marketed. If X was studied in sicker patients or men, and Y was studied in healthier patients or women, X and/or Y might fail those clinical trials and be rejected by the FDA—a result purely due to do bad luck. Wait. Isn't the drug development and approval process supposed to be scientific? Yes, it is. But we can't know what we don't know. What are the lurking variables? We don't know. Therefore, a lot is due to luck.

As we've explored, scientists don't understand the microbiome. Could the microbiome be a key lurking variable in clinical trials? Yes, it could.

Here's a fabricated example positing the microbiome as the lurking variable in a clinical trial. The microbiome is a reasonable example of a lurking variable for the very fact that it is not well characterized and understood. Of course, this is speculative because, by definition, we can't pinpoint lurking variables. Why? Because they are hidden or not understood.

For this thought experiment, 100 patients are given a new drug, Drug X, and 100 are given existing Drug Y. After taking these drugs, some get better and some don't.

Table 8: Drug X Versus Drug Y, Ignoring Microbiome

	Drug X	Drug Y
Patient Gets Better on Drug?	14 better/86 not (14%)	41 better/59 not (41%)

What Percentage of Patients Improve?

If we didn't understand or test for the microbiome, we would say that Drug X doesn't work very well and maybe the FDA should reject Drug X. Why approve new Drug X when existing Drug Y works so much better? When we look deeper, we find different results.

Table 9: Drug X Versus Drug Y, Considering Microbiome

	Drug X	Drug Y
Microbiome C	9 better/1 not (90%)	1 better/9 not (10%)
Microbiome D	5 better/ 85 not (6%)	40 better/50 not (44%)

What Percentage of Patients Improve?

When we do measure the microbiome of each subject, we find that Drug X works better in patients who happen to have Microbiome C (90 percent success), while Drug Y works better in those with Microbiome D (44 percent success).

In this plausible example, the FDA rejects new Drug X, comfortable in the knowledge that patients generally do better on existing Drug Y. However this conclusion is due to the accident that 90 percent of patients have Microbiome D. Years later, when the relationships shown in Table 9 could have been used to successfully treat patients, it's too late. Drug X was rejected and has been long since forgotten.

Are there any real examples of the microbiome wrecking the results of a study? Yes.

Physiologist Laura McCabe was running some experiments, and her results became more interesting with each step she completed.

> In the first experiment, Laura McCabe's lab seemed to hit a home run. The physiologist and her team at Michigan State University in East Lansing were testing how a certain drug affects bone density, and they found that treated lab mice lost bone compared with controls. "I was thinking, 'Hey, great! Let's repeat it one more time to be certain,'" McCabe recalls.
>
> They ordered a seemingly identical batch of mice—same strain, same vendor—and kept them under the same conditions: same type of cage, same bedding, same room. This time, however, treated mice gained bone density. "Maybe one was a fluke," McCabe thought. They did a third run—and saw no effect at all. She was baffled.
>
> She knew that signals from the gut can affect how bone forms and gets reabsorbed, so her team took fecal samples from control mice in each of the three experiments and analyzed their gut microbes. They found something unexpected: Each group had a different microbial makeup to begin with.[40]

Here, the microbiome was the lurking variable. What lurking variables are out there, concealed in the shadows? That's the whole problem. *We don't know!* In most clinical trials, in which approximately half of the patients get better on the drug being tested, there *must be* lurking variables that explain why some improved and others didn't.

It's challenging to analyze clinical trial results and ascertain what's really going on, and we should be concerned about this handicap because bad drugs could potentially be approved while good drugs are thrown on the scrap heap.

Wrap-up

Quite frankly, we're still in the scientific dark ages. There's so much we don't know. Pick any disease, especially a rare one, and study it for some period of time, and you're likely to find that that disease is poorly understood. "We just don't know," is the common refrain.

It's more than just diseases that we don't understand.

Placebos are simultaneously ridiculed by the scientific community and acknowledged for their potency, as they are required as comparators in most clinical trials. Virtually every clinical trial has inadvertently studied and proved the healing power of placebos.

The placebo response makes it difficult for researchers to demonstrate that the drugs they are testing are really working. By comparing the results of the two arms of a clinical trial, what should be a large gap between the active and placebo arms may end up being too small to "prove" an effect. Placebos and nocebos mockingly demonstrate our ignorance. One result is that companies sometimes abandon perfectly good drugs.

In human clinical trials, there may be lurking variables and enough uncertainty about measured relationships that scientists and the FDA could be drawing exactly the opposite conclusion from reality. The FDA and the whole biopharma industry should be concerned with the challenges we face in analyzing clinical trial results and ascertaining the real relationships.

The microbiome could be playing the part of the lurking variable in clinical trials and giving us results in which we might find, for example, that we can explain only 4.8 percent of the variability, meaning that 95.2 percent of the results are being driven by *something else* that wasn't measured.

No scientist would dare ignore the germ theory of disease when developing and testing new drugs, and yet scientists may be making the same mistake with the all-important microbiome, which appears to affect us in a multitude of ways.

[1] Melinda Beck, In Search of Alcoholism Genes, *The Wall Street Journal*, 8 February 2011, pg D1.

[2] Beth Jinks, "ImClone, Bristol to Test for Erbitux Allergy in U.S. South," *Bloomberg*, 12 March 2008.

[3] John Ross, "The Human Cost of a Life-Saving Vaccine," *The Wall Street Journal*, 17 February 2017.

[4] Erika Hayasaki, "Pain Relievers," *Reader's Digest*, May 2018.

[5] So many other riders were also doping that the authorities couldn't find a top racer free of drug taint and the victories remain unclaimed.

[6] Lance Armstrong and Sally Jenkins, *It's Not About the Bike*, 2000, Berkley Books, New York, pg 91 and 104.

[7] Melinda Beck, "Rewiring the Brain to Ease Pain," *The Wall Street Journal*, 15 November 2011.

[8] See, for instance, Bernie Siegel, *Love, Medicine and Miracles: Lessons Learned about Self-Healing from a Surgeon's Experience with Exceptional Patients,* William Morrow Paperbacks, 2011.

[9] Lacy Schley, "Marijuana: The Blunt Truth," *Discover*, July/August 2017.

[10] He and she will be used interchangeably throughout the book

[11] "Study: Placebos Make People Feel Better," Associated Press, 24 August 2005.

[12] Gary Greenberg, "What if the Placebo Effect Isn't a Trick?" *The New York Times Magazine*, 7 November 2018.

[13] "Cholesterol-lowering statin drugs help prevent heart attacks and stroke," *University of California, Berkeley Wellness Letter*, vol 33, issue 1, October 2016.

[14] "When Placebos Make You Sick," *Discover Magazine*, December 2012.

[15] Joseph Sternberg, "A Snickers a Day Keeps the Doctor Away," *The Wall Street Journal*, 29 June 2017.

[16] Maria Cheng, "Survey: Half of US doctors use placebo treatments," Associated Press, 23 October 2008.

[17] Jake Pearson, "Vanessa Trump taken to hospital after white powder scare," The Associated Press, 13 February 2018.

[18] Ajay Gupta, "Adverse events associated with unblinded, but not with blinded, statin therapy in the Anglo-Scandinavian Cardiac Outcomes Trial—Lipid-Lowering Arm (ASCOT-LLA): a randomised double-blind placebo-controlled trial and its non-randomised non-blind extension phase," *The Lancet*, Volume 389, Issue 10088, 24–30 June 2017, Pages 2473-2481.

[19] Steven Nissen, "Efficacy and Tolerability of Evolocumab vs Ezetimibe in Patients With Muscle-Related Statin Intolerance: The GAUSS-3 Randomized Clinical Trial," *JAMA*. 2016 Apr 19;315(15):1580-90.

[20] Russ Roberts, "Gary Greenberg on the Placebo Effect," EconTalk, 4 February 2019.

[21] Often attributed to Albert Einstein. But, instead, it is out of Cameron's 1963 book *Informal Sociology: A Casual Introduction to Sociological Thinking*. https://quoteinvestigator.com/2010/05/26/everything-counts-einstein/

[22] By the Numbers: Bacteria, *Science Illustrated*, September/October 2010, pg 74-75.

[23] Emily Cukier-Meisner, "Community Organizers," *BioCentury*, 9 May 2016.

[24] David Relman, Stanford University, interviewed on Future of Everything, by Russ Altman, 13 January 2018.

[25] David Relman, Stanford University, interviewed on Future of Everything, by Russ Altman, 13 January 2018.

[26] Nathan Collins, "More than 99 percent of the microbes inside us are unknown to science, *Stanford Engineering*, 25 August 2017.

[27] Aristos Georgiou, "Mysterious 'Microbial Dark Matter' Dominates Our Planet," *Newsweek*, Tech & Science, 29 September 2018.

[28] "How Fragrant Poop and Color-Changing Skin May Help Protect Our Health," *NBC News*, 25 July 2017.

[29] "Seres, MD Anderson, Parker in microbiome immunotherapy deal," *BioCentury Extra*, 14 November 2017.

[30] Ian Chant, "A New Movement," *Popular Science*, August 2013.

---

[31] Sam Scott, "Intestinal Fortitude," *Stanford Magazine*, December 2018.

[32] Mark Zipkin, "Rise of the Virome," *BioCentury Innovations*, 24 August, 2017.

[33] Karen Tkach Tuzman, "Viral Goes Diabetes," *BioCentury Innovations*, 24 August, 2017.

[34] James Bellingham, Chief Technologist, Monterey Bay Aquarium Research Institute, *Popular Mechanics*, August 2011, pg 11.

[35] Alan Stahler, "Life Just Got Older," *The Union*, 23 September 2016.

[36] Erin Biba, "From Chimp to Chip," *Popular Science*, December 2013.

[37] Lindsey Tanner, "Coffee May Spell Heart Trouble for Some," Associated Press, 7 May 2006.

[38] Here are the numbers: 34 of 57 men (60%) and 1,000 of 2,000 women (50%) are admitted into graphic arts. For watercolor arts, the numbers are 100 of 500 men (20%) and 333 of 3,333 women (10%), respectively. For mechanical engineering, the numbers are 360 of 379 men (95%) and 100 of 118 women (85%), while for biomedical engineering, the numbers are 900 of 1,500 men (60%) and 16 of 32 women (50%). The overall numbers for engineering are 1,260 men (70%) and 116 women (80%) admitted, while for art we have 134 men (30%) and 1,333 women (40%) admitted. Overall, 1,394 men (66%) and 1,449 woman (43%) are accepted at this university.

[39] Multiple linear regression models produce R-squared values to measure their explanatory value. A value of 1 means the model explains all the results while a value of 0 means the model has no explanatory value. "R-squared = Explained variation / Total variation," according to Jim Frost at the Minitab Blog on 30 May 2013. We know there's variation in the test results. How much of that variation can our model explain?

[40] Kelly Servick, "Mouse microbes may make scientific studies harder to replicate," 16 August 2016, *Science*, http://www.sciencemag.org/news/2016/08/mouse-microbes-may-make-scientific-studies-harder-replicate

Chapter 6: The Real Cost of the FDA

If you talked to ten people about the FDA and the topic of drug regulation, it's probable that all ten could give you reasons that the FDA is beneficial. Paramount among these reasons would be keeping dangerous and useless drugs off the market. The logic is straightforward: dangerous drugs can hurt people directly, and useless drugs can hurt them indirectly, by giving them false hopes, costing them money, and by passing up other, more effective treatments (the opportunity cost argument). Being populated with knowledgeable people, having clear procedures in place to increase the level of sophistication in the pharma industry, relying on solid evidence, and assuming a watchdog role, the FDA helps ensure that these dangerous and useless drugs are kept off the market. Most people can see the putative benefits of the FDA: safer drugs, a more scientific drug development process, and better information about the drugs that are marketed. At least that's the theory.

Most people are not clamoring for changes to the current system. (Most people, it should be noted, don't spend much time thinking about drug development and regulation—you and I are the exceptions.) Of the ten people that we interview, probably six would oppose changing government safety and effectiveness standards to allow for faster approvals of new prescription drugs, while four would likely say they're in favor of speedier FDA action.[1]

How many of these ten people could list any downsides to the FDA's regulation? One? Two? Zero?

Seen and Unseen Costs

Everything has costs, and the costs of the FDA are subtle. It is easy to pinpoint the FDA's budget as a cost, which it is—$6.0 billion in 2020—but there's so much more.

Before we proceed, I would like to introduce a French economist from a century and a half ago, Frederic Bastiat. In one of his famous essays, Bastiat described how good economists should uncover both the seen *and* the unseen in all situations they examine.

What is the "seen" in the FDA? The promise of fewer quack medicines and dangerous drugs like Elixir Sulfanilamide and thalidomide. What is the "unseen" in the FDA? Stumped?

As economists will tell you, the real cost of the FDA stems from the expense, delays, and hassles of getting new medicines approved. With higher costs and lower probabilities of success, fewer companies—especially small ones—will be in business; fewer drugs will be discovered, developed, and marketed for patients who need them; and, with the reduced competition, drug prices will generally be much higher. Plus, even successful drugs will be delayed by many years, precluding their use by patients during that time.

Unlike the man on the street, physicians do think about drug development and regulation. A 2007 survey of American doctors found that three fourths of the doctors who responded believe that the FDA is too slow in approving new medicines. And 73 percent said that the "time it takes for the FDA to approve new drugs and medical devices hurts patients by forcing them to go without beneficial therapies."[2]

Delayed Drug Launches

Consider a drug that has sales of $365 million each year. For this hypothetical product, getting approval and launching just one day earlier is worth $1 million to the pharma company.[3] Based on typical values, it is not unreasonable for a new product to see a value of a few million dollars for *each day* sooner that it is launched. You might not care that drug companies could make more money, but even if, to you, that is a neutral or negative factor, consider the patients that could get potential cures sooner, resulting in real reductions in morbidity and mortality. If patients and society at large are bigger beneficiaries of new drugs than are the pharmaceutical companies themselves—as is typical—then, with this example, American patients and society overall might easily lose $10 million for each day that a hypothetical new drug is delayed by the FDA. That adds up.

With a value of $10 million per day, a six-month delay would cost society approximately $1.8 billion and a 12-month delay would cost $3.6 billion. If there are 25 new drug approvals each year, and the typical drug faces a delay that costs between $1.8 billion and $3.6 billion, using the logic above, the overall cost to society is $45 billion to $90 billion per year, or about seven to fifteen times the FDA's budget.

There's currently a way that companies can pay to speed up the review of their drugs. Companies that develop a treatment for a neglected or rare pediatric disease receive a voucher for a priority review of a subsequent drug. Companies that don't have an immediate need for a priority review can sell the voucher to another company: prices have been in the $67.5 million to $350 million range, with one changing hands in 2019 for $105 million and one in 2020 for $100 million.[4] [5]

Imagine if all companies could pay $105 million and get what would effectively be a priority review for each of their new drugs. Patients, society, and the drug companies themselves would benefit. For the cost of $105 million, we would all derive billions of dollars of benefit.

Unavailable Drugs Cannot Help Patients

One of the main arguments for the FDA's powers rests on the premise that new drugs could potentially hurt patients. But harm is primarily an issue of safety, not efficacy. The harm that inefficacious drugs incur is more of an opportunity cost argument—patients waste their time on ineffective drugs and miss out on better drugs. If the FDA continued its safety gatekeeping role but let markets test for efficacy, there would be substantial benefits. Consider the following example.

There are two drugs. Drug A is efficacious in 70 percent of patients and Drug B is efficacious in 20 percent. The FDA, which bases its decisions on both safety and efficacy, approves Drug A due to its robust benefit, but rejects Drug B due to its paltry benefit. Given this scenario, assume that 100 patients a year try Drug A, and 70 see their condition improve while 30 see no improvement. No patients try Drug B because it isn't on the market due to the lack of FDA approval.

Now, instead, consider what would happen if the FDA approved drugs based purely on safety considerations. In this case, the FDA approves both A and B. As before, 100 patients a year try drug A, and 70 see their condition improve while 30 don't. In addition, another 100 patients a year try drug B, and 20 see their condition improve while 80 don't. One significant but somewhat hidden benefit of this scenario is that both drugs will be available approximately a decade sooner due to the reduced regulatory burden of not needing to prove efficacy.

In the first case, which we'll call the "prove, then market" case, the FDA approves drug A at year ten; from year 11 through year 20, 1,000 patients (100 per year) will try drug A, and a total of 700 will see a benefit while 300 won't. Drug B is not approved, so no patients can even try it.

In the second case, which we'll call the "market and prove" case, the FDA approves Drug A at year one; from year one through year 20, 2,000 patients (100 per year) will try Drug A, and a total of 1,400 will see a benefit while 600 won't. During this same period, 2,000 patients will try Drug B, and a total of 400 will benefit while 1,600 won't.

- Prove, then market: the FDA requires drugs to have evidence of safety and efficacy proven before the drug can be marketed
- Market and prove: the FDA reverts to its pre-1962 rules and only requires proof of safety before marketing; proof of efficacy is not required

The tables below compare the results of the two cases.

Table 1: Prove, Then Market

Number of Patients	Drug A Benefit	Drug A No Benefit	Drug B Benefit	Drug B No Benefit
Years 1-10	0	1,000	0	1,000
Years 11-20	700	300	0	1,000
TOTAL Years 1-20	700	1,300	0	2,000

Number of Patients with "Prove, Then Market" Case

Table 2: Market and Prove

Number of Patients	Drug A Benefit	Drug A No Benefit	Drug B Benefit	Drug B No Benefit
Years 1-10	700	300	200	800
Years 11-20	700	300	200	800
TOTAL Years 1-20	1,400	600	400	1,600

Number of Patients with "Market and Prove" Case

Table 3: Difference

Number of Patients	Drug A Benefit	Drug A No Benefit	Drug B Benefit	Drug B No Benefit
Difference	+700	-700	+400	-400

Difference Equals "Market and Prove" Minus "Prove, Then Market"

Notice that with both drugs, A and B, more people benefit in the "market and prove" scenario. The patients who don't benefit from the drugs are not hurt, per se, except for the time and money they spent trying new drugs that didn't work for them, along with any false hopes they may have held. But they made that choice having some idea of the costs and probabilities; they were never offered any guarantees. They thought they were picking their best choice.

Because, as we've discussed, patients need to personally test every drug prescribed by their physician to ensure that it is safe and effective *for them*, FDA approval for efficacy ("prove, then market") is essentially duplicative and incurs a delay of approximately ten years for each new drug. In this example, when the FDA approves new drugs based on safety alone ("market and prove"), an *additional* 700 patients derive a benefit from drug A, and an *additional* 400 derive a benefit from drug B.

Economic Benefit

Is there an economic benefit from the "market and prove" case? Let's apply some dollars to this example.

Assume that patients who don't benefit from Drug A or Drug B are not physically harmed because both drugs have been certified as safe. Further, assume that the benefit from both drugs, when they work, is $1,000 and that the price of Drug A is $200 and the price of Drug B is $50. Why would they be priced this way? If customers didn't know, a priori, who will benefit, their expectations must be such that they anticipate benefiting economically from each therapy. The expected benefits of the drugs are:

- Drug A: $700 (70 percent times $1,000 value)
- Drug B: $200 (20 percent times $1,000 value)

Given the prices for the drugs, the expected net benefits are:

- Drug A: $500 ($700 expected benefit minus $200 price, or 2.5 times the price)
- Drug B: $150 ($200 expected benefit minus $50 price, or 3 times the price)

Now that we have assumed prices and expected net benefits for individual patients, let's look across all patients.

Table 4: Prove, Then Market

Metric	Drug A	Drug B
People Who Buy	1,000	0
Price per Patient	$200	$50
Total Cost	$200,000	$0
People Who Benefit	700	0
Benefit per Patient	$1,000	$1,000
Total Benefit	$700,000	$0
Net Benefit	$500,000	$0

Financial Results with "Prove, Then Market" Case

Table 5: Market and Prove

Metric	Drug A	Drug B
People Who Buy	2,000	2,000
Price per Patient	$200	$50
Total Cost	$400,000	$100,000
People Who Benefit	1,400	400
Benefit per Patient	$1,000	$1,000
Total Benefit	$1,400,000	$400,000
Net Benefit	$1,000,000	$300,000

Financial Results with "Market and Prove" Case

Table 6: Difference

Net Benefit	Drug A	Drug B
Difference	+$500,000	+$300,000

Difference Equals "Market and Prove" Minus "Prove, Then Market"

The net economic benefit—ignoring any profits accruing to the drug companies involved—of the "market and prove" case is a full $800,000 higher ($1,300,00 versus $500,000). When the FDA considers safety only ("market and prove"), no patients are physically harmed; patients have the opportunity to personally test drugs to see if they work; and the sum of the net economic benefit almost triples. Remember that the FDA wants to ensure that all medications on the market are efficacious to avoid the opportunity cost problem of ineffective drugs: wasted purchase costs, wasted time, and false hopes. By running through this example, however, we highlight an enormous cost of the "prove, then market" case, which is the forgone benefit of the new drugs that are delayed or never approved by the FDA. You might object that this example is merely hypothetical, but the assumptions used might actually be *too conservative*. Harvard economist David Cutler and his colleagues have found that the benefits of new health care technology, such as new medicines, generally outweigh their costs by five to one.[6] Get more medicines on the market and patients benefit.

While we haven't addressed the issues of wasted time and false hopes, based on this analysis the costs of removing the FDA's efficacy requirements—which, as mentioned, were implemented in 1962 based on a non sequitur—are insignificant compared to the overwhelming benefits. The "market and prove" case appears to be clearly better. Based on this, the FDA should be rolled back to its pre-1962 version and should evaluate new drugs for safety only. If this book does nothing else, if it inspires actions to remove or relax the FDA's unnecessary efficacy requirements, it will have served an extremely useful purpose.

Promotion of Unapproved Uses is Illegal

Doctors can use drugs for off-label uses and drug companies can supply them with product. But heaven forbid that companies encourage, support, or promote off-label prescribing.

The FDA doesn't even try to prevent off-label *sales*. How would a government agency prevent sales for off-label uses when sales aren't typically linked with the condition being treated? The FDA wisely looks elsewhere and prohibits drug companies from *promoting* off-label use.

This prohibition may be one of the greatest costs of the FDA's "prove, then market" approach.

Consider this hypothetical conversation:

> Drug company sales rep: Doctor, have you tried Drug X for any of your melanoma patients?

Doctor: Yes. I'm very happy with the results I've seen. What I really need, however, is a drug for my ovarian cancer patients. Do you know of anything that would help those patients?

Drug company sales rep: As a matter of fact, an as-yet unpublished study out of MD Anderson Cancer Center suggests that Drug X benefits patients with ovarian cancer. The results are similar to the results seen in melanoma.

That's the "wrong" answer and this sales representative just exposed his company to potentially billions of dollars of fines from the FDA. The "correct" answer is:

> Drug company sales rep: I'm sorry that your ovarian cancer patients have such a bad prognosis. Unfortunately, the FDA has approved Drug X only for treating melanoma patients.

When we think of governments withholding important information from citizens, we typically think of highly authoritarian governments. For instance, the Soviet government hushed the Chernobyl disaster. More recently, the Chinese government muzzled Li Wenliang, the ophthalmologist who first alerted the world to COVID-19. How many people have died in China and throughout the world as a result of that repression? The FDA is in a similar position in this country. How many patients die or otherwise suffer every day in this country because doctors can't get important information from the company making the drug about to be injected into a patient's arm, or don't even know that a drug is available that should be injected into that patient's arm?

Are there examples of how this prohibition on promotion has hurt actual people? Yes.

In the early 1980s, scientists discovered that the B vitamin, folic acid, taken early in pregnancy, could prevent birth defects.[7] Vitamin manufacturers wanted to share this important news with their customers. However, the FDA directly prohibited them from doing so. To state such a health benefit for folic acid, these companies would have needed to run the gamut of tests required to get their vitamins approved as "drugs." That's one of the outcomes of the 1962 rules: a company can't say that its vitamin, supplement, or drug causes some beneficial result unless it passes all the expensive FDA tests and the data prove that benefit. As a result, the vitamin companies were effectively under a gag order.

Unlike in some other countries, where the word got out and birth defects declined dramatically, researchers estimate that about 25,000 American babies were aborted or unnecessarily born with horrible deformities.[8] In total, this tragedy was worse than the thalidomide tragedy, it was entire avoidable, and it was caused by the very government agency supposedly protecting our health—the FDA.

While this was not technically a case of the companies being prevented from promoting an off-label use, it was a case of companies being prevented from promoting unapproved uses. Warning pregnant mothers of the dangers of folic acid deficiency was a transgression the FDA was not willing to tolerate.

COVID-19 Vaccines

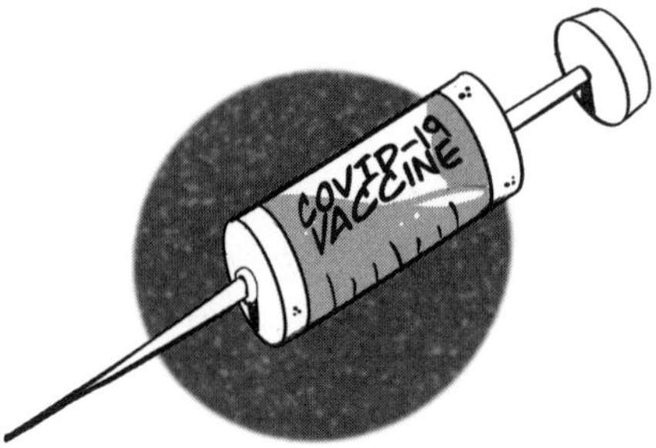

In late 2020, when this was written, hope was delivered to Americans in the form of two vaccines to hasten the resolution of the deadly COVID-19 pandemic. On December 18, the FDA gave emergency authorization to Moderna for the mRNA-1273 vaccine, one week after the FDA had given approval for the similar Pfizer/BioNTech vaccine.

Understandably, and with some justification, the FDA crowed about its role in this achievement. "The FDA's authorization for emergency use of the first COVID-19 vaccine is a significant milestone in battling this devastating pandemic that has affected so many families in the United States and around the world," said FDA Commissioner Stephen Hahn, M.D. Rarely had the FDA acted so quickly. A normal review of a drug application takes six to twelve months. And yet, in this case, the FDA's review took a mere three weeks to review hundreds of thousands of pages of documents. Either the FDA took a crash course in speed-reading or it engaged in some shortcuts given the severity of the pandemic.

One of Pfizer's top scientists commented on how enjoyable it was to work with the FDA when it had a sense of urgency.

> *This was never thought about or possible before in vaccines, where we had real-time feedback from the FDA; not just putting big reports back and saying 'hey, you'll hear from us in a month'; this turned months to weeks, and weeks to days, days to hours.*
>
> *They [the FDA] were willing to take phone calls from us; it sounds strange, but normally it was just letters sent weeks later. Not*

> *everything in R&D can be in this warp speed setting, but this shows we can come together and mount battles against some of the most threatening medical conditions.*[9]
> **Mikael Dolsten**, Chief Science Officer, Pfizer

In what many see as a crowning achievement for the FDA, some see the unnecessary deaths of hundreds of thousands of Americans. Even when the FDA acts incredibly fast, its umbrella of drug regulation dramatically slows access to life saving technologies.

FDA Versus Free Market

Let's compare the case of the Moderna vaccine with the FDA's current rules to a hypothetical case of the Moderna vaccine in a free market.[10] In a free market, any willing seller can sell to any willing buyer. Yes, this can be scary. For instance, Merck began selling morphine commercially in 1827, and any buyer could have acquired morphine from any willing pharmacist. Before you recoil at the concept, remember that opioid abuse didn't become a significant problem until 2010, almost two centuries after Merck started selling morphine and decades after the federal government clamped down on the sale of all so-called scheduled drugs such as morphine.

You may be surprised to learn how quickly and early the Moderna vaccine was developed. On Saturday, January 11, 2020, China's Yong-Zhen Zhang distributed the genetic code of the virus that has since been named SARS-CoV-2. The Moderna lab in Massachusetts took all of *one weekend* to formulate the vaccine, which was ready on Monday. David Wallace-Wells of *New York* magazine writes, "It was completed before China had even acknowledged that the disease could be transmitted from human to human, more than a week before the first confirmed coronavirus case in the United States."[11]

<u>Here's the timeline:</u>

- January 11, genetic code distributed
- January 13, the mRNA-1273 vaccine is formulated
- February 7, the first clinical batch is produced
- February 24, Moderna ships the first batch to the NIH for a Phase 1 clinical trial
- March 4, the FDA gives permission to conduct a Phase 1 clinical trial (safety only)
- March 16, the first human subject is given a dose
- March 23, Moderna begins scaling up for commercial production
- March 27, another Phase 1 clinical trial begins
- April 27, Moderna asks the FDA for permission to run a Phase 2 clinical trial (safety and efficacy in a limited number of test subjects)
- May 1, Moderna and Lonza announce a plan to manufacture a billion doses a year
- May 12, the FDA gives Moderna Fast Track designation for mRNA-1273
- May 18, Moderna announces positive Phase 1 clinical results
- May 29, the first test subjects are dosed in a Phase 2 clinical trial
- July 14, Phase 1 results are published
- July 27, a Phase 3 clinical trial begins (safety and efficacy in a large number of test subjects)
- July 28, non-human primate study results are published
- November 16, Phase 3 results show the vaccine is 94.5 percent effective at preventing infections
- November 30, the FDA announces that it will convene an advisory committee meeting on December 17
- December 2, the U.K. approves a similar vaccine from Pfizer and BioNTech
- December 11, the FDA gives the Pfizer/BioNTech vaccine an emergency use authorization (EUA)
- December 18, the FDA gives an EUA to the Moderna vaccine

When this was written, 537,000 Americans had died and hundreds more were joining them every day. The pandemic had been raging for nearly a year, which means that about 1,500 had died each day. For every day earlier that the pandemic ended, approximately 1,500 Americans wouldn't have unnecessarily died.

While counterfactual timelines are hypothetical, and we don't know the thinking of the Moderna team, we can consider what might have happened with a free market for drugs and vaccines.[12]

The Phase 3 clinical trial for the Moderna vaccine began on July 27 and the results were analyzed and presented on November 16. It took the FDA just a month for emergency approval. While this was fast by traditional standards, it could have been much faster by using a technique called challenge trials. Before explaining challenge trials, we should be clear on how normal Phase 3 clinical trials for vaccines work.

In normal trials, a large number of test subjects are given the experimental vaccine and an equal number are given a placebo. The test subjects then live their normal lives until they become sick or infected through regular day-to-day activities. This can take a long time because, even during a pandemic, only a small percentage of the population becomes infected on any given day.

In the Moderna Phase 3 trial, it took 30,420 adult volunteers, half of whom received the experimental vaccine and half of whom received the placebo, about three months to log 196 cases of symptomatic COVID-19. Then it was a simple matter of seeing what percentage of the 196 had received the vaccine. Eleven had gotten the vaccine while 185 hadn't. Therefore, the vaccine prevented 174 of the 185 infections that the vaccinated group *should have* experienced, hence the efficacy rate was 94.1 percent (174 divided by 185).

In a human challenge trial, we would need only about 400 volunteers. Half of this group would be given the experimental vaccine and half would be given a placebo. All 400 would then be exposed to the SARS-CoV-2 virus. Who would agree to be purposely exposed to a potentially deadly virus? We don't need to speculate. Over 38,000 individuals from around the world signed up through the 1Day Sooner organization. While not all of them would have followed through, many of them would have. This trial would have required only one percent of them to roll up their sleeves.

A challenge trial would have reached the same approximately 95 percent efficacy conclusion and would have had numerous benefits. First, instead of 30,420 volunteers, we would have needed only 400. Second, we would have seen efficacy results at least two months earlier. Third, we would have generated invaluable data on the lifecycle and treatment of COVID-19 from the 200 or so volunteers who would have been "successfully" infected in a controlled medical environment.[13]

Note: In February 2021, the first COVID-19 challenge trial was green lighted in the U.K.[14]

Earlier Sales Save Lives

Even with a free market, sales of Moderna's mRNA-1273 vaccine likely wouldn't have started until after the company began scaling up manufacturing. A company doesn't begin manufacturing until it believes in a product. In the timeline above, that's March 23. But manufacturing takes some time to get going. Let's assume that by April 1, five weeks from the date the first batch was shipped, Moderna begins offering mRNA-1273 for sale.

Sales start slowly. Supplies are limited. Only the bold and brave get inoculated. The rest of us, and Moderna, get some early, albeit messy, safety and efficacy data. These data help Moderna improve the vaccine, dose, and dosing schedule. Having a ready market and a steady source of revenue, Moderna scales up production faster than in the timeline above.

In this scenario, inoculations could have begun at least 8.5 months earlier and, perhaps, the pandemic would have ended 255 days and 375,000 lives earlier. There's little talk of lockdowns and the economy remains resilient.

Perhaps Moderna wouldn't have been comfortable selling a vaccine that hadn't been tested for efficacy. In that case, sales could have begun approximately four months earlier: one month saved from FDA review, two months saved by the human challenge trial, and one month saved from eliminating the necessity of securing FDA permission at various stages of development. In this scenario, the pandemic may have ended 120 days and 175,000 lives earlier.

Moderna certainly would have been willing to sell its vaccine on November 16, when the glowing Phase 3 results were made public. In this scenario, inoculations could begin at least a full month earlier than the FDA would have allowed. In this scenario, the pandemic may have ended 30 days and 44,000 lives earlier.

The range of the results shows that the FDA's processes and actions—even though the FDA had acted incredibly fast in this situation—have killed between 44,000 and 375,000 Americans.[15]

The above counterfactual case is hypothetical. Are there any real examples we can study? Yes.

The influenza pandemic of 1957 (the "Asian flu") was the worst since the Spanish flu of 1918, causing more than 1 million deaths worldwide and 70,000 to 116,000 in the U.S. Maurice Hilleman, discussed in the Introduction, was then chief of the Department of Respiratory Diseases at the Army Medical Center (now the Walter Reed Army Institute of Research). He developed a vaccine for the Asian flu in record time. How did he do it? He was able to work directly with six vaccine manufacturers, bypassing the bureaucratic red tape, as he put it, to begin vaccinating Army recruits in a little over three months after the first *New York Times* report of the outbreak in Hong Kong. In the ensuing three months, millions of doses were administered to Americans and Hilleman was credited with greatly reducing excess mortality in the U.S.[16]

How did Hilleman work so quickly? Simple: he ignored federal drug regulators. "I knew how the system worked," Hilleman said. "So I bypassed the Division of Biologics Standards, called the manufacturers myself, and moved the process quickly."[17] As we can see, the FDA played no part in Hilleman's Asian flu vaccine. This was perhaps as close to the "free market" approach as we may ever see and the result was an unqualified success.

Any discussion of the lives saved by the FDA must include estimates of the lives lost due to that very same agency. The example of the delayed COVID-19 vaccine launch resulted in 400 to 3,500 times as many lives lost as did the Elixir Sulfanilamide disaster that gave the FDA many of its powers. Early in 2021, three thousand Americans were dying each and every day while there was a savior in a syringe sitting in a warehouse, ready to protect us.

Drugs that Never Were

Another cost of the FDA is drugs that we won't have access to.

This is another way in which the FDA really hurts us: the more stringent the FDA's requirements, the more drug development costs increase and probabilities of approval decline. The result? More new drugs end up on the cutting room floor. And yet this is a highly abstract and intellectual argument. It's hard to visualize the drugs that ended up on the cutting room floor and the patients who unnecessarily got sick or died. It's not as if we had the chance to become accustomed to these "could have been" drugs, only to have them taken away; we never got a chance to learn about them, use them, and possibly depend on them in the first place.

Though hard to visualize, it's not impossible because we have one good example to consider here. What follows is one concrete example of a "could have been" drug that will help us put a face, so to speak, on the drugs that have been lost due to the FDA's actions.

The Drug That Never Was

An amazing drug is missing from our medicine cabinets, but it's one that virtually all Americans *should* have access to. Why don't you have it? Because of the FDA, pure and simple. Allow me to explain.

Some years ago, I hit a patch of gravel on a twisty mountain road and my bicycle wheels slipped out from underneath me, resulting in a tumble to the asphalt. I was beaten up, but, luckily, no bones were broken. The doctor at the urgent care facility, after cleaning the gravel from my wounds, wanted to prescribe an analgesic for my acute pain. I told her I disliked Vicodin, and I mentioned Sprix (intranasal ketorolac), which I had helped a client develop over the previous decade. She hadn't heard of Sprix, but she loved ketorolac injections—the IV/IM formulation of the drug ketorolac—and agreed to write me a prescription for Sprix.

The prescription she handed me for Sprix made me consider the sad, stunted success of ketorolac and the absence of a good oral, tablet version of the drug—the formulation I really wanted. The intranasal formulation was fine, but I would have been thrilled with a bottle of oral tablets. Why couldn't I get the prescription I wanted? The answer requires a little history.

Syntex Labs discovered and developed injectable ketorolac, which the FDA approved in 1989, and it was launched under the brand name Toradol IV/IM. Ketorolac is in the NSAID family that includes such popular drugs as Aleve (naproxen), Motrin and Advil (ibuprofen), Celebrex (celecoxib), and aspirin. Ketorolac is an unusual NSAID in that it is far more potent that its cousins. This characteristic allows it to provide opioid—think morphine—levels of pain relief without any of the usual opioid problems, such as addiction, abuse, respiratory depression, nausea, constipation, drowsiness, itching, erectile dysfunction, confusion, and disorientation. Sounds pretty good, right?

> Ketorolac has similar efficacy to morphine and meperidine. A 30-mg dose of ketorolac IM delivers pain relief equivalent to that of morphine 6 mg to 12 mg.
>
> Clinical studies have also demonstrated that combining ketorolac and opioids significantly reduces the need for morphine.[18]

Ketorolac is a great drug, and many doctors, primarily in emergency room settings, swear by it and use it daily. It provides wonderful levels of pain relief without the abuse and addiction aspects of opioids that drive the medical and law enforcement professions crazy.

Ketorolac is not without controversy. Before approval, an FDA employee had an idea based on some mathematical models that Toradol IV/IM should be given with a loading dose—that is, doubling the first dose. Syntex employees didn't think this was a good idea, as the loading dose was completely theoretical, not based on any empirical evidence. But when a government agency that has supreme power over you suggests something, it's often more prudent to comply than to complain.

The loading dose turned out to be an unmitigated disaster: gastrointestinal problems from the loading dose killed 97 patients worldwide.[19] The label for Toradol IV/IM was subsequently changed to eliminate the loading dose, but reputations are hard to dislodge, especially when only a limited number of Syntex and FDA employees knew the real story behind the deaths, and the FDA certainly didn't want that story widely reported. The Syntex employees couldn't make noise about this calamity without potentially transgressing the FDA's rules, goodwill, or both. Sadly, ketorolac's bad reputation persisted for decades, even though the problems with the loading dose were ancient history. For example, this is from Cate Sibley, Pharm.D.:

> The restriction of keeping the max duration of treament [sic] with ketorolac at 5 days does pretty much boil down to the serious GI adverse effects associated with the medication. When I say serious GI adverse effects, I mean GI issues that have resulted in death![20]

All pain relievers, whether OTC or prescription, have known risks. But even today, without any loading dose, ketorolac has a reputation for being more dangerous than other NSAID's. This disparagement simply isn't true. In fact, one long-term, open-label study in Europe showed that ketorolac was *safer* than other NSAID's.

These data weren't available when the FDA approved the tablet formulation of Toradol, called Toradol Oral, in 1991. Worse, the FDA assigned a reviewer who had previously been *fired by the company*. The original FDA reviewer of Toradol Oral—John Harder, who happened to have been one of the few people fired by Syntex during that era—took ketorolac's dangerous history seriously and limited the dose of Toradol Oral to 10 milligrams per day, imposed a strict limit of five days of therapy, and mandated that the oral tablets follow therapy with an injection or intravenous dose of Toradol IV/IM.

The bottom line? You couldn't simply get a bottle of Toradol Oral from your doctor; you had to start with an injection and then transition to the oral. How many people start their pain therapy with an injection? Not many. The requirement to do so effectively destroyed any at-home usage of Toradol Oral. That restriction, along with the super low dose for a limited duration was a recipe for failure. Three strikes, you're out, Toradol Oral.

Crippled Ketorolac

To put this into perspective, the usual dose for the IV/IM is 30-60 mg, and any other delivery system will necessarily require a dose that is as high as, if not higher than, the injected dose. The FDA acknowledged that the proper dose for ketorolac IV/IM was 30-60 mg. Why in the world would the agency think that 10 mg was a good dose for the oral formulation? It's as if John Harder and the FDA *wanted* ketorolac oral to fail; the failure was either conscious and intended or based on gross incompetence. Neither explanation is flattering. With the label restriction of five days, no pharmacy could give a patient more than five tablets at one time, and no insurance company or third-party payer would pay for more than five. Further, any physician who tried to get around this five-day limitation would set herself up for legal liability. And since patients had to start their therapy with a shot, primary care physicians were precluded from writing a prescription for Toradol Oral and sending the patient home via a stop at the pharmacy. Is it any wonder that Toradol Oral was a flop?

With Toradol IV/IM getting a fair bit of usage, but with a reputation for hazard, and the oral formulation effectively crippled, ketorolac, the amazing wonder drug, was effectively neutralized and taken away from us Americans.

Thirty milligram ketorolac oral tablets are the drug that never was. And even if we don't know it, we miss it.

Analgesics are a big problem. On the one hand, they don't provide adequate pain relief to millions of patients. On the other hand, addicted patients sometimes abuse them. A study by the Centers for Disease Control and Prevention reports that prescription opioid-related dependence and abuse cost people in this country $78.5 billion per year.[21] This issue has not escaped the attention of the FDA, which reports: "The FDA is deeply concerned about the growing epidemic of opioid abuse, dependence and overdose in the United States." Scott Gottlieb, appointed head of the FDA in 2017, called opioid abuse "a public emergency on the order of Ebola and Zika."[22] The FDA failed to mention that it's partially responsible for that epidemic.

Ketorolac is relatively safe, works roughly as well as morphine to reduce pain, and is non-addictive and abuse-proof because it doesn't provide an opioid "high." What we really need is an oral formulation that people can use at home, at work, and while traveling. How many problems would 30 mg ketorolac oral tablets solve? Almost all of them.

FDA No Man's Land

A bottle of 30 mg ketorolac oral tablets should be in every American's medicine cabinet. But it isn't and probably never will be. Why? Now that ketorolac is generic, the only way a 30-mg tablet will ever be approved by the FDA is if some drug company invests the time and money to develop it with the full safety and efficacy trials needed to satisfy the FDA—remember, the FDA has never accepted the long-term safety data from Europe, and the approved dose is still 10 mg per day. Then, if and when it garners FDA approval, it would, within a handful of years, face generic competition that would dramatically undercut its price. And, worse, this plan would work only *if* the FDA admitted that ketorolac was safer than it has been saying for the last 30 years, and such an admission would be bad optics for a government agency. Try convincing investors to give you money for that venture!

I did help Roxro Pharma develop a 31.5-mg intranasal formulation of ketorolac— Sprix—which the FDA approved in 2010. But because of serious difficulties working with a revolving carousel of FDA employees, Roxro ran out of money and was sold during the financial crisis to Luitpold, a company that demonstrated an amazing ineptitude for marketing. Sprix was later sold to another company and the price was inflated from $150 to over $1,000 per prescription—yes, $1,000—effectively crippling yet another version of ketorolac.

But the oral tablets, not the intranasal spray, are the prize. Unfortunately, we can't get it, and for that, we can thank the FDA.

Years after ketorolac established itself as an analgesic, clinical trials demonstrated that it had some interesting anti-cancer activity in women who suffered from breast or ovarian cancer. Unfortunately, scientists doing research in this area ran up against the FDA's limit of five days of therapy. "Use is restricted to a 5-day treatment course that could limit application for extended post-operative care in cancer patients."[23] The FDA's limitation on ketorolac as an analgesic now limit its use as a cancer therapy.

As an aside, this would be a good drug for some government agency or non-profit organization to develop because the public health benefit would be far greater than the expected cost of development. But there's little point in an enterprising pharmaceutical company ever trying because, as far as I can tell, the potential profits would be limited.

Drug Shortages

Some drugs have been in short supply. In 2011, President Obama issued an executive order directing the FDA to resolve and prevent critical shortages of vital medicines. "The president's action is a recognition of the fact that this is a serious problem, and we can and should do more to help solve it," said an administration official who asked to remain anonymous. "We can't wait anymore." Unfortunately, yes we can. We're still waiting. Drug shortages are still a problem in 2019. As this was written, 114 to 260 drugs are unavailable or in short supply. Which number is correct depends on how they are counted. [24] [25]

Patients are dying. A 2011 shortage of norepinephrine hampered hospitals' ability to treat septic shock, and a study published in the *Journal of the American Medical Association* concluded: "Patients admitted to these hospitals during times of shortage had higher in-hospital mortality."[26]

Morphine was developed between 1805 and 1816 and became popular after the hypodermic needle was perfected in 1853. Morphine is still, today, the standard analgesic for use in hospitals. Who would imagine that, two hundred years later, we'd have trouble manufacturing enough morphine? But we do. Right now (2019), hospitals and ambulatory surgery centers are grappling with a shortage.

Citing shortages such as these, the Federal Aviation Administration has exempted airlines from requirements that their airplanes stock five key drugs.[27] Those drugs form the core of an emergency medical kit for use during flights. Their absence on airplanes has made air travel more dangerous. Dr. Sherif Badawy, who has published several studies of in-flight medical emergencies, said, "To think you could fly without epinephrine is crazy."

Remember the lesson of French economist Frederic Bastiat: study what is seen and what is unseen. There are the things we see and the things that are hidden from our view, which might be even more important.

The "seen" in this example is the shortage of existing, vital medicines. Can you see what is unseen? What is unseen is the shortage of vital medicines that never were.

> If you'd never been born, well then what would you do?
> If you'd never been born, well then what would you be?
> Why, you might be a WASN'T!
> A Wasn't has no fun at all. No, he doesn't.
> A Wasn't just isn't. He just isn't present.
> But you...You ARE YOU! And, now isn't that pleasant.
> **Dr. Seuss**

"Wasn't drugs" are drugs that failed in clinical trials, that flunked the FDA's tests, or that were never even explored because patents were too short, patients were too few, risks were too high, costs were too prohibitive, marketing was too difficult, third-party payers were too tough, government rebates were too high, lawsuits were too expensive, and investors were just plain worried or had better prospects elsewhere.

These drugs and their victims, due to their "shortage" (their supply is exactly zero—they don't exist), are hard to visualize, and no one is running to Congress or the president to complain that their new miracle drug doesn't exist. Why? It is hard for a particular patient to follow the news in the pharmaceutical industry and then connect the dots to see how a new drug that would have treated her condition—say, Alzheimer's disease or breast cancer—was never developed and approved. This becomes even more difficult for a drug that *prevents* conditions, such as strokes or heart attacks. How would that complaint go? "That drug the

FDA rejected in 2019, or was abandoned by Company ABC in 2016 due to economics, would have prevented my father's heart attack in 2023."

The critical shortages of vital medicines are a far bigger problem than President Obama comprehended because he saw only the existing drugs that were in short supply. The shortages of "could have been" drugs are far worse.

Drug Development Background

To appreciate the interplay of the pharmaceutical industry and the FDA, we must understand a little about how new drugs are developed.

New drugs are discovered in a multitude of places: university labs, government labs, private foundations, hospitals, and the benches at large and small pharmaceutical and biotechnology companies throughout the world. Once they are discovered, the really expensive work begins, and drug companies orchestrate and pay for virtually all new drug development. Some misunderstand the FDA's role: the FDA does not conduct or pay for any drug development or clinical trials; the FDA reviews and assesses results provided by drug companies and either approves or rejects drugs on a case-by-case basis. You can think of biopharma companies as the chefs, while the FDA plays the role of the food critic.

Drug development is a complex and expensive business. And it's getting more so.

Eroom's Law of Drug Development[28]

We've come to expect technology to improve each year. Moore's Law is justifiably famous, with its remarkable ability to explain the past and predict the future. It states that the number of transistors squeezed onto integrated circuits doubles every two years; this pattern has held true for half a century. More transistors on chips allow computers to perform faster mathematical calculations.

Moore's Law is optimistic and reflects the ability of humans to "chip" away at a problem, making sequential, cumulative advances. Much of technology fits this pattern. One glaring exception, tragically, is the drug development conducted by pharmaceutical companies. It is hugely expensive and has gotten more so each year. If costs continue to grow at 7.5 percent per year, real costs will more than double every ten years. The pharmaceutical industry seems to be operating under a reverse-Moore's Law. People call it Eroom's Law. Here's the short version: Drug development costs double every decade. Why? Simple: the FDA is steadily increasing the cost per clinical trial participant and the number of required participants per clinical trial.

Technology and Moore's Law

The Cray 1 supercomputer that I used at NASA in the early 1980s cost an inflation-adjusted $30 million. The iPhone Xs, at a cost of $500, is equal to the computational power of 30,000 Cray 1 supercomputers. Per dollar, the iPhone Xs performs 1.9 billion times as many calculations as the Cray 1. And for that price, you get a phone too.

Why shouldn't drug research and development costs *fall* over time? Every year, scientists learn more about biology, physiology, pharmacology, genetics, and the natural history of diseases. They study what has worked and what hasn't. Their tools become more precise and more powerful. And yet the field of drug research and development seems immune to the powers that drive down the costs for electronic technology.

Drug Development is Expensive

Each year, to launch a certain number of new medicines, companies plow more and more money into research and development. Joseph DiMasi, Henry Grabowski, and Ronald Hansen, in a study performed for the Tufts

Center for the Study of Drug Development, estimated that the cost of bringing a new drug to market, in 2013 dollars, is $2.558 billion ($2.84 billion in 2020 dollars).[29] [30] Further, as a condition for approval, the FDA often requires drug companies to conduct post-marketing clinical trials to answer some remaining questions. Those post-marketing studies add $312 million, on average, to a drug's cost, raising the overall price tag to $2.87 billion in 2013 dollars ($3.19 billion in 2020 dollars).

Why is this number so large? One reason is that much of R&D is spent on the roughly 95 percent of drugs that fail along the way. The 95-percent failure rate is an average; some drugs have a 50 percent chance of success, and others have a 1 percent chance. It depends on the drug, the therapeutic area, and the stage of the drug's development. A 2014 study by researchers at Cleveland Clinic found that 99.6 percent of more than 400 Alzheimer's clinical trials had failed.[31] This high failure rate caused Pfizer, in 2017, to completely abandon its costly and seemingly futile efforts to find treatments for Alzheimer's.[32] The $2.558 billion tab accounts for those "dry holes."

Is this estimate realistic? DiMasi, Grabowski, and Hansen have, over the years, refreshed their analysis regularly. Back in 2003, their figure was $802 million. Shortly thereafter, in 2006, economist Christopher P. Adams and research analyst Van V. Brantner of the U.S. government's Federal Trade Commission tried, using different data, to replicate DiMasi et al.'s 2003 estimate. They found the cost to be slightly higher—$868 million versus $802 million.[33] And they had no dog in the hunt—no reason to overestimate. For that reason, therefore, DiMasi et al.'s methodology for reaching the latest estimate of $2.558 billion appears reasonable.

Drug companies must believe, ahead of time, that they will recoup the money they invest to the extent that it covers the risk of the investment and the return that they could have enjoyed with safer, more conservative investments. A simple example can help. Imagine that a company could invest $100 in a bond and safely earn a six-percent annual return. Alternatively, that company could invest its money in a drug that has a

Figure 1: R&D Costs

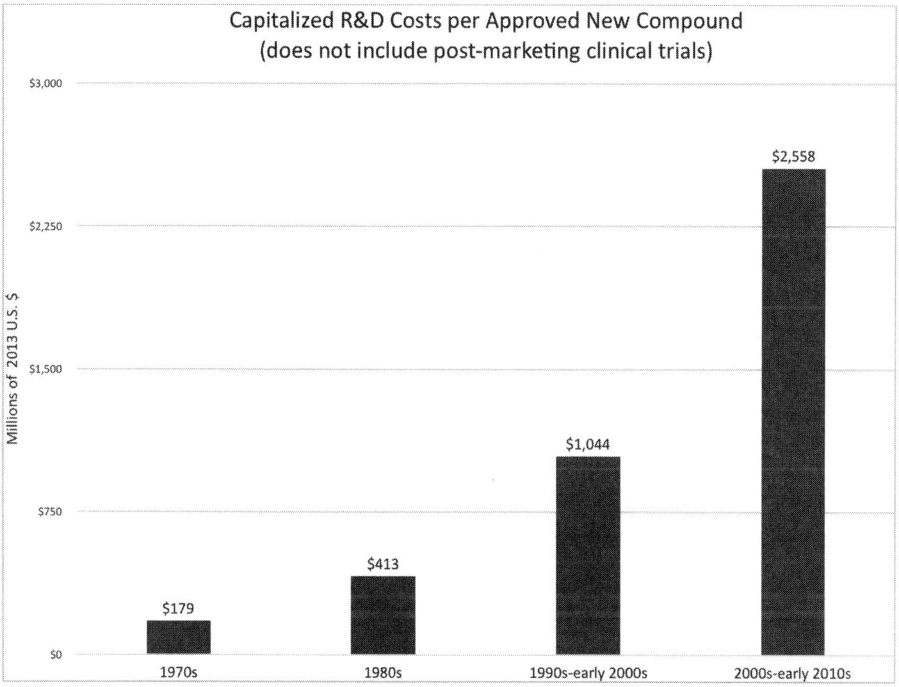

R&D Costs Have Grown Over Time

five-percent chance of successfully reaching the market ten years hence. With the safe investment, the company would have $179 at the end of ten years, for a $79 "profit." This new drug would need to have a profit potential of $1,580 to merely break even ($1,580 times five percent plus $0 times 95 percent equals $79 times 100 percent). And, if this company is risk-averse, as most are, that figure will need to be greater than $1,580.

Drug Development is Getting More Expensive

Capitalized drug development and approval costs have increased at 7.5 percent per year in real terms: $179 million in the 1970s, $413 million in the 1980s, $1,044 million in the 1990s through early 2000s, and $2,558 million in the 2000s through early 2010s (2013 dollars). [34]

If this 7.5 percent annual growth rate persists, costs will more than double every ten years. The annual growth rate over the last decade has been 8.5 percent.[35]

If you want a new drug, pony up $3.2 billion now. In ten years, it will likely cost you $6.4 billion.

Reasons for Expensive Clinical Trials

Why have drugs become more expensive to develop? Some examples help illustrate why.

When I worked at Merck in the early 1990s, Vasotec (enalapril) was one of the company's biggest drugs. It was tested in 2,987 patients before FDA approval. Mevacor (lovastatin), another of Merck's big drugs at the time, was tested in 6,582 patients in the EXCEL Study. At the time, that was thought to be a massive trial.

Now the situation is different.

Orexigen Therapeutics was conducting clinical trials on the obesity compound Contrave (naltrexone/bupropion). In 2011, the FDA asked the company to conduct a trial on between 60,000 and 100,000 patients. This clinical trial would have been enormously expensive, especially considering the resources available for a small company like Orexigen. In response to this request, Orexigen discontinued the development of Contrave and all of its other obesity drugs.[36] During this period, the firm's stock price dropped 70 percent, and Orexigen laid off 40 percent of its staff.

Later, after negotiations with the FDA, Orexigen eventually ran a clinical trial on fewer than 10,000 patients. While this reduced requirement enabled the trial to proceed, this was still a huge and hugely expensive clinical trial.

The REVEAL trial of 2017, in which Merck tested the experimental drug anacetrapib, included a whopping 30,449 subjects and was conducted at 430 hospitals and clinics in the United Kingdom, North America, China, Germany, Italy, and Scandinavia. We will hear more about anacetrapib in the coming pages.

In addition to more patients in each clinical trial, each patient undergoes more tests and procedures.

Between 1999 and 2005, the average length of a clinical trial grew from 460 days to 780 days, while the number of procedures on each patient (e.g., blood draws, scans) grew similarly, from 96 to 158.[37] Comparing the 2001-2005 period to the 2011-2015 period, one study found that the number of study participant visits to care providers (e.g., hospitals, clinics, doctors' offices) increased 23-29 percent; the number of distinct procedures increased 44-59 percent; the total number of procedures performed increased 53-70 percent; and the cost per study volunteer per visit increased 34-61 percent.[38]

The protocols for clinical trials—those written recipes for how patients are to be recruited, dosed, and evaluated—have become more complex, as well. Gerry Messerschmidt, chief medical officer at Precision Oncology, reports, "When I was writing protocols 20 years ago, they were one-third the size that they are now. The change has really been quite dramatic."[39]

In addition to more complicated protocols, clinical trials are more expensive now because the cost per participant has increased at the same time that the number of participants has grown. Why? Again, the answer is the FDA.

This fact was not lost on former FDA Commissioner Margaret Hamburg, who said, "Timelines are long, costs are high, and rates of failure are distressingly high." Janet Woodcock, head of the FDA's Center for Drug Evaluation and Research, admitted that the size and length of clinical trials had grown substantially in recent years but argued that it was necessary for regulators to better identify risks. "We're smarter now [but still] humbled by what we don't know."

Pharmaceutical companies typically estimate the future expenses and revenues for each prospective drug. My consulting company, Objective Insights, helps companies with this process, looking forward 20 or more years. Once we estimate expenses, revenues, and probabilities of success at each phase of development, we compute the financial value of each pharmaceutical project. If the expected value (probability-adjusted value) of the project is negative, or the return on investment is less than for other competing projects, we recommend discontinuing development.

Many new medicines are discarded for reasons that have nothing to do with safety and efficacy. We have looked at the economic case for continued development of many drugs and, when the prospects looked poor, we have suggested killing drugs—drugs for brain cancer, ovarian cancer, melanoma, hemophilia, and other important conditions. All companies do this. In 2017, Merck discontinued the development of two drugs to treat hepatitis C due to their economics.[40] In that same year, Merck discontinued the development of anacetrapib, already in Phase 3 trials as mentioned above, because it was found to reduce the risk of coronary death by only nine percent versus placebo, less than the desired ten-percent target.[41] Even though millions of dollars may have already been spent, a company should never knowingly continue on a path toward losing more money unless some other crucial non-financial objective was being achieved.

This is where the FDA becomes important: the more stringent the FDA's requirements, the more tests each drug is required to pass, the more drugs cost to develop, and the lower their probability of approval becomes—meaning that more of them end up on the cutting room floor. Sounding a warning, Joseph Wu, a professor of cardiovascular medicine and director of the Stanford Cardiovascular Institute, commented that the FDA's requirement that pharma companies test all drugs for cardiac safety has an untoward effect: "[T]he screening is so sensitive that it's killing a lot of potentially good drugs."[42]

The CEO of one public drug company, a cardiologist who had spent the bulk of his career developing new cardiovascular medicines, left the pharma business in his prime. Why? His expertise was in cardiovascular drugs and the FDA had, in his opinion, made it too hard to develop cardiovascular drugs.[43] He shifted to other areas of the medical industry that generally didn't include cardiovascular drugs.

Eroom's Law

Moore's Law is optimistic, with costs dropping 30 percent each year. Eroom's Law is pessimistic, with costs increasing 7.5 percent per year. Moore's Law looks at technology without government interference, while Eroom's Law looks at technology hampered by stiffer and stiffer government regulation.

Unless FDA requirement trends change, for each dollar invested in R&D, expect fewer drugs to be discovered, developed, and marketed. Compared to what we could have, expect fewer therapeutic choices, less competition, higher prices, and some Americans suffering and dying needlessly.

Before-and-After Comparisons

FDA rules are making drug development exorbitantly expensive. These rules haven't been in place forever, which means that a before-and-after comparison of such laws can allow us to analyze whether the rules have helped or hurt, and how much. Economists have ways of digging into and analyzing historical data to answer just such questions, providing needed insights into public policy questions.

New Drug Approvals Drop

Recall that the Food, Drug, and Cosmetics Act of 1938 ("market and prove") was altered by the 1962 Kefauver-Harris Amendments to add a proof-of-efficacy requirement ("prove, then market"), among other things. It heralded an important change in the industry. These discrete before-and-after type situations are fertile ground for economic studies.

In 1973, UCLA economist Sam Peltzman, shortly before he moved to the University of Chicago, analyzed the effect of the Kefauver-Harris Amendments by comparing the number of new chemical entities (i.e., not just reformulations) approved by the FDA before the law changed with the number approved in the decade after the law changed.[44]

For the drug approvals from 1948 through 1961, Peltzman used actual, historical values. He then built a model to project the number of approved drugs from 1962 through 1971 to see how many approvals would have been expected had the law not changed. His model was based on three variables, most notably the size of the prescription drug market lagged by two years. Why two years? Prior to 1962, it took just *two years* to develop a new drug; it now takes 12 to 14 years.[45] [46]

That statistic alone should give us pause because it indicates how drastically things have changed since 1962. Using his projections, Peltzman looked at the actual number of new chemical entities approved and found that it was a shocking *61 percent below his model's projections*.[47]

According to his model, there should have been about 41.8 new approvals each year, but, instead, there were just 16.3, which is 61 percent lower than the predicted value. Compared to a simple linear regression trend, the deficit was 72 percent. Multiple researchers have concluded that it wasn't just inferior drugs that the FDA's process weeded out. Two researchers wrote, "In sum, the hypothesis that the observed decline in new product introductions has largely been concentrated in marginal or ineffective drugs is not generally supported by empirical analyses."[48]

Figure 2: New Drug Approvals

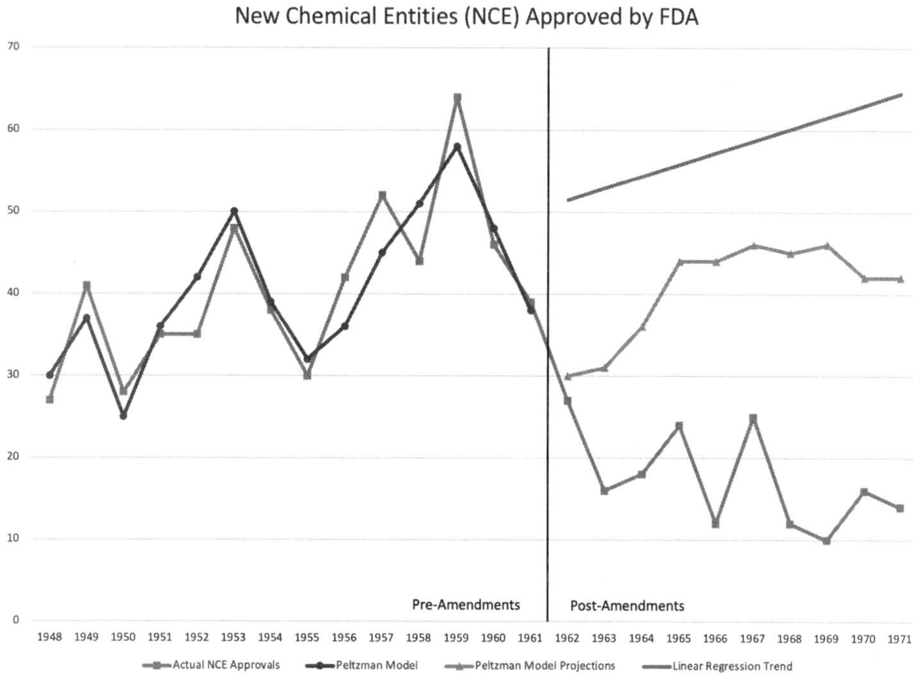

Drug Approvals Dropped After Rules Changed

Peltzman, himself, came to this same conclusion, seeing the culling "as…if an arbitrary marketing quota…had been placed on new drugs after 1962."[49] The Kefauver-Harris Amendments, designed to improve the safety and efficacy of new drugs, appears to have instead resulted in 61 percent fewer new drugs—if we assume no long-term growth in the industry, that means there was a total of approximately 1,475 fewer new drugs since 1962[50]—and no clear evidence that today's drugs are safer or more efficacious than they would have been absent the new rule. Peltzman wrote, "The penalties imposed by the marketplace on sellers of ineffective drugs before 1962 seem to have been sufficient to have left little room for improvement by a regulatory agency."[51]

Some of these drugs, had they been available, may have helped you or your loved ones.

> *This country has a new public health problem—Congress and the FDA.*
> **Dr. Joel J. Nobel**[52]

What good drugs were among those lost after the 1962 Amendments? We'll never know. How would we? What would we do, interview every drug company and every aspiring drug company? "What drugs would you have developed had the FDA's rules not changed?" You can see where that would lead—nowhere. But we do have strong evidence that the FDA and its rules reduced the number of new drugs and, if any of these new drugs were lifesavers, as they certainly were, then the FDA is a killer of both drugs *and* people.

This would not be much of a problem if there were already good medicines available, and all of the subsequent drugs offered only incremental, minor improvements. If our cups had runneth over, we could face the challenges of the medical shortfall with aplomb. But our cups haven't come close to running over.

Meet some of our mortal enemies.

Deadly Diseases Lacking Approved Therapies

What do the following diseases have in common? Zika virus infections, AL amyloidosis, transthyretin-mediated amyloidosis, cholangiocarcinoma, Duchenne muscular dystrophy, transthyretin familial amyloid polyneuropathy (TTR-FAP), upper tract urothelial carcinomas, and non-alcoholic steatohepatitis (NASH)?

They are serious diseases, some of which are always fatal and some that are usually fatal. As of 2018, when I was writing this section, there were no FDA-approved drugs to treat these diseases. Zero. Nada. The FDA acknowledges this fact. As per FDA employees Katherine Needleman and Gumei Liu, "A rare disease, by definition, affects fewer than 200,000 individuals in the United States. Its impact, however, is far from rare. Altogether, about 7,000 known rare diseases affect about 30 million Americans. Yet the vast majority of rare diseases do not have adequate diagnostic tools or treatments."[53]

Treatments for rare diseases do dribble in over time. One affliction that kills one quarter of its victims by liver failure, hepatic veno-occlusive disease, saw the first treatment approved in 2016. Metastatic Merkel cell carcinoma got its first FDA-approved treatment in 2017, as did tardive dyskinesia, Chagas disease, and Batten disease. The latter is a rapidly progressing brain condition that usually kills children between the ages of eight and 12. Medical progress is being made slowly, inch by inch.

Amyotrophic lateral sclerosis, or Lou Gehrig's disease, has a few FDA-approved drugs, but none that cure it or reverse its inexorable march toward death. Most patients die within two to five years after diagnosis.

There are also diseases that *do* have FDA-approved drugs, just severely deficient FDA-approved drugs. One such disease is the previously discussed gastroparesis, treated with the problematic metoclopramide. But for the eight fatal diseases mentioned above, there are no approved medicines—not even one.

There are an estimated 10,000 known disorders (some estimates are as high as 30,000), and yet the National Center for Advancing Translational Sciences says that fewer than 1,000 have effective treatments. The real number is probably lower: one of the key data suppliers in the pharmaceutical industry, IQVIA, tracks approximately 600 diseases. IQVIA is in the business of providing data about therapy usage and is unlikely to knowingly ignore 400 diseases that have effective treatments. Based on this, we can estimate that only two to six percent of known disorders have treatments available, and many of those treatments are deficient in one or more ways.[54]

Was it any wonder that there were no treatments or vaccines available for COVID-19 when it first struck? How and why would a drug company develop a treatment for a disease that didn't exist? While we can't blame drug companies for failing to predict the emergence of a novel virus, we can cheer them along as they develop treatments for that virus. We can also castigate the CDC and FDA for placing unnecessary roadblocks in the way of diagnosing and treating infections. In fact, the CDC and FDA completely botched the testing of patients for COVID-19 by forcing Americans to use a defective test and by resisting widespread testing.

Duchenne Muscular Dystrophy

As I was writing this, an FDA advisory committee had just rejected a drug — Sarepta's eteplirsen—for Duchenne muscular dystrophy (DMD), a genetic disorder that weakens every muscle in the body. The condition usually affects boys, who by age 12 or so can no longer walk, and over time damages the heart and lungs. The fatality rate is 100 percent, and most sufferers do not live past age 25. The drug eteplirsen was being testing in a small clinical trial, and the parents of children suffering from DMD spoke at the FDA review meeting. "Eteplirsen is giving my son a fighting chance," said Beth Perez of Yorktown, Va., who testified with her 12-year-old son, Caden. "He would not be ambulatory without this drug." Others made similar comments.

What do they know, right? They aren't scientists.

The FDA advisory committee rejected the drug (7 to 3, with three abstaining) because of concern about the small size of the clinical trial. "I felt this wasn't a well-controlled study," said panel chairman G. Caleb Alexander, an associate epidemiology professor at the Johns Hopkins School of Public Health. As scientists, those on the FDA's panel weren't convinced by the design of the clinical trial. As parents, those in the audience whose children suffered from this horrible disease were begging for permission to use, or keep using, eteplirsen. If you think as a scientist, you want proof; if you are a parent, you want a fighting chance, any chance, for your child. Physicians who actually treat Duchenne muscular dystrophy sided with the parents. A full 95 percent said that they would use eteplirsen for many of their patients, with some saying they would use it in "essentially all" of their eligible patients.

Here's a disease that is 100-percent fatal, and the FDA is denying suffering patients their only shot at improvement because the evidence isn't undeniably positive. Eteplirsen isn't perfect, but you don't help people by taking away their best alternative.

The FDA claimed that the clinical results weren't persuasive. That's one side of this issue. Here's what several dozen DMD experts on the other side were saying:

> The collective signatories note that the group of 12 eteplirsen treated boys, even accounting for daily deflazacort usage or twice-weekly prednisone, is clearly performing better than our collective clinical experience and the published literature would predict. Collectively, a portion of us represent a group of physicians who have observed over 5,000 DMD patients in our practices over an average of more than 15 years. Published external natural history data and our clinical experience strongly support that the 12 boys treated for over 4 years show a milder clinical progression, likely due to a positive treatment effect of eteplirsen.

As a postscript, after this section was written, Janet Woodcock, Director of the Center for Drug Evaluation and Research at the FDA, countermanded the advisory committee's recommendation and approved Sarepta's drug, Exondys 51 (eteplirsen) in September 2016. The approval raised eyebrows, and Woodcock was challenged by those who, thinking like scientists, correctly questioned the quality of the clinical data. Apparently, though, Woodcock saw the illogic of the FDA rejection.

There's another category of diseases for which there *are* FDA-approved therapies, just no new ones in the last decades. For instance, the FDA approved Dovprela (pretomanid) for tuberculosis in 2019, but it was only the third new TB drug approved in more than 40 years.[55] Progress in these ignored areas has stalled. It's as if these patients are encumbered with the medical equivalents of 1972 Ford Pintos, though perhaps unaware of *why*. The FDA is why.

What, you may wonder, becomes of the hapless patients who require treatment for the serious diseases that lack FDA-approved drugs? That question is answered countless times a day by doctors around the country who, while they are forbidden to use unapproved drugs, are allowed to use drugs, "off-label," for conditions other than what they were approved for. For instance, the patient with AL amyloidosis is often given a drug for multiple myeloma in the hope that the two conditions are closely related enough to help. In another example, in a "you can't make this stuff up," patients with bladder cancer are frequently given an anti-tuberculosis vaccine from 1921.

Wrap-up

The FDA has contributed to an explosion in drug development costs and has kept good drugs out of our hands, harming countless patients who are relying on outdated or repurposed drugs—or who are *waiting* for a drug that might help them.

Costs are growing at a high rate. At a 7.5 percent annual growth rate, drug development costs will more than double every ten years. If you want a new drug, pony up $3.2 billion now. If you wait ten years, it will likely cost you $6.4 billion.

The FDA rules that require proving efficacy prior to marketing ("prove, then market") are largely behind the increase in drug development costs, and these requirements have, in addition to increasing the time for development by ten to 12 years, appear to have reduced the number of new drug approvals by 61 percent. If some new legislation reduced total employment, college applications, new home construction, foreign trade, or oil output by 61 percent, there would be outrage, closely followed by a review of that legislation. In this case, there was Peltzman and a few other researchers, a feeble response from the FDA, and otherwise crickets.

There are roughly 25 drugs each year—1,500 new drugs since 1962—that you and your loved ones will not get access to, primarily because of the FDA's requirements. That deserves more attention.

Only two to six percent of medical disorders have *any* medical treatments available—and many of those have substandard ones—and yet the FDA acts as a Berlin Wall, keeping new cures from suffering patients.

---

[1] According to the poll: https://www.statnews.com/2016/05/11/stat-harvard-poll-drug-approvals/

[2] Gregory Conko, "A Better Way to Increase Access to Prescription Drugs," *TCS Daily*. The study was commissioned by the Competitive Enterprise Institute.

[3] $365 million divided by 365 days is $1 million per day.

[4] "Biohaven Spends $105M for Faster Review of Oral CGRP Inhibitor," *BioCentury*, 18 March 2019.

[5] "Lumos Pharma Announces Sale of Priority Review Voucher." Press Release, 27 July 2020.

---

[6] David Cutler, *Your Money or Your Life: Strong Medicine for America's Health Care System*, Oxford University Press, 2005. Also see David Dranove, *Code Red, An Economist Explains How to Revive the Healthcare System Without Destroying it*, Princeton University Press, 2008, p. 231.

[7] A study in Manchester, Chester, and London showed in 1980 that vitamins containing folic acid reduced the incidence of neural tube defects by half. Smithells R., Sheppard S., Schorah C., Seller M., Nevin N., Harris R. "Possible prevention of neural tube defects by periconceptional vitamin supplementation." *The Lancet*. 1980. The U.S. CDC didn't recommend folic acid until 1991 and 1992.

[8] Mary J. Ruwart, *Death by Regulation* and *Healing Our World*.

[9] Ben Adams, "Pfizer's R&D president Dolsten: Not taking government cash made us more nimble for COVID-19 vaccine," *Fierce Biotech*, 22 January 2021

[10] A version of this article appeared as "The FDA's Deadly Caution," Charles L. Hooper and David R. Henderson, *American Institute for Economic Research*, 16 December 2020. https://www.aier.org/article/the-fdas-deadly-caution/

[11] David Wallace-Wells, "We Had the Vaccine the Whole Time," *New York*, 7 December 2020.

[12] These ideas expand on those of the Hoover Institution's John Cochrane.

[13] Ronald Bailey wrote about this solution on 18 February 2021: "U.K. Approves Clinical Trial That Will Deliberately Expose Volunteers to the COVID-19 Virus," *Reason*.

[14] Jonathan Lambert, "The U.K. approved the world's first COVID-19 human challenge trial," *ScienceNews*, 18 February 2021.

[15] A study published in *Health Affairs* on 18 August 2021 came to the conclusion that the actual vaccination campaign saved 140,000 lives. While an apples and oranges comparison, that number is in the ballpark of the numbers I calculated in this chapter.

[16] Niall Ferguson, "How a More Resilient America Beat a Midcentury Pandemic," *Wall Street Journal*, 30 April 2021.

[17] J. Cavanaugh Simpson, "The Man Who Beat the 1957 Flu Pandemic," *Scientific American*, 19 April 2020.

[18] Sprix website, http://www.sprix.com/meet-sprix/ketorolac-history.aspx

[19] Committee on the Safety of Medicines, Medicines Control Agency: Ketorolac: new restrictions on dose and duration of treatment. *Current Problems in Pharmacovigilance:* June 1993; Volume 19 (pages 5-8).

[20] Cate Sibley, "Limitations of Ketorolac," Get Pharmacy Advice, 17 September 2010, http://www.getpharmacyadvice.com/limitations-of-ketorolac/

[21] National Institute on Drug Abuse, "Opioid Overdose Crisis," NIH website, March 2018.

[22] "The Man Who Knows Too Much," *The Wall Street Journal*, 6 April 2017.

[23] Laurie G. Hudson et al. "Dual Actions of Ketorolac in Metastatic Ovarian Cancer." *Cancers* vol. 11,8 1049. 24 July 2019.

[24] https://www.drugs.com/drug-shortages/.

[25] https://www.accessdata.fda.gov/scripts/drugshortages/default.cfm.

[26] E. Vail et al., "Association between US Norepinephrine Shortage and Mortality among Patients with Septic Shock," *JAMA* 317, no. 14 (11 April 2017) 1433-1442. doi: 10.1001/jama.2017.2841.

[27] Roni Caryn Rabin, "Why Lifesaving Drugs May Be Missing on Your Next Flight," *New York Times,* 3 October 2019.

[28] Charles L. Hooper, "Hooper's Law of Drug Development," originally published as a Featured Article on the Library of Economics and Liberty website, 7 August 2017, http://www.econlib.org/library/Columns/y2017/Hooperdrugdevelopment.html
The title of this article was changed from "Hooper's Law of Drug Development" to "The Dismal Economics of Drug Development" after a reader pointed out that the insight about pharmaceutical R&D costs increasing over time had been described by Jack W. Scannell, Alex Blanckley, Helen Boldon and Brian Warrington in March, 2012. In that paper, "Diagnosing the decline in pharmaceutical R&D efficiency," published in Nature Reviews Drug Discovery, the relationship was termed 'Eroom's Law,' or 'Moore's Law' backwards.

[29] Tufts Center for the Study of Drug Development, Cost of Developing a New Drug, 18 November 2014, http://csdd.tufts.edu/files/uploads/Tufts_CSDD_briefing_on_RD_cost_study_-_Nov_18,_2014.pdf

30 Joseph A. DiMasi, Henry G. Grabowski, and Ronald W. Hansen, "Innovation in the pharmaceutical industry: New Estimates of R&D Costs," *Journal of Health Economics*, Vol. 47, May 2016: 20-33. At: http://www.sciencedirect.com/science/article/pii/S0167629616000291

31 Charley Grant, "Alzheimer's: Pharma's Great White Whale Is Still Worth Hunting," *The Wall Street Journal*, 20 February 2017.

32 Jonathan D. Rockoff, "Pfizer Drops Alzheimer Research," *The Wall Street Journal,* 8 January 2018.

33 Joseph A. DiMasi, Henry G. Grabowski, and Ronald W. Hansen, "Innovation in the pharmaceutical industry: New Estimates of R&D Costs," *Journal of Health Economics*, Vol. 47, May 2016: 20-33. At: http://www.sciencedirect.com/science/article/pii/S0167629616000291

34 Joseph A. DiMasi, "R&D Cost Study Briefing," Boston, MA, November 18, 2014. At: http://csdd.tufts.edu/files/uploads/Tufts_CSDD_briefing_on_RD_cost_study_-_Nov_18,_2014.pdf

35 Joseph A. DiMasi, "R&D Cost Study Briefing," Boston, MA, November 18, 2014. At: http://csdd.tufts.edu/files/uploads/Tufts_CSDD_briefing_on_RD_cost_study_-_Nov_18,_2014.pdf

36 http://www.genengnews.com/gen-news-highlights/orexigen-halts-development-of-anti-obesity-therapies/81245243/?kwrd=Empatic

37 "A Doctor to Heal the FDA," *The Wall Street Journal*, 13 March 2017.

38 Kenneth A. Getz and Rafael A. Campo, "Trends in clinical trial design complexity," *Nature Reviews Drug Discovery*, 16, 307 (2017), 18 April 2017.

39 Denise Myshko, "Trends in Protocol Development, *PharmaVOICE*, March 2017.

40 "Merck discontinues HCV candidates," *BioCentury Extra*, 29 September 2017.

41 "End of the road for Merck's anacetrapib," *BioCentury Extra*, 12 October 2017.

42 Greta Lorge, "Finding the Cures Within Us," *Stanford* alumni magazine, March/April 2017.

[43] This story was reported to me by someone who knows this CEO well. I know the CEO fairly well and the story seems consistent with his behavior.

[44] Sam Peltzman, *Regulation of Pharmaceutical Innovation*, University of Chicago, 1974.

[45] Gail Van Norman, "Drugs, Devices, and the FDA: Part 1: An Overview of Approval Processes for Drugs," JACC: Back to Translational Science, Volume 1, Issue 3, April 2016
https://www.sciencedirect.com/science/article/pii/S2452302X1600036X

[46] Deloitte's Center for Health Solutions annual report, 2016.

[47] Sam Peltzman, *Regulation of Pharmaceutical Innovation*, University of Chicago, 1974.

[48] Grabowski, Henry G., and John M. Vernon, 1983. *The Regulation of Pharmaceuticals: Balancing the Benefits and Risks*. Washington D.C.: American Enterprise Institute for Public Policy Research.

[49] Sam Peltzman, *Regulation of Pharmaceutical Innovation*, University of Chicago, 1974.

[50] 58 years of 25.4 drugs per year equals 1,475 missing new drugs.

[25] Sam Peltzman, *Regulation of Pharmaceutical Innovation*, University of Chicago, 1974.

[52] *Hazardous to Our Health?* Edited by Robert Higgs.

[53] Katherine Needleman and Gumei Liu, "Launching a New Natural History Grants Program: Building a Solid Foundation for Rare Disease Treatments," *FDA Voice,* posted on February 29, 2016.

[54] 600 divided by 30,000 is 0.02. 600 divided by 10,000 is 0.06.

[55] Betsy McKay, "FDA Approves New TB Therapy," *The Wall Street Journal*, 15 August 2019.

Chapter 7: It's Not Easy Being the FDA

Should we feel sorry for the FDA, confronted as it is with a nearly impossible task? Consider some of the challenges it faces.

The Miracle Berry

How do you handle a berry without squishing it?

In 1852, a British surgeon described a strange new fruit that he called a "miraculous" berry. A French explorer first encountered the odd fruit, *Synsepalum dulcificum*, in 1725, in West Africa, where he watched locals eat the fruit before consuming gruel and palm wine.[1] We now know that the fruit has a protein that binds to taste buds, altering the tongue's so-called sweet receptors to activate when sour foods are eaten. For about an hour after you eat it, everything tastes sweet: lime wedges taste like candy, lemons taste like lemonade, and goat cheese tastes as if it were covered in powdered sugar. One modern taster said it was "the strangest gustatory experience I have ever had in my life."

Imagine what this fruit could do for food production and consumption. Would it dramatically reduce global sugar production? Could it help prevent diabetes and tooth decay? Would it affect or even cure the global obesity problem? Imagine, also, how healthy but unpalatable foods could be made irresistibly delicious. Potentially, we could eat impressively nutritious foods that were as sweet as anything from the display cases of a donut shop.

The miracle berry could change everything.

Because the miracle fruit is so delicate, at team of researchers at Tsukuba University in Japan searched for a way to produce the key protein in another, sturdier, food, and they succeeded with lettuce. The result was two grams of lettuce that produced the same effect as one miracle fruit.

You knew there would be a problem with this; there's frequently a problem with these things when a government agency is involved.

The FDA has no issue with you eating the miracle berry as a *fruit*, even though it has never been tested for safety or efficacy. Foods are okay—even the foods that sometimes kill people. But the FDA makes it clear that, if a food company wants to sell you a miracle berry food "additive," even if that additive is essentially a whole food, it will require years of testing and FDA approval. Therein lies the difference. That distinction drove one miracle fruit company out of business. Miralin, the ill-fated company, was on the verge of offering miracle berry foods for sale when it grasped the daunting prospects of the testing required to please the FDA. So, instead, it filed for bankruptcy and fired its 280 employees.

We can grow our own miracle fruit plant at home. But we can't get miracle fruit products.

Impossible Burger

Is that a food additive or a food coloring I'm eating?

The Impossible Foods company makes a meatless burger that looks and tastes like a real ground beef burger. Sound impossible? I've eaten some and they were virtually indistinguishable from beef patties.

The fact that I've tried them means that Impossible Burgers are available to the public...but only through restaurants. As I was writing this in early 2019, Impossible was trying to get approval to sell its raw "meat" to the public in grocery stores, but there was a holdup. The holdup was even stranger than you might imagine.

The FDA had approved a key ingredient in Impossible Burgers, soy leghemoglobin, or heme, as Generally Recognized as Safe (commonly called GRAS). It's heme that gives the Impossible Burger its essential meat-like flavor. If the FDA has approved heme, what's the holdup? This might be, ahem, impossible to believe, but the FDA has approved heme as a "food ingredient," but it hasn't approved it as a "food coloring."[2] Got that?

Heme, which is less than two percent of the Impossible "meat" concoction, is used in Impossible Burgers because it provides a meat-like flavor and it also gives some meat-like color to the uncooked meat. The FDA believes that heme is safe to eat as a food ingredient, but it's not yet sure whether heme is safe to eat as a food coloring. Of course, food colorings are also food ingredients and both are eaten, and while they travel through the same digestive system, they go through different regulatory systems. The necessity for two regulatory pathways was triggered because it was determined that it was the *intention* of Impossible to use heme to provide some red color, and this caused heme to be scrutinized as a food coloring. If the company had added heme just for the taste and texture alone and, low and behold, it just happened to make the meat red, then it wouldn't be scrutinized as a food coloring. The fact that Impossible uses heme partly for its bloody color means that heme must now be proven safe as a food coloring. Say whaaat?

And yet the raw Impossible meat that the FDA says *cannot* be sold to the public is the very same raw Impossible meat that the FDA says *can* be sold to restaurants—and then sold as cooked burgers to the public. One would think that if the burgers were safe in restaurants they would be safe at home, or if they were unsafe at home they would be unsafe in restaurants.

If these rules make sense to you, perhaps there's a promising career for you at the FDA.

Real hamburgers have known health risks, and yet the FDA has never asked beef processors to prove that eating hamburger meat is safe. Those striving to make *better* hamburgers aren't so lucky.

Note: after this chapter was written, the FDA gave a green light to Impossible Foods to sell Impossible meat at retail outlets in August 2019.

The FDA Attacks Bias

What if those who assail biases are themselves biased?

Bias can distort the drug approval process and can lead to bad drugs being approved and good drugs being denied. Many of us can imagine researchers and doctors receiving illicit funds from drug companies in an attempt to get those companies' drugs approved. It can go in the other direction, and we've seen the problematic case of FDA reviewer John Harder reviewing drugs for a company that had recently fired him. In terms of bias, is the FDA part of the solution or part of the problem?

Industry Ties and the FDA's Advisors

In Kevin Costner's comedy *Swing Vote*, the presidential election comes down to a single voter.[3] The premise is absurd. But we don't need to go to the movies to see absurd plots in which big decisions hinge on one voter. The U.S. Congress, via the FDA, has created its own. Except this time, it's not a comedy—it's a tragedy.

When the FDA convenes advisory committees comprised of outsiders (not FDA employees), the members give the FDA a thorough assessment of the new drug's strengths and weaknesses and potential therapeutic role, along with a bit of political cover. Who, after all, can fault the FDA for agreeing with a team of independent experts?

Now, keep in mind that any supposedly "tainted" physicians are excluded from these committees. Who are these "tainted" physicians? Anyone who has any ties to the pharmaceutical industry. In fact, Congress requires the FDA to severely limit independent experts from participating in FDA advisory committees if they have such ties. In my consulting practice, it is common for me to hear my clients complain, "I can't believe that so-and-so wasn't a member of that recent FDA advisory committee." After all, so-and-so is a renowned expert in the field. The reason for this person's absence was his or her ties to the pharmaceutical industry.

But the FDA ran into an intriguing problem when it tried to convene a committee to evaluate a drug for a particular rare disease, infantile spasm. Infantile spasm is a devastating form of epilepsy that strikes about 8,500 American infants in the first year of life; not surprisingly, there are no approved medications for the condition. After Ovation Pharmaceuticals submitted a new drug application to the FDA for Sabril (vigabatrin), the FDA excluded all those with a "conflict of interest" from the advisory committee and ended up with only one available committee member. His name was Gregory Holmes, section chief of neurology at the Dartmouth-Hitchcock Medical Center. Unfortunately, he had served as a principle investigator in clinical trials of epilepsy drugs, and so he, too, faced the threat of being recused. Now, *Swing Vote* becomes *And Then There Were None*.

In true government fashion, all regulatory progress with Sabril, the new drug to treat infantile spasm, ground to a halt until an appropriate committee was convened. Moreover, according to a study commissioned by the FDA, this problem with convening advisory committees will become even more common. Congress's message to patients desperately waiting for new treatments: Tough luck.

Many experts have industry ties, and it is a challenge to keep them off advisory panels. In July 2016, the FDA booted four advisors off an opioid panel because of their ties to pharma companies. In January 2012, after an advisory committee meeting to discuss problems with Bayer's marketed birth control pills, it was discovered that four of the advisers had ties to Bayer, having served as consultants, speakers, or researchers.

The so-called "clean" advisory committees have problems, too. In April 2016, the FDA held an advisory committee to evaluate a drug for Duchenne muscular dystrophy. The 13-member committee included a psychiatrist, a stroke specialist, and several others with no experience in treating Duchenne. These were experts, just, unfortunately, not in the subject at hand, which means they weren't really authorities in the way that mattered. In their statements, the committee members incorrectly presented some of the key facts. Physician Aaron Kesselheim, for instance, stated that the disease is "usually" fatal, when, in fact, the death rate is 100 percent.

Who exactly are these "independent experts"? They are prominent physicians, researchers, and non-FDA government employees, some of whom have run clinical trials for new medicines. Recent conflict of interest (COI) rules have turned this real-world expertise into a liability because the great majority of clinical trials are sponsored by biopharmaceutical companies.

Here's the Catch-22. While the experts were busy being experts, those who sought their expertise, including drug companies, were paying them for their services and advice. This bred suspicion that they were "biased" and couldn't be trusted to impartially evaluate new drugs. So, with this logic, being an expert disqualifies you from being an expert.

Physicians are experts at treating patients. Because pharmaceutical companies develop new drugs that physicians may prescribe, it is immensely valuable for drug companies to find out what types of new medicines they should be developing, what types of information and clinical trial results would best help these new medicines get adopted, and whether any particular new drug should be developed at all. As is typical, multiple biopharma companies are developing drugs that may compete with each other or provide complementary therapeutic benefit. How will the market take shape with these new drugs? Pharmaceutical companies go to doctors for information and assistance throughout the drug development process and, once a drug has been approved, to increase awareness and foster prescribing. Drug companies flock to experts because those experts possess valuable information.

The FDA's suspicion of these experts culminated in an impasse with Sabril for infantile spasm. According to the director of the FDA's Office of New Drugs, John Jenkins, "There are a small number of pediatric epilepsy experts in the country, and they are the experts you go to [to] do a study of a drug. It is likely most of the experts will be conflicted."

Thankfully, we can test the hypothesis that having worked for a drug company corrupts experts. In fact, this hypothesis *has* been tested—and, furthermore, rejected. Moreover, it was rejected via a study done by five researchers, four of whom were employees of the Public Citizen's Health Research Group (PCHRG)—an organization known for its anti-pharma views.

In 2006, Sidney Wolfe—one of the pharmaceutical industry's most vehement critics, a person who, at last count, had helped drive 16 drugs from the market[4]—and three of his fellow PCHRG employees, along with one other author, published an article in the *Journal of the American Medical Association* that drew on 221 meetings of FDA advisory committees, including 76 product-specific meetings that involved yes or no votes on individual drugs. Note that these meetings occurred before the strict conflict of interest rules were in place.

Their findings? None of the 76 voting outcomes would have changed had voters with conflicts of interest been excluded. The authors also found that those with conflicts were no more likely than those without to vote for "their" company's drug. Indeed, those with a conflict were actually *more* likely than those without to vote for drugs that would compete with "their" company's product. That didn't stop Wolfe and his co-authors from concluding, "Ideally, all panels of scientific experts advising a federal decision-making body would be free of financial conflicts of interest with the affected companies."[5] So much for objective, evidence-based policy.

The problem with the corruption hypothesis is that it is based on only one factor: short-term financial incentives. Sure, some of those advisors might have had a small financial reason to favor a particular drug company or a new medicine.[6] But counterbalancing this potential bias are huge reasons not to be biased, including professional reputation, genuine care for patients, the desire to avoid scrutiny, and adherence to professional and scientific norms. If experts lose their reputation for independence by voting like paid shills, they become useless to everyone, including, ironically, pharmaceutical companies.

The FDA can grant COI waivers for outside advisors, but the number of these waivers is limited and declining (thanks to Congress).

If Congress is so interested in removing possible conflicts of interest, it should resign en masse. After all, in one of the most outrageous examples of conflict of interest, senators and representatives vote for pork barrel legislation to get reelected, benefiting from the process in myriad ways. Sadly, Congress seems much less concerned about protecting its reputation than the average pharma expert.

In the meantime, Congress should repeal its absurd, and empirically unsupported, FDA conflict of interest rules. As many as 8,500 American babies a year—and, potentially, millions of the rest of us—would benefit.

Insiders Pick the Outsiders

In 2007, the FDA held an advisory committee meeting to discuss Genta's Genasense (oblimersen sodium) for chronic lymphocytic leukemia (CLL). The FDA recused the only member of the committee who was an expert in CLL. Not one of the committee members appointed by the FDA was an expert in CLL, and two of them worked as consultants for the FDA but failed to disclose that relationship.

Genasense had mixed clinical results and wasn't perfect—few drugs are—but it was better than existing drugs. Genasense had been shown to induce a complete disappearance of disease in 17 percent of advanced CLL patients (a medical Holy Grail), versus seven percent in the control group on old drugs, and responders saw their response last an average of 36 months versus 22 months for the control group. Still, the advisory panel voted seven to three against approval.[7] The FDA sent Genta what's called a Complete Response Letter, meaning that Genasense had been rejected and, as far as the FDA was concerned, the case was closed. CLL experts were surprised and dismayed. Genta promptly laid off a third of its employees, and, today, Genasense sits on the shelf, never having received an FDA approved. Genta closed its doors in 2012.

Do you see a problem with this? An advisory committee is a group of "outside experts." But who determines who the experts are and who invites them to meetings? The FDA. With an ironic twist, the fear of supposed pro-industry biases gives the FDA cover to exclude the true experts and, instead, to convene a panel with a possible pro-FDA bias. This is a like allowing a prosecutor to pack a jury with his buddies.

The FDA does more than just convene the outside panel. The FDA clearly delineates what the advisory committee is to vote on, controlling the discussion in the same way that a lawyer controls a witness in a courtroom. The questions posed to the committee aren't something such as, "Will this new drug help patients?" or "Should we green light this new drug?" The questions are usually far more focused, such as, "Were these clinical trials well controlled?" A voting member may well think that the drug will help patients but might have to concede that the trial could have been better controlled. In November 2020, Biogen's experimental drug for Alzheimer's disease came before an advisory committee. The drug had been tested in two nearly identical Phase 3 clinical trials: EMERGE and ENGAGE. Interestingly, the drug failed one but passed the other. The FDA inscrutably directed the advisory committee to consider the trial that the drug, aducanumab, passed while ignoring the one that it failed.[8] An agency that controls the invitation list, the agenda, and the microphone controls the meeting.

The FDA is supposedly a scientific organization that makes decisions based on empirical data. Unfortunately, the FDA applies this standard to other groups—most notably, drug companies—but not to itself. When it comes to potential conflicts of interest among advisory committee members, the FDA simply rounds up the usual suspects and declares them guilty, without so much as a trial, while engaging in precisely the behavior that it is condemning.

Biases can be a hindrance to good decision-making, of course, and it's a fact that most of us are guilty of bias at one time or another.[9] If the FDA were serious about bias, it would consider *all* kinds of bias and set up systems whereby the expertise of experts could still be extracted, while the effects of their biases were minimized. After all, even a stridently pro- or anti-drug expert might have something valuable to offer. Decision scientists have developed some good techniques to extract information from biased experts, but the FDA continues to employ its amateurish approach.

A bias recognized is a bias sterilized.
Benjamin Haydon, British painter

The problems with FDA advisory committees extend to something that many of us hold dear: voting. Voting is a method that western societies employ to allow people to express preferences for candidates and their policies and to "throw the rascals out" when things head south. The FDA uses voting for something very different, prompting us to ask: How can advisory committee members vote on objective, scientific evidence? Either it's true or it isn't, right? We can't vote on gravity. We can't vote on Maxwell's equations or Newton's laws. When an FDA advisory committee meeting results in a split vote, which often happens—the Duchenne muscular dystrophy panel split 6-7—it means that the panel members disagree, which means that the truth they are seeking isn't black and white. Which means a lot.

Gray Situations and the All-Powerful Arbiter

If you think about it for a moment, it becomes clear that the FDA deals almost exclusively with situations that are gray.

It shouldn't be a wavering line [between statistical certainty on the one hand and getting new therapies to patients on the other], but because there's judgment involved, it turns out to be.
Janet Woodcock, Acting FDA Commissioner[10]

If you were HIV positive, would you treat your condition with chemotherapy and blood thinners? No. Would you treat yourself with daily doses of drain cleaner? Would you guzzle gasoline? No, you wouldn't. You would instead use a drug such as Genvoya (elvitegravir, cobicistat, emtricitabine, & tenofovir) from Gilead Sciences.

This example is black and white, and all reasonable people agree that Genvoya is better for HIV than are chemotherapy, blood thinners, drain cleaner, and gasoline. The FDA does not deal with these black and white situations. The FDA never evaluated drain cleaner for HIV. But not all assessments are black and white, of course; some are shades of gray.

We need to realize that the FDA works almost exclusively in unclear, gray areas, where some knowledgeable, reasonable people say a drug works and others say it doesn't. If all the experts agreed that a drug didn't work, the drug's sponsors would never bring it to the FDA's attention. Every drug that comes before the FDA for evaluation has a number of highly trained champions who are brave enough to put up their hands and publicly state that the new drug is safe and efficacious for some segments of patients. Undoubtedly, there are other people who are less sanguine about the new drug. There are experts on both sides of the issue. The relevant question is: which way does the FDA lean in these ambiguous, gray situations?

In 2011, the FDA revoked the approval of Genentech's Avastin (bevacizumab) for metastatic breast cancer, which was controversial because many people, including breast cancer patients, oncologists, the European Medicines Agency, and the National Comprehensive Cancer Network believed that Avastin *was* an important therapy for such types of breast cancer.[11] The government's solution was, and is, to say that one and only one judgment will prevail—the judgment of the FDA, and it's just a matter of which way the FDA will lean. This issue became one that the FDA needed to resolve *precisely* because some people thought that Avastin worked for metastatic breast cancer and some held the opposite view. Even patient advocates were divided, with some saying, "It shouldn't be approved for breast cancer yet," and others saying, "It should be approved."

Black and white situations are obvious and uncontroversial. Gray situations are not obvious, and they are controversial if one, and only one, opinion will hold legal weight because one side will be validated and the other side will be thwarted. It is exactly in these unclear, gray situations that the FDA finds its vocation. Virtually every time you hear about an FDA ruling, know that there are two sides to the argument, with some experts on one side and others in opposition.

When we look at FDA advisory committee meetings, we can see this grayness in clear detail because the votes are publicly reported. For instance, an FDA advisory committee in April 2016 voted seven to three, with three abstentions, that Sarepta Therapeutics' drug eteplirsen did not have good enough clinical data to warrant FDA approval. Notice that there were three experts on the panel who though that eteplirsen did have enough data. The 2016 advisory committee vote for Cempra's antibiotic solithromycin was even closer, virtually tied at 7-6. Those six voters hadn't flunked out of college, and they weren't fools who walked in off the street. The 2003 advisory committee's vote on Transkaryotic Therapies Replagal (agalsidase alfa) to treat Fabry's disease was 8-7 against. In all likelihood, the curricula vitae of those seven voters could be used to paper one wall of a large room. A vote of 8-7 in 2006 required ADHD drugs to carry "black box" warnings about cardiovascular risks. How easy would it have been for that vote to be 8-7, but in the opposite direction? Split votes are common, but they wouldn't be if all situations were clearly black or white. We don't see physicists voting 8 to 7 that gravity pulls masses toward each other.

Grayness exists both outside and within the FDA.

Normally, we can't penetrate the opaque walls of the FDA to see how employees voted for or against drug approvals, but sometimes that process erupts beyond those walls and gives us a glimpse into this gray zone within the FDA itself. With eteplirsen, which the FDA did eventually approve for Duchenne muscular dystrophy, a consensus was lacking and protests were lodged. On the dissenting side, some of the agency's staffers who had studied eteplirsen's evidence concluded that it "did not provide interpretable evidence of benefit;" the official FDA label slyly said that clinical benefit "has not been established"(then why was it approved?); and some insurers denied coverage, stating that the therapy was "investigational" (it wasn't). Dr. Janet Woodcock, director of the FDA's center for drugs, ultimately decided to overrule her staff and approve the drug anyway. Dr. Ellis Unger, a senior physician in the drug division, objected to her decision and filed a protest that traveled all the way to Dr. Robert Califf, the commissioner. You might have your own opinions about eteplirsen's benefits, but there clearly wasn't unanimity at the FDA, which is the crux of this issue.

The situation was gray, gray, gray.

In another ambiguous case, the FDA approved Biogen's Aduhelm (aducanumab) in June 2021, the first new drug for Alzheimer's disease in two decades. This was controversial because Aduhelm failed one of its key Phase 3 clinical trials and what it does in the human body—reduce amyloid brain plaques—has not been shown to slow the progression of Alzheimer's. The approval triggered waves of criticism. Even many within the FDA disapproved of the approval. An internal document stated that Tristan Massie, a biostatistics reviewer for the FDA, "does not agree that the totality of the data provides sufficient evidence to support the efficacy of aducanumab in Alzheimer's disease and does not recommend approval."

Breast Implants

Consider the complex world of breast implants.

The FDA put an end to routine sales of highly popular silicone breast implants in 1992, restricting them to breast cancer patients because of reports that the implants broke, leaked, and caused serious health problems. In 2003 and 2005, the FDA rejected Inamed Corp.'s bid to bring silicone gel breast implants back to the market. In public testimony before the vote, dozens of women argued that the silicone gel implants left them permanently damaged, while dozens more begged for continued access to them. Some women described their conscious choices to replace salt water-filled implants with silicone-gel implants. Inamed argued that silicone implants broke no more often than saline-filled ones and that they didn't cause life-threatening health problems. Finally, in 2006, long after many of the original manufacturers, who lost billions of dollars in class-action lawsuits, were out of the business, the FDA did again allow the sale of silicone breast implants.

The breast implant issue was and is far from black and white.

If you came across two people arguing over the best ice cream flavor, vanilla or chocolate, what might you tell them? First, both are good. Second, if you prefer vanilla over chocolate, put vanilla in your bowl. If you prefer chocolate over vanilla, put in a scoop of chocolate. The same solution is available for breast implants. If you think saline breast implants will work better, use them. If you think silicone ones are better, choose them instead. If you don't like either, don't use either.

Convalescent Plasma for COVID-19

In August 2020, the FDA granted convalescent plasma—a component of blood taken from recovering patients—an emergency use authorization for treating patients with current infections of SARS-CoV-2, the virus that causes the disease known as COVID-19. Emergency use authorizations are temporary approvals that are to be re-evaluated when better data, especially data from controlled clinical trials, becomes available.

An FDA press release laid out the scientific evidence behind using convalescent plasma, adding that the reduction in mortality could be as high as 37 percent.[12]

Not so fast, said the National Institutes of Health. The NIH concluded there is "currently no data from well-controlled, adequately powered randomized clinical trials that demonstrate the efficacy and safety" of the treatment.[13] Plasma "should not be considered" standard of care for treating COVID-19 patients.

The FDA and the NIH are talking past each other. The FDA's emergency use authorization is granted if there's some clinical evidence that happens to fall short of the more complete evidence that comes from clinical trials.

The temporary approval is given until that better data is available. Essentially, the NIH is telling the FDA to stop granting emergency use authorizations!

This example demonstrates how experts can disagree. We assume that if experts pore over the data, they will arrive at the truth. But here are two experts poring over the same data and yet coming to two diametrically opposed conclusions. They are each seeing their own version of the truth.

All Cases Are Personal

There was a thought-provoking discussion of prostate specific antigen (PSA) tests in a *UC Berkeley Wellness Letter* from 2011. The article critiqued the U.S. Preventive Services Task Force's recommendation in October of that year that all men skip PSA tests for prostate cancer screening.

The article clearly laid out the strengths and weaknesses of the PSA test. In an editorial postscript, the chairman of the editorial board admitted that the male members of the board were split about future testing for themselves. "Two won't, several are considering stopping, while the rest will continue to be tested, though with some ambivalence." Notice anything?

Most medicine is ambiguous, and the PSA discussion merely underscores that fact. Even the educated and informed editorial board of *Wellness Letter* was split on what to do. The final recommendation in the article was: "The decision is a personal one, and men should discuss the pros and cons of PSA testing with their doctors starting at about age 50, earlier if they are high risk."

Let's be frank. This is the recommendation for more than just PSA testing; it is the recommendation for all medical cases. Unless an innocent third party will be harmed, all cases are personal and should be decided by those who are most affected. Men and women should discuss the pros and cons of all medicines with their doctors and make the right choice for themselves, realizing that neither the *Wellness Letter* nor the FDA can make these choices because those organizations are going to fall on one side or the other of a gray area, and they don't possess all the relevant information.

Majority and Minority Opinions

Imagine the uproar among the *Wellness Letter*'s editorial board members if the chairman had decreed that the other members follow his personal decision, effectively forcing his preferences on them, stifling their self-determination, and eliminating the role of individualized treatment and experimentation. Now imagine that he had dictated his preferences to 330 million people and you get a good picture of the FDA. The FDA will never understand the specific circumstances and preferences of 330 million people. Yet the FDA's autocratic approach denies all of us the opportunity to make our own personalized treatment decisions, even when there are qualified experts on both sides of the debate, and even when we have important information about our specific situations, which the FDA cannot possibly know.

In essence, the person with the most power within the FDA lays down the law, requiring all of us, even if we disagree, to comply. And why? Why should one person get to tell the rest of us what to do?

> *If all mankind minus one, were of one opinion, and only one person were of the contrary opinion, mankind would be no more justified in silencing that one person, than he, if he had the power, would be justified in silencing mankind.*
> **John Stuart Mill**

Let's change Mill's quote to better match the situation: If all mankind minus one, were of one opinion, and only one person were of the contrary opinion, mankind would be no more justified in telling that one person what medicines he could take, than he, if he had the power, would be justified in telling all mankind what medicines they could take.

During the SARS-CoV-2 pandemic of 2020, President Trump was criticized for his (claimed) choice to ingest the drug HCQ as a consequence of its unproven efficacy. In defending his actions, he said, "This is an individual decision to make." While you might have strong feelings about Trump's choice, notice two things. First, he wasn't making the error referenced in the J.S. Mill quote of telling us that we should or shouldn't use HCQ. Second, an agency within "his" government disagreed with him—that it's an individual choice—and *is* making that precise J.S. Mill error.

Imagine that there were a well-designed clinical trial of a new medicine showing that 99 percent of the subjects had the expected positive benefit and that one percent didn't. In this scenario, with such a high response rate, this drug would likely be approved by regulatory agencies such as the FDA in the U.S. and the EMA in Europe. Approval would make this drug available to all citizens who could get a prescription from a health care profession.

Now that it is on the market, you try it and either you get the desired response and keep taking it or, if you are in the one-percent category, see no benefit, and stop taking it.

Now reverse the results. In this scenario, only one percent of the subjects had the expected benefit and 99 percent didn't. In this case, it is highly unlikely any regulatory body would approve this drug, and, therefore, it would not be available on the market. But, for the sake of argument, let's say that you came across a bottle of this medicine, tried it and found that, surprisingly, you were one of the rare responders. Now, once you realize that this drug works for you, but that it is unavailable because the regulatory agencies concerned with "all patients" judged the response as insignificant and prevented its marketing, how would you feel? Angry?

Here we have two scenarios. In both, it is obvious who benefits from the drug once they try it. The only difference is the 99/1 split of responders versus non-responders. Note that in the "approval" case, the drug will be on the market and the 99-percent group can use it if they want, while the one-percent group will avoid it. In the other case, the one-percent group, even though they would like to use the drug, are prevented from doing so by the gatekeeping activities of the regulatory agency siding with the majority.

This is, in its essence, a case of the majority oppressing the minority. If this involved religion, politics, free speech, book reading habits, or even coffee drinking behaviors, with the majority telling the minority what to do, we would be outraged. We would argue that this is America! and we have the right to practice our own religion and read our own books, regardless of their popularity. But, according to Congress and the FDA, we don't have that same right when it comes to ingesting therapeutic compounds. The minority must adapt to what the majority will allow.

What Perspective to Embrace?

The theory behind the FDA is that if it, as an expert, pores over the data, it can provide the rest of us non-experts with an accurate and honest assessment of each drug. But what if those very assessments depend on the perspective of the expert involved? We will consider two different perspectives, which we will call the scientific perspective and the decision-maker perspective. Which one should the FDA adopt? Which one does it adopt?

Two Perspectives

Scientist: Scientists are searching for reliable knowledge. Scientists believe that the pursuit of knowledge and objective truth is paramount, and the scientific approach is the path that will lead us there. Scientists ask whether the evidence we have is clear, robust, and convincing. Does the evidence meet our threshold for quality?

Science is the incremental process of finding little truths that can be stacked like blocks on top of each other, cumulatively adding to the overall body of knowledge.[14] Science doesn't try to do too much, lest it find itself with empty hands if one of the building blocks is later determined to be wobbly. As Sir Isaac Newton put it, "Tis much better to do a little with certainty & leave the rest for others that come after than to explain all things by conjecture without making sure of any thing." In other words: make sure you are right; don't make mistakes. Build a solid house.

The FDA is the quintessential scientific organization, exhibiting the scientific perspective. But the scientific perspective knows no urgency and no tradeoffs. If the perfect evidence takes 20 years to be obtained, that's just the way it is. If a million people die in those 20 years, oh well.

> *Science is incredible. But they don't know when to stop. Curiosity killed the cat. Okay, well let's kill 10,000 cats to find out why. That's what science does!*
> **Jon Stewart**, TV talkshow host

Decision maker: The clinician wants to help patients *today*, and giving patients the best therapies and care is paramount, even acknowledging that we have imperfect knowledge. Clinicians assume the perspective of the decision maker.

Doctors usually fall into the decision-maker camp out of nature and necessity. Emerson Perin, an interventional cardiologist at Texas Heart Institute in Houston, said that it's easier to be cautious as a scientist than as a physician. "They [the FDA] don't have patients dying; I do. Daily I have to look them in the eye."[15]

The medical field would be crippled without decision makers because they work in the trenches, diagnosing diseases, determining the best therapies, and providing consistent, caring help to patients. Likewise, the medical field would be rudderless without scientists. When the AIDS epidemic

IT'S NOT EASY BEING THE FDA

exploded in the early 1980s, it was scientists who determined that it was caused by a sexually-transmissible virus. And yet there is tension between the two perspectives; there's a wall between them.

An example of the tension between the scientific and decision-making perspectives arose early in the AIDS epidemic when, during clinical trials for new medicines, some AIDS patients coordinated and mixed their experimental drugs. The thinking was that half each of a good drug and a placebo was better than the 50/50 risk of getting just the placebo.[16] For an individual patient, this made sense (however, it violated the terms of the clinical trial). For scientists and patients who weren't part of the trial, this was a disaster. How could they tell if an experimental drug was working if the results were muddied?

Another interesting scientist/decision-maker issue arose with aspirin some years back.

California physician Lawrence Craven noticed in 1948 that the 400 men to whom he prescribed aspirin hadn't suffered any heart attacks. He regularly preached to all patients and colleagues that "an aspirin a day" could dramatically reduce the risk of heart attack.[17] However, even 70 years later, this topic was still controversial. "Consider the perspective that many people have: 'Why is it so difficult to get a clear answer on a pill [aspirin] that costs a few pennies and is available over-the counter and taken by millions of people?'" asked Michael Thun of the American Cancer Society. That's a good question!

Partly it is a problem of perspective and two different perspectives may reside in the same person at the same time.

In December 2003, an FDA advisory committee declined to endorse the use of aspirin for preventing initial myocardial infarctions, or heart attacks.[18] Does this mean that aspirin, which is approved for the prevention of second heart attacks, doesn't help prevent initial heart attacks? Not necessarily. The story of one of the panelists, Joseph Knapka, can help explain this situation. Knapka, who had lost his father to heart disease at the young age of 34, saw the benefits of aspirin but still voted against the new indication. "As a scientist, I vote, no. As a heart patient, I say, yes." In other words, he had two standards. One standard is the scientific proof that aspirin works beyond any doubt. By this standard, the data on 55,000 patients failed. The other standard is measured by our choices in the real world. By this standard, aspirin passed gloriously. "The question isn't, 'Does aspirin work?' We know it works," explained panelist Thomas Fleming, chairman and professor of the Department of Biostatistics at the University of Washington. "Now in the real world, interestingly, the medical community, and to a large extent the lay community, already accept primary prevention of aspirin," according to Eric Topol, of the Cleveland Clinic Foundation. This is based on evidence that even healthy individuals can cut their heart-attack risk by 30 percent by taking aspirin.[19]

If they thought it worked, why did they vote against it? Two reasons. The first reason was that the clinical data left them with some uncertainty. "The evidence doesn't meet the standards the FDA sets," stated Edward Pritchett, a cardiologist and consulting professor of medicine at Duke

University Medical Center. However, Pritchett was convinced enough that he, himself, had been swallowing an aspirin a day. The second reason is that they were thinking like scientists, not like doctors or patients.

No Evidence?

If you read health care literature, you are bound to come across the following type of phrase: "There's no evidence that X therapy provides Y benefit." Or you will find a doctor who states that she is "not aware of any clinical studies indicating that this therapy regimen is safe." To look at one specific example, perhaps there's no evidence that omega-3 fish oil pills reduce cardiovascular risk. This statement can be interpreted three ways. First, perhaps there have been well-designed long-term studies in humans, and the results show that those who took daily omega-3 fish oil pills had the same cardiovascular risk profile as those who didn't. Second, perhaps the studies have been run, but the results have been equivocal. Third, maybe these studies have never been run. With the first case, the results are in and omega-3 fish oil pills failed. The second case suggests that the studies weren't good enough to illuminate any differences, while in the third case, omega-3 fish oil pills never had their day in court.

Absence of Evidence is Not Evidence of Absence

These results are markedly different and lead us to take different actions. With the first interpretation, perhaps you should forgo omega-3 fish oil pills because they have been proven to be useless for cardiovascular health. With the second and third interpretations, you may continue taking omega-3 fish oil pills because of inferential data suggestive of a cardiovascular benefit.

The problem is that these "no evidence" statements don't usually explain *which* of the three cases leads to this conclusion. To fully explain this tension, we need to introduce and explain the concept of statistical significance.

Statistical Significance

Statistical significance is a tool that statisticians and scientists use to separate real scientific findings from junk science. It's similar to a secret knock that allows entry to genuine scientific findings and keeps fake ones outside in the cold. As with all screens, if it doesn't work as intended, bad results are embraced and good results are shunned. (Note that statistical significance is explored in more detail in Chapter 8.)

A scientist will consider as true only those empirical results that are "statistically significant." The idea behind statistical significance has merit. In one study, researchers separated newborn babies from their mothers and tested whether the mothers could identify their own babies purely by smell alone. If the mothers' choices had been random, the result would have been 33 percent (i.e., they would have randomly picked one baby from the three presented to them). If the mothers could correctly identify their babies, say, 97 percent of the time, you'd be far more impressed than if they could do it only 37 percent of the time, because 97 is far more different from 33 than 37 is. That sense of awe is a proxy for statistical significance.

How did the mothers actually do? They correctly picked their own babies 61 percent of the time.[20] The difference between the 61-percent and the 33-percent results gives us an idea of whether we are seeing a real phenomenon or something resulting from luck, or random chance.[21]

It will be useful to explore what statistical significance means and how it is generated. Statisticians determine statistical significance through a three-step process.

First, they assume that the mothers can't select their babies by smell. Statisticians aren't against mothers, in general. Statisticians take a contrary attitude and assume that everyone and everything is a useless fraud. They start out by assuming that those mothers can't identify their babies.

Second, they collect data. How often did the mothers guess their babies correctly?

Third, they look at the actual results and compare them to the results they would have gotten had their original assumption been true that the mothers were useless. **Statistical significance is a proxy for how much the actual results were unlikely to occur.** If the mothers correctly guessed their babies with a frequency that was unlikely to happen by chance, then statisticians question their original assumption that the mothers were charlatans.

Statistical significance equals: "I was surprised by the results and perhaps my assumption that the mothers (or drug, educational program, public policy, exercise program, diet, etc.) were worthless was incorrect. There might be something going on here because these results were unlikely due to random chance alone."

That is all it does. Statistical significance gives us an indication that there *might be* something actually happening. After statistical significance tells us that we should reject the hypothesis that the mothers can't select their babies by smell, it doesn't lay out a roadmap for what we should do next.

If omega-3 fish oil pills have been tested in thousands of people, with some receiving an inactive drug, or placebo, and some receiving actual omega-3 fish oil pills, statistics could be used to compare the outcomes of the two groups. Statistical significance is a probability threshold that has been settled on by convention to attribute the results either to luck or to true differences between the therapies. Typically, if the probability that the results from a trial are due to luck is less than five percent, the results are anointed "statistically significant" and are added to the scientific library of "things we know." If the probability that the results are due to luck falls above the five-percent threshold, the results are rejected because, per convention, we can't determine whether they were due to luck or not.

Statisticians have, I think, misled people with statistical significance. There are effectively two results: the numerical results and the chance that the results might be spurious. We shouldn't mix them; they both provide value.

What if you studied subjects who took omega-3 fish oil pills, and the clinical data showed that the rates of all-cause mortality, cardiac death, sudden death, myocardial infarction, and stroke were identical between the patients who took the supplements and those who didn't? Well, then you could say that the fish oil pills did not help. That's what an actual newspaper headline implied when it reported: "Omega-3 Supplements Don't Lower Heart Disease Risk After All."[22] But the reality was surprisingly different from the headline.

In an article published in the *Journal of the American Medical Association* in 2012, a meta-analysis of 68,680 patients showed that patients taking omega-3 fish oil pills had a four-percent lower all-cause mortality rate, a nine-percent lower cardiac death rate, a 13-percent lower sudden death rate, an 11-percent lower myocardial infarction rate, and a five-percent higher rate of stroke.[23] Would you like to lower your heart attack risk by 11 percent? I certainly would.

The aforementioned headline referenced this article to report that fish oil pills didn't lower heart disease risk. But these data show that they did. What gives? If you—with your scientist hat on—say that the results must be statistically significant to the 0.63 percent level—in other words, there must be less than a 0.63 percent ($p \leq 0.0063$) chance that the results were due to luck—as this study did, then the results would fall short. In this case, the study results showed that fish pills helped, but that the strength of the findings was deemed insufficient by the statisticians analyzing the data.

To say that fish oil pills didn't work because statisticians are skeptical of the results is to butcher both the English language and logic. It's like someone saying that the Ferrari 458 Italia isn't any faster than the Toyota Prius because that person is skeptical of automotive marketing materials. Perhaps that person is right to be suspicious of marketing materials, but he shouldn't say what isn't true. He shouldn't say the two cars are equally fast. Instead, he should say that the Ferrari is probably faster, or that we have some evidence it is faster, but that company marketing materials are unreliable. Therefore, we can't draw any concrete conclusions about how much faster the Ferrari is. Don't confuse an assessment of the quality of the data with the data itself.

Statisticians—and, by extension, scientists who use statistics—want us to act as if we are in a court of law and question whether the results have been objectively proven (i.e., they are statistically significant) or disproven (not significant). It isn't that straightforward. There are two main weaknesses of statistical significance—the threshold used to show significance and the sample size (i.e., the number of test subjects)—both of which are arbitrary and directly affect the results. One arbitrary number was selected by statisticians, and the other just happened to be the number of people who participated in the studies. If a higher statistical significance threshold had been selected (just as arbitrary as the other one) or if more patients had been studied, then the results might have passed the test and, instead of saying omega-3 supplements are useless, the headline would have roared, "Omega-3 Supplements Lower Heart Disease Risk."

Sometimes the results are nail-bitingly close to significant.

In one study "…FDA statisticians concluded that there was no statistically significant difference between MT 100 [a controlled release combination of metoclopramide 16 mg and naproxen 500 mg] and naproxen for sustained headache response (p=0.063)."[24] Steely statisticians cannot be swayed: if the p-value is above 0.05, and 0.063 is greater than 0.05, the results are thrown in the trash, as they were with MT 100. AstraZeneca's Bydureon (exenatide) suffered the same fate, with a p-value of 0.061, perhaps due solely to the fact that the trial's 14,500 patients were too disparate.[25]

In 2007, Pharmacyclics' Xcytrin (motexafin gadolinium), being developed for lung cancers that have metastasized to the brain, was rejected by the FDA because the p-value was only 0.12, well above the 0.05 threshold. Never mind that Xcytrin was shown to be well-tolerated and to delay the onset of impairment by months.[26] Xcytrin sits on the shelf, still today, never having been approved by the FDA.

In 2007, in a Phase 3 clinical trial with 888 patients, Allergan's Savella (milnacipran) failed three of the four clinical endpoints for which it was being tested. What were the p-values? They were 0.058, 0.053, 0.048, and 0.067. One of the "failed" p-values was a mere 0.005 higher than one of the "successful" p-values. If it seems pretty arbitrary, that's because it is.

In 2011, AstraZeneca announced that Crestor (rosuvastatin) failed to achieve the primary endpoint of a head-to-head clinical trial against Lipitor (atorvastatin) to prevent the progression of atherosclerosis. The results of the SATURN trial showed that Crestor produced a numerically greater reduction in plaque volume, but the difference was not statistically significant (p=0.17).

In 2007, Takeda's Junovan (mifamurtide), a medicine for a rare pediatric bone cancer, was rejected by the FDA, partly because in its key clinical trial, the p-value was 0.06, just slightly above the 0.05 limit. Rephrasing the results, the clinical results had a six-percent probability of being due to random chance, higher than the allowable five-percent probability. Or, flipping it around, we are 94-percent sure that Junovan's results are real, whereas scientists want us to be 95-percent sure.

In 2017, Merck's Keytruda (pembrolizumab) "failed" a clinical trial in patients with previously treated recurrent or metastatic head and neck squamous cell carcinoma. Here's what failure looks like: Keytruda reduced the risk of death by 19 percent and allowed Keytruda patients to live 1.3 months longer than those on standard therapy. Why is this a failure? The p-value for this trial with 495 patients was 0.0204, above the threshold of 0.0175. In other words, scientists wanted to be 98.15 percent sure the results were not due to random chance, but they were only 97.96 percent. Failure ain't what it used to be.

If you have the patience for one more example: In 2021, Amicus' new treatment for Pompe disease allowed, in a clinical trial, patients to walk farther in six minutes, 20.8 meters versus 7.2 meters. That was wonderful news; however, the p-value was "only" 0.072, higher than the 0.05 target.[27]

Again, the use of statistical significance requires that the odds of being wrong—in other words, the results were due to bad luck—are less than a certain threshold, typically five percent. However, sometimes the threshold used by scientists is ten percent, one percent, 0.63 percent, 0.5 percent, or even 0.1 percent. The five-percent level is the conventional choice, but it's still arbitrary. There is a movement currently afoot to officially shift statistical significance from 0.05 to 0.005.[28] Plainly, there isn't one "statistical significance" cutoff engraved on a stone tablet and handed down from a mountaintop.

> *The cut-off level for statistical significance is usually taken at 0.05, but sometimes at 0.01.* ***These cutoffs are arbitrary and have no specific importance.*** [bold in original]
> **Douglas Altman**, *Practical Statistics for Medical Research*[29]

The Power Problem

It is well known that statistical significance is a function of the sample size, and studies are "powered" ahead of time so that they will deliver a clear result X percent of the time. If a study is powered to the 0.8 level, that means that when there is a real effect, we will detect it (declare the result to be "significant") in 80 percent of tests. If AstraZeneca's SATURN trial, described above, was powered at the 0.8 level, and, consequently, 1,385 patients were enrolled to meet that level of power, there's still a 20-percent chance that a real difference between Crestor and Lipitor would *not* have been detected. Conversely, if more than 1,385 patients had been enrolled in the SATURN trial—say, perhaps 3,000—the results might have been significant, and the headlines would have said, "Crestor better than Lipitor," instead of "Crestor miss vs Lipitor." (Note that trial powering is discussed in more detail in Chapter 8.)

The issue of clinical trial power is important. One study found that only 30 percent of the trials analyzed had included enough subjects to find a meaningful result 90 percent of the time.[30] This is shocking. It means that of 100 hypothetical clinical trials similar to the ones in the study, where there actually is a meaningful difference between the two arms being tested, only 27 of the 100 trials would actually produce results showing a difference.[31] Absence of evidence is not evidence of absence. The drugs (or other interventions) being scrutinized in 73 of the 100 trials would appear as if they had no effect when the problem was the trials themselves—the experiments were underpowered.

If the lack of statistical significance shown in the SATURN trial had been due to the arbitrary reason that not enough patients had been enrolled, and the very level used to test significance had been arbitrarily selected, why do so many people uphold statistical significance as a measure of objective, rational truth? Objective, rational truth can't have two arbitrary quantities as its foundation. The answer is that some look at the world as a scientist/statistician and hold that there must be a black and white threshold to elevate some results into the pantheon of "correct results" and to toss lesser results into the trash. They are so anxious to have that black/ white threshold that they allow arbitrariness—something very unscientific —to sneak in the back door.

The Well-Designed Problem

Statistical significance is meaningful only for "well-designed" trials. If the researchers who designed the trial made some fundamental mistakes—even something as simple as not truly splitting the trial participants into two evenly matched groups or giving one drug an unfair advantage over another drug—achieving statistical significance still wouldn't prove that the results were true. Is it possible that two people might disagree on what "well designed" means? Yes. The results of a 24,000-patient study of NSAID analgesics, released in 2016, showed numerically fewer heart attacks, strokes, and heart attack deaths from Pfizer's Celebrex (celecoxib) than from ibuprofen or naproxen. (Recall that Celebrex is a COX-2 inhibitor, like Vioxx, and many thought Celebrex was just as dangerous as Vioxx, which is what motivated this study.) After the encouraging results were presented, was Celebrex's reputation finally cleared? No. Some researchers said the design of the trial meant that Celebrex had an unfair advantage over the other drugs. The study didn't account for how patients took aspirin, they claimed, which was important because Celebrex doesn't block aspirin's heart-protecting effects, while ibuprofen and naproxen can. Steven E. Nissen, chief of cardiovascular medicine at Cleveland Clinic and principal investigator of the study, disagreed and discounted such complaints, calling them a red herring. Assessing patients on a pain scale, the study found "no clinically meaningful differences in pain relief," he said. That would suggest that doses were sufficient to compare the drugs' adverse effects.[32] Do you see where this is going? Some top experts said that that study was well designed and the results were solid. Other top experts questioned the study's design and, therefore, the results. That debate means that there can be no black and white assessment of the "well designed" label for that study; rather, such assessments are at least partly subjective, leaving us with an "objective" result that is based on two arbitrary values and a subjective assessment.

Decision-Maker Approach

In contrast to scientists, decision makers consider statistical significance as just one additional piece of information, useful but not essential. Consider how I, as a decision maker, made the following decision.

In 2008, I purchased a new vehicle. I had narrowed down my choice to the Toyota FJ Cruiser, the Toyota 4Runner, and the Honda Ridgeline. In decision-making parlance, those were my three decision alternatives. I ended up choosing the FJ Cruiser because I found it to be the best alternative for me. In other words, based on my preferences and the available information, the FJ Cruiser was superior to the 4Runner and the Ridgeline.

Here's a question. What role did statistical significance play in my decision?

Did I rely on statistical significance to "prove" that one vehicle was more fuel-efficient? Did I rely on statistical significance for safety results or acceleration or reliability or off-road ability? No to all of these. To see which vehicle was best in each important attribute, I relied on numerical test results, expert opinions, anecdotes, and personal experience, without any statistical significance whatsoever. It became clear pretty quickly that the FJ Cruiser was best for me. Was I remiss?

Information is costly—costing both time and money—and while a statistician wants to collect enough information to be sure beyond a reasonable doubt, a decision maker wants just enough information to show that one alternative is better than the others. Once an alternative is shown to be better, additional information is just wasted time and money.

Scientists tend to compare alternatives to some ideal and see if they pass or fail objective tests. Decision makers compare alternatives against each other, given the available information, and pick the best one. Why does this matter? The first approach is one reason why today it costs $3.2 billion to develop a new drug. Is it possible that some of the information that the FDA requires for new drug approvals is unnecessary? Having been in the industry for three decades, I can answer: Yes.

Scientists with Guns

Scientists will often end discussions of their results with the refrain, "more research is needed." The *UC Berkeley Wellness Letter* frequently ends an article by saying, "We still advise waiting until more research has been done."[33] According to the *Wellness Letter*, it is often best to delay action until you possess flawless information. People's lives pass by without such information.

Scientists compare decision alternatives to some imagined ideal to see if the item or the method in question will "pass." Decision makers compare actual decision alternatives to each other and pick the one they think is best.

That is not to say that scientists are wrong or that we shouldn't greatly admire science and scientists. Science is an important field with important findings. So, what's the problem? When the government gives one group —here, scientists—the power to force scientific approaches and conclusions on those who would prefer to follow their own approaches and conclusions, bad things happen. That's the problem. I am referring to the regulatory power of the FDA, pushing the scientific viewpoint and overriding the clinical, decision making viewpoint of physicians and other health care professions. The FDA is effectively populated by 'scientists with guns,' and when the FDA wins the medical power struggle, as it has, regular doctors and their patients lose. We all lose.

What else could we do? We could grant decision makers the liberty they need to properly treat their patients and convince scientists to trade their guns for carrots. Instead of restricting choices—"if you want a shot at Drug A, you'll need to participate in our trial"—scientists could offer a menu of enticements to potential clinical trial participants: "We will give you X to help us study Drug A."

Comparing Reality with Fantasy

Those who desire perfect information and perfect solutions are really comparing reality with fantasy.

An FDA advisory committee voted that Gilead's Truvada (tenofovir & emtricitabine) was a safe and effective way to prevent HIV infections in high-risk individuals, and the FDA approved Truvada for this usage. Truvada was thus the first drug to protect healthy people from acquiring HIV infections through sexual activity, in what is called pre-exposure prophylaxis, or PrEP. With PrEP, if one sexual partner has HIV but the other doesn't, the healthy partner can take Truvada every day to avoid becoming infected by the other person.

What is interesting was how many people argued against using Truvada for PrEP because it wasn't a perfect solution.

Some health experts bemoaned the fact that people who took Truvada for PrEP were not using condoms. To them, any alternative, other than the "ideal" one of using condoms, was a step in the wrong direction. But they were comparing reality with fantasy. It is pure fantasy to expect all high-risk people to use condoms all the time. And, as we know, condoms are not perfect. Truvada, while not perfect, was a step in the right direction because, according to the CDC, it could lower the risk of HIV infection by as much as 99 percent. That's huge. An alternative doesn't need to be perfect when it is a step in the right direction. And that's reality.

N of 1 Studies

Football star Brian Piccolo died of testicular cancer that had spread to his lungs. His story was so poignant that the movie *Brian's Song* was made about his life and death. Just a handful of years after Piccolo died, real-life doctor Lawrence Einhorn looked at the chest x-rays of Indianapolis schoolteacher John Cleland, who was suffering from the same cancer as Piccolo. "You didn't have to be a medical expert to know that that person was in trouble," Cleland said, "and that person was me." Upon seeing his x-rays, Cleland's heart started pounding in his chest, beating so furiously he thought he could hear it. Einhorn put it as gently as he could: "John, I'm sorry. There's not much more we can do." Then he paused, lost in his thoughts. After moments of thinking, Einhorn told Cleland there *was* one other thing they could try. But it was far from a sure thing. In fact, discouragingly, the only other patient with such widespread cancer who had tried the new therapy had died.

Einhorn did eventually try this new drug on Cleland, who, miraculously, had a profound response and was alive and cancer-free four decades later.[34] This new therapy would go on to transform testicular cancer from a disease that was often deadly to one that could be cured 96 to 99 percent of the time, provided the cancer had not spread too far. Did Einhorn use the new platinum-based drug on Cleland because he had run full clinical trials on thousands of patients and was 95-percent sure that it was safe and effective in patients just like Cleland? No. Cleland was going to die, and Einhorn thought that it was his best, and only, chance. Einhorn was acting as a decision maker, not as a scientist.

During a strategic planning meeting years ago, a person working at an early-stage company with which I was consulting, optimistically—and incorrectly, I must add—exclaimed that his company had already developed a drug. Really? A drug? This company didn't have any drugs. How had he arrived at this startling conclusion? He explained, as the rest of us listened skeptically: one of the employees had dipped his hands into a broth in the laboratory and, later, this person's warts disappeared. There you go! The warts were gone! We've got a drug!

As a "patient" who wanted to cure his warts, the employee found a treatment that worked for him. As scientists, we cringe because this "trial" did not include the things that we normally consider scientific: a known and controlled chemical, double-blindedness, randomization, placebo controls, and large numbers of varied patients. If this pharma company persisted and conducted large-scale clinical trials, then we, as scientists, might be able to conclusively say whether or not the drug worked. But the employee who had dipped his hands in the solution would have *less* information than before: before, he knew that the broth cured his warts; now, with an official drug, he would instead have some data concerning numerous strangers who may or may not be like him. Will he be like the strangers? Or, more precisely, which strangers will he be like, if any? If the new drug from this company helps 70 percent of people clear their warts, will he be like the 30 percent or the 70 percent? And there's the rub. He can't know conclusively without trying the new drug himself because the approved drug might be different than the broth. Even with these gold standard clinical trial results, *no one can know if a drug will work for himself without actually trying it.*

The proof of the pudding is in the eating. Michael Steinman, from the University of California, San Francisco, points out that drug regimens need to be tailored to individual patients. According to Steinman, "We don't know in advance if a patient is going to have side effects, and some drugs are more effective on certain patients than others."[35] We can't look at the chemical structure of a drug and determine who it will help; we must rely on trial and error.

Pfizer's Lipitor (atorvastatin), used for lowering cholesterol levels, had been studied in 400 clinical trials and used for 145 million patient-years of therapy before one particular woman in her 40s starting taking it. You'd think that everything to know about Lipitor was already known. However, when she started taking Lipitor, she was unable to concentrate or recall words. Although tests found nothing amiss, when she stopped taking Lipitor, her symptoms disappeared. When she resumed taking the statin, they returned.[36] Of course, she permanently stopped taking Lipitor to avoid these adverse effects. What had happened to her? We don't know. We just don't know. She had an unusual response to a very common drug, and that's all we know.

Modern clinical trials are designed to meet the needs of scientists; regular patients must still gain personal experience trying a drug to know if it, and how it, works for them. The FDA gets in the way of patients and clinicians. It is not the FDA's scientific/statistical perspective, per se, that is the problem; rather, it is the FDA's coercive powers that directly restrict and inhibit the decision-maker perspective. Scientists with guns trammel medical doctors.

Speaking of guns, the FDA sometimes likens drugs to guns.

The FDA's Weapon Analogy

In addition to the Russian roulette analogy (mentioned in Chapter 2), that some use to explain the FDA's actions, rationale, and raison d'être, the medicines-as-weapons analogy is powerful and has been in use for years. Robert A. Weinstein, Chairman of the Division of Infectious Diseases at Stroger Hospital of Cook County in Chicago, had this to say about the 2003 FDA approval of drug company Cubist's antibiotic Cubicin:

> The approval of CUBICIN is particularly important as we face the growing public health crisis of bacterial resistance. There has been a frightening increase in MRSA infections over the past decade, and the tools currently available to combat this problem have become less effective. The approval of CUBICIN gives physicians a new weapon against cSSS infections, particularly to treat the estimated 600,000 U.S. patients who contract MRSA cSSS infections each year.[37]

He used the term: new weapon. It should be no surprise that people would equate powerful drugs with weapons, given their muscle and their intended uses. But the analogy goes even deeper. Here's where the rationale for the FDA comes into play: How do we know which weapons are safe and which ones aren't?

> *We don't want to put a weapon into the hands of a soldier until it has been tested, and tested under stress.*
> **Dr. Steven Hirschfeld**, FDA employee

While this FDA employee's sentiment is appealing and sounds reasonable, it assumes that having no weapon is better than having a potentially defective weapon. Could that be true? Yes, it could be, but it depends on the situation. Consider Cristy Kessler, a University of Hawaii associate professor who was suffering from three rare autoimmune diseases and was "preparing to die." She went to Turkey to get an unapproved stem cell transplant. Why did she need to go there to get this therapy? Why didn't she stay in Hawaii? Because the FDA wouldn't let her have a stem cell transplant in the United States.

We can think of her Turkish stem cell transplantation as a weapon, one that was largely untested for safety and efficacy. We can also think of her as being in the middle of a pitched military battle. How so? She was already in mortal danger from the three rare autoimmune diseases she was fighting—she was prepared to die. What was the value to her of getting off of that figurative battlefield alive? It was incredibly high.

She had three mortal enemies trying to kill her and was already facing certain death. Her only weapon was an untested one. Does the FDA really want to withhold untested weapons from patients such as Kessler, leaving them unarmed in battle?

Here is a table showing her four possible outcomes:

Table 1: Cristy Kessler' Dire Situation

Kessler's Situation	Use Weapon	Don't Use Weapon
Weapon Works	Good Health	Death
Weapon Doesn't Work	Death	Death

There's only one way to get to "Good Health"

As we can see, her only chance at health was to use that untested weapon and hope that it worked. Fortunately, not all of us face such daunting health challenges. But those of us who do, need better weapons. If we don't get better weapons, and soon, we'll be left with our old, bad weapons or with no weapons at all.

College student Sharon Belvin developed a deadly case of Stage IV metastatic melanoma. After debilitating treatments of chemotherapy and radiation, her hope and her health faded. That's when her oncologist inquired about a clinical trial for a new type of immunotherapy named ipilimumab. "Would you like to try it?" the doctor asked. Belvin jumped at the chance. "The choice was to do nothing and die, or take a chance. It was the easiest decision I ever had to make."[38]

With this treatment, Belvin's tumors vanished and, one year after treatment, she was considered in remission. Later, when she was introduced to the man who had discovered ipilimumab, immunologist James Allison, she burst into tears and hugged him so hard she nearly knocked off his glasses. Allison still chokes up when he recalls the moment.

War on Disease

The number of lethal threats we face is ominous. Occasionally, health risks hit the front page, as we've seen with the COVID-19 coronavirus outbreak in 2020/2021. But most of the time, these threats work in obscurity. Consider one single disease, lung cancer, that kills more Americans *each year* than the combined U.S. casualties from battle in the Revolutionary War, the War of 1812, the Mexican War, the Spanish-American War, World War I, the Korean War, the Vietnam War, and the Persian Gulf War.

Lung cancer is just one type of cancer, and cancer is just one of the threats we face. There are also heart disease, stroke, infectious diseases, pneumonia, diabetes, dementia, depression, Alzheimer's, and influenza, among others. The influenza epidemic of 1918 killed roughly as many Americans—548,000—as the battles of all American wars combined, including both sides in the Civil War.[39] The biggest killer is heart disease, which kills more Americans *each year* than the combined U.S. combat casualties from *all* American wars.[40] In total, these diseases kill about 2.4 million Americans a year. Compared to the average U.S. military monthly death rate during World War II, those 2.4 million deaths are the equivalent of fighting 30 World War II's simultaneously![41]

Imagine if we looked at fighting disease as we looked at fighting World War II, and the newspapers published daily body counts: "Another 6,500

Americans died today in the War on Disease." There could be the Cancer Front, the Heart Front, the Infection Front, and the Diabetes Front. With such a perspective—we got a taste of it with COVID-19—perhaps people would be more attentive to—and become more vocal about—the fight against disease and would be less critical of medicines that aren't perfect.

Disease is the Real Enemy

> *The last enemy that shall be destroyed is death.*
> **The Bible**

War is hell. Disease can be worse.

During the horrifically bloody American Civil War, ten percent of soldiers died from disease, while only six percent died from battle. While not as romantic, disease was the bigger enemy.[42]

We are "fighting" the equivalent of 30 WWII's simultaneously, and the FDA's primary concern is the safety of the weapons we use. Is it prudent for the FDA to be so cautious when four Americans—family, friends, and neighbors—are dying each minute? Remember that we are far more likely to be killed by diseases than we are by dangerous drugs (aka "defective weapons").

Decision makers face critical deadlines. A doctor treating a patient with a bad infection can't tell that patent to come back in ten years when more is known about treatments. That doctor must do something, *now*.

When I first read the following quote, I froze; I've never forgotten this quote and it still haunts me: "If you stay alive for a year-and-a-half, we'll have a drug to really help you." The speaker was Tal Pomeroy, a physician, advising one of his pancreatic cancer patients. When Pomeroy made this chilling pronouncement, the average lifespan of pancreatic cancer patients was a depressingly short 11 months.

Why couldn't Pomeroy give his patient the good drug right then, when both physician and patient could see the promise? The FDA wouldn't allow it. The FDA was essentially saying, "tough." Instead of having a "weapon" that may or may not work, this patient had to go into battle with no weapon at all. Can you imagine President Roosevelt sending American troops into battle in 1944 against German, Italian, and Japanese soldiers without rifles, ammunition, tanks, artillery, or aircraft? If he had, how would history have remembered him? The FDA is effectively sending 330 million Americans into war without adequate weapons. How will history remember the FDA?

Better Safe Than Sorry?

The FDA is nothing if not cautious. Those who favor caution often invoke the precautionary principle to justify their position.

Precautionary Principle

> When an activity raises threats of harm to human health or the environment, precautionary measures should be taken even if some cause and effect relationships are not fully established scientifically.
>
> In this context the proponent of an activity, rather than the public, should bear the burden of proof.[43]

While appealing, the precautionary principle's flaw is that it is asymmetrical. If the fact that I develop a new drug may put people at risk —think of the birth defects from thalidomide—the fact that I *don't* develop that new drug could also put people at risk—think of vaccines for COVID-19. Risk is symmetrical. My action to do something might cause some harm, but my lack of action might also cause some harm. We can't decide which path to take until we have an assessment of the two risks: the risk of developing a COVID-19 vaccine versus the risk of not developing it.

In the situations in which patients are dying or suffering serious morbidity, being overly cautious will lead to even more morbidity and mortality. This is frequently the position the FDA finds itself in. As economist Sam Peltzman said, "…those who will suffer death and disease while a potential drug therapy is evaluated will suffer no less than the victims of a drug disaster, but their number is likely to be much larger than the number of victims of the disaster."[44]

> *The chief danger in life is that you may take too many precautions.*
> **Alfred Adler**, Austrian medical doctor and founder of "Individual Psychology"

We don't have a choice between "safe and effective" drugs and "unsafe and ineffective" drugs. That simplistic choice is unrealistic. Instead, we have a choice between spending more time and money to reduce risk or spending less and accepting greater risk. If we choose to try to reduce risk, we delay potentially life-saving new drugs. That's our only choice. There's a cost and a benefit to reducing risk.

In April 2021, the FDA and CDC "paused" administration of the J&J COVID-19 vaccine because of reports about cerebral venous sinus thrombosis (CVST), or blood clots in the brains of the people who had been vaccinated. This is how the FDA is supposed to work. If there's a potential problem, the FDA should warn us. However, this ended up being an example of how the FDA is *not* supposed to work.

The blood clots occurred in 15 people out of 8 million vaccinated. That's a very low incidence, and might be acceptable even if we knew the clots were caused by the vaccine. But we didn't. CVST occurs naturally in the population and the incidence is estimated to be between 3 and 15.7 per million per year.[45] Given that the vaccine had been available for about eight weeks, we would have expected between 3.7 and 19.3 blood clots in a group of this size.[46] Fifteen is in the middle of that range. In other words, we have little reason to suspect that the vaccine added to or increased the natural incidence rate. But it gets worse. By stopping vaccinations with the J&J shot, the FDA and CDC left millions of Americans at risk for getting COVID-19, which has a risk of CVST one hundred times the natural rate.[47] If there were 10 million Americans who didn't get vaccinated for two months because of the pause and five percent of them caught SARS-CoV-2 during that period, those people might have experienced 150 to 800 cases of CVST.[48] Those number make 15 look pretty insignificant. The FDA's conservatism almost certainly led to *more* occurrences of serious brain blood clots, along with other health problems, including, of course, death. Further, this pause led to more "vaccine hesitancy."

The CDC estimates that 580 to 1,400 American lives will be saved in the next six months by the J&J vaccine.[49] If lives will be *saved* by ending the pause, then lives were *lost* by prosecuting the pause.

When we leave our medical options up to the scientific experts at a government agency, the first thing we get is a bias towards conservatism and risk-aversion. The FDA is acutely aware that of the two ways it can fail, approving a bad drug is significantly worse—*for it*—than failing to approve a good drug. Approving a bad drug may kill or otherwise harm patients, and an investigation of the approval process will lead to finger pointing, causing big problems for the agency and individuals' careers. As former FDA employee Henry Miller put it, "This kind of mistake is highly visible and has immediate consequences—the media pounces, the public denounces, and Congress pronounces."[50] FDA brass are well aware of this dynamic. In 1974, FDA Commissioner Alexander Schmidt explained, "In all our history, we are unable to find one instance where a Congressional hearing investigated the failure of FDA to approve a new drug."[51]

The outcome of approving a bad drug is highly emotional and concrete—pictures, such as those of thalidomide babies, and personal testimonies of suffering are media-friendly—while not approving a good drug is intellectual and abstract. Who would have benefited and by how much? Who will know enough to complain that they were victimized by being denied such a medicine? Such types of protests are difficult to actualize, although AIDS activists have done a decent job of making such an invisible cost visible.

Imagine if Americans had waited for a government agency to "approve" heavier-than-air flight. We might still be waiting. Recall that less than ten years before the Wright brothers' historic flight, scientific experts of such stature as Thomas Edison and the prominent physicist Lord Kelvin flatly stated that such flight was impossible. The U.S. Patent office even rejected the Wright brothers' patent application for a flying machine because it was "incapable of performing its intended function." Left to government risk aversion, we might still be earthbound.

The FDA can only slow the adoption of modern drugs and the resulting increase in life expectancy. It can apply the brakes firmly or less firmly, but it doesn't even own a gas pedal. And while the FDA is applying the brakes, Americans are literally dying for better medicines.

Scientists and Bureaucrats

The distinction made in this chapter—comparing the perspectives of scientists and decision makers, typically clinicians—is unfair to scientists by lumping them together with the FDA. The FDA functions more as a bureaucrat than a scientist. A scientist seeks knowledge and performs experiments and analyses to uncover truths. A bureaucrat checks off boxes. What does the FDA really do? The FDA sets up structures and procedures and then recognizes only those "sponsors" (typically drug companies) that successfully check off the right boxes in the right order.

Consider the important question of which drugs can be used to successfully treat patients suffering from a serious condition known as status epilepticus (SE), in which a person's seizures will not stop. A scientist surveys the field and determines which drugs have proven benefit. The FDA—a bureaucrat—waits for sponsors to check off boxes, which is why, if a sponsor decides not to jump through the hoops, the most successful drug for SE—Keppra (levetiracetam)—never receives FDA approval for that indication and never shows up on an FDA list.[52]

A scientist, seeking knowledge, would consider her approach flawed if her list didn't include Keppra for SE. A bureaucrat, seeking process, would consider her approach sound with the same outcome.

Wrap-up

It's not easy being the FDA, trying to ensure the safety and efficacy of over six thousand medicines and the safety of countless foods for 330 million Americans. Using some straightforward examples, we've seen the problems inherent in the FDA's approach of providing a one-size-fits-all solution for such a large population of unique individuals.

The types of rules the FDA imposes on pharmaceutical companies, which are often able to withstand billion-dollar and multi-year burdens, are generally too costly for food companies, effectively squashing innovation in certain types of food additives.

Those who implicitly or explicitly justify the FDA's powers may be making a conceptual mistake, which is that a body of scientists can look at objective—albeit incomplete—evidence and clearly and unambiguously determine whether a new drug is safe and effective. They can't. Metrics such as statistical significance have substantial limitations, and clinical trial results that show a drug successfully navigating its hurdles may be concealing fundamental problems. At the same time, clinical trials that showed a drug failing its tests might be due to structural problems in the trials themselves, rather than to the drug in question.

The FDA deals almost exclusively with situations that are gray—with experts on both sides of the argument, some saying that a new drug is good and others saying that it isn't. The FDA's involvement in such cases is counter to the basic argument that the benefit of the FDA comes from having an expert on our side, poring over the data, deciding what's true or not and what's best. There are already experts on *both sides* of the argument.

The FDA has been trying to eliminate bias in its advisory committees. However, the particular bias that the FDA is addressing has been shown to be benign, and the most pernicious biases are never addressed; some of them come directly from the FDA's method for selecting outside experts. FDA, heal thyself.

A reliance on experts doesn't remove the need for judgment and vigilance. Which experts should we trust? What if the experts disagree? In which topics does their expertise lie?

The FDA, with its scientist hat on, seeks everlasting knowledge. Your personal doctor wants a therapy that helps you and does so now, or at least very soon. It doesn't matter if the prior sixteen patients got better on a certain medicine if you don't. The benefit that others derive from a certain medicine can help *suggest* whether or not you should use it, but, ultimately, nothing matters except whether you benefit.

Because these two perspectives are so different, we shouldn't be surprised that the two groups make decisions using different approaches, and the FDA's approach might offer little value to your doctor and, ultimately, to you.

The fundamental problem, however, is not that scientists or decision makers are somehow "right" or "wrong." Both perspectives have merit. The fundamental problem occurs when one group has veto power, through coercive force, over the other, and the key actors involved are prevented from pursuing the path that's best for their situation. We would be outraged if scientists were prevented from performing science. We should be just as outranged when the FDA hampers the ability of decision makers to make unfettered decisions.

---

1 Joanna Slater, "To Make Lemons Into Lemonade, Try 'Miracle Fruit'," *The Wall Street Journal*, 30 March 2007.

2 Lydia Mulvany and Deena Shanker, "Meatless Impossible Burger is a hit at restaurants, but you can't buy it at supermarkets until it clears FDA hurdle," *Chicago Tribune*, 26 December 2018.

3 Originally published as David R. Henderson and Charles L. Hooper, "Swing Vote at the FDA," *Medical Progress Today*, 29 August 2008.

4 Alicia Mundy, "A Wolfe in Regulator's Clothing: Drug Industry Critic Joins the FDA," *The Wall Street Journal*, 9 January 2009.

5 Peter Lurie, MD, MPH; Cristina M. Almeida, MD, MPH; Nicholas Stine, BA; et al, "Financial Conflict of Interest Disclosure and Voting Patterns at Food and Drug Administration Drug Advisory Committee Meetings," *JAMA*. 2006;295(16):1921-1928. doi:10.1001/jama.295.16.1921

6 Reasonable assumptions and simple math can show how small the financial incentive can be: these advisors typically own a very small proportion of a particular company's shares, if any at all; the company's success or failure is often based on a portfolio of products; and the probability that the advisor's actions will swing an FDA vote are small, given the number of advisors.

7 Steven Walker, "Drug Czars," *The Wall Street Journal*, 4 May 2007.

8 Amirah Al Idrus, "What could an aducanumab approval mean for future Alzheimer's R&D?," *Fierce Biotech*, 6 November 2020.

9 Decision scientists have identified 175 different biases.

10 Steve Usdin, "FDA's Woodcock reflects on aducanumab, drug approval standards, the future of clinical trials," *BioCentury*, 16 June 2021.

11 "FDA Commissioner announces Avastin decision," FDA News Release, 18 November 2011, http://www.fda.gov/NewsEvents/Newsroom/PressAnnouncements/ucm280536.htm.

12 "FDA Issues Emergency Use Authorization for Convalescent Plasma as Potential Promising COVID–19 Treatment, Another Achievement in Administration's Fight Against Pandemic," FDA Press Release, 23 August 2020

13 Eric Sagonowsky, "Rebuking FDA, NIH experts say 'no data' support plasma as a COVID-19 treatment," *Fierce Pharma*, 2 September 2020.

[14] Technically, science is the process of exposing and rejecting untruths.

[15] Can Stem Cells Save Dying Hearts?, by Cynthia Fox, *Discover Magazine*, September 2005, pg 58-61.

[16] Philipson and Posner, *Private Choices and Public Health, The AIDS Epidemic in an Economic Perspective*, Harvard University Press, 1993.

[17] Craven, Lawrence L. "Acetylsalicylic Acid, Possible Preventive of Coronary Thrombosis." *Annals of Western Medicine* 1950; 4:95-99.

[18] "Broader Use For Aspirin Fails To Win Backing," *The Wall Street Journal*, 9-Dec-03, pg D9.

[19] "Aspirin: Not to be taken lightly," *Consumer Reports On Health*, February 2004, Vol 16, No. 2, pg 3.

[20] Marta Zaraska, "Scents & Sensibility," *Discover Magazine*, November 2017.

[21] More accurately, here's what statistical significance means: "If there were actually no effect (if the true difference between means were zero) then the probability of observing a value for the difference equal to, or greater than, that actually observed would be p=0.05. In other words there is a 5% chance of seeing a difference at least as big as we have done, by chance alone." David Colquhoun, "An investigation of the false discovery rate and the misinterpretation of p-values," Royal Society Open Science, 19 November 2014.

[22] Alice Park, "Omega-3 Supplements Don't Lower Heart Disease Risk After All," *Time*, 12 September 2012.

[23] Evangelos C. Rizos, et al, "Association Between Omega-3 Fatty Acid Supplementation and Risk of Major Cardiovascular Disease Events," *JAMA.* 2012;308(10):1024-1033, http://jamanetwork.com/journals/jama/article-abstract/1357266

[24] "Tough on migraine," *BioCentury*, vol. 13, no. 25, 8 August 2005.

[25] Carly Helfand, "Why did AstraZeneca's Bydureon fail to cut CV risks? A broad paient group, perhaps." *FiercePharma*, 14 September 2017.

[26] Richard Miller, "Drug Disaster," *The Wall Street Journal, 10 May 2007.*

[27] Paul Bonanos, "Short of reaching high bar, Amicus' Pompe treatment still headed for FDA review," *BioCentury*, 12 February 2021.

[28] See “Redefine statistical significance,” *Nature Human Behavior*, Vol. 2, January 2018, 6-10.

[29] Douglas Altman, *Practical Statistics for Medical Research*, Chapman & Hall/CRC, 1991, p. 168

[30] Douglas G. Altman and J. Martin Bland, “Absence of evidence is not evidence of absence,” Statistical Notes, *BMJ*, Vol. 311, 19 August 1995.

[31] 27 equals 0.3 times 0.9 times 100.

[32] Ron Winslow, “Study Suggests Celebrex Isn’t Riskier Than Rival Pain Drugs,” *The Wall Street Journal*, 14 November 2016.

[33] “The Latest on ALA,” *The UC Berkeley Wellness Letter*, Vol 19, Issue 11, August 2003, pg 2.

[34] *It’s Not About the Bike*, Lance Armstrong and Sally Jenkins, 2000, Berkley Books, New York, pg 83.

[35] Laura Landro, “Medication Overload,” *The Wall Street Journal*, 11 October 2016.

[36] Melinda Beck, “Can a Drug That Helps Hearts Be Harmful to the Brain?,” *The Wall Street Journal*, 12 February 2008.

[37] Cubist press release, 12 September 2003.

[38] Kenneth Miller, “Checkmate,” *Discover Magazine*, November 2016.

[39] A soldier must have been killed in battle to be counted as a battle death. There have been 650,604 Americans who have been killed in battle from the Revolutionary War through the Persian Gulf War. This includes battle deaths on both sides of the Civil War.

[40] Battle deaths total 650,604, while other deaths (e.g., accident, infection, disease) total 489,585, for a total of 1,140,189.

[41] The average number of Americans killed in action each month during the 44 months of World War II was 6,639. That’s equal to 79,668 per year. The number of Americans dying each year is 2.4 million, or 30 times the 79,668.

[42] Gary W. Gallagher, Teaching Company, The American Civil War lectures, lecture 27F

[43] Wingspread Statement

[44] Sam Peltzman, *Regulation of Pharmaceutical Innovation*, University of Chicago, 1974, p. 88.

[45] Sharon Devasagayam et al., "Cerebral Venous Sinus Thrombosis Incidence Is Higher Than Previously Thought," *Stroke*, 19 July 2016. Aristotelis Filippidis et al., "Cerebral venous sinus thrombosis: review of the demographics, pathophysiology, current diagnosis, and treatment," *Neurosurg Focus*, November 2009.

[46] 8 million times 3 per million divided by 52 weeks times 8 weeks = 3.69. 8 million times 15.7 per million divided by 52 weeks times 8 weeks = 19.3.

[47] Based on a preprint of an unpublished non-peer reviewed study looking at incidence of Cerebral Venous Thrombosis (CVT) after COVID-19, compared to incidence after receiving an mRNA COVID-19 vaccine (Pfizer or Moderna), or following influenza infection.

[48] Roughly 43% of the U.S. population was infected within the first 14 months of the pandemic. That's 3% per month or 6% for two months. For our purposes, the value of 5% was used.

[49] Aria Bendix, "Continuing to use Johnson & Johnson's vaccine could save 1,400 lives in the next 6 months, the CDC says," *Business Insider*, 27 April 2021.

[50] *To America's Health. A Proposal to Reform the Food and Drug Administration*, Henry I. Miller, M.D., Hoover Institution Press, 2000, p. 42.

[51] Arthur Daemmrich, "Invisible Monuments and the Costs of Pharmaceutical Regulation: Twenty-Five Years of Drug Lag Debate," *Pharmacy in History*, Vol. 45 (2003) No. 1

[52] Keppra is used second line, after benzodiazepines have failed.

Chapter 8: Structural Problems with Drug Regulation

The FDA's approach leads to a number of challenges and odd results. Did Congress think through these issues before it gave the FDA enormous quantities of money and immense power?

Proving a Negative

The FDA and the drug companies it regulates have a fundamental problem: in terms of safety, they are being asked to prove a negative. They are asked to prove that new drugs *will not* have problems with widespread usage. But as those who have studied logic know, proving a negative is impossible. We could test a drug on one billion people and not see any problems, but then it could kill person number one billion and one.

As mentioned in Chapter 7, Lipitor had been studied in 400 clinical trials and used for 145 million patient-years of therapy before one woman found that it gave her some unusual symptoms. She stopped taking it and the symptoms went away.

A drug that has been proven safe in N people might not bc safe for the N-plus-first person who takes it, which is why "safe" drugs can be, at most, just "apparently safe enough" according to our limited information.

Lengthy Clinical Trials

> Scientist in a lab holding a flask and talking to a colleague: *"I finally did it; I discovered a drug that will confer immortality. The trouble is, it will take forever to test it."*

In 2016, to allay fears about testosterone replacement therapies for men, the federal government ran a $50 million, multi-center "Testosterone Trial" among 790 men aged 65 and older. The trial showed that patients who used AbbVie's AndroGel product had improved libido, though the results for energy levels and walking ability were not statistically significant. Some critics were unimpressed, and they pointed out that the long-term risks associated with low-T therapy aren't known. But how long is long enough? If the trial lasted one year, someone could ask about the results at year two. If the trial lasted two years, that person could ask about the results at year three, etc. There is no trial long enough to dissuade someone from asking about the results at year N+1.

This is a bigger problem than it may seem.

Imagine that you are developing a new drug that will allow people to live 20 years longer. How would you ever convince the FDA that your drug is safe and effective? If the FDA accepted biomarkers (such as HbA1c, for example, a blood-based protein), used as surrogates for observable clinical endpoints, you could run a shorter trial. But the FDA doesn't often accept biomarkers and, in this example, there might not be any good ones available; therefore, you would need to run a 100-year clinical trial to capture the hoped-for 20-year-improvement over the status quo of people living to be 70 or 80. Can you imagine lining up money from investors with a small probability of a return after 100 years? Think of the difficulties of tracking those patients and paying for their care during the clinical trial over those 100 years. If any patients dropped out of your tracking system during this clinical trial, they would be lost to you and you couldn't use all of their data. Plus, you would discover the painful truth that your patents would expire long before your patients. Moreover, the political and regulatory regime could change substantially in the interim, and you might never receive approval. It is from these more extreme examples that we learn the limitations of the FDA's current approach.

You might reply that this is an extreme case. Yes. It is. But what if you need a 50-year clinical trial or even a ten-year trial to show results?

Consider type 2 diabetes. The real problems with diabetes— blindness, heart attacks, strokes, and amputations—don't show up for decades. To fully study drugs for type 2 diabetes would require clinical trials that are as long as, or longer than, the patent life on the drugs being studied. Congratulations! Your drug has been found to treat diabetes; however, we're sorry: your patent expired last year. The FDA always grants a minimum period of marketing exclusivity upon approval, but that period might not be long enough to recoup your investment. You, your investors, and your customers are out of luck.

The current system is not set up to handle cases that require lengthy clinical trials. This explains one reason that oncology has been a hot field for pharmaceutical development: if patients typically die in 15 months, a relatively short clinical trial will show that a therapy provides a few extra months, which is often all that a cancer drug needs for approval.

According to the Epilepsy Foundation, clinical trials of new drugs for epilepsy have their own challenges:

> An ongoing difficulty with conducting clinical studies of seizure patterns is the limitation inherent in the methods of data collection. Information obtained from patient reports in diaries may at times be inaccurate, particularly under reported, as patients may not be aware of all seizures or may be amnestic of their occurrence. Data from continuous EEG monitoring are more accurate, but such monitoring is not performed for prolonged periods, and is often performed in the setting of abrupt medication discontinuation, which may obscure natural patterns.[1]

How realistic and reproducible then, are such epilepsy clinical trials and the results they produce? How much can we rely on the data that the FDA requires?

The pharmaceutical industry has a ready solution for this: companies actively avoid developing drugs for diseases for which the clinical trials are too long or too difficult. "Why swim upstream?" they reason. We all lose due to this behavior because, while companies can pick which diseases to *address*, patients cannot choose which diseases to *acquire*. All biopharma companies look at the diseases they want to address and seriously question whether, even if they have a good drug candidate, they can conduct clinical trials that will convince the FDA to green light their new drug. "Can we run clinical trials and get convincing data?" they ask. For many diseases, the answer is a resounding "no." Though this bothers the drug companies for a bit, they don't pout; they simply move onto the next disease target. Patients don't have this luxury; they don't get to choose what afflictions they suffer from. Patients can't vote with their feet. Light on their feet, like deer, biopharma companies shift to diseases with better characteristics; patients stay fixed in place, as trees rooted deeply into the ground, and diseases pick them. And, if after a couple of decades, there are no new therapies for a given disease, the patients afflicted with that disease usually don't know why. There are no front-page news stories reporting that there would have been breakthroughs in a certain disease, but the drug companies didn't think they could generate convincing data for the FDA. Suffering patients don't know that the FDA has made it very difficult to research and develop new drugs for "their" diseases. It is a rare patient who even notices that no new therapies have been developed for a while. There's no blaring headline, no obvious story, and no obvious person to blame.

Picking the Winning Indication

Consider for a moment how the FDA requires biopharma companies to submit new drug applications that clearly spell out the one particular condition to be treated (or "indication"). While these drug companies may eventually receive approval for these specific indications, there may be other, perhaps better, indications that will be discovered only after the drugs are on the market and doctors have had some time to experiment.

What if that biopharma company picked the wrong initial indication, didn't design the clinical trials well, or just got unlucky with a few initial patients who died? Then, that drug might have failed its early trials and suffered FDA rejection, never allowing it to survive long enough to be approved for other, more important, indications. Or, what if that drug had been approved, but endured lackluster results for the first indication? It might not survive long enough to be tested for a second indication. It is worthwhile pondering all the amazing drugs that were never developed or were later rejected by the FDA *simply because the results for the first indication selected by the drug company were lackluster*. These drugs never had the chance to enjoy enough success to give people a reason to subsequently discover even better usages. It would be difficult to compile the list of these drugs, but it is undoubtedly long.

To grasp the magnitude of this problem, consider the difficulty with matching eight young potential athletes with their most appropriate sport.

Before the FDA's 1962 powers—when only safety was required—our athlete-matching exercise may have looked like this:

1. Arthur Unathletic, Bradley Bookish, Alice Unathletic, and Suggs Slug were each tested for a number of sports and failed them all. They were rejected.
2. LeBron James was tested for tennis, swimming, and basketball, and he succeeded wildly in basketball, earning the nickname King James.
3. Lionel Messi was tested for soccer, golf, and swimming. He ended up being a soccer superstar on the Argentinian men's national team.
4. Michael Phelps was tested for basketball, soccer, golf, and swimming. He went on to win 28 Olympic medals in swimming, most of which were gold.
5. Serena Williams was tested for golf, swimming, and tennis. Her tennis skills were obvious, and she went on to win 23 singles tennis titles.

With this approach, we tested eight athletes and found that four had superb athletic skills in at least one sport. The other four athletes were tested and found lacking. Our success rate was 50 percent.

After the FDA's 1962 powers—the two-hurdle approach of safety plus efficacy—our athlete matching exercise might have looked like this:

1. Arthur Unathletic, Bradley Bookish, Alice Unathletic, and Suggs Slug were tested in one sport each—bicycle racing, tennis, golf, and swimming—and were found lacking. Their sponsors, out of resources, stopped further testing.
2. LeBron James was tested for swimming and he failed. His sponsor thought that he could be good at something but was forced to cease all development because of limited resources.
3. Lionel Messi was tested for soccer and succeeded. He became a soccer superstar.
4. Michael Phelps' basketball skills were tested but they didn't impress anyone. He was put into a—ahem—large pool of athletes that had been tested but had failed.
5. Serena Williams was tested for tennis, passed the test, and ended up winning 23 singles titles.

The requirement that athletes be tested for particular sports—often one-and-done due to the costs involved and always-limited sponsor resources— reduced our success rate from 50 percent to 25 percent. Consider the potential benefits to sports fans everywhere if, instead of two successful athletes, we could have four. Can you imagine a world without LeBron James on the basketball court and Michael Phelps in the swimming pool?

The same factors are at play with medicines. If, instead of one-and-done, new drugs with proven safety, but unproven efficacy, could be legally marketed, thousands of doctors could experiment with them, dramatically increasing the probability that those potentially better uses could be found quickly and cheaply, or at least found at all. What might doctors find? For some examples, just review Chapter 3's section on off-label usage.

It is interesting that in the 1950s and 1960s it was common for drug candidates to be provided to physicians who offered the new drugs to a range of patients and carefully observed the clinical results.[2] While there can be problems that arise from this approach, there are also potential benefits.

The current one-and-done approach, with the result that countless good drugs have been consigned to dustbins around the world, might be the single largest cost of the FDA. Without the FDA's influence on this one key dynamic, perhaps we would have twice as many safe and efficacious drugs on the market today. Indeed, if the findings of Sam Peltzman's study reflect this dynamic, since 1963, we could have had 2.6 times as many new drugs as we've actually had.[3]

Some Difficult Truths

Earlier, we exposed the soft underbelly of statistical significance. Here, we explore other troubling consequences of using statistical significance to uncover scientific truths.

More On Statistical Significance

Below, we'll discuss one of the most fundamental weaknesses of using statistical significance—that most study results are actually wrong. But first, here are three reasons that statistical significance is less important than commonly believed.

First, even if a drug is shown in clinical trials to be statistically significantly better than another drug or a placebo, that result applies only to those patients treated by those doctors and nurses at those facilities at that point in time. If any of these variables change, the results might not hold. For instance, if the results come from testing healthier students in the New England area, will sicker patients in the South benefit from the drug? We don't necessarily know.

Second, patients in clinical trials tend to differ from the rest of us. They tend to be younger, better educated, more motivated, and wealthier than other people. Patients in clinical trials are also often altruistic, being motivated by the thought that they are helping future generations.

Finally, some statistically significant results, while statistically significant, aren't "significant" in a real sense—that is, clinically meaningful. If a study shows that blood pressure was reduced by half a percent, on average, will anyone even notice such a small difference? If patients on drug XYZ lived 52 minutes longer, on average, is that truly significant? Statistical significance does not necessarily translate into clinical significance.

Most Study Results are Wrong

The level of statistical significance is usually expressed in terms of a p-value, which indicates the probability that a clinical result might have been due to chance alone. Usually, a p-value less than 0.05 is considered statistically significant. While a bedrock of scientific studies, p-values are more problematic than typically understood.

> *In most circumstances, actually using statistical significance with p-values is not the best way to approach scientific questions. [As a matter of statistical logic] most published research findings are probably false.*
> **John Ioannidis,** Stanford University School of Medicine[4] [5]

Ioannidis isn't the only researcher to have come to such a conclusion.

> *If you use p=0.05 to suggest that you have made a discovery, you will be wrong at least 30% of the time. If, as is often the case, experiments are underpowered, you will be wrong most of the time.*
> **David Colquhoun,** University College London[6]

Translation: many study results are bunk and shouldn't be trusted. If a study reports that subjects given X drug had Y benefit, that result may be wrong. Statistical significance is employed to segregate real results from spurious ones. Yet it turns out that statistical significance isn't well suited to the task.

The conclusions of Ioannidis and Colquhoun can be easily replicated with a few reasonable assumptions:

- Clinical trials are "powered," or designed to find results when they are present "most" of the time. An individual trial might be powered to find results 80 percent of the time. That number could be 30 or 90 percent—it is up to the team designing the trial. If efficacy isn't seen in a clinical trial, it could be that, based on bad luck, the result should have been seen but that the trial was underpowered. As Ioannidis found in both economics and neuroscience papers, the typical study is powered to only 18 percent.[7] This means that even if the effect is present, only one out of five studies will find it; four out of five will miss it. Janet Woodcock, Acting FDA Commissioner, claims that 96 percent of the clinical trails for COVID therapeutics were underpowered.[8]
- Ten percent of new drugs show efficacy. This is likely an overestimate.
- The level for statistical significance is set at p=0.05. Again, a lower or higher number could be used.
- We test 1,000 new drugs, looking for efficacy.

If we were to test 1,000 new drugs, we would expect to see some effect in ten percent of them, or 100 drugs. However, those 100 effective drugs were tested with imperfect trials—there will be true positive and false negative clinical results. In this example, we are assuming that each clinical trial was powered to find an effect in 80 percent of cases, meaning that 80 will have a true positive result and 20 will have a false negative result. We would expect to see no effect in the other 900 drugs. If we assume that five percent of clinical trial results are due to luck, with the 900 drugs with no real effect, we will see a true negative result in 95 percent of the cases, or 855 cases, and a false positive result in five percent of the cases, or 45 cases.[9]

Table 1: Cases that Lead to Spurious Results

Clinical Results	True Result	False Result	Total	Spurious Results
"Positive" Result	80	45	125	**36.0%**
"Negative" Result	855	20	875	2.3%
Total	935	65	1,000	6.5%

More than a third of the positive results are spurious when the true positive rate is 80%

As shown in Table 1, researchers will see 125 results as true (45 false positives, or 0.05 times 900, plus 80 true positives, or 0.80 times 100) and 875 as false (20 of which are really true results). Given these numbers, a third of the "positive" results are really spurious (45 out of 125). In other words, we will be wrong over a third of the time.

Table 2: Cases that Lead to Spurious Results

Clinical Results	True Result	False Result	Total	Spurious Results
"Positive" Result	40	45	85	**52.9%**
"Negative" Result	855	60	915	6.6%

Clinical Results	True Result	False Result	Total	Spurious Results
Total	895	105	1,000	10.5%

A majority of the positive results are specious when the true positive rate is 40%

As shown in Table 2, if the true positive rate is less, not 80 percent but, say, 40 percent, because of low-powered tests, which is more realistic for many fields of study, more than half of the positive results are specious, as shown in the table above, which is what led to Ioannidis and Colquhoun's quotes above.

Table 3: Cases that Lead to Spurious Results

Clinical Results	True Result	False Result	Total	Spurious Results
"Positive" Result	20	45	65	**69.2%**
"Negative" Result	855	80	935	8.6%
Total	875	125	1,000	12.5%

A large percentage of the positive results are specious when the true positive rate is 20%

If the true positive rate is really only 20 percent (in other words, the tests are powered at an even lower level), which is what Ioannidis found for some fields, nearly 70 percent of the positive results are spurious. See Table 3.

Being wrong more than half of the time when you otherwise think that you're right isn't very reassuring. And it just gets worse with more-realistic assumptions. If fewer than ten percent of new drugs have efficacy, the results are worse. If the test subjects aren't randomly and equally split between the test and control groups, the results are worse. We could easily be wrong two thirds of the time—or more.

This conclusion applies to all scientific research results, not just those for pharmaceuticals. Substitute "research results" or "research hypotheses" for "clinical results" in the tables above, and this analysis is then a proxy for all scientific research.

Most research results that get reported are ostensibly true hypotheses. Examples of true hypotheses are: animals given a certain dose of X had a quantifiable response, and people who exercised lowered their blood pressure by Y percent. Ostensibly false hypotheses are simply less interesting and are often discarded because they look like failures: animals given a certain dose of Z had no response, and people who exercised N times a week did no better or worse than those who exercised M times. Such findings are useful but rarely make newspaper headlines because they just aren't that exciting and are hard to parlay into more research money. These studies seem as if they didn't find anything, as if they misfired and failed. Even though these studies uncovered important information, they are seen as duds.

The pressure to find exciting results in the "publish or perish" environment leads to what is called "p-hacking," in which researchers run numerous statistical analyses until they find something with a statistically significant result that is good enough to be published. If these researchers look at enough statistical analyses, they're bound to find something good.

On top of all this depressing news, some results are unusable because the studies themselves never happened! John Ioannidis looked at studies published in the journal *Anaesthesia* that he termed "false" and "zombie." He found very high rates of fake data from Egypt (100 percent), Iran (75 percent), India (54 percent), China (46 percent), Turkey (40 percent), South Korea (25 percent), and Japan (18 percent).[10] According to Ben

Mol, professor of obstetrics and gynecology at Monash Health, who has studied this issue, it is likely that twenty percent of all published studies used falsified data.

For these reasons, the majority of the published research findings we read are really false. They can be neither trusted nor replicated. Wait a minute, though. Wasn't the peer review process supposed to prevent this sort of thing?

Peer Review and Replication

The peer review process—in which experts in the field review a paper before publication—is considered the gold standard and was designed to catch errors in individual studies. Yet it has a mixed record. First, there is no way for reviewers to know whether the results are really true. In the tables above, the reviewers can't tell by reading the paper if the results fall into the true result or false result columns. Second, there have been sting operations wherein completely fabricated results have been submitted using fictitious researchers from fictitious universities, and over half (157 of 304) of the peer-reviewed journals accepted the manuscripts.[11] In another sting, one research paper was doctored with eight deliberate errors in design, analysis, and interpretation. Of 200 regular reviewers for the *British Medical Journal* in 1998, none spotted all eight errors and, on average, each reviewer caught fewer than two.[12]

In 2018, in what was known as Sokal 2.0, a team of three academics successfully submitted hoax papers to peer-reviewed journals. Of their 20 submissions, seven were accepted, four were published online, and three were in process when the hoax was uncovered. This trio targeted humanities journals that specialized in what they called "grievance studies"— an area loosely known as cultural studies, such as gender or identity studies. We can hope that the pranksters would have been less successful trying to fool the higher echelons of scientific journals.

Francis Collins and Lawrence Tabak, both at the U.S. National Institutes of Health, wrote a special paper on the veracity of published research, saying that "[a] growing chorus of concern, from scientists and laypeople, contends that the complex system for ensuring the reproducibility of biomedical research is failing and is in need of restructuring."[13] Consider the seriousness of this problem: "A few years ago, two pharmaceutical companies reported that they could not replicate the vast majority of academic findings in preclinical experiments."[14] The California-based powerhouse biotech company Amgen tried to replicate 53 landmark studies that addressed the basic science of cancer. The Amgen researchers went so far as to cooperate closely with the original researchers to ensure that their experimental techniques matched the original approaches. Still, they could reproduce the original results in just six of the 53 (a mere 11 percent). The German pharma company Bayer tried a similar undertaking, and its researchers reported that they successfully reproduced the results in just a quarter of the 67 seminal studies they considered.

Can it be true that only ten to 25 percent of these seminal studies were reproducible?

This is an important matter: can landmark studies be reproduced? In the field of psychology, 270 researchers set out to do just that, to see if the results from 100 different studies published in leading peer-reviewed psychology journals could be reproduced by other researchers. What happened? They could reproduce just 39 percent of the findings, and those reproduced results were often less statistically significant than the original findings. Sometimes the researchers measured results that went in the opposite direction from the original results.[15]

Reproducing studies is challenging. A *Nature* survey of 1,576 scientists found that "[m]ore than 70% of researchers have tried and failed to reproduce another scientist's experiments." Further, "more than half [of the scientists] have failed to reproduce their own experiments."

Based on what we've seen here, a reasonable estimate could be that 25 percent of study results are correct and 75 percent are incorrect.

Performing Slightly Different Experiments

Collins and Tabak observed that a study sometimes can't be replicated because the replicator is unknowingly performing a slightly different experiment. On the surface, everything is the same between the experiments, but one or more key variables have unknowingly been changed.

The unstated assumption with trials of large numbers of organisms, whether they are mice or humans, is that the organisms are largely fungible, or mutually interchangeable—a mouse is a mouse is a mouse. Or, as the medical world puts it, one mouse is a good "model" for another mouse. Because this isn't literally true and we can see differences between mice, some large number of mice are used to cover up any differences among individuals. If one group of mice has a particularly weak/strong/smart/dumb/energetic/lazy member, then the other group probably does too, making the groups of mice good "models" for each other, especially after the outward differences—sex, age, breed, weight, diet—are accounted for and managed. But what if this just isn't the case? What if one group of mice isn't a good proxy for another group of mice, and the results from the first group won't carry over to the second group?

Scientists at pharmaceutical company Pfizer found that different batches of rats excreted hippuric acid in different amounts, something that is important in studies of rats because it is a key result in laboratory tests. The scientists dug deeper and found that the rats were bred in different rooms. Upon closer examination, the scientists realized that the microbiomes—gut microorganisms, including bacteria, viruses, fungi, protozoa, and single-celled archaea species—of the rats were different, altering their metabolism.[16] This is a big problem.

In Chapter 5, the results of Laura McCabe were discussed. In a study of bone density in mice, she and her team discovered that they got three different results: the drug being tested decreased, increased, and had no effect on bone density. What was different between the three results? The three groups of mice they had started with had different microbial makeups.

In addition to the microbiome, other things affect animal studies. The circadian rhythm influences how a mouse's immune system responds to bacteria, depending upon the time of day. Temperatures in labs may put mice into a state of mild cold stress, causing them to ramp up their metabolisms, making them more prone to inflammation and tumors. Bedding, whether wood, corncob, or paper, can influence hormonal levels and metabolism levels. The height of the animals' cages, on the upper or lower shelf, has been shown to affect retinal degeneration and tumor growth. Even subtle differences between male and female human experimenters can cause problems. Mice given an injection in the presence of men experienced higher levels of stress hormones than when in the presence of women.

If the microbiome—that amazingly complex ecosystem of microbes that occupy our digestive tracts and other parts of our body—makes such a difference in the outcome of a trial, and our basic DNA differs from that of mice, and if our diets and lifestyles differ from those of mice, how can we be sure that those mice are good analogs, or models, for our physiology? We can't. We can't even assume that one group of mice is a good model for another group of mice!

Consider a hypothetical drug being considered by a pharma company, and think about the three clinical trial results found by McCabe above—the drug helps, the drug hurts, or the drug does nothing. The result that shows up in the first preclinical trial that the pharma company runs could have an enormous influence on whether it decides to continue the drug's development. Now consider how many good drugs have, over the years, been shelved because the initial readout on the drug was negative, simply as a result of which group of mice or people happened to be tested first.

One-Size-Fits-All Solutions

The FDA's approach makes it difficult for treatments in which the dose must be tailored to an individual's situation. Because the FDA has little or no visibility into the situations of particular individuals and how the treatment would be tailored for them, the FDA is essentially flying blind.

Titrating Vasotec

If you have hypertension and your physician wants you to try Vasotec (enalapril), a little bit of reading will tell you that there are four strengths available: 2.5, 5, 10, and 20 milligrams. Why not just one? Simple: people are different. Some have mild hypertension while some have severe. Some respond to a low dose of Vasotec and some need more. How do doctors determine the proper dosage for a patient? Good old trial and error, and this particular type of trial and error is called titration by the medical community. The FDA-approved label for Vasotec instructs doctors to titrate (start low and increase) the dose until they find the right one: "The dosage may be titrated upward until blood pressure is controlled or to a maximum of 40 mg daily."

The FDA doesn't know what dose is right for you and won't know what dose you and your doctor settle on.

Sunshine Vitamin

As someone with a fair complexion who grew up in sunny California, I've always needed to be careful about my "dose" of sunshine. When I haven't, I haven't been happy. One summer, my father rented a beach house for a week, and my teenaged brothers, friends, and I spent the whole first day out in the bright sunshine, trying to tan like everyone else on the beach. In retrospect, that was incredibly stupid. I was miserable after that first day

of exposure, lying in bed, moaning, aching, with chills and fever, feeling as if I had the flu. My glorious beach week was completely ruined; even putting on a shirt hurt. At least I got my vitamin D!

Research linking low vitamin D—apparently, it's more a hormone than a vitamin—levels with deaths from heart disease and other causes provides mounting evidence of the "sunshine" vitamin's role in good health. Sunshine, itself, is often an effective way to administer vitamin D and to enhance mood and quality of life.

> *People with low levels of vitamin D in their blood have significantly higher rates of virtually every disease and disorder you can think of: cancer, diabetes, obesity, osteoporosis, heart attack, stroke, depression, cognitive impairment, autoimmune conditions, and more.*
> **Rowan Jacobsen,** *Outside* contributing editor

Consider for a moment what would be involved in prescribing sunshine as a therapy. To get the proper dosage, you would need to know the patient's current blood vitamin D levels, how effectively the patient's body converts sunshine into serum vitamin D, what kind of pigmentation the patient has —how light or dark—along with the current level of tan or burn. If someone had a current sunburn, the "prescription" would be for zero sunlight, to prevent exacerbating the burn. If someone had naturally light skin with a moderate tan, we could prescribe more sunlight. But we, as the prescriber, would also need to know how much of the patient's body would be covered when receiving "therapy." Will the patient be wearing a hat, long sleeves and pants, or just a swimsuit? What time of day will the therapy take place? We, as the prescriber, might not have any knowledge of these factors; however, the patients themselves will certainly know this information.

Herein lies a conundrum. The person getting the prescription knows more about the circumstances of the therapy than does the person doing the prescribing. The person doing the prescribing, however, knows more about the patient's circumstances than FDA employees, residing hundreds or thousands of miles away. And yet for typical medicines the FDA is responsible for telling the doctor what is allowable to prescribe, and the doctor is responsible for telling the patient what to take. When the FDA approves new medicines, it must make educated guesses about average patients. With a new "drug" such as sunshine, what would the FDA do? Would it assume that patients are light or dark? Inside most of the time or mainly outdoors? Covered or not?

What is needed is an algorithm that takes into account every variable and spells out the optimal dosage of sunshine— there's a smartphone app, D Minder Pro, to help people determine what sun exposure they should seek —but that's outside of the FDA's typical approach of approving some drugs and rejecting others, carte blanche. When it comes to our ideal sun exposure, the FDA is completely in the dark.

The FDA's approach leads to a number of strange, but internally consistent, policies.

Rigid Requirements

A company was developing a new drug that appeared to work amazingly well for breaking up solid cancerous tumors. The problem was that once those tumors were lysed—the cells ruptured—some of that cellular material would circulate in the blood and could cause problems. The FDA wanted to know what this company would do, asking the company to specify in great detail in the investigator's brochure—the instruction manual for physicians participating in clinical trials—what procedures would be followed if a patient ran into problems.

Unfortunately, the correct answer is subtle, variable, and spectacularly complex. (There's a reason that doctors go to school for so many years!)

Virtually every patient and every situation is unique. Being formulaic and trying to lay out a flowchart for all these unique situations is bound to lead, when the problem actually arises, to solutions that are not appropriate—meaning that this company's investigator's brochure would instruct doctors to treat their patients incorrectly. Knowing that this could hurt patients and could lead to lawsuits, to say nothing of harming this company's chances for an FDA approval, the company balked. The FDA rebuked the company: "Why aren't you doing what we asked?" To deal with this dilemma, the company laid out the general flowchart for treatment and then offered the caveat that doctors would use their judgment if the situation didn't exactly match what was shown in the flowchart.

Here is a situation in which we should just let doctors do their doctoring. When the FDA requires rigid rules and doctors actually follow them, patients can be hurt. Who wants that?

The FDA Prevents Advice?

Imagine that a friend, in a quiet moment, gives you a frank warning to be careful with your alcohol consumption, commenting that she has observed others in your family having trouble managing their liquor. Or, if you are a man, maybe your friend warned you of the increased risk of heart disease facing men. If you are a woman, perhaps your friend warned you about urinary incontinence, which affects twice as many women as men. Has your friend done anything wrong? Has she done anything illegal? Should the FDA prevent such advice?

Now replace that friend with the genetic testing company, 23andMe. When 23andMe did something similar to what your friend did, the FDA told it to cease and desist.

For four years, the FDA prevented 23andMe from providing any genetic information to its customers, depriving individuals of information about their personal risk of 254 diseases and conditions. Think about that. A company, 23andMe, can use your saliva to access your genetic information. It's then a short step to providing you with any information that 23andMe has about relative risks, derived from associations between the genetic information and health outcomes of others. Perhaps you have a lower than average risk for heart disease but a higher than average risk for Alzheimer's disease. That can help you plan your life. "No," the FDA said. A company cannot use your information to provide an estimate of your likelihood of suffering from a disease. After four years, the FDA relented. But that's how far the FDA's fingers have extended into all things health care related. Should the FDA also prevent your friend from giving you the benefit of her medical knowledge? After all, she and 23andMe were doing the same thing.

We need to remember that spitting into a vial can't hurt us. This isn't an issue of thalidomide hurting fetuses or metoclopramide causing tardive dyskinesia. There is zero risk that the 23andMe test can harm patients. The only "risk" is that you might do something inappropriate with the information provided by your genetic test. But that's some significant mission creep for the FDA: from preventing access to bad drugs to preventing access to our medical information. What if the FDA prevented your doctor from telling you your blood pressure?

Giving Official Advice

By superseding our individual judgments and telling us what therapies we can use, the FDA burdens itself with a different type of problem: expert advisor bias. Both we and the FDA should be aware of and concerned about this potential bias.

One of my brothers once asked me whether the brake pads on his car were too thin and should be replaced. Put yourself in my position. Unless I internalize 100 percent of his costs and benefits, I wouldn't get the benefit of the money he would save by deferring the repair job, but I would get a call back with some amount of blame and guilt if the old, thinning brake pads failed, ruining his disc brake rotors, sending him into a ditch, or worse. My safe response was to suggest that he either have a trained mechanic check the brake pads or simply replace the brake pads.

The costs and benefits that I perceived from that situation were different than the costs and benefits my brother perceived. If the brakes were fine, he would save money and time by delaying a repair job; I would see no such savings. If the brakes were too worn, we would both suffer.

Now, imagine for a moment that you are the newly appointed head of a federal agency making recommendations about automotive brake repairs. Think about it. As an authority figure, you would naturally internalize that responsibility. Also, you, personally, would benefit very little from people delaying brake repairs but, if bad things happened while people were driving with sketchy brakes, you might be held legally or morally accountable. Stated differently, you would bear a substantial portion of the costs of delayed brake repairs while enjoying almost none of the benefits. As the brake repair czar, you would have a very different cost and benefit structure from the rest of us. The recommendations you would make would likely reflect *your* cost and benefit structure and not the cost/benefit calculus of those in your charge. We can call this the **official advisor bias**.

Official Advisor Bias

Authority figures, such as the FDA, have an incentive to give advice based on their own cost/benefit calculus, not yours. The field in economics that studies this is called public choice.

The director of my local hospital was on the radio regularly during the COVID pandemic. His message was clear: we must do everything we can to reduce infections. There are always tradeoffs. One-dimensional solutions are not solutions at all. Was his ultimate objective to help his hospital or us?

Some pages back, we discussed the potential bias of outside experts on advisory committees and how a study showed that those biases hadn't affected behavior (see Chapter 7). This bias, the official advisor bias, *has* affected behavior.

Making Choices for Others

> *You can't make someone else's choices. You shouldn't let someone else make yours.*
> **Colin Powell**

One of my brothers had lived in the same neighborhood for years and noticed a few houses within his budget that had some substantial advantages over his current house. He began to dream. Then, one day, one of these houses came on the market.

He and I talked at length about the advantages and costs of moving versus staying put. The new house was in a much better location, but the price was uncomfortably high and the floorplan left him unexcited. On the other hand, his current lot was small, and, consequently, he was inundated with unpleasant reminders of his neighbors. Moving would entail the usual hassles: staging the old house, negotiating, paying fees, moving, and so on. He was torturing himself with this decision, going back and forth, and looking to me for advice. The only thing I could do was to help him determine which house would work better for him. What I would do and what I thought were largely irrelevant. I wouldn't be living in the new house, and only he could say how much his neighbors' lights and noises bothered him. He was the only one who could say how awesome the new property was or how poorly the new floorplan rated. The decision had to be his and his alone, due purely to the reason that it affected him orders of magnitude more than it did me. My questions and listening helped, but I couldn't know which choice to suggest.

Imagine that the FDA is in charge of houses, and my brother asks the FDA to help him decide whether to move. The FDA knows less than I do about the old house, the new house, the neighborhood, and my brother's situation. Ultimately, my brother's goal was to maximize his utility, not mine, and not the FDA's. I was incapable of making my brother's decision, but the FDA, a government agency lacking even a cursory understanding of my brother or his situation, would be in a far more deficient position.

There are three problems when others make your decisions for you:

- The decision makers don't have the requisite information to make the right decision.
- The decision maker's incentive structure might not match yours.
- The time, cost, and hassle of having that other party review the situation take away from the time and resources you have available.

Are FDA Warnings Useful?

One of the supposed benefits of having a federal government agency monitor our food, drugs, and cosmetics is that, should there be a problem with any of these products, the FDA can require warning labels on them, thus protecting us from harm. Most of us implicitly or explicitly consider this to be a legitimate function of the agency.

But how useful are these warning labels in practice?

I'm currently holding a Mitchum Smart Solid antiperspirant and deodorant. On the back of this innocent-looking product, under warnings, it says, "Ask a doctor before use if you have kidney disease." This warning is one of no fewer than five on this otherwise innocuous-looking personal hygiene product.

The FDA requires this warning because antiperspirants contain small amounts of aluminum, which, if absorbed through the skin, could potentially cause problems in kidney-impaired individuals. Aluminum has also been linked to Alzheimer's disease. Fair enough. But we should ask how big a risk this is. What's the probability that a person would have a problem? Would this problem be significant? How much do we really know about this issue? Prepare to be underwhelmed.

The amount of aluminum in antiperspirant is small and it's not even known whether aluminum *can* be absorbed through the skin. Moreover, one study estimated that the aluminum we get from antiperspirants, if any is absorbed at all, is only 2.5 percent of the amount we get from food (yes, there's aluminum in our food). Further, we get aluminum from water, as municipalities use aluminum-based chemicals for treating drinking water and waste water.[17] We use aluminum food containers and aluminum foil. Plus, even without consuming any aluminum-laden food or storing food in aluminum, there's naturally abundant aluminum around us in our water, air, and soil. In fact, of all the metals listed in the periodic table of the elements, aluminum is the most abundant in our environment.[18] If someone wanted to avoid aluminum, Earth would not be a good place to take up residence.

If you use an antiperspirant, you *may* increase your daily dose of aluminum by a minuscule amount, the harm of which could range from zero to something greater than zero. No one really knows. And for this we get a warning label on our antiperspirants? After explaining the situation, the June 2009 *UC Berkeley Wellness Letter* pointed out that, "the warning may be overly cautious...." Indeed, I think that the *Wellness Letter*'s disclaimer is overly cautious.

Consider how a renally-impaired patient, who takes the warning seriously, would talk to his doctor. "Doc, what should I do? The warning label says I should talk to you before using this antiperspirant." His physician's mind races and settles on one of three responses: the warning is silly and Mitchum should be used regardless; or, wishing to avoid any liability, his doctor may recommend against using the Mitchum; meanwhile, another physician may say that she doesn't really know enough to determine whether or not the man should use the Mitchum.

The man's total aluminum level could be tested before and after usage. Would such a test be valuable for the decision in question? We already know that aluminum is abundant in our environment, so how could we be certain that a raised level is due to the deodorant? Do you see where this argument is going? It's hard to visualize how this warning will help a single patient make good health decisions. And a warning that doesn't help anyone, that provides no useful information, is a useless warning. Worse, this is a case of the boy who cried wolf. If the FDA secretly wants us to become jaded and ignore all warnings, then theirs is the right approach.

Speaking of warning labels, aspirin has a warning about potential hearing loss and tinnitus (ringing in the ears). Ibuprofen and acetaminophen have no such warning. Does this mean that aspirin is more dangerous in this regard than ibuprofen and acetaminophen? No. It does not.

A large Harvard study of middle-aged female nurses found that both ibuprofen and acetaminophen increased the risk of hearing loss by 20 percent. The same study also showed that aspirin does not cause that adverse event.[19] In this case at least, per the Harvard study, the FDA has it exactly backwards, and its warning is useless.

Even sterner warnings can be based on faulty information.

The FDA saw ketorolac as such a dangerous drug that when it approved the drug in oral and injectable forms the early 1990s, the FDA limited its use to five days of treatment. Years later, when Roxro Pharma submitted an intranasal formulation of ketorolac for FDA review, the FDA informed Roxro that it would limit that formulation, too, to five days. However, in the intervening decades, some good data on pain medications had been collected in Europe, showing that ketorolac was *safer* than other non-steroidal anti-inflammatories in its class. Roxro presented these data to the FDA, but the FDA dug in its heels and handed Sprix, the branded name for the intranasal ketorolac, the same five-day limitation.

I suppose that the FDA realized that once it had staked its position on ketorolac being dangerous, it would appear inconsistent to reverse it. Those are bad optics for a government agency. And, really, how many people would ever know about those European data? Data-driven and scientific? Not in this case.

The Information Problem

The FDA regularly asks biopharma companies to collect information about new drugs. Generally, information is good, isn't it? Three clinical trials are better than two, right? Why would anyone complain about the FDA collecting more information about new drugs? Yet, as with many things, information has costs as well as benefits. Given these costs, can gathering too much information be bad? You bet it can; we need to balance the costs and benefits.

Consider the following situation. You were given a job studying trashcans in a moderately-sized city in America. Let's focus on Roseville, California, which has a population of 132,000 and perhaps 100,000 household trashcans. If, as part of your new job, you were tasked with answering one thousand questions (what is in them?, where were they made?, where are they kept?, how much do they weigh?, what temperature are they?, etc.) about each trashcan, and each question took ten minutes to answer, we have a project that will take you one billion minutes to complete. This is 8,333 person-years, or 208 full person-careers. This isn't a job for just one person: you and 207 of your colleagues could spend the rest of your professional lives studying trashcans in Roseville. And why? I have no idea. I made no mention of a mission, objective, goal, or purpose to this exercise. And that's the whole problem.

As professor Ronald A. Howard of Stanford University has observed, and as David R. Henderson and I discussed in our book, *Making Great Decisions in Business and Life*, you should never embark on an information-gathering project without first establishing your objective. If you're designing a new garbage truck, for instance, perhaps you need only be concerned with the size and weight of a representative sample of trashcans. If you are an environmentalist studying refuse and recycling, perhaps you need only study the contents of a few hundred samples to see what is recycled versus what could be recycled. If you are a biologist studying the growth of microorganisms, you can forget about how owners feel about their trashcans. If you are a criminal trying to steal the identity of Roseville's wealthy residents, you can forget about checking the trashcans on the poor side of town.

The pharmaceutical industry and the practice of medicine are, thankfully, quite different from the study of trashcans, but the same principles apply. Because we know that the amount of potential information in the medical universe is unlimited, we realize that we could spend literally the rest of our lives studying one small aspect of one small part of the practice of medicine. Consider this example: does the timing of the consumption of dietary fat over a woman's lifetime affect her risk of developing breast cancer? I'm sure that, if I chose to, I could study this one extensive topic for the rest of my productive life. But, unless I have a good reason to do so, I've wasted my life. In no way does this insight belittle the importance of breast cancer research. It does mean, however, that we should choose our battles carefully and embark on an information-gathering project only after establishing an objective.

Is the FDA simply collecting data or does it have a clear objective? What would a clear FDA objective be? Collect enough data to ensure that a new drug is safe? Safe in the sense that it is 100 percent safe for every person who might take it? No. That's impossible. Safe enough? How safe is safe enough? Safer than the alternatives? In what doses, in what circumstances, for what indications, and for which patients? The whole problem becomes incredibly nuanced, while the depth and breadth of information to be gathered depends on the answers to those questions.

The FDA is in the information-collecting business, and it faces the almost unlimited and intractable "trashcan problem." It should realize that information is costly, and before it takes on any information-gathering project—such as working with a biopharma company to design a clinical trial—the FDA should be clear that for the trial to make sense, the benefits of the information will exceed the costs.

The Principal-Agent Principle

The principal-agent arrangement is ubiquitous due to its necessity and usefulness, but it also provides fertile ground for conflict.

With a principal-agent arrangement, one party—the principal—has some task to be performed, but chooses, for whatever reason, to hire another party—the agent—to perform that task. It follows that the principal must provide some inducement to get the agent to act according to his wishes, and the agent must then actually deliver on the principal's wishes.

An example of a principal-agent arrangement is a medical power of attorney contract. If you, as the principal, will be incapacitated, such as during surgery or due to dementia, you want your agent to make medical decisions as much in accordance with your wishes as possible. In every situation that comes up, but which can't be specified in detail ahead of time, you want your agent to consider what you would want done if you were capable of making the decision yourself.

Now consider a government agency such as the Food and Drug Administration. Because you presumably don't have an advanced scientific or medical degree and don't know the ins and outs of drug development, and you do have a job that keeps you busy all day, you, as the principal, offload the responsibility of assessing drugs and medical devices to the FDA. But, as with the medical power of attorney example, the agent is put in place *to act on your behalf*. Remember that the principal-agent arrangement works only if the agent acts on the behalf of the principal.

The key question with any new medicine or medical device is: if you had the time and expertise to assess it yourself, what would you do? If the FDA does what you would have done, it's a good agent, or agency. (Industry insiders often call the FDA simply "the agency," which is apropos here. One definition of agency is the office or function of an agent.) If the FDA does something else, it's a bad agent/agency and is abusing its power.

If the FDA is overly conservative or overly slow with drug approvals, it is failing in its duties or is abusing its power by following the wishes of someone other than the principal: you. If the FDA puts excessive effort into keeping Congress happy and ignores you, the FDA is abusing its power.

The catch with this agent/principal discussion is that we don't know how you would have rated any new drug or device because you don't have an advanced medical degree and you haven't spent your entire life in that field of specialty. But there *are* other people who have done just that. These are people who don't work for the FDA but, presumably, have your interests at heart because they have spent their whole careers treating people just like you and/or developing new drugs for people just like you.

Who are these people? Some of them work for biopharma companies. Perhaps you don't trust them because of their profit motive. I have a different opinion (please see economist David R. Henderson's excellent article "Make Money off my Sickness...Please"[20]), but I can understand and appreciate your view.

How about another group, also with a profit motive: your trusted doctors—people with advanced medical degrees and long careers in their respective fields of specialty? How about the multitude of treatment guideline-setting bodies, such as the American Academy of Pediatrics, the American Heart Association, the American Thoracic Society, the National Comprehensive Cancer Network, and the National Kidney Foundation. These groups are even *more* knowledgeable and experienced than the FDA in their respective areas.

How about pharmacist-based organizations, such as AHFS, which helps establish the medically accepted uses of drugs, both labeled and off-label?

How about peer-reviewed medical journals? These journals publish cutting-edge research and thinking and, in most areas, are far ahead of the FDA. How about hospitals, where people are treated daily? How about the Susan G. Komen network of cancer survivors, where real cancer survivors share their stories and help each other? How about *U.C. Berkeley Wellness Letter*, *U.S. Pharmacopeia*, *Consumer Reports*, and *Drug Facts and Comparisons*, publications that write about drug and health issues?

How about the Agency for Healthcare Research and Quality, a federal government agency that researches and promulgates information on treatment guidelines and best practices? For instance, the AHRQ helped the American Urological Association and the Society of Urologic Oncology write a 45-page document on the diagnosis and treatment of non-muscle invasive bladder cancer. Not sure if you, as a urologist, should use BCG maintenance therapy on a patient? Consult the AHRQ how-to guide. Not only will it answer your questions, but it also lists its sources and it rates the strength of the evidence.

The National Comprehensive Cancer Network produces similar "how to" documents. The one for cervical cancer is 85 pages in length. The Cochrane Library document on ivermectin for preventing and treating COVID-19 is 277 pages.

How about the equivalent "FDA" government agencies in other countries, such as Health Canada, the European Medicines Agency, Swissmedic in Switzerland, the Medicines and Healthcare products Regulatory Agency in the U.K., the Therapeutic Goods Administration in Australia, the Pharmaceuticals and Medical Devices Agency in Japan, and the China Food and Drug Administration? Surely these agencies are in the same league as the FDA.

How about other government agencies, such as the Department of Defense, which has a budget far greater than the FDA's? This large government agency deals with numerous medical issues, including battlefield medicine.

How about the hand-picked experts who frequent FDA advisory committee meetings? These are the people that the FDA considers experts, and they come with a built-in advantage: they assess new medicines and publicly vote on them.

We don't have just one agent; we have many. And we can look at how the group assesses any new drug.

Imagine a case in which there are 100 agents, and all 100 accept, or approve, a new drug. Then that new drug is highly likely to be worthwhile and should be considered for treating patients. If all 100 agents reject a drug, then that drug is probably a dog and it deserved to be rejected. Yet what should we do if the tally is 50-50, or 20-80, or 80-20? In all three of these cases, if the agents are doing their jobs properly, some of them are saying that the principals—patients—should have access to this new drug.

How should we best deal with such an outcome? We should make the new drug available to 100 percent of principals, realizing that not all of them might use it. Those principals who would not want this new medicine will simply not use it, either because they reject it themselves or their personal agent, their physician, will reject it for them. Making a drug available through a regulatory agency does not mean that everyone *must* use or *will* use the drug in question; it just means that it will still face two key hurdles before any usage: the physician, who must prescribe the medicine, and the patient, who must buy and swallow it.

Grandfathered Drugs

At a campground in California, large warning signs on the water spigots read: "Boil water for five minutes before consuming it."[21] The message was not placed there because of a bacterial infection in the water system or because someone had died drinking from the spigots. Rather, the water had not yet been tested for that year, and though there had never before been problems with the water, camp officials erred on the side of caution and posted the warning sign.

It's a similar story with the FDA and the media's coverage of it. The FDA, using the media as its voice, provides us with alarmist and unhelpful messages about medicines all the time. These messages reflect and expose us to a subtle type of bias—that any drug not specifically evaluated by the FDA must be unsafe. And the awful result is that there are fewer safe drugs on the market and more-expensive drugs overall.

Consider a headline from the *New York Times*: "F.D.A. Says Millions Got Unapproved Heart Pills."[22] One could read that headline and conclude that some shady actor was selling defective or counterfeit heart drugs to American cardiac patients, possibly resulting in injury or even death. As with the water spigot warnings, the truth is quite different.

Consider old drugs that predate the 1938 regulation regarding safety and the 1962 regulation regarding efficacy—not to mention the even older drugs that predate the very existence of the FDA. These 'grandfathered' drugs never received FDA approval. Consequently, aspirin and other grandfathered drugs, including morphine, quinine, pancreatic enzymes, and sublingual nitroglycerin tablets, were available to patients long before the FDA solidified its rules (or, in some cases, existed).

Aspirin, or at least a powder made from the bark and leaves of willow trees, was mentioned in Hippocrates' notes 2,400 years ago. Morphine was developed between 1805 and 1816 and became popular after the hypodermic needle was perfected in 1853. Morphine is still, today, the standard analgesic for use in hospitals. Nitroglycerin has been available for 130 years as a vasodilator to treat heart conditions such as angina and chronic heart failure. It has been spectacularly successful. In 2003, two physicians wrote the following about nitroglycerin in the academic journal *Circulation*:

> Newer drugs quickly replace older remedies. This has not been the case with nitroglycerin, now in continuous medical use for more than a century. Although other applications for it have been found in cardiology, nitroglycerin is the mainstay for affording rapid, indeed almost immediate, relief for angina pectoris. Patients who have mastered the proper use of this agent regard it as a "wonder drug." At a time when the cost of pharmaceuticals is growing out of reach for many, nitroglycerin is still obtainable for pennies and remains one of the best buys in medicine.[23]

But if the FDA gets its way, nitroglycerin will not be obtainable for pennies. The situation was stable until Pfizer went through the time and expense required to test its particular version of nitroglycerin, Nitrostat, which the FDA approved in 2000. Once the FDA did that, other versions became officially "unapproved." In 2010, the FDA sent warning letters to two companies, Glenmark and Konec, ordering them to cease marketing their unapproved versions of sublingual nitroglycerin tablets.

The FDA's action caused Harry M. Lever, a cardiologist at Cleveland Clinic, to say, "If it's not approved and no one has tested it, we can't be sure that it's safe and effective."[24] He added that if patients with angina took substandard or ineffective nitroglycerin tablets, their pain might not subside and the problem could potentially progress to a heart attack.

His statement is false. The unapproved versions have been tested in three important ways: (1) the companies that manufacture these drugs thoroughly vet them to make sure that they are pure and offer a consistent dose of nitroglycerin; (2) these marketed drugs have been tested in the bodies of millions of Americans in regular medical practice over many years; (3) and many different organizations have tested nitroglycerin in countless clinical trials.

One of the manufacturers, Konec, has regularly conducted its own lab tests to ensure that its nitroglycerin pills have the same potency and stability as Pfizer's Nitrostat, the FDA-approved brand-name drug. In the world of medicine, this is basic stuff. We need to remember that nitroglycerin is used to treat acute episodes of angina—chest pain. The benefit that nitroglycerin provides is not theoretical; if patients didn't feel relief from their pain, they wouldn't have continued taking it, and doctors wouldn't have continued prescribing it for the last 130 years.

Lever worried that patients with angina would, if allowed, take substandard or ineffective nitroglycerin tablets. But that's a hypothesis and hypotheses can be tested. Were some nitroglycerin tablets substandard? Were patients harmed? He gave no evidence that they were. He argues for banning first, understanding later.

What have changed over the years are not the sublingual nitroglycerin tablets that millions—including my grandmother—used for decades, but the FDA's own rules. Note that herein lies legal ambiguity. Manufacturers of many drugs, not just sublingual nitroglycerin tablets, have long contended that their medications do not require FDA review because they were grandfathered as pre-1938 drugs. But the agency is now disputing that interpretation of its rules. There has been no legal ruling, and there won't be one unless one of these companies challenges the FDA in court.

The FDA didn't challenge just makers of sublingual nitroglycerin tablets; it went after some other old drugs, as well.

Pancreatic enzymes are digestive aids—some in use for more than a century— taken by people with cystic fibrosis and other conditions. In 2004, the FDA informed three dozen makers of pancreatic enzymes that they would have four years to formally seek FDA approval to stay on the market.

In 2006, the FDA turned its attention to drugs made with quinine. People have been using quinine for, perhaps, five hundred years, meaning that quinine was used long before the FDA was a glint in the eye of a regulator. But it wasn't until one quinine product was approved by the FDA that the "unapproved" ones were told to leave the market. As is typical for the FDA, information about how there are "unapproved" versions of drugs on the market was released with reports of serious adverse events and even deaths from quinine over the years. Of course, the FDA makes no claims that the unapproved versions are somehow deficient or that the new, approved version will be any better. Is quinine wildly dangerous? No. The data show that there is one adverse event for every 300,000 prescriptions filled.[25] You wouldn't get this impression listening to the FDA.

Consider the unapproved drug, orally administered levothyroxine sodium. This drug, produced by Forest and other companies, has been on the market to treat hypothyroidism since the 1950s. After the FDA decided that this older drug was actually a "new drug," Forest was required to navigate the FDA's expensive and difficult new drug approval process. Forest didn't act quickly enough to follow all the proper procedures and, consequently, failed to meet the FDA's deadlines. Then-FDA Commissioner Margaret M. Hamburg, defending the agency's actions, claimed that the government was going after companies like Forest that "pursue profits over the public's health." She knew better. Forest was trying to make profits by *improving* the public's health. It's not that levothyroxine became dangerous to the public overnight; Hamburg was trying to protect the FDA's rules, not Americans' health.

This FDA policy from 2007, requiring tests on grandfathered drugs, turns the old FDA rationale upside down. The only possible justification for the

FDA's regular powers is that it is better to test drugs on thousands of human "guinea pigs" than to release potentially unsafe or ineffective medicines to ordinary patients. But *once* medicines have been used successfully millions of times, why go back to the clinical trials to test them on thousands? There are far more data points on millions of uses than there are on thousands.

Perhaps a bigger issue is how this helps patients who have been successfully treated for decades and are stable on the existing drugs. By removing competitors, the FDA has converted a competitive market into a monopolistic one. Pfizer's Nitrostat, for instance, will be the sole remaining product, leaving the market susceptible to pricing and supply shocks, as we saw with some medical products during the hurricane in Puerto Rico in 2017. In other markets, products that receive FDA approval are typically far more expensive. What if Pfizer, as the sole supplier, has a manufacturing problem and all production ceases, even temporarily? What if Pfizer decides to double the price of Nitrostat? Competition can't step in because the FDA has outlawed competitors. These are potentially serious problems.

Why is the FDA advancing this new approach? One might think that it's to ensure that all medicines that we Americans consume are safe and effective. For a new drug without any long-term evidence, the FDA may have a point. Such a drug *could* be dangerous. But if a drug has been widely used around the world for over a century, and by millions of people, the presumption should be that the drug is both safe and effective. Instead of assuming that existing versions of older drugs are dangerous, the FDA should be required to make a case that they are unsafe and/or efficacious. If they are unsafe or ineffective, proving that should be easy to do with a hundred years' worth of experience. This the FDA has not done.

Why would the FDA even care about grandfathered drugs? Perhaps it cares about the existence of these medicines because they challenge the FDA's justification and, therefore, threaten the FDA's power. After all, if there are drugs on the market that didn't navigate the FDA's review process, and they work well, a reasonable person may question the FDA's burdensome processes.

The FDA's actions over the years have increased and solidified the FDA's power, which looks suspiciously like a power grab. Former FDA employee Henry Miller, founding director of the FDA's Office of Biotechnology, impugning some of the FDA's motives, has reported that FDA employees put an inappropriate amount of effort into empire building and nest feathering.[26]

The FDA wouldn't do this if it were interested purely in the welfare of patients.

Prohibiting Promotion of Off-Label Uses

Do You Mean Million?

Even Google didn't believe it.[27] When we heard about Pfizer's $2.3 billion settlement with the FDA and keyed in the words "Pfizer 2.3 billion legal settlement," Google responded with, "Did you mean: Pfizer 2.3 *million* legal settlement?" (italics in original). Unfortunately, we meant *billion*. What did this drug company do to merit a $2.3 billion record-breaking claim by the federal government? Surely, you might think, it knowingly sold a dangerous drug without government permission, a drug that went on to cause hundreds of needless deaths. Did Pfizer sell a drug as dangerous as, perhaps, thalidomide? Well, no.

What Pfizer did was promote some of its drugs for so-called "off-label" uses—that is, uses for which the FDA had not approved those drugs. Then, when doctors appropriately and legally prescribed these drugs for patients on Medicare and Medicaid, Pfizer had the gall to actually try to charge the government for the drugs the patients received. That led to accusations of fraud against Pfizer and allowed attorneys general to proclaim that they were combating fraud and protecting the American public by slapping Pfizer with this colossal fine. In reality, instead of protecting patients, they were protecting the FDA's dubious powers through the process of extorting a successful American corporation.

As described earlier, many uses of many drugs are off-label. This practice is widespread, legal, and supported by many governmental departments.

Promotion is really speech and the types of speech the FDA prohibits include truthful, actual testimonials. "I felt better so soon that I didn't miss a single day of training," said Eric Bergoust, Olympic gold-medal skier in an ad for Tamiflu (oseltamivir), a flu drug. That's a great testimonial and it's truthful. However, the FDA said that his comments "misleadingly overstate the drug's efficacy." Bergoust didn't quote any statistics about Tamiflu's efficacy; Bergoust simply stated what happened to *him* when he took Tamiflu.

As I create sales forecasts for pharmaceutical and biotech companies, my clients and I are careful to avoid forecasting any potential off-label sales unless those sales will be the fruit of some future indications formally approved by the FDA. Why? Through the process of discovery, if a company's internal documents—such as sales forecast models—show that the company knew about and anticipated off-label sales, a clever prosecutor could claim that the company actually *encouraged* off-label usage.

Why hasn't the FDA's power to prevent off-label prescribing been challenged? It has. In 2005, attorney Ralph F. Hall wrote:

> *After a decade of sporadic litigation, limited legislative action, periodic enforcement actions and numerous continuing legal education programs, the issue remains undecided. Five years ago, Judge Royce Lamberth expressed his frustration with this state of affairs by noting 'after six years [sic] worth of briefs, motions, opinions, congressional acts, and more opinions, the issue remains 100% unresolved.'*[28]

To make companies like Pfizer pay $2.3 billion for such "crimes" violates the principle of proportionality because the damage to anyone, other than the FDA's authority, was essentially zero. Did Pfizer make false statements? No. Did Pfizer defraud doctors or patients? No. Did Pfizer encourage dangerous or inappropriate use of its medicines? No. Were Medicare and Medicaid charged for drugs that patients never received? No. Did Pfizer even know that its drugs were being used off-label? No.

There was no specific instance where Pfizer asked the government to reimburse it for a drug used off-label because Pfizer didn't and couldn't know that information. How would Pfizer ever know, given the large volume of drugs it sells to the government, which particular bottles or vials were for off-label uses?

The prescribing doctors and the patients—the alleged "victims"—were, in fact, both the perpetrators and the beneficiaries. But you'd never know that by listening to government officials. Here's what Kathleen Sebelius, secretary of Health and Human Services, said about the case: "This historic settlement will return nearly one billion dollars to Medicare, Medicaid, and other government insurance programs, securing their future for the Americans who depend on these programs." But the whole point of this lawsuit is to get companies like Pfizer *not* to market beneficial medicines to people on Medicare and Medicaid. How does that help Americans who depend on these programs?

The prohibition of promotion for off-label usage is, in fact, a structural problem with drug regulation, and the FDA would be negligent if it didn't punish offenders. And yet we shouldn't blame those companies that promote off-label uses; we should blame the rules themselves. And rules can be changed.

"Fire That CEO"

In 2011, the U.S. government threatened to exclude Forest Laboratories from future government business unless it removed its hapless CEO, Howard Solomon. It turns out Forest had, in addition to another charged offense, promoted two drugs for "off-label" uses—uses for which the drugs were not approved. It wasn't enough that Forest had agreed to pay the government $313 million in penalties for the alleged violations that the government never directly tied to Mr. Solomon himself.

Multiple arms of the federal government are actively fostering off-label usage. But if a drug manufacturer encourages off-label usage in some small, trifling, or inadvertent way, the government damns that company for supposedly greedily putting profits above public health. And then, in the case of Forest, after extracting a stiff fine from the company, the government goes so far as to pressure the company to fire its CEO, even though the CEO was never convicted of or even charged with a crime.

Department of Veterans Affairs Inspector General George J. Opfer asserted that the government's actions against Forest were, "protecting those veterans from harm done intentionally or indirectly by pharmaceutical companies who promote off label marketing for profit." Perhaps the general can explain how veterans were harmed when physicians *legally* prescribed these medicines; the veterans *voluntarily* took them; and the Veterans Administration, Medicare, and private insurers *voluntarily* paid for them. Who was deceived or intentionally harmed? Show us the victims.

And it wasn't just Forest that supposedly broke this rule; throughout a particularly aggressive enforcement period, Pfizer, as mentioned above, was hit with an oversized $2.3 billion settlement; Eli Lilly paid $1.4 billion; Novartis paid $422 million; Allergan paid $600 million; Elan paid $214 million; and GlaxoSmithKline paid $3 billion for its settlement. In total, for the 2009-2010 period, the Justice Department collected over $6 billion from drug companies for off-label promotion cases.[29]

Fish-Oil Pills and the FDA, Round 1

Amarin Pharma marketed an FDA-approved fish-oil drug called Vascepa. Vascepa had been approved for patients with *very high* levels of triglycerides, but Amarin believed that Vascepa could help patients with lower levels. After discussing this idea with the FDA, Amarin ran an FDA-approved trial that showed that Vascepa was safe and effective at reducing triglyceride levels in patients with merely *high* levels of triglycerides. This should shock no one. If a drug works in patients with very high triglycerides, there's a good chance it will also work in patients with high triglycerides. What's the problem?

The problem comes about because *very high* was on-label, while *high* was off-label. Amarin was sharing the results of its FDA-approved clinical trial with physicians so that they could improve their patients' health. There was no snake oil or fly-by-night salesmen here. This was all about getting the latest scientific findings to physicians to assist them in helping their patients. It would be hard to promote Vascepa and *not* mention the clinical trial results.

The FDA had already extracted many billions of dollars from drug companies as punishment for off-label promotion, and it wasn't going to make an exception of Amarin. Amarin didn't take this lying down and, bravely, sued and won. The ruling from the judges included the following statement:

> *[B]ans against truthful, nonmisleading commercial speech... usually rest solely on the offensive assumption that the public will respond 'irrationally' to the truth....The First Amendment directs us to be especially skeptical of regulations that seek to keep people in the dark for what the government perceives to be their own good.*
>
> **Fourth Circuit Court Ruling**[30]

Why would the FDA have such a policy and enforce it so vigorously? Think about it. If the FDA allowed a biopharma company to promote off-label uses without its specific approbation, the FDA would give up some of its power. Further, if drugs were being used for conditions for which the FDA had not given an official nod, then one could ask why drug companies should be required to garner that initial approval. The whole rationale for the FDA starts to unravel when we can see a precedent for the system working—physicians prescribing drugs and patients being successfully treated—with no visible evidence of FDA control.

The Crime of Writing a Factually Correct Press Release

The "promotion" of off-label uses can take some bizarre turns that hinge on some tenuous interpretations. Consider the case of former InterMune CEO, W. Scott Harkonen, M.D.

InterMune's lead product was Actimmune (interferon gamma-1b), which was approved by the FDA to treat two rare inherited diseases: severe malignant osteoporosis and chronic granulomatosis. InterMune was studying Actimmune for a third disease, idiopathic pulmonary fibrosis (IPF), hoping to expand Actimmune's label. When this incident took place, there was no good treatment—and no FDA-approved drugs—for this nasty, fatal disease that causes lungs to fill with scar tissue and causes death in three to five years.

Some preliminary work showed that Actimmune benefited patients with IPF, so starting in 2000, InterMune ran an FDA-approved clinical trial in 58 hospitals around the world to further explore those preliminary results. The new trial showed that while 17 percent of those on placebo died, only ten percent on Actimmune suffered the same fate. Unfortunately, the statistical significance, or p-value (see Chapter 7), was 0.08, while 0.05 is considered the magic threshold. In other words, while the treatment was promising, according to the norms of statistics, this trial didn't have enough oomph to "prove" that Actimmune worked. InterMune clearly

described these and other failing grades in a press release. That wasn't the problem.

The problem was that InterMune reported that the benefits to a subgroup, mild-to-moderate patients, was highly statistically significant (p=0.004). InterMune laid out the failing and passing results in the press release. The press release essentially said: we narrowly failed our primary objectives due to a lack of statistical significance, but the results showed promise overall and a benefit to one particular subgroup. While this press release seemed innocent enough, the FDA reacted like a bull to a matador waving a red cape.

The FDA claimed that InterMune and Harkonen should have limited the press release to the "we failed" part. The fact that the subgroup results were added, claimed the FDA, comprised off-label promotion and "wire fraud relating to the dissemination of false and misleading statements about the results of a clinical trial." Never mind that everyone involved, including the government prosecutors, agreed that the numbers and conclusions in the InterMune press release were factually correct. "The government has always agreed that there was no falsification of data here," said Allan Gordus, a Justice Department lawyer.

While Harkonen avoided jail, a judge sentenced him to three years' probation with six months of home confinement with frequent monitoring. He was ordered to pay a $20,000 fine and to perform 200 hours of community service. Worse, he is now forbidden to work in any manner with the government's Medicaid and Medicare health programs, effectively ending his careers as a pharmaceutical executive and as a medical doctor.[31]

It all came down to a matter of interpretation and judgment, with InterMune and Harkonen on one side and the federal government on the other.

> *The fact that somebody else doesn't think the evidence is enough—does that foreclose you from holding a different view?*
> **Mark E. Haddad,** Harkonen's attorney

So-called p-hacking and date dredging are a problem (see Chapter 8), but while scorned, they aren't a crime. Scientists everywhere and every day engage in the practice.

> *If you applied this rule to scientists, a sizable proportion of them might be in jail today.*
> **Steven N. Goodman,** Stanford University pediatrician and biostatistician

Stanford's Goodman went on to say, "Part of the issue goes to the level of proof a patient would need when facing a fatal disease with no treatment. If I were a patient, I would want to know [that the drug narrowly missed statistical significance]." That narrow miss "is far from proof that the treatment didn't work."[32]

The message is clear: if you're a CEO and you talk about clinical results in a way that displeases the FDA, you can go to jail.

Conflict with the U.S. Constitution

The Declaration of Independence defined the underlying ideas for this country, and the U.S. Constitution is the basis for its law. While this shouldn't surprise anyone, some still wish it weren't the case, and a subset of those people have been trying for centuries to evade the Constitution's control. But laws are laws and they stay laws until and if they are lawfully changed. Those who don't like what the Constitution says should work toward changing it, as the Constitution allows. But if they ignore it or torture and twist its words according to their masterplan, what they are really advocating is not a society with different laws, but a lawless society. They should think twice before taking that untenable step.

What do these founding documents tell us about the federal regulation of pharmaceuticals?

Read the Declaration of Independence and the Constitution of the United States and identify all the places, or even a single place, where the federal regulation of drugs is mentioned, mandated, or even allowed. You won't find one.

Read those same documents and try to find a place where off-label promotion is prohibited. You won't. You *will* find this statement in the Constitution: "Congress shall make no law…abridging the freedom of speech…." This *should* mean that the prohibition of off-label promotion and, further, the regulation of drug advertising in general, are illegal.

You also won't find a place where the federal government has the authority to prohibit drug companies from selling unapproved drugs.

Try to find a place in the U.S. Constitution where the federal government is given the authority to restrict the freedom of American citizens who are trying to help themselves or, in the extreme, harming themselves. You won't find it.

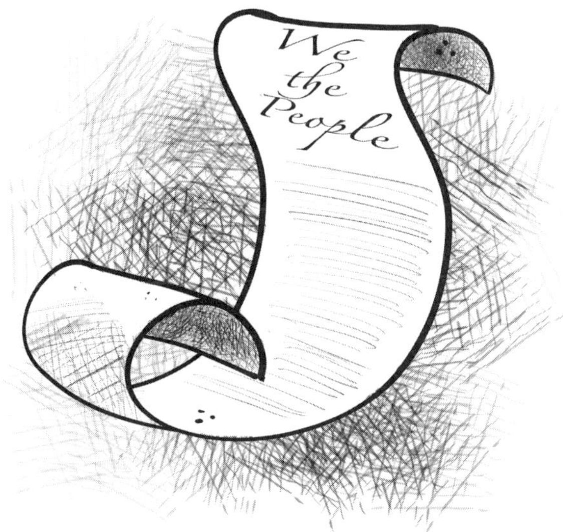

What you will find, however, in the Declaration of Independence is the statement that we have the inalienable rights to life, liberty, and the pursuit of happiness. These rights aren't given to us by the government; these rights exist irrespective of the government. This means that we have the liberty to use whatever food and drugs we see fit. This means that if the FDA withholds life-saving drugs, it is denying our right to life. Our pursuit of happiness may involve the usage of medicines that we consider to be therapeutic, and to deny us this inalienable right is to deny one of our most basic human rights.

You will also read the Ninth and Tenth Amendments in the Constitution, which clearly state, "The enumeration in the Constitution, of certain rights, shall not be construed to deny or disparage others retained by the people," and "The powers not delegated to the United States by the Constitution, nor prohibited by it to the States, are reserved to the States respectively, or to the people." Based on the Declaration of Independence and the Constitution of the United States, states and individuals have expansive powers, while the federal government has clearly delineated powers and was left by the Founders strictly limited and highly constrained.

Some believe that they've found wiggle room in the "general welfare" clause. Article I, section 8 of the Constitution grants Congress the power to "lay and collect Taxes, Duties, Imposts, and Excises, to pay the Debts and provide for the common defense and general Welfare of the United States." This "general welfare" clause—which also appears in the introductory paragraph of the Constitution—does not mean, as some assume and hope, that Congress has essentially unlimited power and can write any legislation if it can be argued to be for the "general welfare." First, promoting the general welfare was a *goal*—an overall objective of the Constitution—which is why it was in the "We the People" introduction; designing the specifically limited government described in the Constitution was the Founders' considered plan for *achieving* that goal.

The federal government can do only those things that are allowed by the Constitution. If Congress, the president, and the rest of the federal government could do *anything* they felt like doing, the Founders would never have seen the need to write the Ninth and Tenth Amendments in order to constrain the federal government—they would have been unnecessary.

Another clause sometimes used to justify federal government actions—the one providing the power to regulate "commerce among the states"—was intended to prevent the states, which were essentially operating as sovereign countries at the time, from limiting commerce by, say, charging tariffs or limiting the free movement of goods through their territories. Again, some may interpret "commerce among the states" to mean anything and everything, which could imply that Congress has been given unlimited power. We need to remember that the Founders of this country wrote the Constitution to define what the federal government can do—i.e., its powers—and primarily how those powers are limited. If the Founders wanted the federal government to have unlimited powers, the Constitution would either have been unnecessary or it would have been written completely differently, saying something such as, "The Congress is free to make any and all decisions affecting the citizens of the country." You'll notice that the Constitution doesn't say this or anything like it.

If for no other reason than our Founding Fathers wanting to constrain the federal government's powers via the Declaration of Independence and the Constitution, the FDA should be abolished, or at least it should be relegated from the federal to the state government level, enabling us to have fifty different approaches and the concomitant experimentation and competition therein.

FDA Violates Separation of Powers and Due Process

The FDA violates the separation of powers that the Constitution spells out between the legislative, judicial, and executive branches. The FDA creates rules, enforces those rules, and often adjudicates disputed matters.

A study by the Pacific Legal Foundation found that 98 percent of FDA rules over a recent 17-year period were unconstitutional.[33] A primary reason was that low-level civil servants often signed and issued new rules. These employees were never nominated by the president and confirmed by the Senate, meaning they could not be an "officer of the United States" as the Constitution requires. Career employees, while important players, are not democratically accountable for significant policy decisions.[34]

The FDA also violates the principles of due process.

For example, the federal government has stepped up its use of the so-called "responsible corporate officer doctrine" to hold pharmaceutical company executives personally and criminally responsible for FDA laws. This enforcement approach doesn't require the executives to be personally responsible for an offense or even to be aware that an offense has been committed. As we know, all residents of the United States are innocent until proven guilty, which requires prosecutors to prove criminal intent and criminal behavior. With the responsible corporate officer doctrine, prosecutors simply prove that a law was broken somewhere in the company, and it automatically follows that the executive(s) at the top of the organization must be guilty.

One conviction is worse than merely a fine and jail time; it can mean the end of that executive's career because the government's punishments actively ban convicted individuals from doing business with the government's health care arms, Medicaid and Medicare. No drug company can afford to forgo those large segments of business, and, therefore, no drug company would ever hire an employee with such a conviction, whose cost to the company could run into the billions of dollars. You've heard of three strikes and you're out? Welcome to "one strike by someone else and you're out."

Wrap-up

The FDA's approach leads to a number of challenges and some very odd results. Did Congress anticipate and consider these issues before it gave the FDA enormous power and money? Apparently not.

Patients can't vote with their feet. They don't get to pick diseases; diseases pick them. If the FDA makes it hard to develop new drugs for certain diseases, patients suffer, whether they see that connection or not. Pharmaceutical companies, on the other hand, deal with FDA-imposed handicaps with aplomb. They simply move on to other therapeutic areas and other diseases.

We've seen that the FDA has limited the number of new medicines available to doctors and patients. In this chapter, we've explored one mechanism behind that—the requirement that drug companies pick indications first and then test drugs for efficacy. Using a sports analogy, half of the athletes with star potential fell through the cracks if they were tested first in sports outside of their expertise. The same process causes some drugs to incorrectly appear to be losers.

In a serious challenge to the practices of science and medicine, we used realistic examples to explore how the majority of published research findings are actually false. They can't be trusted or replicated. That's painful for all of us who love and rely on science.

We also explored the startling case of a CEO who was criminally convicted for the offense of writing a balanced and factually correct press release.

In a serious challenge to the FDA and the federal government, we discussed how the Declaration of Independence—which spelled out the core tenets for this country—and the Constitution—which is the footing for all American law—have created a federal government whose limited powers prohibit it from regulating drugs. To argue otherwise, without actually changing the Constitution, is to advocate not a society with different laws, but a lawless society.

---

[1] Seizure Clusters, Epilepsy Foundation, http://www.epilepsy.com/information/professionals/refractory-seizures/potentially-remediable-causes/seizure-clusters#1

[2] Scannell, J., Blanckley, A., Boldon, H. et al. "Diagnosing the decline in pharmaceutical R&D efficiency." *Nature Reviews Drug Discovery* 11, 191–200 (2012). https://doi.org/10.1038/nrd3681

[3] Sam Peltzman estimated that FDA new drug approvals dropped by 60.9 percent since the FDA instituted its new rules in 1962. One divided by 0.391 equals 2.56.

[4] Russ Roberts interview of John Ioannidis, EconTalk, "John Ioannidis on Statistical Significance, Economics, and Replication," 20 January 2018.

[5] "Trouble at the Lab," *The Economist*, 19 October 2013, http://www.economist.com/news/briefing/21588057-scientists-think-science-self-correcting-alarming-degree-it-not-trouble

[6] David Colquhoun, "An investigation of the false discovery rate and the misinterpretation of p-values," Royal Society Open Science, 19 November 2014.

[7] The January 20, 2018 episode of EconTalk with Russ Roberts and John Ioannidis: "Statistical Significance, Economics, and Replication."

[8] Steve Usdin, "FDA's Woodcock reflects on aducanumab, drug approval standards, the future of clinical trials," BioCentury, 16 June 2021.

[9] David Colquhoun, "An investigation of the false discovery rate and the misinterpretation of p-values," Royal Society Open Science, 19 November 2014.

[10] John Ioannidis, "Hundreds of thousands of zombie randomised trials circulate among us," *Anaesthesia*, 2021.

[11] "Trouble at the lab," *The Economist*, 19 October 2013

[12] "Trouble at the lab," *The Economist*, 19 October 2013.

[13] Francis S. Collins and Lawrence A. Tabak, "NIH plans to enhance reproducibility," *Nature*. 2014 Jan 30; 505(7485): 612–613.

[14] Kelly Servick, "Mouse microbes may make scientific studies harder to replicate," 16 August 2016, *Science*, http://www.sciencemag.org/news/2016/08/mouse-microbes-may-make-scientific-studies-harder-replicate

[15] Steve Connor, "Study reveals that a lot of psychology research really is just 'psycho-babble'," Independent, 27 August 2015.

[16] Gunjan Sinha, "Bugs and Drugs," *Scientific American*, 14 November 2005.

[17] Robert Ashley, "Ask the Doctors," 4 October 2017.

[18] "Aluminum is the most abundant metal in the earth's crust." Jefferson Lab, http://education.jlab.org/itselemental/ele013.html, accessed 18 May 2009.

[19] "Wellness Made Easy," University of California, Berkeley, *Wellness Letter*, Vol 29, Issue 6, February 2013, pg 8.

[20] David R. Henderson, "Make Money off my Sickness...Please," Defining Ideas, Hoover Institution, 28 August 2000. http://www.hoover.org/research/make-money-my-sickness-please

[21] Originally published as: David R. Henderson and Charles L. Hooper, "The FDA's Power Grab," *Defining Ideas*, Hoover Institution, 8 September 2016.

[22] Natasha Singer, "F.D.A. Says Millions Got Unapproved Heart Pills," *The New York Times*, 26 March 2010.

[23] Thomas B. Graboys, MD; Bernard Lown, MD, "Nitroglyerin: The 'Mini' Wonder Drug," *Circulation*. 2003; 108: e78-e79.

[24] Natasha Singer, "F.D.A. Says Millions Got Unapproved Heart Pills," *The New York Times*, 26 March 2010.

[25] "The FDA vs. Small Pharma," *The Wall Street Journal*, Review & Outlook, 21 September 2007.

[26] Source: a personal conversation.

[27] Originally published as: David R. Henderson and Charles L. Hooper, "Pfizer's $2.3 Billion-Dollar Settlement," *Forbes*, 9 September 2009.

[28] Washington Legal Foundation v. Henney, 128 F. Supp. 2d 11, 15, D.D.C. 2000.

[29] "Pharmaceutical Companies to Pay $214.5 Million to Resolve Allegations of Off-label Promotion of Zonegran," Press Release, The U.S. Department of Justice, 15 December 2010.

[30] "Fourth Circuit Holds that a Regulation Largely Prohibiting Alcohol Advertisements in College Newspapers Is Constitutional," Harvard Law Review, Liquormart, 517 U.S. at 503 https://www.jstor.org/stable/25763031?seq=1#page_scan_tab_contents

[31] David Brown, "The press-release conviction of a biotech CEO and its impact on scientific research," *Washington Post*, September 23, 2020.

[32] David Brown, "The press-release conviction of a biotech CEO and its impact on scientific research," *The Washington Post*, 23 September 2013.

[33] https://pacificlegal.org/press-release/new-study-finds-98-of-fda-rules-over-17-years-are-unconstitutional/

[34] https://thehill.com/opinion/judiciary/440710-1860-unconstitutional-fda-rules

Chapter 9: FDA Myths

The FDA was given great powers based on some widely held but incorrect assumptions. What were those myths?

Myth: We're From the FDA and We're Here to Help You

The FDA was instituted to protect Americans from useless and dangerous drugs. It fulfills its duties by following Plato's ideal of the philosopher king, the benevolent dictator. The agency is saying, in effect, that it will pore over the data and decide what is best for us. Who could criticize such a worthy-sounding organization? Nonetheless, you may be shocked to learn that the FDA sometimes makes our lives more, not less, dangerous, and that at a fundamental level, it is unable to make some of the difficult tradeoffs necessary to help us get the best medical treatment. Frequently, the FDA eliminates our best alternatives.

Many believe that the FDA exists only to help us. Perhaps the FDA *should* exist purely to help us, but let's be realistic. The FDA is populated with individuals, just like you and me, who have hopes, dreams, and career aspirations. According to Sheldon Richman, "[g]overnment officials are no less devoted to their careers and prestige than people outside the government; indeed, power is what may have attracted many to government 'service.'"[1] It is entirely reasonable to see how these forces might incentivize FDA employees to act in ways that have more to do with *their* success than with *ours*.

And think about this: even if the FDA's true purpose were to make the best decisions about our healthcare, does this agency have the information it needs to properly address our health and welfare? How much can the FDA possibly know about each individual's particular situation, diagnosis, prognosis, and needs? The FDA *may* care about you, but it has zero knowledge of you—as a patient and as a human being.

Myth: When Experts Pore Over the Data, Clarity Ensues

Filgotinib

In 2020, the FDA and Japan's Ministry of Health, Labour and Welfare both reviewed a new drug application for Gilead Sciences and Galapagos' filgotinib, for rheumatoid arthritis. The two agencies looked at the results from the Phase 3 FINCH and Phase 2 DARWIN clinical trials.[2] Based on the clinical results, partners Gilead and Galapagos were optimistic about filgotinib's chances.

"After more than 4,544 patient-years' exposure thus far, the FINCH and DARWIN programs continue to show that filgotinib has a consistent efficacy and safety profile and has the potential to help more people living with RA achieve meaningful symptom control," said Walid Abi-Saab, MD, Chief Medical Officer at Galapagos.[3]

Gilead Sciences and Galapagos received mixed and disappointing results.

Even though the two government agencies looked at the same data, they came to different conclusions. The agency in Japan approved filgotinib with the data provided; the agency in the U.S. handed Gilead a complete response letter, which is FDA-speak for, "We can't approve your new drug until you show us more—and better—clinical trial data."

BPA

Consider the controversial and feared bisphenol A (BPA), a chemical used in certain plastic products, such as water bottles and food packaging. Many of my friends energetically avoid products that contain it and even avoid products, such as water bottles, that don't contain it but give the appearance that they could.

The State of California, based on the "State's Qualified Experts," has determined that BPA has been shown to be toxic to the female reproductive system.[4] The state feels so strongly about BPA that it required a sporting goods store that I visited to post prominent warnings about BPA at the customer checkout. My reaction was, "Really? Is BPA *that* dangerous?" The Centers for Disease Control isn't so certain about the health risks of BPA, saying that "[m]ore research is needed to understand the human health effects of exposure to BPA."[5] The FDA, after reviewing

more than 300 scientific studies over four years, is sticking to its conclusion that BPA remains safe in food contact materials.[6] The European Food Safety Authority has some doubt and will be re-evaluating BPA. The U.S. Environmental Protection Agency labels BPA a "chemical concern" and will continue to study its effects on the environment. The BPA industry maintains that "actual [human] exposure to BPA is hundreds to thousands [of] times below the safe intake limit."[7]

There you have it. Experts here and experts there, and there's no clear consensus.

Frustrated with differing opinions, the National Toxicology Program, the National Institute of Environmental Health Sciences, and the FDA developed a consortium-based research program known as the Consortium Linking Academic and Regulatory Insights on BPA Toxicity, or CLARITY-BPA, to answer the question once and for all. The program was designed specifically to limit possible biases and cheating. The current findings of this $8 million study? No adverse health effects were seen in animals exposed to low doses of BPA.[8] Is that the final answer? Or just one more opinion to be added to the list?

Regardless of which answer/opinion you think holds more water, the BPA case exposes the myth that if experts pore over the data, everything will become clear.

Pornography

Rarely, with new drug approvals, is there an objective, scientific truth that is incontrovertible and unambiguous. There are, instead, a variety of opinions and states of information that run the gamut. Even the "game" itself has ill-defined rules. Those involved often cannot define, beforehand, what they would consider "enough" to judge that a new drug has passed the twin hurdles of safety and efficacy. Consider the following quote from a different, earlier controversy:

> I shall not today attempt further to define the kinds of material I understand to be embraced within that shorthand description "hard-core pornography," and perhaps I could never succeed in intelligibly doing so. But *I know it when I see it*, and the motion picture involved in this case is not that. [italics added]

The famous quote above is from U.S. Supreme Court Justice Potter Stewart in 1964, when he was describing a threshold test for obscenity in

Jacobellis v. Ohio. "We" can't define pornography, but "we" can know it when "we" see it was the upshot. The pharma industry is no different. The problem is that we don't all see the same thing and we don't all agree.

The premise of the pharmaceutical regulatory regime is to test all new drugs for safety and efficacy and allow on the market only those drugs that pass some undefined and undefinable hurdles. But, as with pornography, definitions on which we all agree are difficult, if not impossible, to come by, and so we usually fall back on "we'll know it when we see it." Of course, one person's "we see it" is another person's "we don't see it." It's unrealistic, ultimately, to expect everyone to agree on complex, sometimes ambiguous, and possibly conflicting data, tentatively measured against undefined criteria. For complex issues like these, there doesn't need to be just one right answer. In fact, that is the strength of a decentralized system and the Achilles heel of a centralized system. The multitude of views and states of information in a decentralized system is a feature, not a bug.

Throughout this amorphous and mutable environment, pharmaceutical companies need to make long-term decisions about which projects to fund. With such uncertainty, it's amazing that companies can plan at all.

Myth: Experts Know Stuff. You, on the Other Hand...

Let's assume that you have psoriasis and use an ointment for it. This ointment was discovered, tested, and manufactured by some company, say Company A. Does Company A know how well the ointment has worked for you? No. In the absence of an adverse event, there's no direct feedback to Company A. Company A might talk to a small number of patients for market research purposes, but Company A never talked to you. Company A might buy data from an organized panel of patients. But unless you're in this panel, Company A won't hear from you. This ointment was approved by the FDA. Does the FDA know how well the ointment has worked for you? No. Again, the FDA doesn't call your home and ask you whether the ointment has been effective on your psoriasis. In fact, the FDA doesn't even know who you are, that you have psoriasis, and that you are using that salve. If you report an adverse event, the drug manufacturer and the FDA will hear from you, but that's relatively rare. Does your insurance company, doctor, or pharmacist know whether the salve has worked for you? Unless you directly tell them so, no. Your doctor diagnosed your psoriasis and prescribed the salve, but doctors frequently hear nothing back from patients about the success of their prescribed therapies unless there is a troublesome adverse event.

You, alone, know whether this ointment has worked for you.

Over the last century, the trend has been to shift the responsibility for medical care away from the individual and toward the "expert." Physicians and the FDA are seen as having more expertise than patients. If you want someone who can explain how COX-2 inhibitors or HMG-CoA reductase inhibitors work, good luck finding the average person on the street who can answer such a question. That's a job for an expert. However, you'd be even *less* likely to find someone at the FDA who knows whether that ointment worked for you. That's *your* relative expertise. You should recognize this fact and avoid being complicit in letting the authorities undercut your authority.

There are multiple types of information, and one can be considered an "expert" in many different areas. Some at the FDA are experts in how COX-2 inhibitors work, and we can appreciate their scientific knowledge. But that's just one type of information. There's also information that economists refer to as *local knowledge*. Locals know where the best river swimming spots are, where you can find good pizza, where to find the best deals on gasoline, and which nearby company is currently hiring. These people might not be experts on swimming, petroleum markets, pizza, or job markets in general, but they have special knowledge of time, place, and situation, knowledge that typically eludes a centralized government agency. Our psoriasis example demonstrates local knowledge.

Friedrich Hayek's Knowledge Insight

In 1974, Friedrich Hayek shared the Nobel Prize in economics with Gunnar Myrdal. One of Hayek's insights shed light on the source and use of knowledge in society, and particularly the difficulties faced by central planners attempting to organize an economy. Hayek's insights can be applied to the FDA, which is a type of central planner. Here, in a nutshell, is a summary of Hayek's view:

> But Hayek pointed out that the data are not "given." The data do not exist, and cannot exist, in any one mind or small number of minds. Rather, each individual has knowledge about particular resources and potential opportunities for using these resources that a central planner can never have. The virtue of the free market, argued Hayek, is that it gives the maximum latitude for people to use information that only they have.[9]

You have much better local knowledge of your psoriasis and the effect of that ointment than anyone else. And you have the most at stake, too. You are not an expert on psoriasis in general, but you are an expert on your psoriatic condition, and you have the most skin in the game (pun intended). You need to be viewed as a primary expert, not as a secondary expert, or worse, someone to be ignored.

Because of the advantages of having local knowledge, markets are able to solve fundamental problems that vex central planners. If Drug B works for you, as determined by your personal assessment, take it. If Drug B doesn't work, don't take it. If Drug B's extra cost isn't worth it to you, don't buy it. It's impossible for a central planner to make informed decisions and take appropriate actions for each and every individual.

Look at virtually every other product and service that touches our lives. The solution is the same: let those who want to supply it, supply it, and let those who want to purchase it, purchase it, assuming that those on both sides of the transaction are adults acting voluntarily and that both parties are held responsible for their actions. We can apply the same solutions to medicines. Our country did just such an intelligent thing in the past, and it can again.

Myth: The FDA Follows the Science[10]

The FDA claims to follow the science. According to the agency, "The FDA's job is to carefully evaluate the scientific data on a drug to be sure that it is both safe and effective for a particular use, and then to decide whether or not to approve it."[11] So why in 2021 did it attack ivermectin, a medication it certified as safe and effective in 1996?

The agency put out a special warning that "you should not use ivermectin to treat or prevent COVID-19."[12] The FDA's statement included words and phrases such as "serious harm," "hospitalized," "dangerous," "very dangerous," "seizures," "coma and even death" and "highly toxic." Any reader would think the FDA was warning against poison pills. In fact, the drug is FDA-approved as a safe and effective anti-parasitic.

Ivermectin was developed and marketed by Merck & Co. while I worked there years ago. William C. Campbell and Satoshi Omura won the 2015 Nobel Prize for Physiology or Medicine for discovering and developing avermectin, which Mr. Campbell and associates modified to create ivermectin.

Ivermectin is on the World Health Organization's List of Essential Medicines. Merck has donated four billion doses to prevent river blindness and other diseases in Africa and other places where parasites are common. A group of 10 doctors who call themselves the Front Line Covid-19 Critical Care Alliance have said ivermectin is "one of the safest, low-cost, and widely available drugs in the history of medicine."

Ivermectin fights 21 viruses, including SARS-CoV-2, the cause of COVID-19. A single dose reduced the viral load of SARS-CoV-2 in cell cultures by 99.8% in 24 hours and 99.98% in 48 hours, according to a June 2020 study published in the journal *Antiviral Research*.

At the time of writing, 75 clinical trials were evaluating the use of ivermectin for treating COVID-19. The statistically significant evidence at the time suggested that it is safe and works for both treating and preventing the disease.

In 115 patients with COVID-19 who received a single dose of ivermectin, none developed pneumonia or cardiovascular complications, while 11.4% of those in the control group did. In other trials, fewer ivermectin patients developed respiratory distress (2.6% vs. 15.8%); fewer required oxygen (9.6% vs. 45.9%); fewer required antibiotics (15.7% vs. 60.2%); and fewer entered intensive care (0.1% vs. 8.3%). Ivermectin-treated patients tested negative faster, in four days instead of 15, and stayed in the hospital nine days on average instead of 15. Ivermectin patients experienced 13.3% mortality compared with 24.5% in the control group.

Moreover, the drug can help prevent COVID-19. One 2020 article in *Biochemical and Biophysical Research Communications* looked at what happened after the drug was given to family members of confirmed COVID-19 patients. Less than 8% became infected, versus 58.4% of those untreated.

Despite the FDA's claims, ivermectin is safe at approved doses. Out of four billion doses administered since 1987, there have been only 28 cases of serious neurological adverse events, according to an article published in the *American Journal of Therapeutics*. The same study found that ivermectin has been used safely in pregnant women, children and infants.

If the FDA were driven by science and evidence, it would give an emergency-use authorization for ivermectin for COVID-19. Instead, the FDA asserts without evidence that ivermectin is dangerous.

Myth: The FDA is the Final Authority on Medical Matters

Juries

I have long been amazed by the combination of two irreconcilable facts: most people think that the FDA is the paramount expert on medical matters, but when patients feel that a drug has hurt them and they want recompense, they take the matter to the courts and, perhaps, a jury trial. If the FDA is such an esteemed authority and has the sole power to assess and approve medicines, why do the courts ignore the FDA's proclamations or, conversely, not seek retribution—or at least input—from the FDA when problems occur? What justification is there for jury trials to determine scientific issues? And if juries can determine scientific issues, then should the FDA be discharged from its drug approval role and be replaced by juries comprised of average Americans?

The scientists at the FDA proclaimed that Vioxx was a useful therapy option when it was green lighted in 1999. When Merck & Co. removed Vioxx from the market due to the risk of heart attack and stroke, the courts then tried to determine liability for drug harms, but they ignored the elephant in the room: the FDA. In August 2005, a jury of 12 non-scientists in Texas produced a $253 million verdict against Merck because of Vioxx. Also in 2005, Merck won a major court victory when a New Jersey jury found that the drug company properly warned patients about the risks of Vioxx, refusing to hold the company liable for some bad outcomes suffered by some.[13]

Isn't this the FDA's job? The FDA was, and is, tasked with ensuring that all medicines are safe and effective, and the FDA is charged with writing, in conjunction with the drug company, the package insert or "label" for each drug. If the label is incorrect or misleading, the FDA must share the blame. And if regular people, and not the experts at the FDA, can assess such matters, then why do we need the FDA in the first place?

Status Epilepticus

The FDA approves drugs as "safe and efficacious" for given indications, or specific diseases. One could assume that to treat a specific disease, the treatments to consider should come from a list of those drugs with the FDA's blessing for that indication.

For the serious and dangerous epileptic condition known as status epilepticus (SE), benzodiazepines are the typical first-line treatment. Patients that aren't helped with benzodiazepines, however, need a second-line therapy to bring their life-threatening seizures under control. The list of approved second-line drugs for SE includes Cerebyx (fosphenytoin), Dilantin (phenytoin), and phenobarbital.

Many would assume that, because they are FDA-approved, these drugs are the best for SE, as determined by scientific studies and a thorough review by the FDA.

However, consider for a moment that Keppra (levetiracetam)—not on the FDA's list—is the most widely used drug for this condition.[14] What gives? Have doctors been duped by aggressive drug company promotions? No. It would be outright illegal for the drug company that developed Keppra, UCB, to promote Keppra for status epilepticus without an approved indication. There is no promotion of Keppra by UCB.

Solid science supports the widespread use of Keppra. The results of a double-blind, response-adaptive, randomized controlled clinical trial in 2020 suggest that Keppra is as good as or better than Cerebyx.[15] A study in Japan supported this conclusion.

If you listened to the FDA, you'd never know this. The FDA's list of "best" drugs for SE ignores the premier scientific studies and leaves off arguably the best product; the FDA doesn't seem to care about this.

Doctors don't think the FDA is the final authority on medical matters. Instead, they follow their own experience, the experience of their peers, and the scientific literature. Patients experiencing deadly seizures are glad they do.

Myth: The FDA is Consistent and Logical

Are the federal government and, by extension, the FDA consistent and logical?

COVID-19 Vaccines

Before the FDA approves any new vaccine, it must conduct a manufacturing facility inspection. The thinking is that vaccines are used to inoculate millions of people and any problems with safety and reliability would be profound.

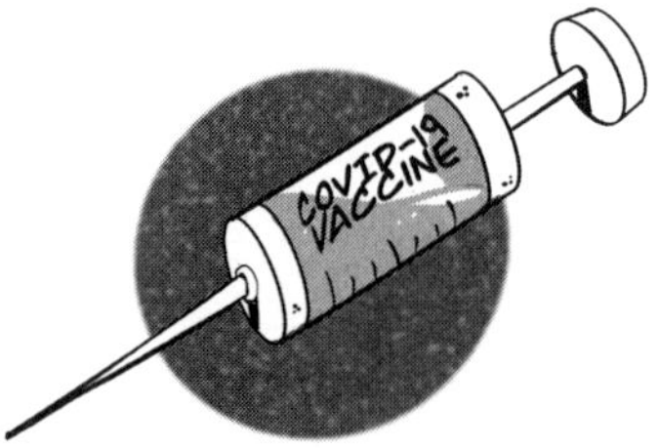

However, with new vaccines designed to immunize people against the virus that causes COVID-19, the FDA was planning on waiving the pre-launch manufacturing inspection requirement.[16] What makes this more striking is that some of the companies developing vaccines in this area are using new technologies and have never had any prior vaccines approved, meaning they and their new technologies have never faced an FDA manufacturing inspection. Plus, COVID-19 vaccines might be administered to billions of people in a short period of time, magnifying potential problems.

Arguments can be made for or against pre-approval FDA inspections, but if pre-approval inspections are a good idea for typical vaccines, then they are certainly a good idea for COVID-19 vaccines. And if inspections aren't needed for COVID-19 vaccines, then they certainly aren't needed for regular vaccines.

Is a little consistency too much to ask?

Marijuana

The federal government has a marijuana problem.

The U.S. government maintains marijuana's status as a Schedule I controlled substance, placing it in company with infamous drugs such as heroin, LSD, ecstasy, and PCP. A Schedule I drug is defined as having a very high potential for abuse, no accepted medical use, and a lack of accepted safety data for use under medical supervision.

In 2006, the FDA, concurring with this assessment, rejected marijuana for medical purposes, saying that "no sound scientific studies supported medical use of marijuana for treatment in the United States, and no animal or human data supported the safety or efficacy of marijuana for general medical use."

This action, however, is at odds with other FDA actions, which include approving, as safe and effective, Marinol and Cesamet, both synthetic versions of delta-9-tetrahydrocannabinol (THC), the main active ingredient in marijuana. Here's what the FDA had to say about Marinol. "MARINOL® (Dronabinol) Capsules is indicated for the treatment of: (1) anorexia associated with weight loss in patients with AIDS; and (2) nausea and vomiting associated with cancer chemotherapy in patents who have failed to respond adequately to conventional antiemetic treatments."

If the synthetic versions are so good, why didn't the FDA, in 2006, embrace the natural version? After all, in the Marinol statements above, the FDA was basically agreeing with marijuana advocates. It took more than a decade, but the FDA eventually approved the (mostly) natural version. In 2018, the FDA approved Epidiolex (cannabidiol) oral solution for the treatment of seizures associated with Lennox-Gastaut syndrome or Dravet syndrome. The FDA hasn't yet embraced natural, unprocessed marijuana and may never.

Still, if one federal agency says that marijuana has medical benefits, then how can another part of the federal government say that it has no medical use? It appears that the government is talking out of both sides of its mouth.

Special Protocol Agreements

A special protocol agreement (SPA) is a written agreement that a manufacturer may enter into with the FDA. The SPA sets out the design and parameters for the clinical trials of a new drug and the performance characteristics for which the FDA would approve the drug. For the FDA, such an agreement lets it spell out what it is looking for. For a drug company, such an agreement minimizes development risk by providing regulatory predictability, such that if the drug company follows the procedure set in the SPA and the drug meets the benchmarks specified in the agreement, the FDA *must approve the drug.*

Wikipedia says this about SPA's: "A Special Protocol Assessment (SPA) is an advanced declaration from the Food and Drug Administration that an uncompleted Phase 3 trial's design, clinical endpoints, and statistical analyses are acceptable for FDA approval." Under this agreement, if the drug company delivers the data, it will get an approval.

SPA's would be useful contracts if the FDA abided by them. But it doesn't always comply. And that's a problem. Consider the case of Amarin Pharma.

Fish-Oil Pills and the FDA, Round 2

Amarin Pharma was trying to secure an expanded label for its fish-oil-derived drug Vascepa (discussed in another context in Chapter 8). Here, what is important is that Amarin entered into a SPA with the FDA. Later, when the clinical trial of Vascepa showed that it had met all the requirements for approval set out in the SPA, Amarin expected that the FDA would approve Vascepa for that additional patient pool. Instead, the FDA rescinded the agreement. Some contract! The FDA believed that, although the drug did reduce triglyceride levels, as agreed upon, such a result was insufficient because the company didn't take an additional step and prove that reducing triglyceride levels would reduce cardiovascular events.

Here we have a government agency that normally operates opaquely to achieve unknown objectives and criteria. Then when it does—occasionally—specify those criteria ahead of time in a clear legal agreement, it sometimes still capriciously backs out of that agreement once those criteria have been met. That SPA was worth the paper it was printed on.

Flu Vaccines and the FDA

Pop quiz: Can drug companies market influenza vaccines even if the vaccines haven't been proven in clinical trials to attain some level of effectiveness?

The answer is yes. Such vaccines are sold first, and efficacy is determined later ("market and prove"). The FDA *doesn't* require the testing of flu vaccines each year, although we should note that our neighbor to the north, Health Canada, does.

If the FDA can relax its rules about clinical testing in one situation—for flu vaccines—why not in other situations? Follow the FDA and you'll see an organization that is, shall we say, "flexible" with its own rules.

KV Pharmaceutical

Here's another example of a fickle FDA ignoring its own rules.[17]

In 2012, the drug company KV Pharmaceutical had problems with its drug Makena (17P) and filed for Chapter 11 bankruptcy protection after its run-in with Congress and the FDA. Although KV played by the rules, it experienced the capriciousness of Congress and the FDA and, shortly thereafter, the immutability of economic laws.

A long-acting form of progesterone, 17 alpha-hydroxyprogesterone caproate (or 17P, for short), helped prospective mothers reduce the risk to their babies of preterm birth. With 17P not available through normal drug channels, compounding pharmacies—pharmacies that produce their own pharmaceutical products—had stepped in to produce and sell unapproved "home brew" doses of 17P for $10 to $20 each.

Why was 17P sold in such a way? In 1956, the FDA approved Squibb's Delalutin (the original version of 17P), but for conditions *other than* reducing the risk of preterm birth. After some time, Squibb (now part of Bristol-Myers Squibb) stopped marketing and manufacturing Delalutin. This abandonment opened the possibility of another company applying to the FDA to receive marketing approval and marketing exclusivity for a "new" branded version of 17P.

It wasn't until 2003 that 17P was actually studied for reducing the risk of preterm birth—meaning babies born before 37 weeks of pregnancy. A clinical trial involving pregnant women with a history of preterm delivery showed that weekly injections of 17P substantially reduced the rate of preterm delivery among these women and reduced health problems among their infants. This led to the "off-label" compounding by pharmacists and home brew doses.

Old "square peg" drugs, such as 17P, cast doubt on the whole rationale for the FDA. Do we really need the FDA to ensure that the medicines we consume are safe and effective? If so, then how do we explain the existence of a corner of the market where unproven home brew drugs are being used—and the sky hasn't fallen? Quite clearly, FDA approval is *not* a necessary condition for the successful use of medicines.

Not surprisingly, given its tendency to seek greater control, the FDA's long-term goal is to bring these misfit drugs into compliance. As a carrot, the FDA rewards pharmaceutical companies that take such products through the expensive and lengthy approval process with multi-year marketing exclusivity under the Orphan Drug Act. KV bought into this promise. In February 2011, the FDA approved Makena to reduce the risk of preterm birth in pregnant women with a history of at least one spontaneous preterm birth, giving Makena seven years of marketing exclusivity.

As someone whose child was born prematurely, at 2 pounds 11 ounces, I can tell you that preterm births are both scary and expensive. (Thankfully, my son is now a healthy and happy 25-year-old.) While we were lucky, not everyone is, and preterm births remain a serious problem. According to Sandra Kweder, M.D., deputy director of the Office of New Drugs at the FDA's Center for Drug Evaluation and Research, "Preterm birth is a significant public health issue in the United States. This [Makena] is the first drug approved by the FDA that is indicated to specifically reduce this risk."

That was the honeymoon period. And then KV announced the launch price. Makena's price was set at $1,500 per dose, increasing the cost of a complete therapy from $300 to $30,000.

As a next step, the FDA was supposed to shut down all compounding operations because, according to the FDA's own compliance policy, when the FDA approves new, commercially available drugs, all production of compounded copies must cease.[18] After all, how can it be "marketing exclusivity" if other producers are allowed to sell their own versions?

However, during the uproar over the high price of Makena, the FDA broke its own rules, presumably due to pressure from Congress. In a letter to the Federal Trade Commission, Senators Sherrod Brown, D-Ohio, and Amy Klobuchar, D-Minn., argued that Makena's price would reduce access to 17P and exhorted the FTC to investigate potential price-gouging and anti-competitive conduct by KV. The Senators expressed concern that KV was "taking advantage" of the FDA's approval and Makena's orphan-drug status, leading to "a monopolization of treatments to address preterm labors."[19] [20] Brown didn't stop with the FTC. At a Senate Appropriations Hearing, Brown grilled FDA Commissioner Margaret Hamburg on the "outrageous" price of Makena and asked her to "take leadership within HHS to find a strategy or path quickly to get this company to price its drug responsibly."[21] [22]

Were Brown and Klobuchar serious? Of course KV had taken advantage of its situation with Makena. That's what companies do.

In this case, of course, the federal government had essentially handed KV its advantage. Brown and Klobuchar were disingenuous for blaming the company for taking advantage of something that Congress gave it. And what is the FDA's award of market exclusivity other than a temporary, government-granted "anti-competitive" monopoly? The Senators should have started their investigation of anti-competitive conduct by looking in the mirror.

Under wilting political pressure, Hamburg and the FDA neglected to stop the compounding pharmacies, and the cheap doses of 17P continued. This put KV in a difficult position. Feeling stress from both the government inquiry and cheap competition, KV reduced the price of Makena to $690 per dose. This symbolic gesture didn't help matters, though, because competitors were still selling 17P at two percent of KV's price.

KV forced the issue by reversing roles with the FDA and analyzing some compounded versions of 17P, finding that most failed to meet at least one FDA quality standard for potency and/or purity. The FDA retorted, after analyzing some compounded 17P products itself, that it had found no major safety problems, but it reserved the right to take enforcement action against the compounding pharmacies, if warranted. But did the FDA really want to set a precedent of allowing unapproved drugs on the market and then acting only if there were a problem with them? Perhaps seeing the rhetorical corner it was boxing itself into, the FDA reiterated its belief that approved drug products such as Makena "provide a greater assurance of safety and effectiveness than do compounded products."

In August 2012, hopelessly trapped and facing disappointing sales, KV Pharmaceutical filed for Chapter 11 bankruptcy protection, blaming the FDA's lack of enforcement of market exclusivity for Makena. KV explained that it had been "unable to realize the full value" of Makena after the FDA gave de facto approval to the compounded products, which "effectively nullified" Makena's seven years of exclusivity. KV had earlier sued the FDA to take "sufficient enforcement actions" to stop the distribution of compounded 17P, but in September 2012, U.S. District Court Judge Amy Berman Jackson dismissed the suit on the grounds that the case pertained to the FDA's "discretionary enforcement activities."

Was KV gullible for actually believing that it would get the seven years of marketing exclusivity promised by the FDA? Perhaps. The FDA has demonstrated that it is, at its heart, a political organization that bends its rules to accommodate the prevailing political winds. In the choice between following their own rules and keeping their jobs secure, the FDA's top brass chose the latter.

Many people believe that the FDA needs to ensure that the medicines we Americans consume have been proven safe and effective long before we ever get a chance to use them. Yet the Makena story gives us a peek into an area of medical practice where unproven home brew drugs rule the market, where even the FDA seems to agree that FDA approval is superfluous.

Myth: Unregulated Drug Companies Will Harm Patients

> *Manufacturers have vested interests. Between those interests and the interests of patients, the FDA must be the arbiter. To argue that people ought to be able to choose their own risks, that government should not intervene, even in the face of inadequate information, is to impose an unrealistic burden on people when they are most vulnerable to manufacturers' assertions: when they are desperately ill, when they are hoping against hope for a cure, or when they are seeking to enhance their physical appearance.*
> **David Kessler**, former Commissioner of the FDA

Numerous complaints, many discussed in this book, have been leveled against the FDA. But we should ask: if the FDA didn't exist, or if it were scaled back, would patients be at increased risk from unregulated drugs? Are manufacturers' "vested interests" such that they would purposely or inadvertently hurt patients? These are important questions.

Nisha Gupta was a medical resident who, while treating a patient, accidentally poked herself with a needle. Unfortunately, that incident infected Gupta with chronic hepatitis C and led her on a harrowing multi-decade path of liver transplantation, encephalopathy, and cancer. "We were all stressed out. I was going to die soon and I was prepared," she recalls.[23]

That was her prognosis at the time, but Gupta was kept alive by a drug that wasn't commercially available at the time. Gupta, through her doctor, contacted Bristol-Myers Squibb to acquire compassionate use—really "expanded access"—doses of BMS's Daklinza (daclatasvir), while Daklinza was still in early clinical trials. The BMS drug worked miracles and Gupta was afterwards completely hepatitis C free. She was cured, and Daklinza has since been green lighted by the FDA to treat hepatitis C virus infections.

Interestingly, Gupta had first contacted the drug companies Merck & Co. and Vertex to obtain expanded access doses of boceprevir and telaprevir—both since approved by the FDA—but the companies were worried that their unapproved drugs would interact with the other drugs the woman was taking. "As a company, and a physician, we were taught not to do harm. We thought we would do harm," Vertex's chief medical director, Dr. Robert Kauffman, explained.

We have been told for decades that without the FDA to protect us, drug companies would sell us all manner of dangerous and ineffective drugs. If we ever doubted that, two words were on standby to make us cower: thalidomide babies. "If the FDA doesn't protect us, we will have more thalidomide babies!" Yet here was a gravely ill patient begging two drug companies to let her try their hepatitis C drugs—drugs that were eventually approved as safe and effective—and they refused. Does that make sense? Yes, it does. Drug companies are run by people, often physicians, or other medically trained people, who want to help patients, not hurt them. Executives and employees alike hold their heads high when they consider the progress they have made in the war against disease—such as curing hepatitis C. Drug companies make money when they successfully treat medical conditions, and they risk going out of business if they don't or, even worse, if they hurt patients. Just look at the Vioxx fiasco, the army of lawyers that filed cases, and Merck's near brush with corporate death. Vioxx was a misstep that Merck, and every other biopharma company, hopes to never repeat. Merck doesn't need a government agency, such as the FDA, to state the obvious: the world is watching and if you hurt patients, you will suffer in so many ways that it will make your head spin!

The Vioxx Chronicle

It is important to remember and understand the history of the ill-fated Vioxx.[24]

After running the APPROVe clinical trial, designed to test whether Vioxx could prevent the recurrence of colon polyps, Merck & Co. determined that Vioxx increased the risk of heart attacks by 80 percent after 18 months of therapy (25 events on placebo versus 45 events on drug). Just days after the data became available and even though *no patients died* from these cardiovascular events in the trial,[25] Merck decided to voluntarily stop selling its blockbuster Vioxx. *The Wall Street Journal* wrote:

> Even in the case of Vioxx, the likelihood that an individual taking the drug would have a heart attack or stroke is relatively small. In a study of 2,600 patients, there were 15 heart attacks or stroke[s] per 1,000 patients among those who took Vioxx for longer than 18 months. Among those who took a placebo, there were 7.5 heart attacks or strokes per 1,000 patients. And those who took Vioxx for less than 18 months had no increased cardiovascular risk.[26]

The risk of a patient having a cardiovascular event related to Vioxx was "very small," according to then Acting FDA Commissioner Lester M. Crawford, but "overall, patients taking the drug chronically face twice the risk of a heart attack compared to patients receiving a placebo."

An empirical comparison of risks can help frame the Vioxx danger. Based on a paper in *Health Affairs*, the fatality risk of Vioxx was 76 per 100,000 person-years, which is about the same as for another, currently marketed drug, Tysabri (natalizumab) for multiple sclerosis, at 65. This is about twice the fatality risk of rock climbers, construction workers, taxi drivers, chauffeurs, and truck drivers, per person-year. But the risk of Vioxx use is far lower than that for logging workers, tree fallers, and motorcycle riders.

Vioxx is off the market now due to concerns about safety, but one can still legally climb rocks, cut trees, drive trucks, and ride motorcycles.

As an aside, perhaps Merck should have kept Vioxx on the market and, instead, limited its usage to those patients with the best benefit/risk profile. The withdrawal gave ammunition to those who argued that Vioxx's benefits weren't significant enough to warrant *any* increased risks. And, as we will have seen elsewhere (see Chapter 2), there were patients who strongly preferred Vioxx over other drugs, even with the increased cardiovascular risk. This approach would have helped Merck squash the image of Vioxx being a wildly dangerous drug, and it may have prevented some proportion of the subsequent lawsuits. Nevertheless, Merck bravely pulled the plug on its blockbuster.

Some claimed that Merck had hid bad Vioxx data. CBS's *60 Minutes* joined that list of detractors when it reported, shortly after Vioxx was pulled from the market:

> However, according to internal Merck documents ***60 Minutes*** has seen, and interviews with outside scientists, Merck had concerns that Vioxx could possibly cause cardiovascular risks long before it was pulled off the market.

CBS's report clearly gives the impression that Merck hid this information. But here's a simple fact: **Merck had been warning patients about the cardiovascular risks for years**. The package insert ("prescribing information" or "label") from September 2002, and reprinted in the widely used *Physicians' Desk Reference*, devotes two full tables and a number of paragraphs to the risk of cardiovascular problems. The package insert reports data from the VIGOR study showing that 45 of 4,047 patients on Vioxx experienced a "cardiovascular thrombotic event" (strokes and heart attacks) compared to only 19 of 4,029 patients on naproxen. The package insert goes on to say that Vioxx is not a substitute for aspirin and that patients who need cardiovascular protection should continue taking aspirin. Printing such risks in the package insert is not a good way to hide any of Vioxx's warts. Instead, it is a way to allow doctors and patients to make informed choices.

I should clarify that most strokes and heart attacks are not fatal. Only five patients on Vioxx and four on naproxen died of heart attacks in the VIGOR study. In other words, there was one extra death from a heart attack out of 4,000 people on Vioxx at double the maximum recommended daily dose. That seems like a small risk. But the key point is that Merck broadcast those results to the world and didn't hide them.

CBS doubled down on its bad reporting.

The network showed a healthy, beautiful 39-year old, Janet Huggins, who died within a month of starting to take Vioxx. CBS added:

> Instead, Merck found something potentially worse: Patients taking Vioxx for longer than 18 months were twice as likely to suffer a heart attack or stroke than those taking a placebo.

But 18 months is *not* one month. What was CBS thinking? Merck has solid evidence that Vioxx shows no additional cardiovascular risk until after 18 months of therapy; Huggins died in one month. To blame everything on Vioxx is sloppy thinking.

When I worked at Merck in the late 1980s/early 1990s, employees proudly quoted George W. Merck's 1950-era credo: "We try never to forget that medicine is for the people. It is not for the profits. The profits follow, and if we have remembered that, they have never failed to appear." Not for nothing did *Fortune* magazine name Merck America's Most Admired Corporation seven years in a row around that same time.

It's interesting that the ultimate insider, Merck's then-CEO, Ray Gilmartin, told a congressional committee that his wife took Vioxx until the day the company withdrew the drug. Unless we speculate that he was out to kill his wife slowly, and was willing to accept a low probability of succeeding, his and her behavior are powerful evidence that Merck was selling a drug it considered relatively safe.

Anyone who thinks that established, reputable pharmaceutical companies would foist dangerous products on the American public absent the FDA should study this situation carefully. As the first bulwark, the employees within these companies would stop such drugs and, if that didn't do the trick, their shareholders would try to apply the brakes, followed by doctors, pharmacists, hospitals, third-party payers, and industry watchdogs. And if a company persisted and marketed a bad drug, trial lawyers would gleefully bring it to its knees. Pharmaceutical companies clearly understand this situation. The world is watching, and companies that hurt patients will suffer in manifold ways. It's time the public and policy makers learned this insight.

This is why we will not return to the days of snake oil sales. If we somehow rewound automobile regulations back to those of 1965, pre-U.S. Department of Transportation, our cars wouldn't suddenly revert to Dodge Darts, Rambler Americans, and Chevrolet Corvairs. Likewise, if we rewound drug regulations to the pre-FDA era, our medicines wouldn't revert to quinine and digitalis.

Myth: The FDA Prevents Harm to Americans

If a pharmaceutical company's drug severely harms or kills a patient, that could be front-page news. But that's not the only way that patients can be harmed. A patient who isn't given a helpful medicine at the right time is also harmed and may suffer severe consequences or even die. But this type of harm, which includes the cases in which the drug isn't provided because *it doesn't exist,* doesn't make it onto the front page or even page 13 or 33 of the newspaper because the victim and the harm caused are typically invisible. Who was the victim? We usually don't know. What drug would have helped the person and to what extent? We usually don't know.

Recall that economist Frederic Bastiat's lesson (see Chapter 6) was to study both what is seen and what is unseen. (His short essay, "What Is Seen and What Is Not Seen," is worth reading.[27]) The "seen" in the first example is a specific drug harming a specific person, for a Type 1 error. The "unseen" in the second example is a good drug not helping a person, for a Type 2 error. This unseen situation often results from a drug not being developed, perhaps because a company didn't see a clear development path or economic payback, or because the drug was explicitly rejected by the FDA.

Eteplirsen

Sometimes, however, the unseen can be observed with careful observation. Consider two young boys with the same deadly disease— Duchenne muscular dystrophy (DMD). Max Leclaire, age ten, was in a clinical trial for a new drug that had miraculously reversed some of his debilitating symptoms. His brother Austin, age 13, had tried to enter the clinical trial but didn't meet the exacting criteria. (Drug development is serious business for biopharma companies, and they often severely limit the types of patients that can enter clinical trials to improve their chances of an ultimate FDA approval.)

Sarepta Therapeutics was, at the time, developing eteplirsen for DMD. For the previous year Max had received a once-weekly IV infusion in a double-blind clinical trial. After just four months, Max's parents realized that their son was getting the active drug because it had not only slowed the progression of the disease but had dramatically improved his symptoms—something that, for this disease, was highly unlikely to happen with a placebo. They just wished that their second boy, who had steadily worsened, could have had the same chance.

The juxtaposition of the two boys' conditions allows us to say with some confidence that Austin was being harmed by *not* receiving eteplirsen. Why wouldn't Sarepta give eteplirsen to Austin? After all, there was evidence from Max's case that the drug was having a positive effect. Essentially, the

FDA simply wouldn't allow it because, according to the agency, the proof of eteplirsen's efficacy and safety had not yet been established. Would Austin's parents, given everything they knew about eteplirsen, willingly give to it to Austin? Definitely. And they had attended meetings with the FDA to make their feelings known.

So, Austin's parents were forced to follow the FDA's assessment of what constitutes an acceptable risk—for all drugs, not just for those in clinical trials—instead of relying on their own judgment. Austin's situation gives us a rare opportunity to shine a light on a typically unseen problem and to actually see how the FDA can harm patients.

As economist Milton Friedman once said, "I don't think the state has any more right to tell me what to put into my mouth than it has to tell me what can come out of my mouth." Of course, the state doesn't agree, and the FDA's whole raison d'être is to tell us what we can put into our mouths (and eyes, noses, muscles, veins, and skin).

Not Available Here

We've been told that Elixir Sulfanilamide- and thalidomide-type troubles result from a pharmaceutical market devoid of government control. While there's some truth to that, these types of problems can still arise in markets *with* government control and, worse, government control can actually cause different types of problems. Problems will crop up in self-regulated markets—yes. However, those same types of problems, and others, can also crop up in government-regulated markets.

Alodorm (nitrazepam), a hypnotic drug of the benzodiazepine class, provides short-term relief from severe, disabling anxiety, plus insomnia, and was approved in the U.S. in 1971. Providing fuel for the "drug lag" argument, the approval abroad had come a full five years earlier. Alodorm provided an advantage over other drugs at the time, leading to fewer deaths from overdoses. Dr. William Wardell, co-founder of Tufts University's Center for the Study of Drug Development, analyzed the delay in the FDA's approval of Alodorm and concluded that 3,700 lives had been lost.[28] This one "drug lag" resulted in 34 times as many lives lost as did the Elixir Sulfanilamide disaster. Wardell also looked at the delay in the FDA approval of beta blockers and estimated that that one event accounted for tens of thousands of deaths, or some multiple of the entire thalidomide disaster.

Can the FDA really be keeping good therapies from us?

Robert Goldberg of Brandeis University estimated that at least 200,000 Americans died over a 30-year period due to drugs that they couldn't get but that were available overseas.[29] If that number is correct, that death toll is equal to about 2,000 Elixir Sulfanilamide disasters.

The time taken for the FDA's review of Cytotec (misoprostol), a drug for stomach ulcers, may have led to the deaths of 15,000 people. Similarly, the time to review streptokinase, a so-called clot buster, may have precipitated 22,000 deaths.

Another specific case highlights tens of thousands of needless deaths per year, making the thalidomide and Elixir Sulfanilamide disaster pale in comparison. The FDA's officially approved uses for aspirin include the temporary relief of minor aches and pains associated with a cold, headache, backache, toothache, premenstrual and menstrual cramps, and minor pain of arthritis. Aspirin can also be used to temporarily reduce a fever. What is missing? According to economist David R. Henderson, "... millions of people are unaware of the strong clinical evidence that aspirin can reduce deaths caused by heart disease. But because the FDA has never approved aspirin for preventing heart disease, drug companies are legally prohibited from advertising that information. As Paul Rubin, an economist at Emory University, has said, 'The ban on aspirin advertising causes tens of thousands of needless deaths per year.' This is all thanks to regulation by the FDA."[30]

On 20 November 2020, Pfizer and partner BioNTech submitted a request to the FDA for an Emergency Use Authorization (EUA) of their vaccine candidate against the SARS-CoV-2 virus. The request was based on a final analysis of the clinical trial results from November 18. The FDA scheduled an advisory committee to meet on December 10 to review the EUA application and approval was given the following day. This means that the FDA gave limited approval to the vaccine 23 days after the glowing clinical results were fully analyzed and released. Considering that approximately two thousand Americans were dying each day due to COVID-19, the FDA's admittedly expeditious process still cost at least 46,000 lives.[31] That human cost far exceeded the cost of the Elixir Sulfanilamide and thalidomide tragedies that gave the FDA its powers.

Am I advancing an unsupportable, pro-industry spin by providing these specific examples? Not at all. Consider the work of Columbia University's Frank R. Lichtenberg. He studied the effects of pharmaceutical innovation using an approach whereby he compared the vintage (the launch year) of drugs used in a country with the increase in national life expectancy at birth. This research was motivated, interestingly enough, by research that showed higher productivity in manufacturing firms that used more modern, or later-vintage, equipment. Could a similar pattern be seen with drug usage? Here's what he's found:

> For the 30 countries in our sample, between 2000 and 2009 population-weighted mean life expectancy at birth increased by 1.74 years. The estimates indicate that the increase in life expectancy at birth due to the increase in the fraction of drugs consumed that were launched after 1990 was 1.27 years—73% of the actual increase in life expectancy at birth.[32]

Of course, like all retrospective studies, this study shows only correlations and is incapable of showing cause and effect. Yet if these findings are correct, *three quarters of the increase in life expectancy we've enjoyed in recent times is due solely to our adoption of modern drugs*. New pharmaceuticals are friends, not foes.

Scrutinizing new drugs from an economic perspective further highlights their value. As pointed out in the Introduction, only two percent of the total value of vaccines ends up in the pockets of the companies that develop and manufacture them, while 98 percent is enjoyed by those patients who are vaccinated and by society overall.[33] Nobel prize-winning economist William Nordhaus found a similar conclusion across other industries: "Innovators were able to capture about 4 percent of the total social surplus from innovation."[34] *We* are the primary recipients of the value of new innovations and *we* should encourage innovators to keep innovating.

The FDA can only slow the adoption of modern drugs and the resulting increase in life expectancy and other economic benefits. It can apply the brakes firmly or less firmly; it doesn't even own a gas pedal.

Myth: The FDA Would Approve Itself

Recall that the FDA employee who suggested the higher loading dose for Toradol IV/IM based that recommendation on a hypothesis and some mathematical modeling, not on empirical evidence. Now contrast that with what the FDA requires of the companies it regulates.

Some years after Toradol Oral was approved (barely) by the FDA, one of my clients, Roxro Pharma, tried to develop an intranasal formulation of ketorolac, named Sprix. As you can imagine, in the intervening 15 years since Toradol IV/IM had been approved, ketorolac had been widely used by patients and physicians and studied by researchers. Through this process, it was determined that serum (blood) concentrations of ketorolac determined the effectiveness of the dose. So, when Roxro built its case to convince the FDA of intranasal ketorolac's safety and efficacy, it should have been as simple as showing that proper serum concentrations were quickly attained without any adverse effects at the point of delivery—the nostrils. Roxro could have shown that intranasal ketorolac was just like the other formulations of ketorolac—in that it gave similar serum levels—and it did not irritate nasal tissue.

A reasonable person might think that this new drug should have been approved based on that information alone. But the FDA is not a "reasonable person." Roxro had a perfectly logical argument for seeking approval of its intranasal formulation without the need for further empirical, clinical data. The FDA, though, does not typically accept logical arguments, no matter how reasonable and compelling; the FDA accepts only cold, hard data based on well-controlled experiments. That is, at least, when the FDA isn't the one pushing the logic.

Perhaps empirical data *is* of paramount importance, and logical arguments can be seriously flawed, as we saw with the Toradol IV/IM loading dose. Perhaps we should act only if we have empirical data clearly saying we should act; otherwise, we should obey the status quo and wait to act.

Now consider for a moment how the FDA came into being in the first place. The FDA exists because of congressional action. There were no cold, hard data. There were no tests and trials run. There was no experimentation. As we already discussed, some problems in the usage of certain drugs were identified; Congress thought about these problems for a bit and then gave the FDA beefy regulatory powers. And yet, "Americans will be healthier with the FDA than without" is a hypothesis amenable to testing and proof, and nothing more.

Have we Americans been healthier with the FDA and all its regulatory power? Are drugs on the market safer? Are drugs on the market more efficacious? Has the FDA helped increase or reduce the number of drugs on the market? Has the FDA increased or decreased the quality-adjusted life years of us Americans? (See Chapter 10 for the answer.) And, if it has increased the quality-adjusted life years, at what cost? Have we gotten a good deal?

Has the FDA employed empirical evidence to prove that we can be 95-percent sure that its approach to drug regulation is the best approach? If not—and I've personally never seen a hint of proof—then the FDA fails its own tests and should reject itself. In the ultimate ironic, existential paradox, if the FDA were a new drug, it would, indeed, reject itself.

The FDA's current approach to drug regulation is not the only alternative. The FDA could approve drugs based on safety only and let the medical ecosystem determine which drugs work and for whom. As part of that approach, the FDA could even retain the right to pull drugs that are later found to have no effectiveness. The FDA could be an advisory agency instead of a gatekeeping agency. It could sometimes substitute logic for empirical data, as in the Sprix case. It could ensure that medicines are labeled correctly and nothing else. The FDA could rely more heavily on outside experts. Or, perhaps, the FDA could simply disappear. The point is, Congress and the FDA adopted an approach without exploring other approaches and without empirical evidence. That was unscientific. The motivation was political, and no scientific testing and empirical evidence was considered or required.

The government demands empirical evidence when the "bad guys" need to prove something, but not when the "good guys" desire something. For instance, the *Wall Street Journal* reported in May 2013 that, based on a randomized, prospective, scientific study in Oregon, having Medicaid insurance was no better than having no insurance.

> On Wednesday the *New England Journal* published the results from year two of the Oregon project, which "showed that Medicaid coverage generated no significant improvements in measured physical health outcomes" versus being uninsured. If Medicaid were a new drug, in other words, the FDA would reject it.[35]

So how did the federal government respond to this? By curtailing, restructuring, or canceling Medicaid? No. The government further *expanded* Medicaid. Imagine the outrage and surge of lawsuits if a private company charged customers $580 billion a year for a program that provided zero benefits. With a governmental program, such a monumental failure simply draws yawns, as if we expected it all along.

As with Medicaid, we should not be afraid to ask hard questions about the efficacy of the FDA itself; the FDA regularly asks tougher questions of drug companies, day in and day out. Turnabout is fair play.

In 1962, Congress failed in its due diligence and even got the logic completely wrong: thalidomide had a problem with *safety*, an issue for which the FDA already had regulations, but the laws were changed in 1962 to add proof of *efficacy*. Thalidomide was unsafe, but only for fetuses, not for everyone, and even the new laws may not have prevented the thalidomide tragedy due to the prevailing level of scientific knowledge at the time.

It is important to note that thalidomide, along with some new thalidomide derivatives, is back on the market today for a variety of conditions and is successfully treating patients daily. Revlimid (lenalidomide) is closely related to thalidomide and has been proven effective at treating myelodysplastic syndrome, mantle cell lymphoma, and multiple myeloma.

The Elixir Sulfanilamide disaster in 1937 was not a case of a dangerous drug but of a gross mistake. The mistake was corrected almost immediately under the pre-FDA system. The Elixir Sulfanilamide problem arose without the FDA and it was quickly resolved without the FDA's involvement. It's true that the FDA, had it been in place, likely would have prevented the Elixir Sulfanilamide disaster, but at what cost? Is preventing a relatively small, quickly corrected problem enough to justify the enormous cost of the FDA and the 60-percent reduction in new drug approvals? In 2006, in an eerie repeat of the first tragedy, there were 94 deaths in Panama from a cough syrup tainted with diethylene glycol. This medication had not been produced by a greedy drug company hungry for profits, but by Panama's very own national health system.[36] Problems can occur no matter who's at the wheel, and those problems can be quickly corrected without panicking and driving into a tree. Further, we need to retain perspective: the 107 children killed by Elixir Sulfanilamide account for less than three percent of the children who voluntarily, but unknowingly, drink sweet and tasty ethylene glycol *every year*.[37] Of course, not all of them die, but many do.

A couple of tragedies were leveraged to give the FDA enormous, intractable power. Was it worth it?

Thinking people can disagree, a priori and ex ante, about whether the FDA will help or hurt people on balance, and it is hard to tell without empirical evidence. Will the FDA's focus on safety reduce problems with dangerous drugs? Will the presence of the FDA keep drug companies honest? Will the FDA's expensive requirements for new drugs reduce the development and marketing of newer, better drugs and, therefore, deny people the benefit of those good drugs? Will reduced competition drive up drug prices, compromising choice and access? How will these competing forces balance out? Will the FDA, on net, help or hurt? One person could hypothesize that the FDA will, on balance, help, while another could hypothesize that it will, overall, hurt.

Clearly, without solid supporting data, the FDA would never approve itself.

Myth: Congress Thoroughly Vetted the FDA Concept

If empirical data and experiments are the way to go, and logic is not to be believed, why did Congress institute a vast new bureaucracy without conducting even a single experiment? In an ironic twist, Congress used logic and hypotheses to set up a government agency that doesn't believe in using logic and hypotheses. Congress collected no new data to empower an agency that requires others to collect voluminous amounts of expensive data.

We can do better.

What else could Congress have done? We can reasonably ask: if all new medicines must be rigorously tested for both safety and efficacy, lest innocent people might be harmed, why should government agencies evade such scrutiny? After all, government agencies and their policies are far more impactful than any single drug, and they may be harming innocent people, either directly or indirectly. If they are, we have a right and an obligation to know.

Congress could have, and *should* have, tested the FDA for safety and efficacy. Luckily, it's not too late. How, you might wonder, can an agency be tested for these traits? We could split the country in some manner and run an experiment. The best approach might be to assign half of Americans to a test group and half to a control group. Perhaps we could use the last digit of Social Security numbers, with even-numbered individuals under the control of the FDA and odd-numbered individuals not. That way, people could move geographically without disturbing the system, and we would avoid confounding factors such as regional variations in genetics, affluence, medical care, diet, and lifestyle. Children would fall into their mother's category until they reached age 18. Half of all Americans would be under the regulations of the current FDA, while half would have a relatively free market with none of the FDA's regulations.[38] We could then check back in 20 or 30 years and see which group did better by any number of metrics. Scientists, statisticians, economists, and market researchers would think they'd died and landed in heaven with the plethora of data.

As an aside, imagine how people would react if, by design, the experiment divided them not by Social Security numbers, but by residence relative to the Mississippi River; those east of the Mississippi would be under the control of the FDA, and those west of that great river would not be. Would there be lawsuits by those in the East, claiming that they were being discriminated against? Or, what if women were under the FDA's control but men weren't? Would that be sexist *against* women? Or, perhaps, what if minorities were under the control of the FDA and whites were not? Would that be racist *against* minorities?

Instead of just the two groups described above, there could be three groups: Group 1 would follow the FDA's safety and efficacy rules; Group 2 would follow just the FDA's safety rules; and Group 3 would follow neither. Twenty or 30 years would be required to give biopharma companies time to develop medicines for the three groups and to get a good reading on the health outcomes of the groups. True, it would take some time. But the sooner we started, the sooner we'd know.

The above approach is empirical and could demonstrate whether the FDA helps or hurts Americans. And yet many would be uncomfortable with such an approach for the same reasons that it is considered unethical in a clinical trial to give a sick person a placebo when there's an accepted treatment available. Giving a person a placebo in place of an effective treatment is highly likely to cause that person harm. The fear is that those in Group 3 (the non-FDA group) would be free to purchase and use useless products such as Dr. Quack's Curesall Placebo, effectively hurting themselves.

This logic, while appealing, is flawed because it assumes that the FDA protects people, which is exactly what we want to discover. Such a conclusion merely begs the question: it assumes as given that which is to be shown. But what if the FDA hurts people? If the FDA hurts people, the approach described above is unethical, not because some people will be unprotected by the FDA, but, rather, because some people will be unnecessarily encumbered by the FDA. To say that it is unethical to leave people without FDA protection presupposes that the FDA is beneficial. Yet that's exactly what we seek to know; the FDA could be beneficial, neutral, or detrimental. Absent this proof, Congress and the FDA are simply playing with our lives.

We should, nonetheless, directly address the concern that many would have with running such an experiment: would people, unencumbered by the FDA, do stupid things?

Stupidity is not new—people did stupid things long before the FDA existed and, even with the FDA firmly in place, people still do stupid things today. But if patients are so hopelessly incompetent that they can't, say, figure out how to take the drug that they've been prescribed, why do pharmacies dispense whole bottles of 30 or more pills at a time? Don't they worry that patients might consume them all in one sitting? If people are so stupid, won't they confuse their vitamins with their heart medications? I won't say that these things never happen, but they are not the norm.

People aren't the only ones who do stupid things. The FDA does stupid things and we, not the FDA, suffer for them. Look at the ketorolac loading dose fiasco described previously. The body count included people like us, not FDA employees.

The FDA's mistakes hurt a lot of people.

Aligning Decisions and Outcomes

Our general tendency as humans is to learn from our mistakes. The FDA, unfortunately, hinders this learning process by disassociating actions from their costs. The best way to encourage people to learn from their actions is to have decision makers receive the reward of good outcomes and bear the cost of any bad outcomes, which generally leads to quick resolutions and better decisions. Bearing the costs of our mistakes gives us the incentive to change our behavior. When the FDA makes mistakes—such as incorrectly rejecting a good drug—we often bear the costs, and the FDA has no incentive to change its behavior. And we have little recourse for altering the FDA's behavior. How much control, really, do we have over federal bureaucracies? Once the FDA has made its decision public, it will resist changing its decision or giving people reason to doubt the appropriateness of that decision. That's a problem.

Judging Markets

Many can look at a given market and point to some of the poor choices that people make. For instance, someone gets duped or purchases too much or too little, or someone buys something that causes us to scratch our collective heads. Consider the impetuous 18-year-old boy who gets the name of his girlfriend of three weeks tattooed on his arm. Those of us who are wiser (and probably older) find ourselves scratching our heads and asking, "What was that dumb kid *thinking*?"

The market for nutritional supplements provides disturbing examples, with people taking things that have been proven not to work or consuming supplements that are likely dangerous. Some come to the conclusion that people are not competent and, therefore, should not be free to make their own choices in such an important arena. However, in making these judgments, they're comparing the way that people behave in the real world with some idealized, hypothetical solution that is probably impossible to realize. Once they compare reality with fantasy and determine that reality has fallen short, they usually advocate a heavy-handed government solution—a solution that might have its own serious consequences, that might actually be worse than the situation they are trying to fix. This is faulty thinking.

Economists Vilfredo Pareto and Howard Demsetz will help us debunk the next myth and see a path through these woods.

Myth: Market Failures Require Government Solutions

Nirvana Fallacy

Discussions of "market failure" have been a mainstay of economics for years, with economists highlighting occasional market shortcomings. As many can readily see, if markets have failed in some way, one solution is to have governments try to fix the unsolved problems. Howard Demsetz, an economist at UCLA and the University of Chicago, conceded that *ideal* government interventions might make markets more efficient. But he challenged his colleagues to show that *actual* government inventions would. He coined the term "nirvana fallacy" to pinpoint the logical flaw in his colleagues' thinking. "Those who adopt the nirvana viewpoint seek to discover discrepancies between the ideal and the real and if discrepancies are found, they deduce that the real is inefficient."[39]

If reality is flawed, then a government intervention will fix it, or so the claim goes. The problem with that idea is that the actual, flawed government intervention may be no better than our actual, flawed status quo. We need to do more than point fingers; we need to put our finger on solutions that actually work.

Pareto Improvements

To return to our empirical test of the FDA's worth, another way to separate people into these three groups (FDA safety prohibition only, FDA safety and efficacy prohibition, and no FDA prohibitions) would be through self-selection. Those who want the safety of FDA oversight would join Groups 1 or 2. Those who are comfortable with less oversight could join Groups 2 or 3. In essence, this self-selection approach makes the FDA an oversight and information agency that does not have the power to force anyone to abide by its proclamations and prohibitions. This would allow reasonable people to make reasonable decisions and choose the level of protection they want. This self-selection process completely obviates subjective value judgments and the faulty comparison of reality with fantasy. With this approach, no one forces others to abide by their value judgments; none are worse off than under our current approach, and some are better off.

This suggested reform is something that economists call a Pareto improvement.

Nineteenth century Italian economist Vilfredo Pareto is widely known for his law of income distribution. He also studied economic efficiency and developed the concept of a Pareto improvement: changes that can improve one person's situation without making anyone worse off. A Pareto improvement is a step in the right direction.

Consider a hypothetical example. Let's assume that a third-world dictator requires everyone in that benighted country to eat dinner at precisely 6:00 PM. If surveyed, some people might admit to wanting dinner at 6:00, but others might confess to preferring an evening meal at 7:00. A Pareto improvement would occur if the dictator relaxed the rules a bit and let people eat at either 6:00 or 7:00. The first group would be no worse off than before— they would still eat at 6:00—and the second group could eat at 7:00 and be better off than before. One's situation is unchanged, and one's situation is changed for the better. In economic terms, the utility —or satisfaction—of the first diners is unchanged, while the utility of the second group is increased.[40] The generalized solution, of course, is for the dictator to "allow" everyone to eat dinner at a time that each diner prefers. Thankfully, in our enlightened country, we can eat dinner whenever we please.

Now, consider again the self-selection proposal from above. What would it do?

The more cautious, conservative, and generally healthier patients could voluntarily wait for a full FDA review of safety and efficacy and the subsequent official approval. The bolder and, perhaps, more desperate patients could try new drugs sooner. Patients who didn't want to wait wouldn't have to, and cautious patients would still get the assurance of reams of efficacy data derived from the bolder patients' earlier use of certain drugs. Both parties would be better off than—or at least equally as well off as—they are today. Even those patients who wouldn't consider their situation improved would still be no worse off.

Such a solution is a Pareto improvement, in that everyone is at least as satisfied as under the current system. This does not mean that none of them will suffer poor outcomes; being free to choose does not confer protection from poor choices, bad luck, and adverse outcomes.

The only people worse off would be those who derive value from being able to restrict and regulate the behavior of others. These people fall into two camps: those who derive psychological or financial benefit from controlling others and those who derive a scientific benefit, as they find it easier to recruit subjects for clinical trials when the subjects have nowhere else to turn. The second group provides value to society; the first doesn't.

When Congress gave the FDA its powers, Congress was basing its actions on a hypothesis, whether consciously or not: give a government agency the power to restrict the availability of medicines until those medicines have been appropriately vetted, and Americans will be healthier and wealthier—due to the beneficial health economics of good medicines—overall.

But why should we speculate about whether the FDA has helped or hurt Americans? There is something we can do to finally get an answer: let's test the value of the FDA and get a definitive read. Let's run an ambitious, audacious trial and find out once and for all. Our children and their children will thank us.

Wrap-up

Scott Gottlieb was appointed FDA Commissioner in 2017. To his new staff, he counseled: "We need to be patient-centric and science-based in everything we do. And, we must make sure that in all our efforts, we maintain the gold standard for regulatory science and independent, science-led decision-making, all led by a strong career workforce."[41]

With these marching orders, the FDA tells drug companies that they must rely on the FDA's process to uncover the scientific truth, lest we Americans suffer dangerous and ineffective drugs.

If this objective, scientific approach is important for one *single* drug approval, consider how important it is for *all* drug approvals *in total*.

Each of those new drugs has been, or is being, rigorously tested. Which is why it is unfortunate and inconsistent that the overall approach to drug regulation—the FDA in its current form—responsible for *all* drug approvals—was never tested with even a modicum of the rigor that goes into each and every new drug evaluation.

Does the FDA help us? Does the FDA hurt us? Should the FDA employ hurdles for both efficacy and safety or just for safety? Should it be an information agency? Should it focus on product labeling? Should it do something else? Should it exist at all? We don't have direct, prospective, empirical evidence to answer these questions because *the FDA itself was never tested*; it was just *assumed* that it would help. That's a hypothesis, and hypotheses—especially important ones—can and should be tested.

[1] Sheldon Richman, "What Does It Mean to Have a 'Right' to Health Care?" *Reason*, 19 March 2017.

[2] Angus Liu, "Gilead's rheumatoid arthritis med filgotinib, after cold shoulder from FDA, wins global-first nod in Japan," *Fierce Pharma*, 25 September 2020.

[3] Gilead Sciences press release, "Filgotinib Demonstrates Durable Efficacy and Consistent Safety Profile at 52 Weeks in FINCH 1 and 3 Studies in Rheumatoid Arthritis," 4 June 2020.

[4] California Proposition 65 website: https://www.p65warnings.ca.gov/chemicals/bisphenol-bpa

[5] CDC website: https://www.cdc.gov/biomonitoring/pdf/BisphenolA_FactSheet.pdf

[6] FDA website: https://www.fda.gov/Food/IngredientsPackagingLabeling/FoodAdditivesIngredients/ucm166145.htm

[7] Bisphenol A industry group website: http://bisphenol-a.org/whatsNew/20170727.html

[8] Steve Milloy, "Bad Science May Banish Paper Receipts," *The Wall Street Journal*, 25 February 2019.

[9] Friedrich August Hayek biography, *The Concise Encyclopedia of Economics*, available for free on the web: http://www.econlib.org/library/Enc/bios/Hayek.html

[10] A version of this was published as "Why Is the FDA Attacking a Safe, Effective Drug?" *The Wall Street Journal*, 28 July 2021, by David R. Henderson and Charles L. Hooper.

[11] FDA consumer update, "Why You Should Not Use Ivermectin to Treat or Prevent COVID-19," on FDA website, 2021.

[12] FDA consumer update, "Why You Should Not Use Ivermectin to Treat or Prevent COVID-19," on FDA website, 2021.

[13] John Curran, "Jury clears Merck in Vioxx liability case," Associated Press, http://napavalleyregister.com/business/jury-clears-merck-in-vioxx-liability-case/article_b242f1df-498d-5636-a87f-448d6e9a5c08.html.

[14] Fifty percent more widely used than the next product. Based on industry usage data from Symphony Health and proprietary market research conducted in September 2020.

[15] Chamberlain, et al, "Efficacy of levetiracetam, fosphenytoin, and valproate for established status epilepticus by age group (ESETT): a double-blind, responsive-adaptive, randomised controlled trial," *The Lancet*, vol. 395, 11 April 2020.

[16] Eric Sagonowsky, "FDA won't require manufacturing inspections for emergency COVID vaccine use: Bloomberg," Fierce Pharma, 26 October 2020.

[17] Originally published as: Charles L. Hooper, "Never Mind: FDA Changes Own Rules in Midstream," *Library of Economics and Liberty*, 5 November 2012. http://www.econlib.org/library/Columns/y2012/Hooperdrugs.html

[18]http://www.fda.gov/ICECI/ComplianceManuals/CompliancePolicyGuidanceManual/ucm116791.htm

[19] "Brown Leads Effort to Demand Federal Investigation Into Price Gouging of Pre-Term Labor Drug for Expectant Mothers," Senator Sherrod Brown press release, March 17, 2011.

[20] "Senators seek investigation into KV drug pricing," Lisa Brown, *St. Louis Post-Dispatch*, March 19, 2011.

[21] "Senators demand action on Makena price," *BioCentury Extra*, BioCentury Publications, March 17, 2011.

[22] "Contradicting itself," *BioCentury*, The Bernstein Report on BioBusiness, BioCentury Publications, week of April 18, 2011.

[23] Jennifer Corbett Dooren, "Connecting Patients With Experimental Drugs," *The Wall Street Journal*, 22 October 2012.

[24] Articles on Vioxx originally published in *Reason* (David Henderson and Charles Hooper, "Clear Thinking About Vioxx, *Reason*, 3 January 2005) and *TCS Daily* (David R. Henderson and Charles L. Hooper, "Grey Matter," *TCS Daily*, 19 November 2004).

[25] According to Dr. François Bertrand, executive director of medical research for Merck Frosst Canada

[26] Andrea Petersen, "Despite Vioxx Withdrawal, The Benefits of Medicines Can Outweigh the Risks," *The Wall Street Journal*, October 5, 2004.

---

27 https://www.econlib.org/library/Bastiat/basEss.html?chapter_num=4#book-reader

28 Daniel Henninger, "Drug Lag," *The Concise Encyclopedia of Economics*, David R. Henderson, editor. https://www.econlib.org/cee/

29 Doug Bandow, "The FDA Can Be Dangerous to Your Health," *Commentary*, Cato Institute, 11 November 1996.

30 See FDAreview.org for other good information on this topic.

31 This does not assume that the vaccine would have been given immediately and would have saved Americans immediately. It instead assumes that the pandemic would have ended 23 days earlier than it otherwise would have.

32 Frank R. Lichtenberg, "Pharmaceutical Innovation and Longevity Growth in 30 Developing and High-Income Countries, 2000-2009," *NBER Working Paper Series*, Working Paper 18235, 2012

33 Tomas Phillipson, Julia Snider, et al, "The Social Value of Childhood Vaccination in the United States," *American Journal of Managed Care*, 5 December 2016, 2017;23(1):41-47.

34 William Nordhaus, paper for National Bureau of Economic Research, 2006.

35 "The Oregon Trial," *Wall Street Journal*, 20 May 2013

36 "4 More Die of Tainted Meds in Panama," Associated Press, 30 October 2006.

37 Every year 4,000 children drink delicious and deadly ethylene glycol. Brandan Koerner, "Why is Antifreeze So Delicious?" *Slate*, 13 July 2004.

38 Physicians would need to check a patient's Social Security number and a database of drugs by category before prescribing a drug for a patient. Over time, physicians would tend to learn which medicines were available to each group of patients.

39 David R. Henderson, "Chicago's Lesser-Known Free Marketeer," *The Wall Street Journal*, 13 January 2019.

40 Of course, life is not perfect. If two people wanted to eat dinner together and one preferred 6:00 while the other preferred 7:00, one or both would have to compromise.

---

41 Phil Taylor, "Gottlieb tells staffers FDA can help—indirectly—to cut medicine prices," *FierceBiotech*, 16-May-17.

Chapter 10: Investigating a World Without the FDA

Treatment with the blood thinner Coumadin (warfarin) can turn patients' toes purple. Not surprisingly, this condition is known as purple toes syndrome. While this and many other side effects are rare, more than half of the 32-page FDA-approved package insert for Coumadin consists of warnings and the side effects and drug-drug interactions patients may experience.

Is Coumadin safe?

GW Pharmaceuticals' cannabis-based treatment for epilepsy, Epidiolex (cannabidiol), was approved by the FDA in June 2018. In one clinical trial, 39 percent of the Epidiolex patients registered a median reduction in monthly seizures, compared with only 13 percent on placebo.

The FDA claims that it approves only effective drugs, but for 61 percent of patients, if these results hold up, Epidiolex will be no better than snake oil, offering false hope and nothing more. For more than half of the potential patients who might take Epidiolex, their usage will be a waste of time and money, concomitant with some risk of adverse events.

Is Epidiolex effective?

The fact that Epidiolex won't help 61 percent of patients and that Coumadin has hazardous aspects is proof that things aren't perfect with our current system of drug regulation. The "FDA-world" that we live in can be considered better than a counterfactual "no-FDA-world" only if our situation would be worse absent the FDA. And yet there's strong evidence that it would be better.

As discussed in Chapter 9, the FDA was never tested the way new drugs are: prospectively and empirically. As a reminder, in a typical clinical trial, patients are typically split into two seemingly equal groups, with one group receiving the active drug and the other getting an inactive placebo. The clinical results for the two groups of patients are compared to see if the active drug benefited those who got it. Such a test was never conducted to evaluate the FDA, leaving us only two ways to empirically determine if the FDA has helped or hurt Americans:

- We can compare the outcomes experienced by rich, developed countries that did and did not adopt an FDA-like drug regulatory scheme. However, the potential for this approach is limited because drug regulation has been standardized in recent years.
- We can run retrospective analyses, which use before/after comparisons to ascertain how the FDA has affected us.

We will briefly touch on the country-to-country comparison approach later in this chapter. But first, let's examine the retrospective analysis approach.

Retrospective Analysis Approach

The simple-minded approach for a retrospective analysis would be to compare the drugs that were available in, say, 1936 (i.e., pre-1938) to the drugs available now and ask whether those drugs from the early 20th century were better than the drugs from today. Naturally, it's not a fair comparison because the "FDA-world" has the benefit of eight decades of advancement, while the "no-FDA-world" is stuck in 1936, the era of the Great Depression, Franklin Roosevelt, Jesse Owens, and Adolf Hitler.

Imagine going to your doctor and requesting only those drugs and medical treatment that were available in 1936. Your doctor would have a fool for a patient. And that's just what a simplistic 1936 versus circa 2020 comparison would show. However, while we don't necessarily want the *therapies* from 1936 or 1960, we might still want the *rules* from those eras.

We know what happened with the FDA in place—that's the world we have now. What would have happened had the FDA not received such tremendous powers? Some other drugs, perhaps good or maybe bad, would have become available. Which drugs? For which diseases? How good would they have been? What would they have cost? We can't know. It's impossible to know which drugs the FDA stopped directly, through its gatekeeping process, or indirectly, due to its onerous approval process and resulting costs and delays. One can only speculate. What else can we do?

Shotgun Therapy

The best we can do is to study the situation just before and after any major new tranche of FDA regulations, and that is exactly what economist Sam Peltzman did in his analysis of the 1962 Kefauver Amendments, which he documented in his 1974 book, *Regulation of Pharmaceutical Innovation*.[1] Some may complain that his analysis is dated, but it occurred at precisely the best time to be close to the action. (Do historians dismiss Alexis de Tocqueville's *Democracy in America* because it is almost 200 years old? No. It was written *in* the age it was written *about*.)

Without repeating his whole book, which is worth reading, a summary of Peltzman's findings bear emphasis and repeating. His research helped us to see the dramatic results produced by the 1962 amendments.

Prior to 1962, it took just two years to develop a new drug; it now takes 12 to 14 years.[2][3] The latest estimate from IQVIA is 13.6 years from patent filing to launch.

> *We went from synthesis to the commercial drug in three years. That is absolutely impossible today.*
> **George Hitchings**, recipient of the Nobel Prize for chemistry, discussing an antileukemia drug he helped develop before the 1962 amendments[4]

Peltzman found that research and development costs had doubled.[5] R&D costs had been increasing, but in the 1962 to 1969 period, they were twice what would have been expected had the growth rate in evidence prior to the 1962 amendments continued.

His most startling finding was that the number of successful new drugs had declined by 61 percent.

> *In the decade before the amendments, an average of forty-three NCEs [new chemical entities—not just reformulations of old drugs] was introduced annually compared with an annual average of sixteen in the subsequent decade.*
> **Sam Peltzman**[6]

The FDA itself concluded that the number of "truly important" drugs approved before and after the amendments dropped either from 7.1 to 5.8 or from 12.3 to 9.1, depending on which study we reference. Striking another blow to the 1962 amendments, Peltzman found that ineffective drugs were kept off the market in the same proportion as effective ones, "…as if an arbitrary marketing quota had been placed on new drugs after 1962."[7] Any ham-fisted bureaucrat can arbitrarily limit the number of new drugs launched; we expected more from the FDA.

Before the new FDA regulations, the magnitude of the alleged problems in the pharmaceutical industry was small and, therefore, the new regulations couldn't have been expected to help very much. Peltzman found that, even before the new regulations, consumers gradually learned from experience which drugs worked and which didn't. This meant that the medical profession deemed less than ten percent—and possibly as little as five percent—of drugs sold on the market ineffective.

> *The penalties imposed by the marketplace on sellers of ineffective drugs before 1962 seem to have been sufficient to have left little room for improvement by a regulatory agency.*
> **Sam Peltzman**[8]

Peltzman found that the FDA used a faulty net to keep out inefficacious drugs.

> Even after the amendments were passed, there were still some ineffective drugs that managed to get through the FDA tests and onto the market. So the advantages of the amendments could actually be less than it appears—and it appears that they are very small.

The FDA's efforts weren't completely wasted, and Peltzman concluded that some ineffective drugs had been kept off the market, but that the benefit was "too small to compensate for the benefits consumers have had to forgo because of reduced drug innovation."[9] Once we realize that consumers typically gain more from the benefits of new drugs than they suffer from the costs of ineffective drugs, we are forced to conclude that "the losses from [the] inefficacious drugs [were] trivial compared with the surplus generated by other new drugs."[10]

> It appears that a form of 'shot-gun therapy' has been applied to the problem of ineffective drugs: for the sake of excising (part of) the potentially offending 10 percent, 60 percent of potential innovation is eliminated.[11]

How did Peltzman tally the pros and cons on the new amendments? Overall, Peltzman found that consumers had, on balance, lost. They gained a little from reduced waste on purchases of ineffective drugs, but they lost a lot due to a reduced flow of new, beneficial drugs and due to higher prices. Peltzman concluded that the best way to improve the situation was to roll back the changes.

> *Any administrative change which shortens the NDA review process, decreases the attendant expense, and permits greater risk taking is likely to yield net benefits.*
> **Sam Peltzman**[12]

Peltzman's results suggest that the 1962 amendments have been harming patients. There weren't many ineffective drugs on the market before 1962, which meant that the room for improvement was small. One typically tries not to change an efficient system for the worse, but that's exactly what Congress appears to have done, as we can see from the dramatic reduction in the number of new chemical entities approved. The attempt to cut fat resulted in cuts to muscle and bone.

Consumers gain substantially more from the benefits of new drugs than they suffer from the costs of ineffective drugs. Further, if only five to ten percent of pre-1962 drugs were ineffective, we know that 90 to 95 percent *were* effective. Thus, a 60-percent decline in the availability of *all* new drugs must adversely affect consumers, because effective drugs constituted most of decline.

Mathematics is fighting the FDA: the value of good drugs is so much more than the cost of bad (ineffective) drugs, and the great majority of drugs are already good. There just isn't very much room for improvement, and any missteps—delays in approvals, good drugs rejected, and fewer new drugs overall—come with a steep cost.

Formidable Roadblock

Sam Peltzman wasn't the only researcher to study the FDA during this period. The 1975 *Economic Report of the President of the United States* questioned and criticized the new efficacy amendments, arguing that, in addition to the increased costs and unnecessary delays, "[i]t is not clear that the average efficacy of drugs introduced after 1962 is any higher than that of drugs previously introduced."

Shortly thereafter, in 1976, the President's Biomedical Research Panel declared that the FDA "has become a formidable roadblock" to the development of "potentially useful drugs."[13] "It is indeed ironic," said Louis Lasagna of the University of Rochester, "that what was supposed to be a

program to protect consumers is actually increasing their exposure to greater disease by taking away possible cures."[14]

Economist Steven Wiggins agreed with these conclusions, finding that increased FDA regulations raised costs and reduced the number of new drugs.[15]

Howard Hughes Medical Institute researcher Barry Bloom conducted an analysis of FDA approvals from 1945 through 1970, broken down into five-year groupings. Bloom noticed a significant slowdown in the 1961-1965 and 1966-1970 periods. He commented on the abundance of breakthrough medicines launched in the late 1950s and the paucity of breakthroughs after that time.

Using the fact that the 1962 amendments affected only American drug reviews, researchers were able to contrast the results in this country with those in other countries. Notably, researchers did not see a similar decline in new drug launches in the United Kingdom, suggesting that the root cause here was the new legislation. William Wardell, who coined the term "drug lag," found that four times as many new drugs were launched in the U.K. as in the U.S. during the 1962-1971 period. Such types of comparisons have subsequently lost their luster, as there has been significant standardization of drug regulation around the world. Wardell did still find some differences between countries and a country-to-country comparison can serve other purposes. For instance, Wardell and Lasagna examined drugs that were approved in both the U.S. and prominent European countries and found a 1.0- to 2.1-year lag in U.S. approvals. This was the genesis of the so-called drug lag argument.

Frank Lichtenberg, Round 2

Recall that we were introduced to Columbia University economist Frank Lichtenberg in Chapter 9. That chapter highlighted his study suggesting that modern drugs were associated with 73 percent of the increase in life expectancy that we've enjoyed in the last few decades. That's huge. But there's more.

Lichtenberg has focused on the value of pharmaceuticals. Why does that matter? If pharmaceuticals are generally harmful, the FDA's efforts to restrain the entry of new drugs are justifiable. If pharmaceuticals are beneficial, and especially if they are hugely beneficial, then the FDA's efforts are harder to justify. Lichtenberg has a study that suggests just how amazingly beneficial new drugs are.

Lichtenberg's research found that the pharmaceutical expenditure per life-year saved was $2,837.[16] This represents an incredible deal. The Environmental Protection Agency uses the figure of $9.6 million (2021 dollars) for the value of a statistical life. Economists estimate the value of a statistical life by observing how much extra pay workers require to accept dangerous jobs. If we assume that each life represents 78 years, the EPA's value per life year saved is 43 times the cost of each life year saved by a pharmaceutical. In other words, pharmaceuticals provide a value 43 times their cost. Spend a dollar, get forty-three back (4,338 percent

ROI).[17] Who wouldn't want to make that investment in their most important asset, their life?

Lichtenberg found that drugs launched since 1982 have been adding 150 million life-years, each and every year, to the citizens of the 22 countries he studied.[18] If, based on research from Peltzman and others, we assume that the FDA has reduced the number of new drugs by half, then we can conclude that FDA-type regulations have cost the people in those 22 countries 150 million life-years per annum. How did I get that figure? They would have benefited with 300 million life-years per year but actually got only 150 million.

True, had the 1962 version of the FDA not been in place, there might have been more ineffective drugs that ended up on pharmacists' shelves and in our medicine cabinets. But the FDA already had rules for safety—so these "bad" drugs might have been ineffective but not unsafe—and Peltzman found that prior to 1962, only five to ten percent of drugs were ineffective, and there are still some ineffective drugs today. And, further, Peltzman saw a 61 percent decline in new drugs.

What does this mean for you, your family, and your friends? It suggests that **the 1962 amendments have cut short each American life by an average of ten years**.

How did I calculate this? Life expectancy increased from 70.11 in 1962 to 78.81 in 2020. If newer pharmaceuticals were responsible for 73 percent of this 8.7 year increase, they added 6.35 years. If the FDA's 1962 amendments reduced the benefit of new drugs by 61 percent, then new pharmaceuticals should have provided 16.3 years of increased life expectancy. The difference between 16.3 and 6.35 is ten years. If Peltzman and Lichtenberg are correct, the 1962 amendments cost, on average, every American ten years. Based on the EPA's value of a statistical life, **the 1962 amendments have cost you and everyone you know $1.2 million dollars in lost expected life.**

While there have been many things which could have affected life expectancy since 1961, as shown in Figure 1, actual life expectancy in 2020 was about 9.0 years below the trend from 1900 through 1961. While far from proving that the 1962 amendments reduced our life expectancy by ten years, this analysis does generally support that conclusion.

Figure 1: U.S. Life Expectancy

Actual Life Expectancy is Below the Pre-1962 Trend

In summary, it appears as though the FDA has denied you and me 61 percent of the value of life-saving drugs—ten years of life expectancy—since 1962. Can a conservative government bureaucracy hurt us? Yes, we have strong evidence it can.

Wrap-up

We will never fully understand what would have happened had the FDA *not* gotten its awesome powers in 1938 and 1962. We can, however, review the writings of the economists who have studied the situation thoroughly and note their conclusions about how the FDA has harmed— and continues to harm— Americans. If the FDA were scientific and objective, it would act on those conclusions to mitigate that harm. It hasn't, and it is unlikely that it will.

Even better than studying retrospective analyses, we could run a prospective trial to study the FDA in the same way that the FDA requires drug companies to study new drugs. One cannot simultaneously argue that individual drugs should be studied thoroughly, while also arguing that the *process* for studying, approving, and regulating these same drugs should not adhere to similar standards of evidence.

It seems clear that without the FDA's powers, particularly those gained in 1962, there would have been more drugs on the market. And, while some of those drugs would have caused a small increase in morbidity and mortality from adverse events, that effect would have been more than offset by a large decrease in morbidity and mortality from the therapeutic benefits of those medicines. The net effect would have been healthier and longer-lived Americans: ten years longer

We would be foolish to use a wrecking ball on our house to alleviate a minor rodent problem. We would be just as foolish using a wrecking ball on the whole pharmaceutical industry to address a few ineffective drugs. Unfortunately, that's generally what happened.

The FDA is killing us; it's a fact, not hyperbole.

---

[1] Sam Peltzman, *Regulation of Pharmaceutical Innovation*, University of Chicago, 1974.

[2] Gail Van Norman, "Drugs, Devices, and the FDA: Part 1: An Overview of Approval Processes for Drugs," JACC: Back to Translational Science, Volume 1, Issue 3, April 2016 https://www.sciencedirect.com/science/article/pii/S2452302X1600036X

[3] Deloitte's Center for Health Solutions annual report, 2016.

[4] Daniel Henninger, "Drug Lag," *The Concise Encyclopedia of Economics*, David R. Henderson, editor. https://www.econlib.org/cee/

[5] Sam Peltzman, *Regulation of Pharmaceutical Innovation,* page 29.

[6] Sam Peltzman, *Regulation of Pharmaceutical Innovation,* page 13.

[7] Sam Peltzman, *Regulation of Pharmaceutical Innovation,* page 45.

[8] Sam Peltzman, *Regulation of Pharmaceutical Innovation,* page 45.

[9] Sam Peltzman, *Regulation of Pharmaceutical Innovation,* page 48.

[10] Sam Peltzman, *Regulation of Pharmaceutical Innovation,* page 46.

[11] Sam Peltzman, *Regulation of Pharmaceutical Innovation,* page 67.

[12] Sam Peltzman, *Regulation of Pharmaceutical Innovation,* page 89.

[13] Michael Silver, "The FDA efficacy requirements have boosted the costs of drugs, slashed their rate of introduction, and deprived the sick and dying of vital medicines," *Reason*, 1 October 1978. http://reason.com/archives/1978/10/01/regulations-that-are-killing-u/print

[14] Michael Silver, "The FDA efficacy requirements have boosted the costs of drugs, slashed their rate of introduction, and deprived the sick and dying of vital medicines," *Reason*, 1 October 1978. http://reason.com/archives/1978/10/01/regulations-that-are-killing-u/print

[15] Steven Wiggins, "Product Quality Regulation and New Drug Introductions: Some New Evidence from the 1970s." *Review of Economics and Statistics*, 63(4): 615-19, 1981.

[16] Frank Lichtenberg, "How Many Life-Years Have New Drugs Saved? A 3-Way Fixed-Effects Analysis of 66 Diseases in 27 Countries, 2000-2013," working paper 25483, January 2019.

[17] $9.6 million divided by 78 years is $123,077 per year. $123,077 per year divided by $2,837 per year is 43.38. New drugs provide a benefit that is 43 times their cost, or show a return on investment of 4,338%.

[18] Stephen Kurczy, "Calculating the Benefits of Drugs," *Ideas and Insights*, Columbia University, 12 February 2019.

Chapter 11: Greatest Good for the Greatest Number?

Many think that the FDA pursues the path of the greatest good for the greatest number, but that's difficult to square with observation. For instance, Emory University economist Paul Rubin has concluded that FDA regulations have saved between 500 and 1,000 injuries (injuries, not deaths) per year but have cost between 2,100 and 12,000 lives annually.[1] That's not a good tradeoff. Could it really be that bad? If so, how could that happen?

Consider a few specific cases and determine for yourself whether the FDA is working toward the greatest good for the greatest number.

Diseases Versus Treatments for Diseases

In the U.S. alone, the death toll from all diseases is about 2.4 million per year.[2] The "big two," heart disease and cancer, are responsible for half of these deaths. (Even in the pandemic year of 2020, COVID-19 didn't unseat the big two.) Compare that with the estimated death toll from the FDA-approved drugs used to treat those diseases: about 100,000.[3] In the "game" of life, diseases "win" by a factor of 24 to 1. What does this mean? Well, if we ignore other causes of death—such as the abuse of illicit drugs, alcoholism, car crashes, work accidents, homicides, and suicides—which, together, total roughly 300,000 per year, 96 percent of Americans die from diseases and only four percent die from adverse drug reactions.

We don't hear about this because it's rarely in the headlines (2020 was an exception). What garners the headlines are risks that are relatively minor in comparison. Terrorism kills, on average, only 160 Americans per year, and that's if we include the September 11 attacks. Shark attacks leave one

American dead every two years. U.S. commercial airplane crashes produce so few fatalities that we need to look back to 2009 to see any passenger deaths. Gun homicides yield 14,400 victims per year.[4] All illicit drug abuse and overdoses result in 70,000 fatalities per year.[5] Taken together, these deaths, which the media tend to sensationalize, produce just seven percent of the fatalities caused by heart disease and cancer and just 3.5 percent of the fatalities from all diseases.

"If it bleeds, it leads" is an understandable tactic for news outlets wanting to sell advertising, but not for the supposedly objective and scientific FDA. If the FDA is, in fact, working for the greatest good for the greatest number, it should be 24 times as concerned with the diseases themselves as it is with the safety of the drugs used to treat those diseases. But that isn't the FDA we have. Our FDA puts more effort into pruning the garden of new drugs than it does into nurturing promising candidates.

Over-The-Counter Mevacor

Consider Merck's abandoned efforts to take its prescription-only cholesterol-reducing drug Mevacor (lovastatin) over-the-counter, or OTC. Doing so would have made it more accessible to patients who could have gotten it directly from a grocery store or pharmacy instead of needing the extra step of getting a doctor's prescription. Merck's goals collided with a determined FDA that rejected its application not once, but three times. After that, Merck understandably gave up.

Although more than 13 million Americans take statins, according to the government's National Cholesterol Education Program guidelines, three times as many people should be taking them. Why is usage so low? One reason is that some are leery of Western medicine and pharmaceuticals. Also, many of us see no need for medicine when we feel fine and have no symptoms. Add in the expense and hassle of continually going to a doctor for a prescription, on top of the copayment, and the cost of obtaining even generic lovastatin adds up. The more something costs, the less of it people will purchase.

The result is that 27 million Americans who would benefit from one of modern medicine's greatest inventions are doing without it. The *UC Berkeley Wellness Letter* estimates that 1,500 heart attacks and strokes are prevented within each group of 100,000 statin users per year.[6] That means that the 13 million statin users are being spared 195,000 heart attacks and strokes each year and that 405,000 equivalent events befall those who do not take statins but would benefit from them.

The side effects of statins, moreover, are rare and seldom serious. According to the *Wellness Letter*, "[t]hese proven lifesavers are considered very safe by all expert organizations, including the American College of Cardiology, American Heart Association, and National Heart, Lung, and Blood Institute." As we saw in Chapter 2, one study showed that more patients on placebos than on statins complained of adverse events.

The FDA has, for years, agreed that the prescription-only 20 mg dose of Mevacor is safe and effective. And yet the FDA hasn't been convinced that consumers would make informed decisions about how to use OTC Mevacor, even though Zocor (simvastatin) has been available OTC in Britain since 2004.

Merck's SELECT trial among 1,497 potential lovastatin OTC customers indicated that some patients would use it in a way that the FDA didn't consider ideal. Within this set of "non-ideal" users are two main groups. Patients in the first group should have been on something stronger than OTC lovastatin. But many of them would have taken nothing; therefore, it's hard to argue that OTC lovastatin would make them worse off. The second group was at low cardiovascular risk and probably didn't need to be on a statin. But even for this group, the drug was safe and had some therapeutic benefit.

Let's put some lopsided numbers to these two groups to see just how overblown the FDA's concerns are. Assume that five million appropriate patients would take an OTC statin each year. Assume, too, that a whopping five million "inappropriate" (by FDA standards) patients would also take an OTC statin. Among the appropriate patients, the statin would prevent 75,000 heart attacks and strokes. Of the inappropriate patients, almost all of whom would derive *some* cardiovascular benefit, 10,000 would experience mild muscle pain due to their statin; 250 would experience muscle pain (myopathy) serious enough to stop taking their drug; and about 75 would suffer potentially fatal rhabdomyolysis. Rhabdomyolysis has a mortality rate of 20 percent.[7] That means that millions would benefit and 15 would potentially die. And this is a worst case scenario.

Clearly, Mevacor as an OTC drug isn't perfect—what is?—but it is far superior to the status quo. With the benefits and risks being so asymmetrical, the OTC statin alternative continues to be better even if we make the assumption that a whopping 99 percent of all OTC statin customers would be inappropriate. Yet the FDA seems to see two classes in America: uninformed consumers who matter and informed consumers who don't. How else can the negative experience of hundreds overrule the stellar outcome of millions? If the FDA views this as the greatest good for the greatest number, its logic certainly isn't the greatest.

Statins, moreover, are known to be safer than some other OTC products that the FDA does embrace. Consider aspirin and other drugs in the NSAID class. These products are already available OTC, but they are far from safe even when used as directed. One researcher reported that at least 6,000 U.S. deaths per year result from NSAID-induced gastrointestinal bleeding. To be consistent, the FDA should either allow OTC Mevacor or pull non-steroidal anti-inflammatory drugs from the market. (I'd argue for the former.)

The FDA considered one alternative in isolation—allowing Mevacor to be sold over the counter—found it less than perfect, and then rejected it. By doing this, the FDA has chosen the status quo under which Americans are suffering 405,000 unnecessary heart attacks and strokes each year.[8]

If the FDA is to address the 2.4 million Americans who die from disease each year, it should care as much about those who go without drugs as it does about those who take them.

Over-The-Counter Ulcer Drugs

Another big benefit of over-the-counter drugs is lower prices. OTC proton pump inhibitors and H2 antagonists—used to treat gastroesophageal reflux disease, stomach ulcers, and acid reflux disease—are priced at about ten percent of their prescription versions.[9] The main reason: consumers, spending their own money out-of-pocket, are more price-conscious than health insurers. Moreover, simply comparing OTC prices with Rx prices substantially understates the saving realized by patients who avoid unnecessary doctor visits to procure prescriptions. Consumers save both time and money when they aren't required to visit doctors and pharmacists.

Once again, a policy of the greatest good for the greatest number would heavily favor OTC drugs.

Over-The-Counter Erectile Dysfunction Drugs

Virtually everyone is familiar with the erectile dysfunction drug Viagra (sildenafil), one of the most widely discussed, advertised, and prescribed drugs in recent memory. Did you know that Viagra is available OTC in the U.K. but not in the U.S.? Why not?

Whether patients swallow OTC or prescription pills, they receive the benefits and face the risks of those drugs. Prescription-only drugs—with patients having to pass through one gatekeeper authorized to write prescriptions and one gatekeeper authorized to fill prescriptions—are obviously more difficult to obtain than OTC drugs, which can be purchased at grocery and drug stores.

If gatekeepers provide a valuable service, then there may be good reason to employ their services. What benefit do these gatekeepers offer in the case of erectile dysfunction (ED)? Consider the diagnosis of ED. Are men going to lie about their ED in order to obtain Viagra illegitimately? This is not a condition that men fabricate and brag about. Plus, since there's no blood test for ED, doctors must rely on their patients' own assessments of ED for a diagnosis—there's no objective, non-invasive way to tell if a man really has it or not.

With Viagra available OTC, a man who thinks he needs it can simply buy some at a store. With Viagra available by prescription only, a man who thinks he needs it must first make an appointment with his doctor, attend that appointment, usually during business hours, and then make a special trip to a pharmacy, usually during business hours, all the while advertising his very personal problem. If patients think that these gatekeepers provide value, they can still get drugs for erectile dysfunction the traditional way. But why require men, as the FDA does, to pass through two gatekeepers when it is not at all clear that they provide value?

Vaping and Public Health

Consider the smoking of tobacco cigarettes and the vaping of e-cigarettes. Smoking is one of the biggest public health risks, with the World Health Organization projecting a billion early deaths due to cigarettes during the 21st century. Vaping with e-cigarettes has become very popular. Should the FDA crack down on this new form of smoking?

In 2016, the FDA announced a slew of new regulations on e-cigarettes, including prohibiting correct, factual claims about how much safer e-cigarette are than tobacco cigarettes. These regulations appear to be motivated more by the desire for power and control than for public health because any government actions that successfully dissuade people from vaping will probably have the unintended consequence of pushing some people to use tobacco products and, thus, buoy the cigarette smoking rate. Vaping might not be completely safe, but it is far safer than smoking, which means that the FDA's new rules, if they nudge even a small number

of vapers toward more-dangerous cigarettes, may directly harm Americans.

What might happen with the new FDA rules? We can put some numbers on this harm.

Using 2017 numbers, we can estimate that there are 3.5 million non-smoking adult American vapers.[10] Assume further that vaping is one-twentieth as dangerous as smoking[11] and that ten percent of vapers will shift to smoking if the clampdown on vaping continues. According to a study by researchers at Columbia University, an 18-year-old non-smoker will have a quality-adjusted life expectancy of 11.0 years more than an equivalent smoker.[12] Because not all vapers are so young, let's cut that estimate to 5.5 extra years. In other words, the average non-smoker can expect to live an additional 5.5 "optimal health" years. Applying our estimate that vaping is only five percent as dangerous as smoking, we find that vapers will live, compared to smokers, an additional 5.2 optimal health years.[13]

Based on our ten-percent assumption, under the new FDA rules, 350,000 of the 3.5 million current vapers will shift to smoking. Each smoker will see a quality-adjusted life expectancy reduction of 5.2 years. That works out to a reduction of 1,820,000 quality-adjusted life years. If each vaper has a remaining life expectancy of 50 years, this is equivalent to 36,400 people dying,[14] which means that those FDA rules perpetrate the equivalent of almost thirteen September 11 attacks on current vapers.[15]

The Royal College of Physicians came to a similar conclusion of the potential of vaping: "Large-scale substitution of e-cigarettes, or other non-tobacco nicotine products, for tobacco smoking has the potential to prevent almost all the harm from smoking in society."[16]

The greatest good for the greatest number? That opinion just went up in smoke.

Ask What Changed[17]

One of the more startling public-health-related developments was the 660-percent increase in the number of overdose deaths involving heroin between 2002 and 2017. Curiously, most of the increase happened after 2010.[18]

What caused this increase and why after 2010? Was it the greed of heroin dealers or a flood of heroin into the illicit market? The second explanation is not an explanation at all. The first explanation doesn't make sense on its own terms: greed is usually used to explain price increases, and if the price of heroin had increased substantially, then, absent other factors, one would expect less heroin usage and fewer deaths from heroin overdoses.

A third explanation comes from the Centers for Disease Control: "The increased availability of heroin, combined with its relatively low price (compared with diverted prescription opioids) and high purity appear to be major drivers of the upward trend in heroin use and overdose."[19] But this doesn't explain much either. Why was heroin more available, and isn't the CDC saying that the price and purity were relatively constant?

What else could explain the increase in the demand for heroin? How about a reduction in the supply of its substitutes, such as prescription painkillers?

In a 2018 paper published online, economists William N. Evans and Ethan Lieber of the University of Notre Dame and Patrick Power of Boston University explain what changed:

> We attribute the recent quadrupling of heroin death rates to the August, 2010 reformulation of an oft-abused prescription opioid, OxyContin. The new abuse-deterrent formulation led many

> consumers to substitute to an inexpensive alternative, heroin. Using structural break techniques and variation in substitution risk, we find that opioid consumption stops rising in August, 2010, heroin deaths begin climbing the following month, and growth in heroin deaths was greater in areas with greater pre-reformulation access to heroin and opioids. The reformulation did not generate a reduction in combined heroin and opioid mortality—each prevented opioid death was replaced with a heroin death.[20]

The FDA, in an attempt to prevent the abuse of prescription painkillers, inadvertently drove drug abusers to that notorious street drug: heroin. In doing so, the FDA swapped prescription opioid deaths for heroin deaths. The FDA didn't save lives, it merely changed the cause of death. So much for the greatest good for the greatest number.

The Opioid Crisis

One of the most persistent greatest-good arguments involves addiction and the "opioid addiction crisis." The argument centers on the need for the government to restrict access to opioids to prevent addiction, with the fear that if the gates are cracked opened, addiction will spread, and the nation will be overcome with opioid-addicted zombies. We need, in short, a metaphorical Great Wall of China between the susceptible American population and the evil opioid-pushing drug companies. Unfortunately, by keeping opioids away from addicts, the government also makes them harder for legitimate pain patients to acquire. That's a real problem. My friend just suffered through an episode of shingles without access to opioid analgesics.

The common fear—a fear behind much of the desire to crack down on opioid usage—is that normal, otherwise healthy, people can become easily addicted to opioids prescribed to them for pain. The reality is that most opioid users will typically not resort to abuse, while those prone to addiction will abuse whatever drug "works" for them.

According to the National Institute on Drug Abuse, abuse of narcotic analgesics is rare among legitimate pain patients taking proper doses. Based on a 2015 study from North Carolina, if you take the pain medications your doctor prescribes and don't combine them with illicit drugs, the annual probability of death is 0.022 percent, or about two out of 10,000 patients.[21] In other words, those who are at risk are not the typical patients who complete their analgesic prescription as directed. We do know that some patients can develop problems and their stories are unfortunate and doleful.[22]

Drug abusers are different. Those on "oxy," the so-called "Hillbilly Heroin," know what they are doing—they are *trying* to get high, and they experiment with drug cocktails. The 2002 National Household Survey on Drug Abuse reported that among those who took OxyContin (oxycodone) without a prescription, 98 percent had used other pain relievers for non-medical purposes, and more than a quarter had injected heroin. These are not typical Americans. In 2003, the *Journal of Analytical Toxicology* reported that in less than two percent of oxycodone-related deaths, oxycodone was the only drug found at autopsy.[23] Those who are abusing prescription pain relievers are also abusing illicit drugs.

Those few who actively abuse opioids are doing so purposely and willfully, however shortsighted and destructive their behavior might seem to the rest of us. Why should we, the majority, be denied some valuable drugs because someone somewhere is engaging in self-destructive behavior, and, if denied this one drug, those drug-seekers will simply move on to the next drug on the list? Can't get drug X? Use drug Y. People who abuse drugs, after all, will get high on *something*: prescription opioids, illicit opioids, alcohol, marijuana, heroin, etc.

We can't forget that opioid addiction crisis has arisen despite the efforts of the FDA and the rest of the federal government to control the ingredients, manufacturing, supply, and prescriptions of drugs to an exceptional degree. Drug companies manufacturing "controlled drugs" are required to work within a production quota and must get permission from the Drug Enforcement Administration (DEA) to even purchase raw ingredients.

The government plays other roles in the opioid addition crisis. According to the Centers for Medicare and Medicaid Services (CMS), "Medicaid beneficiaries are prescribed painkillers at twice the rate of non-Medicaid patients,"[24] and they are three to six times more at risk for overdose. OxyContin isn't cheap. Medicaid's low copays have insulated potential abusers from the real cost.

One in three Medicare Part D beneficiaries received an opioid prescription in 2016, according to the HHS Inspector General. Further, some 500,000 beneficiaries received the equivalent of 12 tablets a day of 10 mg Vicodin (acetaminophen & hydrocodone) for at least three months.[25] That's over a thousand pills! What is going on?

The fact that opioids are abused by addicts and are more difficult to obtain because of government rules has led many physicians and patients to fear them, fear persecution, and to underuse such painkillers in general. I have heard of patients with chronic pain begging for more analgesics, as anyone in pain might do. One of my clients' proprietary market research studies from March 2017 showed that over half of physicians agreed with the statement: "I worry about opioid addiction issues." Over a third said that they prescribed fewer opioids than they did five years ago.

As a result of the crackdown, opioids have been prescribed less frequently; however, this hasn't translated into fewer problems. One study looked at the relationship between opioid prescriptions and injury-related deaths, including unintentional deaths and suicides. The authors concluded: "In every state examined [all 50 U.S. states and D.C.], there was no consistent relationship between the amount of prescription opioids delivered and total injury-related mortality or any subgroups, suggesting that there is not a direct association between prescription opioids and injury-related mortality."[26] In other words, the crackdown didn't prevent deaths. These results are consistent with conclusions reached by the Centers for Disease Control and Prevention.

Notice what has happened with this drug crackdown policy. At the macro level, drug abusers "matter," but regular pain patients, even though they far outnumber drug abusers and are innocent victims, don't "matter." I'd bet that most pain sufferers think that they *do* matter. They probably matter to their kids and to their spouses, parents, friends, neighbors, customers, bosses, and coworkers.

Any crackdown on opioids will employ the same techniques used by the current War on Drugs and the 20th century Alcohol Prohibition: demand stays the same; the quantity supplied drops; prices skyrocket; transactions happen outside legitimate, regulated commercial channels; and users are driven to ever more powerful drugs of questionable content and quality. First, consider that addicts are moving to drugs with a stronger kick: fentanyl, which is 50 to 100 times as potent as morphine, and carfentanil —sometimes used as an elephant tranquilizer—which is 10,000 times as potent as morphine.[27] Second, prescription drugs aren't currently the problem; there's been a wave of illicitly manufactured fentanyl from labs based in China and Mexico.[28] U.S. Customs officials at JFK Airport report that they are able to intercept just 40 percent of the opioid fentanyl that is hidden in the one million pieces of international mail that is processed *each day*.[29] And that's just for the fentanyl coming through one port of entry, and just for packages sent through the U.S. Postal Service.

Yes, some people are getting high on opioids. Yes, some drug companies produce opioids. But opioids from drug companies aren't the primary problem. To those suffering from pain, however, they are the primary solution—if only the government wouldn't enact legislation with untoward unintended consequences.

When the government limits access to opioids, it is doing little to treat addicts, and, meanwhile, the limits cause substantial collateral damage to the many Americans who suffer from pain.

Wrap-up

Many people assume that the FDA is pursuing a policy of the greatest good for the greatest number, helping Americans live longer and healthier lives. If this were the case, the FDA's actions could be seen increasing the quality-adjusted life years (i.e., healthier and/or longer lives) that Americans live. What if it is, instead, *reducing* quality-adjusted life years? (See Chapter 10).

If Paul Rubin is right and FDA regulations count in the positive column between 500 and 1,000 injuries prevented per year but show in the negative column between 2,100 and 12,000 lives lost, then the FDA is indeed reducing quality-adjusted life years and following a policy of the greatest damage to the greatest number.

The FDA does not seem to understand—or acknowledge—its role in creating the greatest harm to the greatest number.

---

[1] Paul H. Rubin, "An Opportunity Or a Threat: How to Have Safer, Less Expensive Drugs," Independent Institute, 7 December 2004

[2] The Centers for Disease Control and Prevention (CDC).

[3] See Chapter 2. Note that a substantial number of people who die due to "disease" actually die due to medical errors by health care professions in the process of treating those diseases. For instance, researchers from Johns Hopkins estimated in 2016 that more than 250,000 die annually due to medical errors in the United States. That puts medical errors as the third leading cause of death in the country. BMJ 2016;353:i2139

[4] The Centers for Disease Control and Prevention (CDC).

[5] The Centers for Disease Control and Prevention (CDC).

[6] *U.C. Berkeley Wellness Letter*, November 2007.

[7] Huerta-Alardín AL; Varon J; Marik PE. "Bench-to-bedside review: rhabdomyolysis – an overview for clinicians". Critical Care. 9 (2): 158–69, 2005.

[8] To calculate this: 1,500 heart attacks and strokes are prevented each year per 100,000 statin users and 27 million should be on statins but aren't (27 million divided by 100,000 times 1,500 is 405,000).

[9] "Using the Proton Pump Inhibitors to Treat Heartburn and Stomach Acid Reflux: Comparing Effectiveness, Safety, and Price," *Consumer Reports*, Updated July 2013.

[10] Jim McDonald, "How Many Vapers Are There?," *Vaping360*, 14 July 2016.

[11] Royal College of Physicians https://www.forbes.com/sites/jacobsullum/2016/04/28/royal-college-of-physicians-says-e-cigarettes-can-prevent-almost-all-the-harm-from-smoking/#3ff32eb349b8

[12] Haomiao Jia, et al, "Quality-adjusted life expectancy (QALE) loss due to smoking in the United States," Qual Life Res. 2013 Feb; 22(1): 27–35. https://www.ncbi.nlm.nih.gov/pmc/articles/PMC4590979/

[13] 5.2 is 5.5 times 0.95.

[14] 3.5 million vapers times 10% equals 350,000. 350,000 people times 5.2 years equals 1,820,000 years total. 1,820,000 years divided by 50 years per person equals 36,400 lives.

[15] 2,902 died on American soil during the September 11 attacks. 36,400 divided by 2,902 is 12.5. 36,400 deaths is equivalent to the deaths of 12.5 September 11 attacks.

[16] Jacob Sullum, "Royal College Of Physicians Says E-Cigarettes Can 'Prevent Almost All The Harm From Smoking'," *Forbes*, 28 April 2016.

[17] Originally published as: David R. Henderson and Charles L. Hooper, "Economists Know: Ask What Changed," *Library of Economics and Liberty*, 29 January 2019.

[18] "Overdose Death Rates," National Institute on Drug Abuse, August 2018 https://www.drugabuse.gov/related-topics/trends-statistics/overdose-death-rates

[19] Rose A. Rudd et al, "Increases in Drug and Opioid Overdose Deaths — United States, 2000–2014," Centers for Disease Control and Prevention (CDC), 1 January 2016.
https://www.cdc.gov/mmwr/preview/mmwrhtml/mm6450a3.htm?s_cid=mm6450a3_w

[20] William N. Evans, Ethan Lieber, and Patrick Power, "How the Reformulation of OxyContin Ignited the Heroin Epidemic, February 14, 2018.
https://www3.nd.edu/~elieber/research/ELP.pdf

[21] Jacob Sullum, "Are You More Likely to be Killed by Opioids Than a Car Crash?" *Reason*, 17 January 2019.

[22] Travis Rieder, "The Perilous Blessings of Opioids," *The Wall Street Journal*, 15-16 June 2019.

[23] Sally Satel, "Oxy Morons," *The Wall Street Journal*, 15 May 2017.

[24] CMS services bulletin, 2016.

[25] "The Opioid Puzzle," *The Wall Street Journal*, 26 October 2017.

[26] Evelyn Truong, et al., "Opioids and Injury Deaths: A population-based analysis of the United States from 2006 to 2017," *Injury*, 10 March 2010.

[27] Anyssa Garza, "Illicitly Produced Fentanyl: A Growing Cause of Synthetic Opioid Deaths," *Pharmacy Times*, 29 August 2018.

---

28 Anyssa Garza, “Illicitly Produced Fentanyl: A Growing Cause of Synthetic Opioid Deaths,” *Pharmacy Times*, 29 August 2018.

29 Deirdre Shesgreen, “An inside look at the hunt for fentanyl, the deadly opioid driving the overdose crisis,” *USA Today*, 17 September 2017

Chapter 12: Micromedical and Macromedical Perspectives

Economists make a distinction between microeconomics and macroeconomics: they call the large-scale, top-down approach macroeconomics and the small-scale, bottom-up approach microeconomics. Analogously, there are macromedical and micromedical views that we should understand.

Making Decisions

The Macromedical Way

The macromedical approach is familiar to most of us. A new drug, X, is tested on thousands of people and the results are statistically analyzed in an attempt to find true differences between X and a placebo. The therapeutic benefits are then judged against the risk of adverse events, considering the groups most likely to take Drug X. The FDA employs a macromedical view, generally considering the overall situation.

If Drug X is seen to be a positive addition, the FDA approves it. If not, the FDA rcjccts it.

The Micromedical Way

Patients, doctors, and other clinicians generally focus on the micromedical view, considering the health of one individual patient, because that's the mountain they need to summit. A physician takes all the data available and applies it to an individual patient. Therein lies both a problem and an opportunity.

What really matters to you, as an individual, is whether the drug you are about to take is safe and efficacious for *you*. The fact that a drug works for 40 percent of strangers increases the odds that it will work for you, but those odds are what you rely on *before* you put Drug X to the test; those odds help you decide whether or not to try Drug X. Once you do consume Drug X and resolve your conundrum, the success of those strangers becomes academic.

The micromedical approach focuses on the good of the individual in question and relies heavily on decision analysis, trial and error, and personal introspection. We've touched on some of the building blocks of decision analysis and will now put those pieces together.

Decision Analysis

Decision analysis is the study of decision making within uncertain and sometimes risky situations—in other words, almost all situations.[1] For example, buying a house is an uncertain and risky venture. Things might turn out really well or you might rue the day that you signed on the dotted line. Decision analysis is forward-looking and relies on a clearly defined decision maker.

The following medical example from Stanford University's Ronald Howard demonstrates the micromedical/decision analysis approach.

Imagine that you are blind but otherwise healthy and are offered a free procedure—someone else will pay for it—that will leave you in one of two states: healthy with good vision or dead. The probability that you will end up healthy and sighted is *p* and the probability that you will die is 1 – *p*. At the moment, we don't know *p*, but it is a key factor in determining which alternative you will choose. How high must *p* be for you to accept the procedure? Fifty percent, 80 percent, 99 percent, or 99.9 percent?

Figure 1: Vision Procedure?

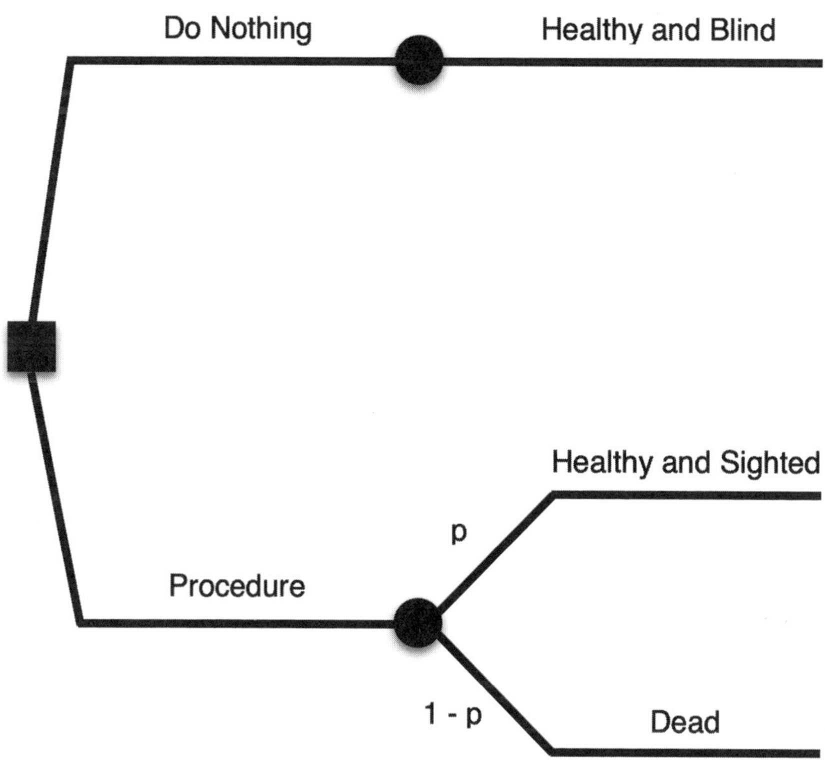

How high must *p* be to accept the procedure?

Two very reasonable, thoughtful people could give very different answers.

If one person's answer is 50 percent and another's is 99 percent, then the first person might happily join a clinical trial for some new, but risky, vision procedure to get a benefit quickly. The second person, however, might prefer to wait many years, until the procedure has matured through usage by numerous patients, and thereby reduce the risk. These two people face the same decision, but they have different preferences and may, therefore, take different paths.

The square box on the left of Figure 1 represents a decision. You can do nothing or have the procedure. If you do nothing, you will remain healthy and blind. If you have the procedure, one of two things will happen: you will end up healthy and sighted or dead. The circle represents an uncertainty node. Once you pick the "Procedure" alternative, you will have a probability of p of ending up healthy and sighted and a probability of $1 - p$ (the two branch probabilities must add to 100 percent) of dying.

Here's another example, shown in Figure 2. You have bladder cancer and are not responding to the standard treatments. The normal next step is a cystectomy—a surgeon will remove your bladder. As part of that procedure, your surgeon will create a urinary diversion—a new way to store and expel urine. If you decide against the cystectomy, there's some chance your cancer will metastasize and kill you. Neither outcome is appealing.

The probability that the cancer will metastasize and kill you is p and the probability that it won't is $1 - p$. Again, we don't know p at the moment, but how high must p be for you to accept the cystectomy procedure? Twenty percent, 50 percent, or 80 percent?

People who would strongly prefer to skip the cystectomy and keep their bladder, even if it kills them, will require a high percentage, perhaps 80 percent to push them toward the Cystectomy alternative. People who are

Figure 2: Cystectomy?

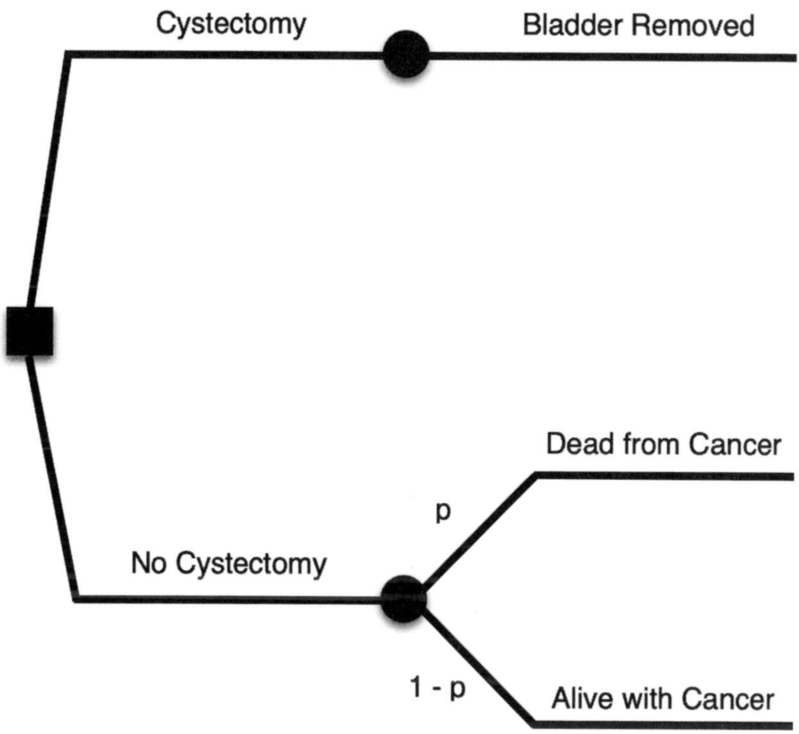

How high must *p* be to accept the cystectomy?

willing to cope with the difficulties of living without a bladder and strongly want to live a longer life will require a lower probability, perhaps 10 or 20 percent, to push them toward the Cystectomy alternative. Again, these two people face the same decision, but they have different preferences and may, therefore, take different paths.

Preferences

There are two important points about preferences: first, they are often discovered more clearly via actions than statements; second, they aren't right or wrong—they just *are*.

Economists have noted that our preferences are revealed, not expressed. If you ask a 16-year-old girl whether she will ever have children, she might give you a confident-sounding yes or no. It will probably be something such as, “of course,” or “no way!” However, if we check back in 15 or so years, we might be surprised at the actual result. People often find that they can’t really appreciate a situation until they are actually faced with it. That 16-year-old has a limited appreciation of what’s involved with having or not having children. None of us will ever exactly know what’s involved until we *actually have* children, but those of us making the decision at 24 or 34 can much better estimate the tradeoffs and consequences than we could have at 16.

This “we can’t know until we’re there” can partly explain how every generation looks at the younger generation and asks how the world can survive with these lazy, selfish, self-centered, unaware, fill in the blank, _______, kids. But, of course, our parents’ generation said that about us and our grandparents’ generation said it about our parents, etc. “That kid, George Washington. He’ll never amount to anything!” Let’s face it—it’s only when we get older and come face-to-face with the problems and opportunities of adulthood that we tend to grow up and act as adults. And that growth manifests itself by revealing some behaviors and preferences that we weren’t aware of as children.

That means that we can’t simply survey a representative sample of Americans and ask them what probability of success they would need to accept the vision surgery alternative described in Figure 1. Most Americans are *not* blind, and those who are know their answer needn’t be authentic because the situation is hypothetical.

Further, preferences are not right or wrong—they just *are*. Because of this, it is problematic to judge a person based solely on his or her expressed or actualized preferences. As you’ve probably noticed, we humans do quite frequently make such judgments. To judge others is normal; we see that “those people” are different from us, and their different choices force us to evaluate our own choices and challenge us to prove to ourselves that our choices are "right." If, in our minds, we deem our choices as right, then we naturally assume that the choices of the others are "wrong." If we leave it at that, there's no substantial problem. There is a problem, however, if we force others to abandon their preferences and to follow our own preference system instead.

We discussed Pareto improvements in Chapter 9. When we force others to follow our preference system, we have what could be called a Pareto deterioration. As an example of such coercion, we considered a tinpot dictator who required everyone to eat dinner at precisely 6:00 PM to show that it was suboptimal from a Pareto standpoint. Relaxing that dinnertime requirement would be a Pareto improvement and would make some people better off without hurting others.

There's no fundamental reason why eating dinner at 6:00 is universally better than at 7:00. Let people decide for themselves based on their own preferences.

Medical Choices

Preferences are important in the medical field because they lead people to select certain medical interventions and to reject other ones.

A patient's choice between therapies (with the help of an agent—a doctor) is based on many variables: efficacy, tolerability, convenience, ease of use, side effects, risk, possible embarrassment, pain, monetary cost, other non-monetary costs (e.g., hassle), speed of action, and long-term consequences. These therapy costs and benefits must be judged within the context of numerous personal values and tradeoffs: the fear of death, the fear of surgery, the fear of hospitals, tolerance for pain, health profile, financial status, value of time, value of health, risk tolerance, self-image, and personal goals.

Let's go back to the hypotheticals presented above. How important is it to you to regain your sight or to retain your bladder?

Furthermore, we should think about how preferences and values can manifest as thresholds. A psoriasis drug helps clear up your skin. That's great. But does it improve your skin enough for you to comfortably wear summer clothes without embarrassment? An ophthalmic drug improves your vision. Does it improve your vision enough for you to drive? To drive at night? An alopecia therapy grows more hair on your scalp. Does it grow enough hair to allow you to forgo a wig at social functions? A cancer drug helps you live longer. Will you live long enough to attend your granddaughter's wedding? These are the outcomes that really matter to patients, and they crystalize the way that many view therapy choices.

These assessments must come from their only confidant—the individual himself—and must be mapped against the particular situation that that individual finds himself in. Any outside agency, such as the FDA, can never frame the problem from the individual's perspective.

It's as if the individual patient is solving a complicated word problem (Train A leaves the station at time 0 traveling at 50 MPH, while train B leaves the station an hour later traveling at 55 MPH, and train C is 500 miles away, coming toward them at 30 MPH, etc.). We've all seen these types of problems. The individual making a medical decision must solve this problem, which can be difficult. But consider the situation from the FDA's perspective: the FDA knows that a word problem involving travel is being solved, but it knows nothing about A, B, or C, and it isn't aware of the setup or the speeds and distances. Try solving that problem!

The FDA looks at groups of people, guesses at a reasonable word problem setup, and then solves that problem. But that's just a made-up problem; it's not the real problem that the individual must solve, and we don't know if it's even close. The FDA might have math geniuses on staff, but those geniuses are provided with ill-framed math problems. To solve these types of problems, the FDA needs clairvoyants, not mathematicians.

Now imagine that each of one million individual patients has a unique word problem to solve. The FDA can probably guess what some of these word problems are like and can probably estimate some reasonable parameters, but it will never be quite right for the typical patient and it may be wildly off for the atypical patient.

Ludwig von Mises

The word problems above serve simply as an analogy. What patients are doing is looking at a complex system of information, alternatives, preferences, tradeoffs, probabilities, and possible outcomes to come up with a preferred therapy alternative. To assume that the FDA can determine the best alternative from this complex problem is unreasonable, given that it is incapable of framing the problem from the individual patient's perspective—quite simply, the FDA does not have—and never will have—the necessary information about every individual to do so. This is one of the insights of Ludwig von Mises, the noted Austrian economist.[2] In what is called the "socialist calculation problem," Mises demonstrated that a lack of essential information would cripple socialist economies. Stated differently, centralized bureaucrats cannot make the proper decisions for the individuals that those bureaucracies represent because they lack the requisite information.

What if the FDA, instead of poring over clinical trial results, merely guessed at the safety and efficacy of the new medicines it was evaluating? Critics would protest, and for good reason! How can the FDA make good decisions if it is guessing about crucial information? But the FDA guesses anyway. We've seen that the FDA has little, if any, information about your particular state of health, your situation, and your preferences. So, how does the FDA make many of its decisions? It guesses.

Guessing was not the right way to get good grades in school and guessing is not the right way to solve medical problems.

Let's look at a hypothetical, but realistic, case to highlight how unhelpful the FDA is to individuals making medical choices.

Treatment of AL Amyloidosis

Imagine for the following thought experiment that you have had the bad luck to be diagnosed with AL (systemic light chain) amyloidosis, which is a condition whereby your bone marrow produces misfolded proteins that circulate in your blood stream and, when they deposit in your organs, understandably cause problems. AL amyloidosis is rare, affecting only ten patients per million in the population and, because doctors are not looking for it, it is poorly diagnosed. When it is finally diagnosed, American patients don't live much longer than five to ten years. The sad truth is that, as this was being written in 2020, there were no FDA-approved medicines available to treat it. None.

The goal of ALA treatment is to eliminate the production of the misfolded proteins and to clear out the deposits from any organs where they may have collected. To stop the production of the misfolded proteins, doctors may give patients chemotherapeutic agents, such as dexamethasone or cyclophosphamide, with or without Velcade (bortezomib). Velcade for ALA is off-label, having been approved only for multiple myeloma and mantle cell lymphoma.

Are chemotherapy and Velcade the only treatment alternatives? Because I'm not a medical doctor—I don't even play one on TV—I can deviate from the standard medical script and tell you more than your doctor ever would.

You *do* have other choices. You always have other alternatives. You could skip all treatments and follow the "status quo/do nothing" path. You have any number of other "medications" available. You could try miracle healing at church. You could take a homeopathic medicine, take pain pills, or even choose to swallow Drano drain cleaner. Please understand that I'm not trying to be funny—I'm making the point that, though very few of us would ever choose to consume Drano, we are *free* to do so. No one will stop us. So, you see, there are *always* other alternatives, no matter how absurd some of them may be.

Here are your treatment alternatives:

- Status quo/do nothing
- Take chemotherapeutics without Velcade
- Take chemotherapeutics with Velcade
- Take pain medications
- Take a homeopathic medicine
- Miracle healing by God
- Take Drano drain cleaner

One very important alternative is missing from this list: take a New Drug. The one therapy that is unavailable at this time is the "New Drug" that the FDA forbids you to use because it hasn't been approved, meaning that it hasn't received marketing authorization. Let's discuss the others, one at a time.

Doing nothing, while a feasible alternative, is probably foolish in this case, as ALA will kill you in a handful of years. However, the "do nothing" or "watchful waiting" status quo alternative should always be considered, as it is the baseline to which the others must be compared.

Taking pain medications would just mask the pain but not help with the disease. This is not a good alternative, but it's an alternative nonetheless.

Taking a homeopathic medicine would be equivalent to doing nothing, in the best case. I'm not aware of any homeopathic medicine on the planet that can help with ALA. If you disagree with me, when you set up your own decision tree, you can feature the homeopathic medicine alternative.

Some people believe that miracle healing works. Google it and you'll get over half a million hits. If you think it may work for you, the FDA won't—and can't—stop you, because God doesn't follow FDA edicts.

Drano: Naturally, this is a really stupid alternative that was added for shock value. Every list of alternatives can include some "treatments," such as antifreeze, arsenic, hot lava, dehydration, a mound of sleeping pills, and rattlesnake bites, that no reasonable person would choose because they are clearly bad. But they are there, nonetheless. There are literally thousands of unconventional things that could be considered for therapy; we don't consider them seriously because they are so ridiculous. But they are there, available for patients to use if they *want* them.

There are multiple lessons from this. First, the FDA can't protect us from treatments that are unsafe because there are already literally thousands of dramatically dangerous substances, such as Drano, that are readily available. Second, people aren't as stupid as the FDA would have us believe and, hence, aren't in need of as much protection as many assume. The fact that people aren't treating ALA with hot lava or Drano demonstrates that they clearly understand the dangers of those alternatives. Third, by prohibiting "New Drug," the FDA reduces the alternatives available to physicians and their patients. And for some people, sometimes, those alternatives are their best alternative.

Next, we put all these decision alternatives into a decision tree. See Figure 3. The square on the left signifies a decision that we will make from among the alternatives listed on the right.

For each alternative, there is a range of uncertainty around the outcome received (see Figure 4). The circles in the middle signify uncertainty nodes. For example, there are a number of possible outcomes from the "Chemo without Velcade" alternative. Not shown are the branching

Figure 3: AL Amyloidosis Treatment Alternatives

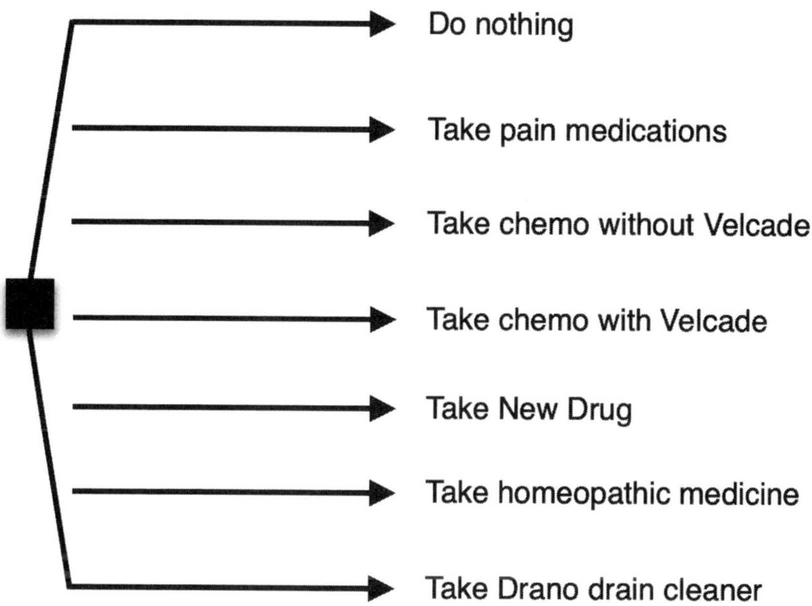

Pick one treatment alternative

structures for the other decision alternatives. [Note that "VG partial response" stands for "very good partial response" and "progression" means the disease continues unabated.]

The actual decision alternatives are finer than the coarse ones shown here. What type of chemotherapeutic should be used with Velcade? What dose of Velcade and at what frequency? How long should the patient stay on Velcade?

Opportunity costs enter the picture because by choosing "Chemo with Velcade," you give up other alternatives, such as "Chemo without Velcade." Will using Velcade now preclude the use of Velcade or some other better drug in the future?

Figure 4: ALA Treatment Uncertainties

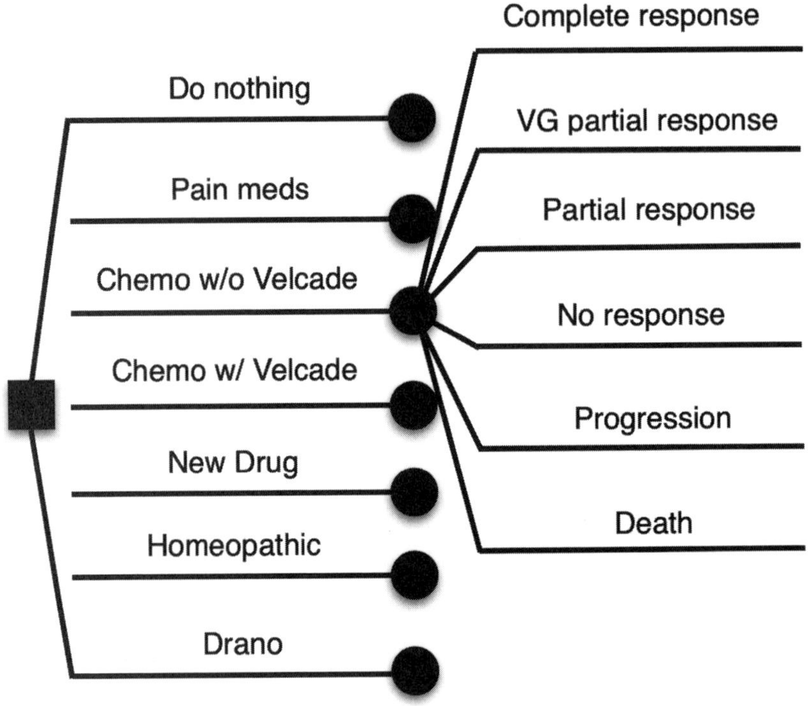

After picking one treatment, a number of outcomes are possible

Information is key. Can we get better information on the alternatives and the probabilities of success and failure? Can we get information on better drugs working their way through clinical trials that we might choose to wait for?

Thinking on the margin is important. Let's say that you've chosen "Chemo with Velcade." What's the best thing to do next, after you've gone through a course of treatment of chemo with Velcade? Increase the dose? Decrease the dose? It's not all or nothing; it can be more or less.

Which decision alternative should you choose? Unfortunately, we can't know yet because there's a huge gap in our understanding. What is your medical situation? Are you otherwise healthy or on your death bed? What are your preferences?

Role of the FDA in Micromedical Decisions

Within the micromedical perspective, where does the FDA fit into the ALA decision trees above? How can the FDA help this patient (you, hypothetically) fight ALA—or other diseases?

Let's consider how the FDA can help.

Information and Outcomes

The FDA can collect, assimilate, and propagate information about each decision alternative. For instance, what are the probabilities of each outcome from using Velcade? What are good doses? What evidence has been collected and how solid is it? What can patients expect from Velcade? What adverse events have others experienced?

The FDA can disseminate information about bad therapies, such as homeopathic remedies for ALA and, in the extreme case, Drano. In this regard, the FDA functions as a tour guide, pointing out local features to see and ones to avoid.

The FDA can also ensure that products are labeled correctly. Is that 10 mL vial supposedly containing 3.5 mg of Velcade really an unadulterated vial of Velcade? Is it counterfeit? Was it made in a musty basement in Pittsburgh by someone with half a cigar hanging out of his mouth?

While the FDA can *potentially* help with information, the agency has a complicated relationship with the free availability of information, and it often prevents truthful information from being disseminated, as we have seen with off-label promotion and press releases. But there's more.

The FDA can also act *against* the dissemination of information that might help people to seek treatments. One case involved Apple, which dropped a planned glucometer—a device that measures the blood's glucose level—from its first-generation Apple Watch after it discovered that the device would fall under the FDA's purview if it helped people make medical decisions. Apple wanted to increase the information available to individuals with diabetes, and the FDA scuttled the project. The next case, discussed in Chapter 8, involved 23andMe, a company that provides mail-order, direct-to-consumer personalized genetic testing services that quantify disease risks. Is genetic information dangerous? The FDA must have thought so, because in November 2013, the FDA ordered 23andMe to "immediately discontinue" the marketing of its testing service until the FDA reviewed and approved it. The FDA later rescinded that ban in April 2017, and now our genes can share their secrets with us.

Beyond these abilities to inform—or refuse to inform—the public, things start looking even worse for the FDA as we assess its role in micromedical decision making.

Preferences

The one with the best insight into your preferences is, of course, you. You are the expert. Your family and friends are next on the list, followed, perhaps, by your doctor. Pharmaceutical companies and the FDA are dead last. The FDA has little to offer. The FDA doesn't even know that you exist.

Opportunity Costs

While the FDA can state the obvious and say that taking Drug A means that you can't take Drug B, it can't provide insight into your particular situation and what opportunity costs really mean to you. By choosing one drug over the other, what do you potentially gain and what do you potentially give up? Again, the FDA has little to offer.

Thresholds

The FDA has little insight into how much better your skin needs to be before you can wear summer clothes without embarrassment. The FDA doesn't know how much a cancer drug will need to prolong your life for you to celebrate your granddaughter's wedding.

The FDA has little to offer.

Tradeoffs

If you had cancer, would you prefer a stronger medicine that may cause more side effects or a gentler medicine that causes fewer side effects but has less efficacy? Nothing is perfect. How do you make the tradeoff between efficacy and tolerability?

If you begin another chemotherapy regimen, you may lose the ability to work, travel, or attend an important event, such as your granddaughter's wedding. You can clearly see this tradeoff, but the FDA has literally zero knowledge about the tradeoffs you are facing. The FDA has no idea that your granddaughter will be trying the knot this summer.

The FDA has little to offer.

Uncertainty and Risk

While the FDA might know about the range of outcomes for a given therapy, how you feel about the range of those outcomes is highly dependent on your particular situation and your preferences. The FDA is, at best, an outsider looking in.

Consider the risk that you will be hospitalized after a particular therapy. For a retired person with a flush bank account and a solid support network, being hospitalized my not be that bad. For a single mom supporting a family, being hospitalized could be devastating.

The FDA has little to offer in terms of understanding how the risk of being hospitalized could affect you.

Alternatives

We've painted an unflattering picture of the FDA, but here's where the agency absolutely falls flat on its face.

The FDA can't create new alternatives. The FDA merely regulates the foods, drugs, and medical devices that others do the hard work of developing. The FDA's primary job is to push the drug development brake pedal, not to step on the accelerator. The FDA doesn't even *have* a gas pedal

The FDA is a retardant, not a catalyst, of medical innovation. The only real action that the FDA can and does take is to delay new therapies. Whether it delays the New Drug alternative a little or a lot, it still, at least temporarily, removes an important alternative from our decision tree. Remember that new drugs cannot be used legally until the FDA has approved them, and the FDA's process can only delay drugs, never accelerate them.[3] If you think that New Drug would have been your best choice, you're out of luck.

Advocates of the FDA will say that this is an incomplete assessment. One important aspect of the FDA's work, they will say, is to keep dangerous drugs off the list of alternatives. But this argument doesn't stand up to logic. Think of all the other dangerous substances that are, or could be, on the list. We have Drano on our list. We could add antifreeze, arsenic, hot lava, dehydration, three bottles of Viagra tablets in one dose, and electroshock therapy. There are literally thousands of dangerous and/or ineffective things that could be considered for therapy; we don't consider them because they are often ridiculous. But they are there, available for patients to use if they *want* them. The only alternatives kept off the list by the FDA are drugs that are in that gray area, where some people say they will help and others don't.

The FDA has tremendous power to prohibit potentially good (gray) therapies, but it can't prevent all bad therapies.

Advocates of the FDA point to the FDA's success at keeping inefficacious drugs off the market, as these drugs give patients false hopes and encourage pointless usage when better therapies may be available. While this is an appealing argument, we have little reason to believe that the FDA has succeeded in this regard, and our micromedical framework shows this. Why? Long before the FDA was created, the medical system was striving to use only effective drugs, and it looks as though it has done a reasonable job.

The only fallback for FDA advocates would be to say that the FDA has more or better information about drugs than the rest of us. Even if this were true now, it needn't stay that way. This is the information age, and the Internet can provide truckloads of information to anyone energetic enough to wade through it.

Wrap-up

The field of medicine is really the science and practice of finding the best therapy for each patient and then skillfully applying and monitoring that treatment until some therapeutic goal is achieved.

The macromedical approach seeks the best therapies for populations of people, while the micromedical approach seeks the best therapy for one individual.

Your personal doctor treats you as an individual. It doesn't matter if the prior 16 patients got better on a certain statin, if you don't. The benefit that others derive from a certain drug can help *suggest* whether you should use that drug, but, ultimately, nothing matters except whether you benefit.

And the way you find out is the way people found out before the FDA existed: good old fashioned trial and error.

Using insights from the field of decision analysis, we can see that the FDA has a fundamentally limited ability to help us. The FDA *can* help with information, although it often forgets this. However, for preferences, opportunity costs, thresholds, tradeoffs, thinking on the margin, uncertainty and risk, and alternatives, the FDA is about as useful to us as a golf club is to a fish.

---

[1] For more on this, please see David R. Henderson and Charles L. Hooper, *Making Great Decisions in Business and Life*, Chicago Park Press, 2006.

[2] Austrian here refers to a branch of economics, not the nationality. See Peter J. Boettke, "Austrian School of Economics," *Concise Encyclopedia of Economics* (free on the web).

[3] The expanded access program allows some patients to take some drugs before they are approved by the FDA.

Chapter 13: A Vision for The Future

Our lives would improve without the FDA acting as a capricious gatekeeper. That's my bold claim. Are you skeptical?

When we consider scaling back the FDA's powers, there are always those ready and willing to cry thalidomide—a threatening call intended to stop us in our tracks and remind us that situations can and have gone off the rails. Without the FDA to protect us, would we have more thalidomides? Instead of turning off our brains and freezing when we hear the word thalidomide, we need to calm our frayed nerves and step back. To think clearly about this, perhaps we can learn from another industry: consider cars and trucks.

By virtually every measure, automobiles are much better today than they were 100 years ago. They are more powerful, faster, quieter, cleaner, safer, more efficient, more comfortable, more solidly built, more reliable, require less maintenance, handle better, and last longer.

Modern cars have:

- Environmental controls for heating and cooling
- Crumple zones for crash protection
- Tires that can last 70,000 miles without flats
- Bright, high-tech headlamps
- Smart keys
- On-board diagnostics
- Electrical connectors that connect securely and don't corrode over time
- Rust protection
- Turbochargers for additional power with fuel efficiency
- Stereo systems that connect to our smartphones
- Cruise control that matches the speed of the car being followed
- Platinum and iridium spark plugs that last 100,000 miles
- Digital instrument panels
- Safety glass
- Collapsible steering columns
- Knock sensors that retard the ignition, when needed, to prevent dangerous cylinder "knocking"
- Suspensions that absorb bumps and maintain control
- Hydraulic, fade-resistant power disc brakes
- Beautiful paints and finishes
- Room to comfortably fit an entire family
- Windshield wipers
- Theft protection
- Steering wheel controls
- Locking gas caps
- Safety locks for hoods
- Automatic starting systems
- GPS anti-theft devices
- Tinted glass
- Backup cameras
- Radial steel-belted tires
- Engines and transmissions that can last 200,000 miles
- Aerodynamics to reduce noise and fuel consumption
- Power steering
- Anti-lock brake systems

- Sound insulation
- Driving ranges of 600 miles
- Sophisticated six-speed automatic transmissions with paddle shifters
- Airbags and three-point seatbelts
- Cabin air filters
- Self-parking technologies
- "Miles remaining" calculations
- Cup holders
- Electrical outlets
- Pollution controls
- All-wheel drive
- Navigation systems
- Computer systems to help with operations and diagnostics
- Long service intervals
- Stability control
- Maintenance reminders
- Limited self-driving capabilities
- Gas, diesel, hybrid gas/electric, and electric drivetrains
- Electric motors with lithium ion, nickel-cobalt-aluminum oxide, and nickel-manganese-cobalt batteries

That's an impressive list.

Certainly, there have been some wonderful cars made in the last 100 years, and some are highly sought after by collectors. However, other than car collectors and those with sentimental attachments to their classic cars, many people who own an older car do so because they can't afford a new one.

Even those attached to their older cars and trucks sometimes slyly add modern features, getting a boost by fitting modern tires, brakes, batteries, electronics, and even transmissions and engines. Even if it's not their aim, classic car owners get the benefit of modern oils, antifreeze, and gasoline.

While there are regulatory bodies and regulations that have mandated improvements to cars, most of the improvements have happened via market forces. Where regulations have been enacted, those regulations have often codified the current trajectory of automotive enhancements, effectively jumping in front of the parade and pretending to lead it.

If you doubt this, how can we explain the fact that cars improved substantially and U.S. motor vehicle deaths per mile traveled dropped by a factor of seven *before* the National Highway Traffic Safety Administration (NHTSA) was established in 1965?[1] Of course, part of the improvement can be credited to better roads, signage, lighting, and safer drivers, among other things. But better cars were a significant factor.

Consider motor vehicle deaths per 100 million miles, as shown in Figure 1. The vertical line demarcates the year that the NHTSA was established. The trend, using 1913 through 1965 data, is also shown[2] and it overlaps the actual, historical data, meaning the recent improvements in safety appear to be a result of the long-term trend, not government regulations. If the government regulations had had an appreciable effect, the actual post-NHTSA deaths would have been lower than the trend of the pre-NHTSA data. We don't see that.

Why would cars be getting safer without government regulators, ahem, driving the process? Car companies don't want to kill their customers—that's always a bad business practice. Car companies don't want bad public relations, don't want to be sued, and don't want nasty books written about them (see Ralph Nader's *Unsafe at Any Speed*). Car companies do want to be seen as leaders in innovation, and they want to make a lot of money. They can do that only if customers choose to buy their cars and are satisfied enough to recommend their vehicles to friends.

Why do cars keep getting better? The forces for improvement are tremendous. Engineers are habitual problem solvers who work behind the scenes, improving thousands of aspects of automotive design and manufacturing. Customers, in their role, keep the pressure on car companies to build better and better cars. Customers seek out awesome cars and, ideally, the prestige that comes from their choices. (Think of the

Figure 1: U.S. Motor Vehicle Deaths

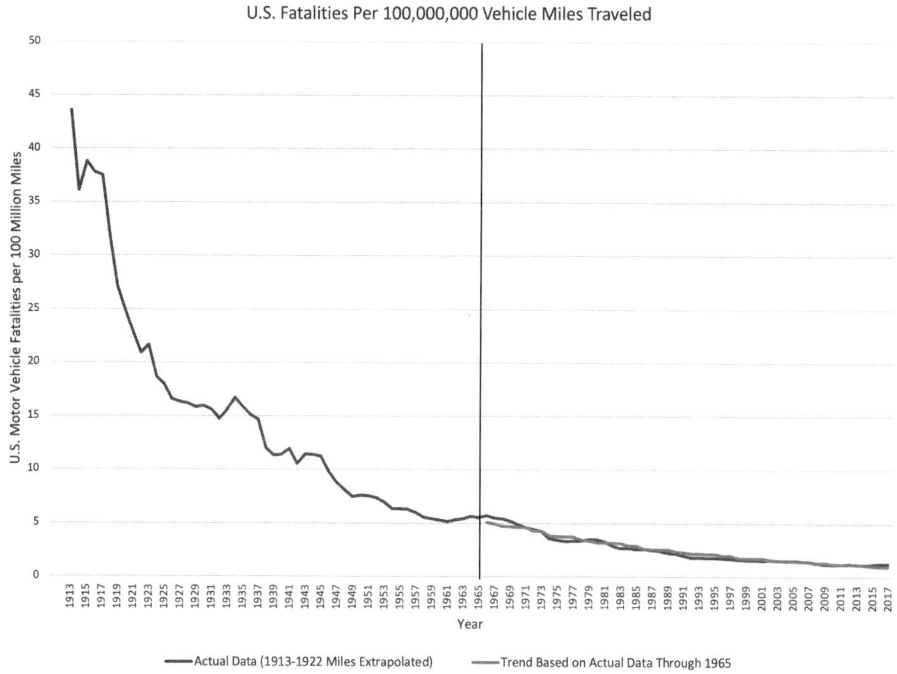

U.S. motor vehicle deaths declined before and after NHTSA was established in 1965

kudos that Tesla owners get from their friends and colleagues; owning a Tesla signals to others certain positive traits.)

Car magazines such as *Road & Track* and *Car & Driver* write monthly about the glories of well-built cars. Car review publications, such as *Consumer Reports*, scrutinize the attributes and reliability of the cars available in dealerships. The press employs both carrots, such as "best of" lists, and sticks, by quickly pouncing on any car company that stumbles. Missteps like the Ford Pinto gas tank bolts are a painful reminder for auto executives.

Almost every force works toward making cars better, and we have 100 years of proof that these forces are powerful indeed.

It could be the same for the pharmaceutical industry.

Every force in the automotive industry that entices and compels car companies to keep improving their products is also at play in the pharmaceutical industry—if we would let it.

What is the pharmaceutical industry that we have? Sure, there are awesome new products such as cancer fighters, cholesterol reducers, gene therapies, and hepatitis C cures. But we also have bladder cancer patients who have 100-year-old tuberculosis vaccines injected into their bladders because there's nothing better. We have AL amyloidosis with no approved therapies. We faced the COVID-19 pandemic without adequate diagnostics, therapeutics, and vaccines. A mere two to six percent of known disorders have any sort of treatments available, and many of those treatments are deficient in one or more ways. The industry is rife with ineffective and dangerous drugs. It's as if we live in Cuba and are told by the ruling elite that we should be thankful that we get to drive Buick Roadmasters and Ford Fairlanes from the 1950s.

What could the pharmaceutical industry be like?

Think about innovative people such as Steven Spielberg, Steve Jobs, Elon Musk, Jony Ive, Jeff Bezos, and J.K. Rowling. Look at innovative companies such as Amazon, Apple, Ford, Google, Honda, PayPal, Pixar, Porsche, Robinhood, Rockstar Games, Samsung, SpaceX, Tesla, and Toyota. Think of innovative government agencies such as NASA during the space race days, leaping from the first manned space flight to landing on the moon in eight short years. Think of Lockheed's Skunk Works®, that in 1943 built the U.S. Army's first jet fighter, the XP-80 Shooting Star, in a mere 143 days. That same type of spirit could be behind new drug discovery and development.

Consider, again, the example of the Apple Watch. Without the FDA's hurdles, Apple may have included a glucometer in its first-generation Apple Watch, helping countless diabetics.

Consider, again, the case of Sprix (intranasal ketorolac). Without the FDA's hoops to jump through, Roxro Pharma could have developed an intranasal formulation of ketorolac. Once it determined that serum (blood) concentrations of ketorolac quickly reached the desired levels and that there were no adverse effects in the nostrils, Roxro could have launched Sprix as soon as manufacturing had been finalized. Better yet, we would never have needed Sprix because we could have enjoyed the advantages of 30-milligram oral ketorolac tablets.

Consider, again, the case of Impossible Burgers. Without the FDA's twisted rules about food coloring, we could have been cooking meatless Impossible Burgers in our own homes years earlier.

Without the FDA's interference, Allen Tower could provide sick children with customized cardiological devices.

Now, imagine an employee who sees a way to make a product safer, more efficacious, or easier to manufacture. This employee would make a presentation to management, and if management found the idea appealing, a pilot project would be launched. If the results of the manufacturing and testing were good, the improved product would be rolled out in the market as a whole.

Innovation won't come from just new and improved products. The pharmaceutical industry has a veritable warehouse of "failed" products that failed simply because of FDA rules. There are certainly gold nuggets in that warehouse. We simply need to get out of the way of people who know how to bring useful therapeutics to doctors and patients.

This sensible, straightforward, market-based process is how we get better food, cars, smartphones, computers, and movies. A similar process could be giving us better medicines, too. What possible reason could we have for looking at a process that delivers an abundance of quality services and products—i.e., the free market—and saying that it will fail when applied to one particular product: medicines? Normally, one must argue about "market failures" to advance governmental solutions. As economists have pointed out, there is no solid market failure rationale for the FDA's powers.[3]

Recall the story of Maurice Hilleman, who used his oldest daughter's mumps infection to isolate the offending virus and develop a promising vaccine, which he then tested in his younger daughter. Hilleman brought a classic childhood disease to the verge of extinction. This is the kind of medical breakthrough we should expect to hear about day in and day out.

We did enjoy some spectacular and, frankly, unexpected success against the novel coronavirus of 2019 with the public–private partnership named Operation Warp Speed. Previously, the record for fastest vaccine development was three months—by Hilleman—for the influenza vaccine of 1959 and four years— by Hilleman—for a non-influenza vaccine. In 2020, we saw a few vaccines developed in under a year. This was fortuitous, as COVID-19 was killing approximately 8,000 people a day.

The examples in this book provides a glimpse of a world in which the FDA has too much power—in other words, the world as it is. Imagine shifting that power from a single, centralized authority to the market, made up of drug discoverers, scientific researchers, medical professionals, and most important of all, the individuals who face disease and seek solutions based on their preferences, their situations, and their medical needs.

That vision of a healthy future inspired this book. In turn, I hope this book inspires others to help realize a future that will be better than our past and present.

[1] Based on an analysis of U.S. traffic fatality data. The number of deaths due to motor vehicle collisions is known from 1913 through 2017. The number of miles is known from 1923 through 2017. The values for 1913 through 1922 were extrapolated. Fatalities per 100,000,000 miles traveled were about 39 from 1913 to 1916 and 5.5 in 1965 (39 divided by 5.5 is 7.1). Therefore, fatalities per 100,000,000 miles traveled have dropped by a factor of seven before the National Traffic Safety Administration was established.

[2] Data from 1913 through 1965 were trended using exponential smoothing, multiplicative trend and multiplicative seasonality. This method was selected over dozens of others via a technique of holding out actual data and seeing which trending methods best predicted the actual data. Grading was via MAPE scores.

[3] "Where Is the Market Failure Argument for the Interventions We Have?" *FDAReview.org*.

Chapter 14: Possible Solutions

This book has highlighted a number of deficiencies in the current regulatory environment for biotechnology and pharmaceutical medicines and, to a lesser degree, medical devices, diagnostics, vaccines, and food in the United States. What are some possible solutions to the shortcomings discussed here? What can we do to make things better for our country, our children, and our friends, and ourselves?

Status Quo

The "do nothing," status quo, alternative should always be considered. It is the baseline alternative against which all other alternatives should be considered. It consists of keeping the FDA's regulations the same and working to ensure that the FDA is populated with capable employees. In other words, more of the same.

While realizing that, by changing things, we could make matters worse, here, in no particular order, are some possible solutions to think about. Some may be better than others, but since, as this book has tried to make very clear, the status quo is wanting, these are worth considering.

Make Animal Testing Ancillary

As discussed in Chapter 4, the FDA's reliance on and requirements for animal testing are problematic. Nonetheless, pre-clinical animal studies do often provide important findings. What needs to change is the FDA's animal testing requirements. Animal studies should be ancillary, not central, to the drug development process. The results from animal studies at super high doses should be taken with a grain of salt.

Smartphone App for Drug Feedback

We could set up and promote a smartphone app that would be similar to Yelp, but for drugs. With this app, patients could report efficacy results, adverse events, and drug-drug interactions. Pharmacists and physicians could encourage the use of the app. While the quality of any particular individual data element might be low—witness Yelp restaurant reviews—the sheer abundance of data would allow for productive analyses by all manner of researchers. Many questions could be answered that would help the medical profession better understand how patients adhere to therapy regimens, what side effects they experience, which drugs work for which conditions, and what combination of drugs might be interacting.

In 2021, the CDC offered v-safe to individuals who received one of the COVID-19 vaccines. V-safe was a smartphone-based tool that used text messaging and web surveys to provide personalized health check-ins for those who had received a vaccine. It was very easy to use. One's smartphone's camera would scan a QR code to start the process and, once set up, v-safe would send a daily reminder to patients to report overall health and side effects that potentially could have resulted from the vaccine. Something similar to v-safe could be used for other medicines.

Organize a Large Panel of Patients

With the smartphone app mentioned above, the risk is that we might get responses from the two tails of the distribution: those who love a new drug and those who hate it. This is a problem on Yelp with restaurant reviews.

A related but different idea would be to convene a large panel of patients who would be willing to provide regular input. When I say large, I mean large: on the order of 10 million Americans. These patients would be paid on a monthly and per-interaction basis to participate, and key medical and pharmacological information would be collected and analyzed. This information, once de-personalized, could be sold to universities, researchers, third-party payers, pharmacy benefit managers, and drug companies. The FDA could use the information to look for drug efficacy and safety issues.

This panel would have other benefits. The pandemic of 2020/2021 highlighted the lack of serial infection and antibody data for the SARS-CoV-2 virus. What percentage of the population was infected? Was the rate of infections increasing or declining? What percentage of the population had antibodies from a prior infection? It's hard to fight an enemy when we lack information about the enemy's location and strength. No general would ever want to enter battle without good intelligence information. Had this panel been in place, we could have had solid, near real-time surveillance data about the progression of the virus through society.

The National Institutes of Health is organizing something along these lines. The "All of Us" research program seeks to enroll one million Americans and collect data for ten years or more.

Move Drug Regulation to the State Level

As discussed in Chapter 8, the FDA, a federal drug regulatory agency, is not allowed by the U.S. Constitution. However, state governments could take up the cause and regulate drugs at the state level. While this approach to drug regulation would be more complicated and somewhat duplicative, fifty different approaches would give us far more experimentation. Some states could band together and work under one umbrella. Americans could then make their choice of residency based partly on the drug regulation schemes employed by the different state governments.

Reward the FDA for Improving the Health of Americans

To better align the interests of a drug regulatory agency—here the FDA—and regular Americans, we could change the FDA's reward structure to make some fraction of FDA employees' pay and promotion determined by objective metrics that derive from the overall health of Americans. FDA employees would get bonuses based on how many—actually, how few—ischemic strokes strike Americans each year, for instance, and the length of the resulting hospital stays, rehabilitations, and disability periods.

With this policy in place, consider a hypothetical scenario. The FDA can approve a new drug that will prevent ischemic strokes. Based on the best available information, 100 patients per year will die due to adverse events from the drug but 100,000 patients, who otherwise would have died, will now live. With the existing FDA, this drug might be rejected because the agency wouldn't want to face scrutiny for approving a drug that killed 100 Americans. With a properly incentivized FDA, this drug would probably be approved for marketing because saving 100,000 and allowing 100 to die is a clear net positive.

Ultimately, we don't necessarily care how many drugs the FDA approves or rejects or whether, in its role as gatekeeper, it is too stingy or generous; we care about having powerful therapies to help us live long and healthy lives and, in the long run, we care about actually living those long and healthy lives. We care about being well, however we get there.

Framed this way and with appropriate incentives, the FDA might actually find a way to advance some therapies. The FDA might, instead of acting as a critic and stern gatekeeper, reach out to companies working on therapies for ischemic stroke and help them shepherd their products through the discovery, development, review, approval, and marketing processes. With the correct incentives, the FDA could be a powerful partner instead of a stout opponent.

Approve Drugs That Receive at Least Three Votes

The FDA could automatically approve any drug that received three or more votes in an advisory committee meeting. Currently, advisory committee votes are informational and advisory, and the FDA may or may not follow the committee's advice. With this change, if an advisory committee has at least three outside experts who think that a new drug should be approved, the FDA would be required to approve it.

No More FDA Judge, Jury, and Executioner

Remember the case of Sprix in earlier chapters (see Chapters 6, 8, and 9)? Sprix was being developed by Roxro Pharma through the 505(b)(2) regulatory pathway, with the promise that such drug development was to be faster and cheaper by not requiring duplicative clinical trial data.[1]

In the case of Sprix, however, the FDA reviewer, Harvard's Lee S. Simon, required Roxro to conduct full clinical trials as if Sprix were a completely new product with no history. This set Roxro back two years and millions of dollars, crippling the tiny company during the Great Recession.

When Simon returned to Harvard, the FDA reviewers who replaced him seemed perplexed by Simon's demands on Roxro. They would not have required those extra clinical trials. While sensitive to how they made the FDA appear to outsiders, they indicated that they had no idea why Simon placed such demands on Roxro and communicated that they would have acted differently. Apparently, Roxro wasn't alone: more than a third of biopharmaceutical companies complained in a 2006 survey that FDA regulators changed their position while the companies were in the middle of testing a drug.[2]

In a somewhat related note, not too long afterwards, Simon was forced to resign from Harvard Medical School after it was discovered that about half of the text of a medical journal article he had written was taken verbatim from another published paper.[3] You can understand Roxro's wish that he had been fired earlier. After Roxro spent millions of dollars and several years to get the cold, hard data that Simon required, the data proved what we already knew: Sprix worked just like other formulations of ketorolac, and blood levels are what matter. What a waste of time and money.

When this was happening, Roxro knew that Simon was wrong and wasn't following the rules. But what can a six-person company do when facing a huge, powerful bureaucracy? Sue? Roxro was trying to save cash, not spend it. And even if Roxro won in court, suing the government agency responsible for approving your product is a dangerous proposition.

The problem that Roxro ran into could have been avoided in a simple way. Instead of allowing the FDA to act as the judge, jury, and executioner, all future conflicts like this one could be resolved in front of an independent third party. The two sides—Simon's team and Roxro's team—would argue their case in front of an independent panel or judge.

This wouldn't be a full-blown lawsuit by a company against the FDA. This would be an inexpensive and faster way for contentious, important drug development—but not drug approval—decisions to be heard in front of an unbiased third party. In the Roxro/Simon example, I have little doubt that an independent judge would have ruled in Roxro's favor. Further, with this kind of process, FDA reviewers would likely be more careful, knowing that their key decisions would be scrutinized by an independent judge.

Adaptive Clinical Trials

Standard clinical trials are double-blind, placebo-controlled, randomized trials. The researchers set objectives for the trials, recruit patients, half of whom get the active drug with the rest getting a placebo, and the study proceeds as designed until the end. This prevents biases and makes for cleaner analysis of the results. Unfortunately, this structure is rigid, expensive, and slow.

Adaptive clinical trials can adjust as discoveries are made. For example, during the COVID-19 pandemic, Gilead Science's drug Veklury (remdesivir) was tested in the Adaptive COVID-19 Treatment Trial. The first drug being tested was actually hydroxychloroquine, but as unimpressive results rolled in, the key drug was switched to Veklury. When a separate trial found that patients who received five days of Veklury did as well as patients that had gotten ten days, the patients in the adaptive trial were put on five-day regimens.

Adaptive clinical trials have the potential to be faster and cheaper.

Allow Promotion of Off-Label Uses

Remember that drug companies are forbidden to "promote" drugs for off-label uses (uses for diseases that aren't officially spelled out on the package insert). This means that doctors and the representatives of pharma companies can have an in-depth, back and forth conversation about the use of a drug for pain, if that drug has been formally approved for pain. But once the doctor changes the topic to migraines—a use not officially sanctioned—the representative must remain silent. Should a higher dose be used? The representative can't say. Are there potential problems and ways to circumvent those problems? The representative can't say.

Products that have received FDA approval for one indication are, according to the FDA, safe, which is why they were approved in the first place. So why not let doctors and patients experiment with off-label uses, as they do now, but with the additional benefit of information possessed by the drug companies that discovered, manufacture, and understand the drugs? Don't you want your doctor to be able to talk to the company that developed the drug being injected into your body? Don't you want your doctor to be able to talk to a drug company that might have a better drug for you to take? Off-label prescribing will happen with or without this information, and all parties will benefit from the additional information, which is one reason, after all, that *all* speech is protected by the First Amendment.

We should liberate information.

Truly Grandfather Older, Grandfathered Drugs

Instead of trying to bring older drugs, such as sublingual nitroglycerin, into compliance with newer regulations, the FDA could truly grandfather these useful, older drugs and simply leave them alone. FDA meddling just makes the situation worse, as in the cases of aspirin, morphine, quinine, pancreatic enzymes, and sublingual nitroglycerin pills.

Drugs that have been used successfully by millions of patients for many years should be treated as innocent until proven guilty. The FDA is free to mount a campaign to prove that the old drugs are bad drugs, but many problems arise when manufacturers are required to prove that old drugs are good drugs. See Chapter 8 for more.

Shift from Pre-Marketing Gatekeeping to Post-Marketing Surveillance

Instead of the FDA's guilty-until-proven-innocent framework, the FDA could shift to an innocent-until-proven-guilty approach, and after safety had been determined sufficiently, any new drug could be marketed, even absent efficacy data.

The FDA would then surveil each new drug, carefully watching for problems.

In such a post-marketing situation, the FDA could assess efficacy through clinical trials, regular medical practice, peer-reviewed journals, patient-based or disease-based organizations, third-party payers, third-party rating organizations, longitudinal patient insurance claims data, social media, patient panels, market research, the smartphone app described above, among other methods. The FDA could watch for problems, warn companies about problems, and then, with due process, pull offensive products directly from the market.

Some may scoff at the value of discovering the truth through regular medical practice because of a perception of imperfect people trying everything under the sun. That *is* its weakness, of course, but it's also its *strength*. In terms of sheer numerical advantage, 330 million individual Americans, along with a million or so doctors, can run far more experiments than are possible from limited and artificial clinical trials. It's a feature, not a bug.

Researchers at Stanford University are already using sophisticated "big data" searches of social media sources and FDA reports to uncover rare problems with drugs and drug-drug interactions.[4]

There are, certainly, pitfalls to avoid with post-marketing surveillance. Determining the truth can be tricky. Here is one example.

Imagine that there are two drugs, D and S, on the market for a particular condition. Wanting to know more about the use of these drugs, we analyze retrospective data and notice something startling: D was associated with three times as many adverse events, perhaps heart attacks, as S. Does this mean that S is the safer and, therefore, the better drug? Does it mean that D is particularly dangerous? Should the FDA pull D from the market?

Perhaps. Perhaps not. We don't have enough information.

Drugs S and D might be used for the same broad condition, but they might be given to different types of patients at different times. S might be given to patients with mild or moderate disease while D might be given to patients who present with severe disease. Or, patients might start on S, while they are healthier, and then be upgraded to D, when they become sicker. D might be a last-line therapy given to patients just before they die.

The higher frequency of adverse events with D is a correlation, but without further digging, we can't tell if that is merely an association or a true cause and effect.

We can see a similar result in other areas. Fewer of the patients that are seen by school nurses die than those treated by paramedics. Does that mean that paramedics are less capable than school nurses? Should victims of car crashes request treatment from school nurses? No, of course not. School nurses tend to treat young people for bumps and bruises, and that's why so few of their patients die.

This idea for post-marketing surveillance is not new. Former FDA Commissioner Andrew von Eschenbach proposed, in 2012, that "after proof of concept and safety testing, the [new therapeutic] product could be approved for marketing with every eligible patient entered in a registry so the company and the FDA can establish efficacy through post-market studies."[5] He argued that reducing dependency on expensive and lengthy Phase 3 clinical trials would have a positive effect on medical innovation and the U.S. economy. He pointed out that doctors, payers, and patients would be, and should be, the ultimate judge of the quality of new drugs and that biopharma companies would learn from that experience to develop superior products.

We could give von Eschenbach's idea a chance.

Allow Human Safety Data to Supersede Animal Safety Data

In an effort to prevent the debacle that XenoPort faced with Horizant, where a small study with animals nearly derailed a drug that *already* had good human safety data (see Chapter 4), the FDA should refrain from rejecting any new drug or pulling an already marketed drug when good human safety data exists. If the drug is designed for humans, animal safety data should never be allowed to override human safety data.

The FDA should care more about us humans than it does about rodents. Who, but a rat, could argue otherwise?

Use Longitudinal Insurance Claims Data for Virtual Clinical Trials

When a drug company wants to test a new drug, it typically designs a clinical trial in which some large percentage of the trial participants get the standard of care. For example, if patients today are using triptans to prevent their migraines, a test of a new drug to prevent migraines will require a clinical trial in which half of the patients get the current standard of care: triptans.

The research question to be answered is whether the new drug is better than triptans (or at least non-inferior to triptans).

However, there are millions of occurrences of people already taking triptans—that's what standard of care means. If we could see what has happened to the people already taking triptans, we could reduce the size of the clinical trial by up to half. Thankfully, there's a way to do this using the mountains of data that the medical profession records and submits to insurance companies to receive reimbursement.

By appropriately "mining" this mountain of data using what are called business rules (for example: pull all the patient records where a patient got a diagnosis of migraine from a neurologist and was prescribed a triptan drug within three months), we can look at the success of triptans for preventing migraines. Then the results of the clinical trial of the new drug can be compared to the results of patients already on triptans to see which therapy appears to be best.

This technique has the potential to reduce the cost of clinical trials by up to 50 percent and it also is more realistic because those patients on triptans are real patients in real settings, not artificial clinical trials. Plus, instead of having perhaps 1,000 triptan users in a clinical trial, we could effectively look at ten times that number. Further, this would facilitate enrollment in clinical trials by reducing the risk that participants would end up getting the placebo.

Use Statistical Significance More Wisely

To better assess new medicines and existing medicines that are being tested for new conditions, the FDA shouldn't arbitrarily reject clinical trials if statistical significance is not reached, saying that the trial "failed." Instead, the FDA, and the medical community at large, should present the unvarnished truth—the absolute results along with the statistical significance reached—and use a combination of the two to ascertain the merits of any drug or procedure.

A drug with a small clinical benefit might be worthless even if statistical significance is met. A drug with a large clinical benefit might still be worthwhile even if statistical significance isn't met, especially if the statistical significance target wasn't met because the clinical trial itself wasn't "powered" properly, as is commonly the case.

Consider this real example from a scientific paper looking at survival rates of patients with metastatic malignant melanoma. "Although the death probability of a patient with brain metastasis in the study was almost twice [that] of a patient with digestive metastasis, hazard ratio (HR) being of 1.98, the difference was not statistically significant ($p = 0.1333$)."[6] Translation: patients with brain metastases died at twice the rate of patients with digestive (gut) metastases. However, there was a 13.3 percent probability that this result was due to random chance.

When we read the quoted sentence above, if we think like a scientist, we might discount the result. After all, the results weren't statistically significant. If we think like a doctor, we'll pay attention because the death rate was twice as high and the result was highly likely a real result (86.7 percent probability). It didn't meet the 95 percent threshold, but it came close.

If you were a doctor treating patients with brain and digestive metastases, this finding would be important to you and your patients.

See Chapters 7, 8, and 12.

Offer Substantial Protection for New Uses of Off-Patent Drugs

Recall the drug that may never be: 30-milligram tablets of oral ketorolac. The FDA could encourage incremental innovation by offering market exclusivity for such drugs. If a drug developer could have, say, ten to twelve years of market exclusivity for robust oral ketorolac tablets, someone would likely step forward and develop such a drug. Instead, the FDA offers a measly five years of market exclusivity for new uses for existing drugs (so-called 505(b)(2) approvals). When most products take five to 12 years just to reach their peak earnings, and most of the marketing expenses are front-loaded, five years of protection is generally not enough time for a company to earn a return on its investment and, consequently, not enough to entice it to invest in such types of products.

If you want something from another party, make sure the other party will benefit.

With such a change to the rules, all the risk would be incurred by the drug company. If a new product were successful, both the company and the patients who ended up using it would benefit. Then, in a handful of years after the exclusivity expired, customers would be able to purchase competitors' versions of the new product at reduced prices. If, conversely, doctors and patients didn't prefer the new product, they would avoid it and the product would flop, sparing patients any exposure. If the product failed in the clinic, the only loser would be the pharma company. There are many possible winners but only one possible loser: the company doing the development.

Heads, we win; tails, we don't lose. It's as close as we (customers) can come to a sure thing.

Return the FDA to Considerations of Safety and Efficacy

Instead of the FDA rejecting drugs that it doesn't think are "better," or rejecting drugs for which the FDA doesn't think there's a "need," the FDA should return to its lawful requirement to approve *all* drugs that are deemed safe and efficacious, regardless of whether or not the FDA thinks that they are superior to existing drugs.

This has two substantial benefits. First, drug development companies would perceive a higher probability of approval if they produced "merely" safe and efficacious drugs, avoiding the risk of developing a drug that the FDA somehow didn't think was necessary. With less capriciousness comes more certainty and lower overall development costs. Second, customers of all types would benefit from the additional choices and the competition that would arise from more approved drugs, even if they were considered similar to existing drugs.

Not all patients respond to all drugs. In addition to their competitive benefit, so-called me-too drugs are important because they give doctors and patients other therapy choices.

With more similar drugs available, prices would be lower. Far lower. Saying that a product is a me-too admits that, at a minimum, the product's availability increases competition. That's good, not bad.

Competition works in the pharmaceutical industry. There's no question about it. Compare pharmaceutical markets that contain low-priced, competitive, me-too products—such as drugs for hypertension—to markets with one or two very expensive products—such as cancer drugs—and the benefits of competition become clear. There's an order of magnitude difference.

This solution would also prevent the problem seen with Versartis' growth hormone drug somavaratan (see Chapter 1). Recall that the FDA didn't see *a need*. The FDA had shifted from its role as an approver of drugs to a *chooser* of drugs.

All drugs that are safe and efficacious benefit the practice of medicine. No drug should be rejected because the FDA doesn't see a need (see Chapter 1).

Have Pharma Companies Provide "Bumper to Bumper" Warranties

If biopharma companies provided life and disability insurance along with their bottles of drugs, they would assume greater responsibility for any adverse events arising from their drugs, while the benefits from the successful use of the drugs would continue to accrue to the patients.

This idea could reduce or eliminate the need for the FDA to be a gatekeeper because the biopharma companies would incur most of the risk from questionable drugs. There are two ways to keep bad drugs off the market: First, have a government agency act as a gatekeeper. Second, push the risk of bad drugs back onto those organizations originating and promoting them. This proposal strengthens the second approach.

The feedback that biopharma companies currently get from the market, and the corresponding incentives, should be enough to ensure safe and efficacious drugs. However, if it isn't enough, some form of insurance could supplement those incentives.

Of course, biopharma companies would necessarily charge more for their products. To the customers, whose risk would be reduced, a drug with a warranty is worth more than a drug without a warranty. To the manufacturer, whose risk would be increased, a drug with a warranty is more expensive than a drug without a warranty. TANSTAAFL.[7]

Allow More Rx-to-OTC Switches

One proven way to get medications into the hands of patients quickly and cheaply is Rx-to-OTC (prescription to over-the-counter) switches. Prescription drugs require patients to first visit a doctor to get a prescription and then to visit a pharmacy to have that prescription filled by a trained pharmacist. Those difficult and expensive visits are eliminated with over-the-counter products because OTC drugs are available in a wide range of stores, from grocery stores to pharmacies, and are available without prescriptions. See Chapter 11 for more on this topic.

Let an Outside Group Invite Experts to Advisory Panels

The FDA has its finger on the scale when it comes to drug approvals because it picks the advisory committee members that sometimes provide advice about new drug reviews. An advisory committee is a group of ostensibly outside experts. But who determines who the experts are, who invites them to meetings, and who controls the meeting? The FDA, the ultimate insider, does. This is analogous to allowing a prosecutor to pack a jury with his family and friends. For more, please see Chapter 7.

The FDA has no particular built-in advantage in selecting panels of experts. Why not eliminate this potential source of bias and let an impartial, outside group take over that role? The FDA would request an advisory committee for a particular disease and the third party would select the group, provided that the experts were chosen based on clear criteria, such as their expertise in that specific disease. This would eliminate one possible source of bias in advisory committees.

Outsource the FDA's Functions

Safety

As economist Milton Friedman pointed out long ago, by outsourcing, a government can achieve a certain outcome without performing that activity directly. For instance, by hiring an outside company, a city government can collect trash at curbside each week without directly buying trucks and hiring and managing trash collectors. The FDA could do this with drug safety. The FDA could conceivably have a stable of perhaps a dozen safety-certifying organizations that would be bonded and thoroughly vetted by the FDA, with their licenses subject to discontinuation in the event of sloppy or dishonest work. Pharmaceutical companies would rely on these organizations to assess the safety of their medicines. The organizations would contract with the federal government for a negotiated amount per new drug review, an amount below current FDA review costs—the amount could potentially be very low or even zero. The organizations would then be free to charge pharmaceutical companies a fee for each drug review and, given competition, would compete on quality, service, and price. In this way, the government could save money, and drug safety evaluations could be performed more quickly and more efficiently.

These safety-certifying organizations would be responsible for the initial and all subsequent safety assessments of those medicines they took on. Depending on other rules, these organizations would be responsible for certifying that a medicine is "safe" before it is marketed, and then, once the new drug is on the market, they would monitor safety via multiple channels.

Efficacy

These same organizations, or different ones, could also assess new products for efficacy. There is no fundamental difference between outside organizations assessing new drugs for safety and for efficacy.

What are the advantages of this approach? Government functions can typically be handled more cheaply by an outsourced company. In addition, these companies would compete on price, quality, and service, allowing drug development to proceed more quickly and efficiently. It could be a win-win-win: helping taxpayers with lower taxes, drug companies with faster approvals, and both patients and drug companies by increasing the probability that newer, often better drugs would actually reach the market. The FDA could provide oversight.

As shown in Chapter 6, faster drug approvals could potentially provide a $45 to $90 billion per year benefit.

While many kinds of outside companies could perform this outsourced function, insurance companies, pharmacy benefit managers, hospitals, treatment guidelines organizations, and managed care organizations already create drug formularies and/or review scores of drugs in detail, making them likely candidates for this new role.

If necessary, for extra security, two outside companies would be required to review and approve each drug, both giving a thumbs up before efficacy is certified, thus greatly reducing the possibility of carelessness, bias, or bribery.

This approach would address another problem in the current environment: companies are often afraid of the FDA. Sometimes these companies kowtow to the agency's demands, lest they suffer retribution. This can't be the best approach because whenever one party has such power over another, the search for the truth is the first casualty.

Denationalize Drug Approvals

Government Agencies in This Country

If we can consider outsourcing drug evaluation functions to private companies and organizations, surely we can consider outsourcing these functions to other, competent U.S. government agencies.

In one interesting case, there was a bill being considered in November 2017 that would have allowed the Defense Department (DoD) to approve drugs and medical devices for the armed forces, resulting in a strange intergovernmental conflict. Why was this even an issue? According to the DoD spokesperson, Claude Chafin, "The FDA has denied freeze-dried plasma to troops in the field for 10 years."[8] The FDA's response to this claim? "FDA has been working closely with DoD to bring freeze-dried plasma to our troops and anticipates that these products will be fully approved for safe and effective use for our armed forces as early as 2018."[9] In effect, the DoD said that the FDA was too slow. The FDA asked for patience. Tell that to the soldiers in the field.

There's amusement mixed with frustration when observing such an internecine conflict, when one government bureaucracy is too slow to address the needs of another government bureaucracy.

Isn't it possible that a government agency with a budget of approximately $600 billion—100 times as large as the FDA's—and millions of employees would be able to assess the merits of freeze-dried plasma for those military personnel in harm's way? Remember, we can't use the argument that FDA protection is needed because a profit-seeking private company might try to dupe some uneducated and desperate patients. This is the DoD we're talking about. Whatever advantages one large government agency has, another larger one would, or at least could, conceivably have, too. There is no market failure here. This freeze-dried plasma will be used internally at the DoD; there will be no marketing, prescriptions, etc. Further, the DoD is *already* using freeze-dried plasma with elite troops and, therefore, probably knows far more about these blood products than the FDA knows. It shouldn't be much of a stretch to apply that experience more broadly and extend the availability of this life-saving product from elite troops to the military's ordinary troops.

Government Agencies in Other Countries

The issue of "drug lag" has been a topic of discussion in the drug development industry. Drug lag refers to the FDA approving drugs months or years after comparable regulatory bodies elsewhere have done so. Americans aren't fundamentally different from Canadians, Germans, Australians, the English, or the Japanese. Why should one group get new drugs years before the others? Why should residents in Bellingham, WA get access to new drugs potentially years after their neighbors across the border in Vancouver, BC?

Not long after the Vioxx fiasco that sullied the FDA's image, the FDA rejected Arcoxia (etoricoxib), a new COX-2 inhibitor from Merck. The FDA explained that it didn't see the need for another drug such as this. Robert Myer, director of the FDA's Office of Drug Evaluation II, told reporters that, "simply having another drug on the market wasn't sufficient reason to approve the product unless there was a unique role defined." Others didn't agree. Arcoxia had already been approved in 63 other countries, and one physician, James Fries, a Stanford University rheumatologist, said there was a "crying need" for more treatment options.[10]

Don't be misled into believing that Arcoxia, which had been tested in over 34,000 patients, was a dangerous drug. According to Merck, "there is more long-term safety data from controlled clinical trials, in terms of patient-years on treatment, for Arcoxia than for any other NSAID, including traditional NSAIDs and COX-2 selective inhibitors."[11] Do the English or Germans seem careless or inept? No? Those countries already allowed patients to use Arcoxia, as did 61 other countries in Asia, Latin America and Europe.

As of 2002, Casodex (bicalutamide), used to treat prostate cancer, had been approved in 40 countries, but not the U.S.[12] The FDA finally approved it in 2008. Did American men really need to wait those six years? By 2002, Risperdal Consta (risperidone), used to treat bipolar disorder and schizophrenia, had already been approved in 23 countries outside the U.S.[13] The FDA approved it in 2003.

This problem is symmetrical, and patients in other countries sometimes suffer from the tardiness of *their* government agencies. Pulmozyme (dornase alfa) for cystic fibrosis was approved in January 2001 in the United States and was marketed in about 70 countries throughout the world before it was finally approved in Japan in 2012.[14]

The issue of drug lag was more pronounced in the past, and there are indications that the FDA is now leading, rather than following, the pack. The FDA reported that "about two-thirds of the novel drugs approved in 2015 (29 of 45, 64%) were approved in the United States before receiving approval in any other country."[15] In more recent periods, the FDA has been arguably faster than the European Medicines Agency (EMA). "The FDA's median review time was 66 days shorter than the European Medicines Agency on 142 drugs approved by both agencies between 2011 and 2015, and 77 days shorter on all drugs approved by either agency over the same time period, according to an analysis published in *The New England Journal of Medicine*."[16]

With COVID-19 vaccines, the FDA was far ahead of the EMA. The FDA approved (with limited emergency use authorizations) the first two vaccines so fast that it startled industry veterans. If anything, the FDA showed what it could do if properly motivated. While we don't hope for another pandemic, we can hope for a motivated FDA.

Nevertheless, while drug lag is important, it is a relative measure and doesn't address the more important issue: does it really matter if the FDA is a bit slower or a bit faster than its compatriots, if, altogether, they are a bale of slow-moving turtles?

The issue of drug lag and slow drug approvals has even distressed some FDA insiders. Henry Miller, a former FDA employee, was criticized by others in the agency for approving genetically engineered human growth hormone products "too fast." They had wanted him to sit on the application until "enough" time had expired to avoid the impression that the application had been rushed. Miller studied the data, realized that these growth hormone products were safe and effective, and then approved them. Now, decades later, he has been proven right over and over again by the experiences of millions of children.

As discussed in Chapter 6, drug approval delays could reasonably be costing our society $45 to $90 billion per year. Consider the potential value gained if drug companies could shop around and find faster drug review agencies, even if those agencies charged additional fees of tens of millions of dollars. One can imagine a world, some years into the future, where drug review agencies charge steep fees—even $100 million might be reasonable—but review and approve drugs months or years faster than they do now. And drug safety and efficacy need not suffer at all, as all regulatory agencies could use the same efficacy and safety data.

U.S. government bureaucracies have no monopoly on merit. It is perfectly reasonable to consider outsourcing drug review functions to other, competent non-U.S. government agencies. This solution can be called *denationalized drug approvals*, as originally described by George Mason University economist Daniel Klein.

Denationalization would continue the tradition that drugs be proven safe and effective by a government agency, but it would end the FDA's monopoly on being that agency. This would open up drug approvals to a dozen or so respected government regulatory bodies around the world, such as the European Medicines Agency, Health Canada, Swissmedic in Switzerland, the Therapeutic Goods Administration in Australia, the

Pharmaceuticals and Medical Devices Agency in Japan, the Medicines & Healthcare products Regulatory Agency in the U.K., and the China Food and Drug Administration. When appropriate, the list could include other American agencies, such as the DoD. Even if one could argue that government agencies should prohibit access to drugs not yet proven to be safe and effective, there's no reason to think that the FDA is the best or most efficient government agency to handle that responsibility. Daniel Klein writes: "Under the proposal, the FDA would have to *compete in giving permission*." [17] [italics in original] Generally, when there's competition among providers, the customers of those providers—here, drug companies and patients alike—benefit.

To make this scheme work, we could either supplant the FDA's authority as the sole determiner of which drugs and medical devices can be marketed in the U.S., and/or we could require the FDA to approve any drug that has already been approved by one of its counterparts in developed countries.[18] Consider the Indian government, which, in 2019, started automatically approving new drugs that had been approved for use in the European Union, United Kingdom, Australia, Japan, and United States, provided that the clinical trials included some Indian patients.[19] With denationalized drug approval, safety and efficacy would still be paramount, of course, but regulatory agencies would compete on cost, efficiency, and reasonableness.

Delink Gatekeeping, Information, and Process

Newspapers reported in 1908 that, "In Kingston, New York, a mixup between automobile oil and maple syrup, both in identical containers, led to the destruction of several motorcar engines."[20] The destruction of motorcar engines?! We are left to wonder about the consumers who poured motor oil on their pancakes!

The very serious issue of counterfeit drugs can be disconcerting: "Rick Roberts, a San Francisco college professor with AIDS, felt an odd stinging sensation when he injected Serostim by Serono SA, an antiwasting drug he got at a pharmacy in December, 2000. Then he noticed other anomalies with the packaging, such as a rubber stopper in a vial normally sealed with plastic. 'I was very afraid,' says Mr. Roberts, who confirmed his batch of medicine was fake when he checked Serono's Web site."[21] The FDA's role in ensuring proper labeling and preventing counterfeit drugs is a foundational and widely accepted function of drug regulation.

The FDA is currently an information agency, a quality assurer, a penalizer, and a gatekeeper. It could cease being the latter and focus on the former three roles.

Even without being a gatekeeper, proffering marketing authorizations, the FDA could still provide useful facts on safety, efficacy, tolerability, dosing, and appropriate patient segments, and ensure that products are unadulterated and not mislabeled.

With this solution, the FDA could analyze and compile the data, provide recommendations and stern warnings, and then get out of the way. The Food and Drug Administration makes a better window than a wall.

Set up a Tiered System to Allow Earlier Access to Some Drugs

Right to Try legislation was one way to get drugs to patients who were desperate and very likely to die anyway. Another, more graduated, and thorough solution would be to segregate patients into four categories: in immediate danger of dying (e.g., with advanced cancer); living with a serious medical condition (e.g., with epilepsy); generally healthy but in clear need of some medical care (e.g., with hypertension requiring treatment); and healthy. The level of proof and the tradeoff between safety and efficacy would differ among the medicines available to each group to better match the risk tolerance of the patients in each.

Those who are dying would get access to any drug that has passed basic Phase 1 safety testing. Those with a serious medical condition would have access to all drugs that have passed Phase 2 clinical testing. Those who are generally healthy but in clear need of some medical care would have access to drugs approved through the current FDA approach (Phases 1 through 3). The last group, healthy patients, such as healthy children getting vaccines, might have access to drugs only after those drugs have passed even more rigorous safety testing than is typically conducted today, such as after Phase 4, post-marketing studies.

With this solution, we more appropriately match the level of risk and reward for each segment of patients.

Consider amyotrophic lateral sclerosis, also known as Lou Gehrig's disease. In September 2020, Amylyx Pharmaceuticals published a paper describing the benefits that some patients received in a clinical trial of its experimental drug to treat ALS. This promising news was welcomed by the ALS community. "Anything that can slow down the rate of decline in a disease that has no cure—or no treatment to reverse symptoms—is good," said Jinsy Andrews, who treats ALS patients and directs clinical trials at Columbia University Irving Medical Center.[22]

Given current FDA approaches, another large clinical trial would need to be run before the FDA would allow widespread availability of the new medicine. Yet given the life expectancy of ALS patients of just two to five years, *many current ALS patients would have progressed and died before that second trial could be run*. With the solution outlined here, today's ALS patients would receive access to the Amylyx treatment. While this would make it harder to run a placebo-controlled trial—who would want to risk participating in the trial and getting the placebo?—it would give patients the hope of living longer than just a few years. ALS is already a death sentence; the FDA shouldn't concur.

Allow People to Opt Out

It's simple: for a variety of reasons, some Americans don't want to be controlled by the FDA. In the interest of liberty and Pareto improvements —some patients would be better off and no patients would be worse off— we could set up a process to allow those people to opt out.

Allowing people who want to be free of the FDA's restrictions and its infringements on their liberty would be a Pareto improvement for society. See Chapter 9.

Those who did opt out would be free to use any drug that a willing manufacturer offered for sale. Those who didn't opt out would see no change to their situation.

While intellectually appealing, this solution might not have much of an effect unless wide swaths of the population opted out. Why? Any bad experiences that these patients might encounter on unapproved drugs could hinder the chances of those drugs ever being approved by the FDA. The opted-out population would need to be substantial enough to give biopharma companies lucrative markets even ignoring the non-opted-out, FDA-controlled population.

Allow Patients to Take Unapproved Drugs as Long as They are Clearly Labeled

With this proposed solution, companies that desired to sell drugs without FDA approval could do so if the label said clearly, in big letters, "This drug has NOT been approved by the FDA." Pharmacists could help emphasize and disseminate that cautionary message. While this reform may sound radical, some patients would be better off and no patients would be worse off, based on their assessment of their own situation. (See Chapter 9 for more.)

Some patients would continue to insist on taking only FDA-approved drugs—the situation we all face today—while other patients would be willing to trust other sources of information.

Where could people get information about new drugs, if not from the FDA? There is a plethora of information organizations: U.S. Pharmacopeia (now called USP); *U.C. Berkeley Wellness Letter*; *Consumer Reports*; *Drug Facts & Comparisons*; health maintenance organizations; hospitals; health insurers; medical journals; the multitude of guideline-setting bodies (e.g., American Academy of Pediatrics, American Thoracic Society, National Comprehensive Cancer Network, National Kidney Foundation, and American Heart Association); the Agency for Healthcare Research and Quality; medical journals; the news media; and individual physicians.

It's not outrageous to take drugs that aren't FDA-approved.

While it may initially strike us that only daredevils and fools would take drugs without FDA certifications, if we consider the prevalence of off-label uses and uses of non-approved drugs, such as aspirin until 1980 (when it was approved for some limited uses), there is reason to think a large majority of the population would behave that way.

In April 2021, I received an injection of the Pfizer-BioNTech COVID-19 vaccine. On the fact sheet I was given, I was informed that this product was "an unapproved vaccine that may prevent COVID-19. There is no FDA-approved vaccine to prevent COVID-19." Not only was I thrilled to receive this vaccine, so were the dozen other people in line with me. And it wasn't just us. Approximately 100 million other Americans had already received one of the COVID-19 vaccines and more were joining them daily. In all likelihood, more than half of adult Americans will soon willingly take an unapproved drug and the FDA is collaborating with this transgression of its normal decrees.

We are already comfortable with consuming unapproved drugs, and have been for a century, so why not extend it to its logical conclusion?

Make the FDA a Safety Agency; Markets Can Determine Efficacy

With this solution, the FDA could still analyze and make assessments about safety and efficacy, but the efficacy recommendations would be informational and not prohibitive. Once the FDA determined that a drug had been adequately tested for safety and had passed those tests, it would be available to physicians and patients.

The biggest holdup in getting drugs to market is not how long it takes to show that they're safe but, rather, the time and expense to show, to the FDA's satisfaction, that they are efficacious for particular uses.[23] Approximately 35 percent of drug development costs are for safety testing, while 65 percent are for efficacy testing.[24]

By reverting to pre-1962 law and ending the FDA's power to require efficacy for particular uses, or "indications," as much as a decade and hundreds of millions of dollars could be trimmed from the time and expense required to bring each new drug to patients.

With this approach, biopharmaceutical companies, scientists, hospitals, doctors, universities, insurance companies, managed care companies, health newsletters, peer-reviewed medical journals, guideline-setting bodies, and patients, working individually and together, would establish efficacy, or the lack thereof. Could there be ineffective drugs? Sure. But as doctors and patients learn, such drugs would tend to disappear over time. Recall Peltzman's finding: "The penalties imposed by the marketplace on sellers of ineffective drugs before 1962 seem to have been sufficient to have left little room for improvement by a regulatory agency."[25]

This makes sense. In reality, patients participate every day in a similar process of drug testing, regardless of an FDA certification of efficacy, making FDA certification neither necessary nor sufficient. In practice, an FDA certification of efficacy is just a starting point; doctors and patients regularly evaluate drugs for efficacy.

We've already discussed how patients on Vasotec are titrated (see Chapter 8). Consider these other examples.

About 70 percent of migraine suffers benefit from treatment with a drug from the triptan class.[26] Even when the FDA finally approves a drug, such as a new triptan, as "safe and efficacious," doctors must still evaluate the drug to find out how efficacious it is for each particular patient. Migraine sufferers discover whether a triptan works for them through old-fashioned trial and error. This process of trial and error can take a long time, and for some patients suffering from, say, depression, the process of finding the right drug can take years.[27]

One patient on Lynparza (olaparib), Seana Roubinek, was taking it to help with her ovarian cancer. Unfortunately, the drug caused a steep drop in her red blood cells. Luckily, her physicians dealt with the problem by simply cutting her dose in half.[28] As much as it would like to, the FDA can't tell Roubinek beforehand whether Lynparza will work for her. The FDA can't tell her, ahead of time, which dose will be best for her. These facts are determined the old-fashioned way, the way that doctors and their patients have always done, with trial and error.

This raises a question: If patients and their doctors will engage in personal experimentation even if the FDA proclaims a drug efficacious, why not simplify and speed up the process by allowing patients access to new, potentially efficacious drugs sooner, so that they can get busy with the trial and error process?

With this policy change, drug approvals would be faster and cheaper because drug companies wouldn't need to convince the FDA about efficacy. More drugs would be on the market because of cheaper and faster drug approvals. This would lead to more physician and patient choices and more competition, which is the only thing that consistently holds down drugs prices.

The FDA successfully used this approach from 1938 through 1961. There's no reason it can't again.

Run a Trial to Test the FDA

As mentioned in Chapter 9, Congress could test the FDA for safety and efficacy. We could split the country by some manner and run an experiment. The best approach might be to assign one third of Americans to each of the following groups: no FDA prohibitions; FDA prohibition for drugs that haven't yet proven safety; and FDA prohibition for drugs that haven't yet proven safety and efficacy. We could use the last two digits of Social Security numbers, with numbers 00-32 in the first group, 33-65 in the second, and 66-99 in the third. That way people could move without ruining the trial, and all the confounding factors, such as regional variations in genetics, affluence, medical care, diet, smoking, and lifestyle attributes, would be minimized. Children would fall into their mother's category until they reached age 18.

Let's call them groups 1, 2 and 3. In group 1, one third of all Americans would be under the regulations of the current FDA (i.e., post-1962 rules); in group 2, one third would have access to new drugs sooner (i.e., 1938-1961 rules); and in group 3, one third would face a relatively free market with none of the FDA's prohibitions (i.e., pre-1938 rules). We could then check back in 20 or 30 years and see which group did best by any number of economic and medical metrics. Twenty or 30 years would be required to give biopharma companies time to develop drugs for the three groups—currently infeasible drugs might become feasible—and to get a good reading on the health outcomes of the groups.

With these data, we could assess the FDA's cost per additional quality-adjusted life year.

Assume, for the sake of discussion, that people in group 1—those subjected to FDA prohibitions—enjoyed, on average, two extra quality-adjusted life years. Assume, further, that the per-capita lifetime cost of the FDA were $20,000. Then, each person in group 1 would face a cost for a quality-adjusted life year of $10,000, which is a great bargain. (Would you choose to live one more healthy year for a cost of $10,000? I would!) With these results, economists could make a strong case for FDA regulation. However, the numbers could instead go against the FDA if the cost per quality-adjusted life year were, say, $1 million—a value far greater than what is generally accepted as "efficient"—or if the quality-adjusted life years were *negative*. If the quality-adjusted life years were negative, we would conclude that the FDA was costly and didn't help. While a bitter pill to swallow for the FDA and its advocates, such an outcome would make for (relatively) easy policy decisions, as there's no point in paying for something that's detrimental.

It would be like finding that the sunscreen you lather on your kids *causes* skin cancer. There's a simple solution: stop using it.

Abolish the FDA

What if we took the straightforward path and simply abolished the FDA? We have reason to think that the FDA has reduced the life expectancy of Americans by a whole decade.

With this solution, the U.S. government would completely abolish the FDA and let markets assess labeling, safety, and efficacy. Scare tactics about more thalidomide babies aside, pharmaceutical customers would not be left high and dry.

The FDA is designed to address the fear that biopharma companies will unleash unsafe or useless drugs on vulnerable Americans. And yet drug companies are more subordinate and compliant than the FDA, as well as more vulnerable to social pressure and media criticisms. Think of drug companies not as unstoppable forces but, rather, as organizations that have posted billion-dollar escrow accounts—their stock market capitalizations—with instructions to financial institutions: "If we do anything wrong, please disperse some proportion of this money to the victims."

The bigger the company, the deeper the pockets and the less we have to fear.

The intention in creating the FDA was admirable: drugs should be proven safe and efficacious. But note what changes when we switch from a free market, where the consumer is king, to a regulated market, where the FDA is king. Costs increase, and product development timelines increase. That much is clear. Drug prices also increase because of the increased cost, risk, and time for development, combined with reduced competition. But the real change is even more subtle than that: drug companies will work on only the limited set of drugs and for the patient cohorts for whom they can *prove* efficacy to a skeptical government agency.

Let's use treatment of Duchenne muscular dystrophy as an example. If the only straightforward way to *prove* that a medicine is successfully treating DMD is through a six-minute walk test (a measurement of how far patients can walk in six minutes), then patients who can't walk for any reason—perhaps their disease is so advanced that they are confined to a wheelchair—are purposely excluded. They will be excluded from the clinical trials and from the drug's label. Without being listed on the label, all usage in boys confined to wheelchairs will be considered "off-label" and, hence, typically not covered by insurance companies.

And yet a new drug could potentially help both ambulatory and wheelchair-bound patients. In a free market, both the walking and wheelchair-bound might get new DMD drugs. With the FDA around, only the currently walking patients will get the new drug.

Even more subtle: with the FDA in place, we cease to be the ultimate customer; instead, that customer is Congress. The FDA doesn't really care whether you're happy as long as Congress is happy. You and I have lost control over our health care.

> *If members of our society were empowered to make their own decisions about the entire range of products for which the FDA has responsibility, however, then the whole rationale for the agency would cease to exist.*
> **David Kessler**, FDA Commissioner, 1992 [29]

He has a good point. Let's take back our power. Let the agency cease to exist.

Wrap-up

This chapter presents a number of possible solutions to the problems outlined in this book. These solutions are intended to foster useful discussion, and astute readers will note that some of the possible solutions overlap or contradict other solutions. Regardless, the alternatives presented here should receive attention, scrutiny, and consideration, not because they are buttoned up and ready to be implemented, but because the topic of drug regulation is so important to so many people, and our current system is crying out for improvement.

---

[1] "The provisions of 505(b)(2) were created, in part, to help avoid unnecessary duplication of studies already performed on a previously approved ('reference' or 'listed') drug; the section gives the FDA express permission to rely on data not developed by the NDA applicant." Camargo Pharmaceutical Services, https://camargopharma.com/what-is-505b2/

[2] Henry I. Miller, "Why It Takes a Village (To Afford a Prescription)," *TCS Daily*, 4 December 2007.

[3] Laura Mirviss, "HMS Professor Simon Resigns," *The Harvard Crimson*, 13 March 2009, http://www.thecrimson.com/article/2009/3/13/hms-professor-simon-resigns-a-harvard/

---

[4] See work by Russ Altman, a Stanford professor of bioengineering, genetics, and medicine.

[5] Andrew von Eschenbach, *The Wall Street Journal*, 14 February 2012.

[6] Sandru A, Voinea S, Panaitescu E, Blidaru A. "Survival rates of patients with metastatic malignant melanoma." *J Med Life*. 2014;7(4):572-576.

[7] TANSTAAFL: there ain't no such thing as a free lunch.

[8] Dan Diamond, "Lawmakers defend 'unprecedented' Pentagon health panel, which could undermine FDA," *Politico*, 6 November 2017.

[9] Dan Diamond, "Lawmakers defend 'unprecedented' Pentagon health panel, which could undermine FDA," *Politico*, 6 November 2017.

[10] Andrew Bridges, "FDA Panel Frowns on Vioxx Successor," Associated Press, 12 April 2007.

[11] "Press Release: Merck Receives Non Approvable Letter from FDA for Arcoxia," *FierceBiotech*, 27 April 2007.

[12] Otesa Middletown, "FDA Panel Rejects Appeal For Prostate-Cancer Drug," *The Wall Street Journal*, 18 December 2002.

[13] Alkermes press release, 29 April 2003.

[14] Chugai Pharmaceutical press release (translated), 7 June 2012.

[15] From FDA website: "Comparing approval to other countries offers another measure of approval efficiency. Although regulatory processes differ widely between FDA and those of regulatory agencies in other countries, about two-thirds of the novel drugs approved in 2015 (29 of 45, 64%) were approved in the United States before receiving approval in any other country."

[16] "FDA beats EMA on drug application turnaround," *BIO SmartBrief*, 7 April 2017.

[17] See Daniel B. Klein, "Drug-Approval Denationalization," *Library of Economics and Liberty*, April 6, 2009.

[18] See Daniel B. Klein, "Drug-Approval Denationalization," *Library of Economics and Liberty*, April 6, 2009.

[19] Gayathri Vaidyanathan, "India's clinical-trial rules to speed up drug approvals," *Nature*, 3 April 2019.

---

20 Brad Prowse, "100 years ago from the files of The Union," *The Union*, 20 November 2009.

21 "Fakes in the Medicine Chest,' *The Wall Street Journal*, 22-Sep-03, pg B1.

22 Jonathan D. Rockoff, "Study Shows Progress in Treating ALS," *The Wall Street Journal*, 6-Sep-20.

23 David R. Henderson and Charles L. Hooper, "Markets Can Determine Drug Efficacy," *Forbes*, July 8, 2009. At: http://www.forbes.com/2009/07/08/waxman-fda-bill-efficacy-opinions-contributors-biologic-drugs.html

24 Joseph A. DiMasi, Henry G. Grabowski, and Ronald W. Hansen, " The price of innovation: new estimates of drug development costs," *Journal of Health Economics*, Journal of Health Economics 22 (2003) 151–185, Table 5.

25 Sam Peltzman, *Regulation of Pharmaceutical Innovation*, University of Chicago, 1974.

26 "Heading off Headaches," University of California, Berkeley, *Wellness Letter*, vol 33, issue 2, Fall 2016

27 "To Dose or Not to Dose?" Breakthroughs, Briefly, *Stanford* alumni magazine, January/February 2017.

28 Joseph Walker, New Drugs for Ovarian Cancer Patients," *The Wall Street Journal*, 5 September 2016.

29 "David Kessler's Legacy at the FDA," Robert Goldberg, *Quick Study*, Institute for Policy Innovation, 1997.

Chapter 15: Conclusion

Twisted Mysteries

Have you ever read a mystery novel in which your top suspect was ultimately proven innocent while the real crook seemed above suspicion? Undoubtedly you have. That's the modus operandi of some mystery writers. These authors encourage us to pay close attention to subtle clues and regularly employ plot twists to keep us on our toes.

We can find the same relationship in history books, with no creative writing necessary.

People in medieval Europe perceived cats as evil, actively killed them, and even passed laws against keeping them as pets. Despite these beliefs, some people kept their cats and, lo and behold, were less susceptible to the black plague pandemic that swept through Europe. Then came the

forehead-slapping moment. Doh! It was the *rats* that were the problem, not the *cats*! The cats were the solution. Felines were keeping the rodent population in check and limiting the risk of the plague, which relied on the bacteria residing in the fleas that the rats carried. The cat-rat-flea-bacteria-plague insight came too late for many unfortunate feline and human victims.

Thankfully, the plague is no longer a threat, and we can legally keep cats as companions.

Of course, there are still threats to our health. The interplay between the characters involved today may be no more obvious to us than the cat-rat-flea-bacteria-plague connection was to medieval Europeans, but the risk is just as real. A current storyline suggests that pharmaceutical companies can harm our health directly and indirectly, and that unless the federal government dons the role of savior, we are at mortal risk. But is that the complete story?

Just as in Sir Arthur Conan Doyle and Dame Agatha Christie's entertaining stories, people are dying, and we need to stay alert for subtle clues and plot twists.

Argument for the FDA

Recall the official storyline. Pundits say that we need the FDA to, effectively, "keep the bar high" and "keep out the riffraff." Here are three such arguments:

> *It [the FDA] forces companies to innovate, to come up with things that are worthy of close scrutiny, and it simultaneously discourages shortcuts and sloppiness. The worry is that if someone tries to do the world a favor by getting the big ol' slow FDA out of the way, that the result will not be a flood of grateful innovation, but rather a flood of lower-quality drug submissions.*[1]
>
> In the Pipeline blogger and pharma chemist **Derek Lowe**

The FDA's standards actually promote innovation because patients don't want just any old drug - they want drugs that work.[2]
Aaron Kesselheim, Harvard Medical School

Our patients deserve the same quality therapies as everyone else, and to weaken the standards will only threaten our population with unsafe, ineffective therapies.[3]
National Organization for Rare Disorders

The view many proponents of the FDA hold is that there are effectively three bins—good drugs, dangerous drugs, and ineffective drugs—and the FDA is well suited to sorting new drugs into those three bins. By doing this job, the FDA enforces scientific rigor and keeps us safe and healthy.

As we've explored in this book, the FDA ostensibly protects us from unsafe and ineffective medicines. This is how proponents might see the situation:

Table 1: Effect of FDA

No. of Drugs Available	Without FDA	With FDA
Good Drugs	100	100
Dangerous Drugs	50	0
Ineffective Drugs	70	0

The FDA improves the situation

From this simplistic point of view, the FDA's only effect is on bad drugs, as it thwarts dangerous and ineffective drugs while still allowing good drugs to pass through its filters.

Argument Against the FDA

Scientists haven't figured out every nuance of the world—far from it. The large gaps in our knowledge are rather surprising. The things that scientists don't understand range from small items, like what triggers our bodies to demand a breath of fresh air, to big ones, like the mysterious dark matter and dark energy that surround us and constitute 95.5 percent of the universe. Even though we spend a third of our lives asleep, scientists understanding of sleep is spotty.

> *Despite decades of research, scientists don't understand exactly why we sleep and how it benefits us.*[4]
> ***Berkeley Wellness Letter***

Sleep is a mystery. Dark matter is a mystery. You are a mystery. The chemical compounds we call drugs are a mystery. Genetics are a mystery. Diseases are a mystery. Growing old is a mystery. Your microbiome is a mystery. The interactions of you, your genetics, diseases, growing old, your microbiome, your environment, and drugs are a mystery squared.

The challenge that the FDA faces isn't to say that Drug A is dangerous, Drug B is safe but useless, and that Drug C is safe and effective. Rather, the FDA, to be accurate and to help improve the health of Americans, needs to say that 50 mg is the safe and effective dose for Person A; 10 mg is the safe and effective dose for Person B; no dose, no matter how high, will be effective for Person C; and no dose, no matter how high or low, will be both safe and effective for Person D.

Even that's too simplistic. For effective treatment, we need to know that Person A should be on a low dose of Drug X, Person B should be on a high dose of Drug Y, Person C should be on a combination of Drug Y and Drug Z, and Person D should receive no therapy other than diet and exercise.

The FDA will never get to this point with its current approach. The FDA's job, as currently framed, is impossible.

The medical profession does eventually reach a rough approximation of the desired solution, via fits and starts, because it employs the micromedical view (see Chapter 12). There are many possible approaches and technologies to assist the medical profession in its pursuit of optimal treatment, but the FDA's simplistic approach isn't one of them.

We observed above how the pro-FDA person might view the situation. Let's supplement that view.

Unsafe and Ineffective Drugs

FDA proponents would probably name Elixir Sulfanilamide, with its deadly diethylene glycol base, as one of the unsafe drugs that the FDA could protect us from. However, that drug was a mistake and was withdrawn from the market as quickly as it appeared. It lived for only a moment. It doesn't belong in the "Without FDA" column unless Table 1 was constructed at precisely the moment when the ephemeral Elixir Sulfanilamide materialized. Realistically, it can't be counted in either the "Without FDA" or the "With FDA" column; one system *actually* rejected it and the other almost certainly *would* have. We should not be overly worried about such rare occurrences.

Another "unsafe drug" in Table 1 is thalidomide. But thalidomide is available today and is helping my friend. If it can be counted in the "Without FDA" column, it must also be counted in the "With FDA" column. Realistically, thalidomide shouldn't be considered an unsafe drug once people learned how to properly use it. As we now know, thalidomide is harmful to fetuses but helpful to adults with multiple myeloma.

Look at the zeros in the "With FDA" column in Table 1. As explained in Chapters 2 and 3, there are, today, many drugs of questionable efficacy and safety. Overall, we have little reason to believe that the FDA has been successful at keeping harmful drugs off the market. If we give the FDA some credit, however, the table might properly look like Table 2. Notice the slight differences between the two columns.

Table 2: Effect of FDA

No. of Drugs Available	Without FDA	With FDA
Good Drugs	100	100
Dangerous Drugs	50	47
Ineffective Drugs	70	66

The FDA helps a little

However, we do have strong evidence that the FDA has reduced, as if by an arbitrary quota, the *total* number of new drugs available. Sam Peltzman found that the number of new drugs fell by 61 percent. Even the FDA acknowledged that the number of important new drugs declined after it was given greater powers. The table might actually look like Table 3.

Table 3: Effect of FDA

No. of Drugs Available	Without FDA	With FDA
Good Drugs	100	50
Dangerous Drugs	50	24
Ineffective Drugs	70	33

The FDA generally makes things worse

Given Table 3, most people would tend to choose the "Without FDA" column, especially once they factor in years-long delays, higher drug prices, and a laundry list of other problems caused by the FDA, not the least of which is ten lost years of life expectancy. The "With FDA" column has roughly the same percentage of dangerous and ineffective drugs as the "Without FDA" column, however there are fewer drugs available. That's not what Congress had in mind when it gave the FDA truckloads of money and power.

The forehead-slapping moment here is that market-regulated pharmaceutical companies—the characters we were suspecting all along—are part of the solution. The federal government—the FDA—has its fingers in all things drug-related and is part of the problem. The FDA is largely mucking things up. Ah! We weren't expecting that conclusion because we weren't paying close enough attention to the clues.

Concluding Remarks

If the pro-FDA narrative were true, then FDA-approved drugs should be universally safe. They're not. FDA-approved drugs should be universally effective. They're not. If the FDA is such an expert, it should be able to tell patients which drugs will give them adverse effects. It can't. The FDA should be able to warn patients to avoid drugs that will be ineffective for them. It can't. The FDA should be able to tell a particular patient that a particular drug will work well. It can't.

The FDA boldly states that the medicines it approves are effective at treating diseases. And yet, many times, only a small minority of patients benefit. This means that the FDA cannot tell you, in advance, whether *you* will benefit from any given drug and what *your* response will be. The only way for you to determine if a particular drug will work for you is to try it yourself and, if it doesn't work, try another one. This has always been the approach, independent of the FDA's powers. Doctors and patients needed to use a trial and error approach before the FDA and they still use the same approach today.

Even the categorization of safe and effective is problematic. We've seen that there aren't safe drugs and unsafe drugs: even the safest food or drug can cause harm in the right circumstances, just as the most dangerous substance can be a lifesaver if used properly. The dose truly makes the poison.

Is water safe? Drink two gallons of it and you might die from hyponatremia, as did Jennifer Strange. Conversely, reduce your dose of water enough and you'll die from dehydration. The safest thing we know can be unsafe.

The approach that the FDA requires for testing new drugs in animals has some value, but it is also inhumane and logically flawed. The observed safety of drugs in laboratory animals is poorly correlated with safety in humans, and common foods and drugs that are consumed daily by people are hazardous to animals, while the opposite is also true. Worse, there are drugs that are effective at *killing* certain animals that still offer therapeutic value to humans. If we can't comfortably reject drugs that, in the extreme, directly *kill* laboratory animals, how can any drug that has a poor safety signal in animals be rejected for human consumption?

If that's not damning enough, there are drugs that are productively and widely used every day around the world that were originally designed as, or at least moonlight as, *people-killers*. If drugs that were designed to cause a fatal response in humans can still find a use in the medicine cabinets of medical professionals, why should the FDA ever reject any drug that merely has a poor safety profile?

The most unsafe thing we know can be used safely. The most toxic substance known to mankind has been certified as safe and efficacious by the FDA, meaning that to be considered unsafe, any new drug must be, at a minimum, *even more toxic*. That's not likely.

Struggling to keep some composure while doing an impossible job, the FDA has placed undue burdens on pharmaceutical companies, resulting in increased costs for drug development, a reduction in the number of new drugs approved, and our inability to access some good medicines. If any of

these missing drugs would have saved lives—which is a certainty—then the FDA's actions have killed Americans.

The FDA a silent killer. Silent, like the seemingly innocent character in a mystery novel who is surreptitiously perpetrating brutal murders. When we find out in the final chapter who the real villain is, we are as shocked as when we learn how the FDA, our supposed savior, has hurt us all.

Pundits talk about evidence-based medicine when it applies to the utility of individual drugs, and some are incredulous and critical when biopharma companies launch new drugs without adequate evidence of benefit. But evidence-based medicine can have wider implications and can apply to the FDA itself, as well as to the entire system of drug regulation. It's about time.

Shark Attack Fallacy

The FDA has never been subjected to the testing that it daily requires of drug companies. But it should be. If one individual drug should face scrutiny to prevent harm, the whole drug approval process should face scrutiny orders of magnitude greater; so many lives are at stake. If the

FDA were tested scientifically, it likely would fail spectacularly. Where is the evidence that the FDA actually helps? It exists in our imaginations.

The FDA and its proponents make assertions that unregulated drug companies will take advantage of people when, in the words of former FDA Commissioner David Kessler, "they are most vulnerable to manufacturers' assertions: when they are desperately ill, when they are hoping against hope for a cure, or when they are seeking to enhance their physical appearance." This is a hypothesis and hypotheses are amenable to testing. We can all understand that sometimes, some people might be taken advantage of by some companies. But where is the empirical evidence of the nature and extent of the abuses? Are one percent of people mildly harmed one percent of the time? Or is it 80 percent of people harmed significantly 80 percent of the time?

The FDA and its proponents are playing to our fears. You've probably been warned that if you swim in the ocean, "you could be killed by a shark!" This statement loses its power when the evidence is consulted: there were two deaths from unprovoked shark attacks in the whole world in 2019.[5] In the pharmaceutical industry, the cry is "without the FDA, we would have more thalidomide babies!" For every "you could be killed by a shark" or "we would have more thalidomide babies" statement that plays to our fears, we should ask to see the data.

Policy should be based on actual risks, not hypotheticals and rare cases.

The risk we incur from drugs is highly dependent on our situations and preferences. The FDA can't recommend a particular drug for you because it doesn't know the particulars of your situation—it doesn't know your preferences and what tradeoffs you are willing to make, and, even after you try a drug, the critical information about whether it worked and whether it caused you any harm rarely makes it back to the FDA. The FDA is flying blind because it lacks some of the most essential information. When the FDA rejects or approves a drug, it is guessing at key patient attributes. If the FDA guessed at the clinical attributes of a drug, there would be universal outrage. But the FDA regularly guesses at data that are just as fundamental.

How can a federal government agency hope to tell us what drugs are good and bad? People aren't fungible. We are complicated, unique individuals. Our physiologies, genetics, diets, habits, and pretty much everything else about us are unique. That is why one person chooses to live in the heart of Boston while another prefers the woods of Maine.

A patient makes a choice between therapies (with the help of her agent, the doctor) based on many variables: efficacy, tolerability, side effects, riskiness, monetary cost, non-monetary cost, and speed of action. These drug costs and benefits must be judged within the context of many personal values and tradeoffs: the fear of death, the fear of surgery, the fear of hospitals, the fear of needles, potential pain, and the individual's health profile, financial status, value of time, value of health, courage, optimism, and risk tolerance. Further, people make decisions based on thresholds. Will a new therapy allow me to drive to work? Will a therapy allow me to wear summer clothes without fear of unsightly skin? Will a therapy allow me to live long enough to see my granddaughter's wedding? For the FDA to decide what compounds pass this complex tradeoff is preposterous, given that the FDA can never frame the problem from the individual patient's perspective. Just as with the choice between living amid the hustle and bustle of Boston or in the solitude of a Maine forest, one individual's best alternative could be another's worst.

If, instead of medical therapies, this federal government agency were telling us what kind of shoes to buy or where to go on vacation, we would consider it laughable. It doesn't matter how many Ph.D.'s and M.D.'s walk the halls at the FDA. Centralized bureaucrats cannot make the proper decisions for us because they lack the requisite information and incentives. We *should* laugh at the concept of the FDA.

Problem Misdiagnosed

We've been lied to and otherwise misled. People in positions of power sold us a "solution" after they, themselves, misdiagnosed the problem. And these people didn't recognize that their so-called solution was actually something else: a hypothesis. Their hypothesis was that their shiny new agency would fix the problem that they had misdiagnosed in the first place. Then, they effectively skipped town, never checking to find out whether their solution had actually worked.

The hucksters who pushed this approach worked in the Capitol Building. Their solution consisted of heavy-handed, centralized, government regulation. It's time to pull back the curtain and expose the machinery of such regulation, which is nothing more than drug regulation theater—all show and little go. As in any mystery novel, the ending might shock us, but if we reread the story, we'll see that the evidence was there all along.

It isn't a matter of the FDA not doing its job. The problem is that the FDA's approach is simply unworkable. The FDA's approach is the wrong tool for the job and using the wrong tool is a way to make things worse.

Thirteen Concepts

The following thirteen concepts, first discussed in the Introduction, explain why the FDA will never be able to deliver on its promises:

One: substances themselves aren't dangerous or safe. The safety of a substance depends on the situation and the exposure of the individual.

Two: efficacy can't be determined without decentralized trial and error by doctors and patients. The FDA's assessments of efficacy are duplicative.

Three: drugs work for some but not others. The FDA often can't tell which patients will benefit.

Four: animal studies and human clinical trials often can't tell us which drugs work and which don't. When they do give a clear answer, that answer is often wrong.

Five: with the FDA's rules, new drugs are presumed guilty until proven innocent. The FDA reduces our therapeutic choices by making it difficult for companies to develop new medicines.

Six: pharmaceuticals are more beneficial than they are detrimental; they should be presumed innocent until proven guilty.

Seven: the FDA slows new drug development and availability.

Eight: the FDA doesn't bring any unique skills to the table. There are other organizations that can and do evaluate drugs.

Nine: doctors and researchers, when given the freedom to do so, find the best uses for each new drug, accentuating the positive aspects and reducing the negative.

Ten: both you and your doctors seek drugs that work and have manageable side effects and reject drugs that don't work or have bad side effects.

Eleven: you are a unique individual and you will sometimes make different choices than others who appear to be similar. The FDA has little or no idea who you are and what you want.

Twelve: the FDA has a fundamentally different perspective from you and your doctor, and that perspective has some serious shortcomings.

Thirteen: politicians and government employees are no less attached to their jobs and the prospect of potential gain than the rest of us. Sometimes that leads them to act in ways which directly or indirectly harm us.

Legislative Binge

We have, for the last eight decades, been living with the consequences of an emotionally-induced legislative binge fueled by fears of perpetual thalidomide babies. This legislative binge bestowed a government agency with great powers, based not on logic and reason, but on a hypothesis that was never perceived, by its supporters or the general public, as warranting verification. As discordant as this is to many, we don't need the centralized, Soviet-style FDA to act as a gatekeeper to block drugs that haven't satisfied some inscrutable standards for safety and efficacy. Self-regulating markets can perform these functions and have so many other advantages. Look around and notice how other complex goods and services—including mutual funds, mortgages, motorcycles, airplanes, computers, smartphones, dentistry, estate planning, home remodeling, running shoes, and app-based ride-sharing services—are successfully provided by the free market, day after day.

Are these solutions perfect? No; we don't live in nirvana. Our goal isn't to find the elusive "perfect" solution, it is to find the best one or, at a minimum, a better one. Occasionally the centralized governmental solution will be better; most of the time it will be worse.

The evidence suggests that the FDA has reduced our life expectancies, metaphorically, as if we all took up smoking. Our life expectancies have increased, it's true, but they would have increased substantially more had the FDA not been blocking new therapies. The FDA is a public health risk on the order of smoking.

The FDA stands between us and our medicine cabinets, preventing us from accessing life-improving, life-saving drugs. Americans will, I am convinced, live longer and healthier sans the FDA. The greatest good for the greatest number relies on us abolishing or weakening the FDA.

Regardless of promises and threats from its proponents, the FDA is bad medicine. There are some remedies worse than the disease and the FDA is one of them. *The FDA should reject itself.*

---

1 Derek Lowe, "A New FDA Commissioner, Suddenly," *In the Pipeline*, Science Translational Medicine, 6 March 2019.

2 Deena Beasley, "Pompe drug lauded by Trump costs $300,000 a year," Reuters, 1 March 2017.

3 Deena Beasley, "Pompe drug lauded by Trump costs $300,000 a year," Reuters, 1 March 2017.

4 "Why sleep?", University of California, Berkeley, *U.C. Berkeley Wellness Letter*, special issue 2019.

5 Florida Museum. https://www.floridamuseum.ufl.edu/shark-attacks/yearly-worldwide-summary/

About the Author

For when an interest is already intrenched in law and habit of thought, those who are not against it are for it.
Henry George, 1886

I grew up, as did many people, believing that government agencies protect us in the same ways our parents protected us when we were young; they understand the world thoroughly, know us well, and put our interests before their own. As I became older and studied more deeply, I learned of the problems inherent in the regulations and actions of government agencies and the extensive benefits of freedom and voluntary transactions. I questioned my earlier views, and one of the agencies that drew my attention was the U.S. Food and Drug Administration (FDA), which I began to see in a new, more critical light. Years later, my perception changed yet again, slowly and mostly imperceptibly, when I worked in the pharmaceutical industry, first at Merck & Co. and then at Syntex Labs. I was so busy dealing with my new responsibilities that I virtually stopped thinking about public policy issues. Then, one day, I realized that I had begun to believe in the FDA again. If we didn't have the FDA, I thought, what menagerie of dangerous and inefficacious drugs would be on the market? Oh, the suffering that would result! My thinking had come full circle.

Some may be surprised that this happened while I worked at a drug company, a supposed enemy of the FDA—a dogged myth that may never die.

To say that I developed a fondness for the FDA would be an exaggeration, as I heard damning stories of the FDA's internal workings, inconsistencies, bureaucratic delays, and occasional incompetence. However, my views were largely consistent with, perhaps, those of most employees in the pharmaceutical industry, even today: the FDA is an imperfect government bureaucracy with an ever-challenging job that still performs a critically important function. If we didn't have the FDA, what dire problems would we have?

Whatever your view of the FDA, I've probably held it at one time or another.

One day, I started to reconsider the topic of drug regulation with fresh eyes. That thinking led slowly, but directly, to this book. Instead of simply holding the common view that regulation is essential, I started from first principles and questioned the common view. The more I thought about the issue, the more I saw both the benefits and the costs of drug regulation. As I continued to think more keenly, the less I saw the benefits and the more I saw the costs. The result of those years of thinking: this book.

If you want to discover your views on a topic, write a book.

This book explores the issues from first principles. What does drug safety mean? What does drug efficacy mean? Is the FDA scientific? Why do pharmaceutical and biotechnology companies develop new drugs? What could stop them? What could help them? What is the FDA's role in this? How do patients and their physicians make therapy decisions? Do they share goals with the FDA? What health risks do American face? Why and how do bad drugs enter the market? How did the FDA come about? Would Americans be better off with the current FDA, a revised FDA, or no FDA at all? What laws could be changed to improve the situation?

This book is a result of my earnest attempt to explore a topic that too often gets ignored or relegated to commonly accepted "views" and to clarify my own thinking, and perhaps yours, too.

Economist David R. Henderson, quoting the late Nobel Prize-winning economist Friedrich Hayek, has explained that people's views are like assets. To change someone's mind about a topic is to cause him or her to suffer a capital loss, which is why people don't like having their views challenged. That's probably what economist John Kenneth Galbraith had in mind when he delivered the following quote.

> *In the choice between changing one's mind and proving there's no need to do so, most people get busy on the proof.*
> **John Kenneth Galbraith**

The ideal, I have come to realize, is to hold the search for truth as the one paramount asset and to jettison falsehoods as you would rubbish, because the truth is what is valuable; ideas, information, and views are merely pointers to the truth. We should modify and discharge them if they cease providing value.

> *When my information changes, I change my mind.*
> *What do you do?*
> Economist **Paul Samuelson** paraphrasing economist
> **John Maynard Keynes**[1]

Some may be suspicious of a book written by a pharmaceutical industry insider. Good. Every reader should be suspicious about everything he or she reads. As for me, yes, I'm an insider. But don't for a minute think that I'm an industry shill. This book doesn't repeat industry perspectives; it challenges them.

None of my pharmaceutical clients asked me to write this book or have any idea I'm writing it. No one is paying me to write it, and, if those in the industry ever read it, some will agree with it, some will disagree with it, and others will scratch their heads and wonder why I wasted my time. No advocacy groups or industry organizations are, as this book was written, even aware of its existence. The ideas expressed here are mine and mine alone, formulated and scribbled on my own time, and paid for out of my own pocket.

My allegiance lies with the regular people who do the living, breathing, and dying in this world. If the FDA-regulated pharmaceutical industry helps people live long and prosperous lives, great. If it doesn't, that's a problem. I want the truth.

Why did I write this book? Because I care about people and I want them to live long and healthy lives. Too many of my loved ones have been snatched from my world decades before their time. I want that to stop, and I want you to help me.

I want to increase the number of live-saving and life-improving vitamins, supplements, diagnostics, devices, procedures, vaccines, and medicines available to people everywhere, and I want to increase the speed of their development and availability. I want people to live long, healthy, productive, and satisfying lives.

While no one other than me is responsible for this book, and the views expressed do not necessarily reflect the views of my clients, friends, or coworkers, I have had the help of Russell T. Hooper and Ronald A. Howard, who have reviewed and discussed certain sections. Without their help, this book would have been less successful. Further, I would like to thank the countless people with whom I've conversed over the years.

David R. Henderson didn't actually write any part of this book, but he might believe he did with all the passages I've borrowed from the articles we've coauthored over the years. Thank you, David, for a wealth of clear thinking and productive conversations. I owe a debt of gratitude to my business partner, Brett V. Gaspers, for his encyclopedic knowledge of the life sciences and for giving me the freedom to think and write, and to my wife, Lisa, for her inspirational life and enduring support.

Rena Henderson, editor extraordinaire, patiently read through a draft and provided numerous useful edits to help make this book flow better. However, if problems remain, I take full responsibility.

Kudos are in order for Mark Lawler, whose brilliant illustrations provide some welcome insights and eye candy, and Jeff Ishikawa, who demonstrated his prodigious art skills on the cover illustration. Russell T. Hooper, a true Renaissance man, edited sections of the book and developed the cover design.

Short Biography

Charles L. Hooper is president and co-founder of Objective Insights, Inc., a consulting firm dedicated to providing life science companies with the marketing and financial analyses they need to make informed decisions about their business opportunities. Objective Insights has been in business for 27 years and has successfully completed more than 420 projects for over seventy health care companies. He worked for seven years at NASA/ Ames Research Center, three years at Merck & Co., and two years at Syntex Labs. All told, he has spent the last three decades in the biopharmaceutical industry. He was a Visiting Fellow at Stanford's Hoover Institution for a decade. He has a B.S. in Computer Science Engineering from Santa Clara University and an M.S. in Engineering-Economic Systems (now Management Science Engineering) from Stanford University. He has started four companies. His writing has appeared in the *Journal of Clinical Pathways*, the Hoover Institution's *Defining Ideas, American Institute for Economic Research, Forbes, Medical Progress Today, Reason, The Goodman Institute, The Library of Economics and Liberty, The Washington Times, The Washington Post, The Concise Encyclopedia of Economics*, Cato's *Regulation*, and *The Wall Street Journal*. He coauthored *Making Great Decisions in Business and Life* (Chicago Park Press, 2006) with David R. Henderson and it has been translated into Chinese (Mandarin), Japanese, Korean, and Spanish. He can be reached at Hooper@ObjectiveInsights.com.

Charles and Lisa have two grown sons and enjoy living in Grass Valley, a small community in northern California with ample outdoor recreational opportunities.

[1] The original source and wording of this quote is in dispute.

Index